State of the Art TESOL Essays

Celebrating 25 Years of the Discipline

Sandra Silberstein, Editor

Typeset in Highland, Garamond
and printed by
Pantagraph Printing, Bloomington, Illinois USA

Helen Kornblum *Director of Communications and Marketing*
Deborah Green, Marilyn Kupetz *Copy Editors*
Ann Kammerer *Cover Design*

Teachers of English to Speakers of Other Languages, Inc.
1600 Cameron Street, Suite 300
Alexandria, Virginia 22314 USA
Tel 703-836-0774 • Fax 703-836-7864

ISBN 0-939791-48-X
Library of Congress Catalogue No. 93-060565

Editor's Preface

Most of the papers in this volume were commissioned for the 25th-anniversary issues of the *TESOL Quarterly*, appearing in 1991. Others, pertaining to the history of our professional organization and K-12 classroom practice in the U.S., have been added for this volume. The goal of this anthology is to convey a sense of the diversity of perspectives in the field of teaching English to speakers of other languages—to examine the field through prisms that subdivide the image in multiple and intersecting ways. The volume balances research and theoretical analyses of language learning with pedagogical approaches. It links broad-based overarching perspectives with discussions of specific locations and practices.

The authors represented in this volume are distinguished scholars in their respective areas. Their charge was to anchor overviews of current practice and future directions with historical summary. It is my hope that the volume will prove of use to students of second language learning and teaching, teacher trainers, administrators, and materials developers who desire a synthesis of the state of the art of our field and a vision of its future.

As befits a volume intended to be both retrospective and prospective, Overview articles compose the first of its four sections. These examine the field as it is and as it might be, addressing fundamental issues of what it means to be language educators in a global society.

The second section, Perspectives on the Field, observes the profession through a variety of lenses. Views represented include those favoring communicative, whole language, and ESP (English for specific purposes) approaches, as well as perspectives on SLA (second language acquisition) research and testing.

In The Skill Areas and Beyond, readers will find state-of-the-art discussions of research and practice during the past quarter century. Although they do not necessarily endorse a "skills approach" to language teaching, the authors share the view that much can be learned about specific elements of language and language use; these insights must inform any approach we adopt.

The two articles that compose the last section look historically at the TESOL association, exploring its relationship to the field of applied linguistics and its growth from a learned society to a professional organization.

As in any rapidly evolving discipline, were the articles to be commissioned today, several currently developing perspectives might be more conspicuous. Among these would be various commentaries on teaching beyond so-called methods, including critiques of the very concept of method (cf. Pennycook, 1989, Prabhu, 1990), examinations of the day-to-day life of the classroom (cf. Prabhu, 1992), and reconceptualizations of teaching and teacher training (cf. Freeman & Richards, 1993).

Another area we might see explored comprises approaches to "critical" pedagogy and research, which seek to make language teaching and research (self-)conscious of their perspectives and empowering to learners and "subjects." For recent discussions in this area, see, for example, Cameron, Frazer, Harvey, Rampton, & Richardson (1992); Kress (1991); and Simon (1992).

Finally, I am grateful to those who made this volume possible: the authors for their extraordinary efforts on behalf of the field and two able assistant editors: Deborah Green and Marilyn Kupetz.

REFERENCES

Cameron, D., Frazer, E., Harvey, P., Rampton, M. B. H., & Richardson, K. (1992). *Researching language*. London: Routledge.

Freeman, D., & Richards, J. C. (1993). Conceptions of teaching and the education of second language teachers. *TESOL Quarterly, 27*(2), 193-216.

Kress, G. (1991). Critical discourse analysis. *Annual Review of Applied Linguistics 1990, 11,* 84-99.

Pennycook, A. (1989). The concept of method, interested knowledge, and the politics of language teaching. *TESOL Quarterly, 23*(4), 589-618.

Prabhu, N. S. (1990). There is no best method—Why? *TESOL Quarterly, 24*(2), 161-176.

Prabhu, N. S. (1992). The dynamics of the language lesson. *TESOL Quarterly, 26*(2), 225-241.

Simon, R. I. (1992). *Teaching against the grain: Texts for a pedagogy of possibility.* New York: Bergin & Garvey.

Sandra Silberstein
Seattle, Washington
Spring 1993

CONTENTS

OVERVIEWS

PERSPECTIVES ON THE FIELD

THE SKILL AREAS AND BEYOND

ORGANIZATIONAL PERSPECTIVES

OVERVIEWS

Internationalism and Our "Strenuous Family"*

MARY ASHWORTH
University of British Columbia

This paper explores what internationalism can mean in the context of TESOL's "strenuous" (active, determined, eager, and spirited) family. As an organization and as individual professionals, we can advocate—for peace, literacy, language rights, and education; we can work to protect multiculturalism within and outside North America; and we can network to support international goals.

More years ago than I care to remember, when I closed the door on high school teaching and crept through the back door to university teaching, I left with one deep regret: that I would no longer be able to read poetry to a captive audience. But as I gained courage and confidence as a university professor, I dropped a little poem in here, a longer one there, and then as I received more invitations to speak in public, I decided that, provided I didn't overdo it, I could continue to engage my pleasure—or as Joseph Campbell (1988) might have put it—to "follow [my] bliss" (p. 118). I don't do it because I like the sound of my voice—indeed, I don't always like the sound of my voice—but because the poet can say succinctly, yet with passion, the core of what I want to say and what will take me much longer to say.

The title of my address is "Internationalism and Our 'Strenuous Family'" and "strenuous family" is in quotation marks for a reason—it is a quotation from a poem by Robert Louis Stevenson (1918), whom you will recall was a sickly youth, the son of a lighthouse engineer, a profession he was expected to follow. But his rebellious spirit and his urge to write sent him around the world. In one poem he expresses concern that people may think poorly of him because he "fled the sea . . . to play at home with paper like a child." He goes on,

*This is a slightly revised version of the closing plenary address delivered at the 25th Annual TESOL Convention, New York, March 1991; the oral character of the text has been preserved.

In the afternoon of time
A strenuous family dusted from its hands
The sands of granite, and beholding far
Along the sounding coast its pyramids
And tall memorials catch the dying sun
Smiled well content,

("Skerryvore: The Parallel")

Perhaps TESOL too is in "the afternoon of time" and may smile "well content" at its achievements so far, at "the pyramids and tall memorials" it has built, but there remains more to be done. But let me take a few moments to look at the strenuous family of TESOL before I move on to the wider world, and from there to an examination of the future, and what it may hold for us and require from us.

Strenuous has at least 16 synonyms. No, I won't list them all—just four: active, determined, eager, and spirited; these four characterized TESOL in its early days, along with vision. As a result the TESOL family grew quickly, both in North America and around the world. The aims and objectives of TESOL were such that they appealed to ESL/EFL individuals and associations. The first 10 non-U.S. associations to affiliate with TESOL were based in Puerto Rico, Venezuela, the Dominican Republic, Mexico, British Columbia, Quebec, Italy, Spain, Ontario, and Japan.

Today there are about 18,000 individual members, 43 U.S. affiliates and 30 non-U.S. affiliates worldwide. You should understand that TESOL does not proselytize. Neither the President nor the Executive Director travel around the world selling TESOL as if it were a product everyone ought to have. They provide information when asked—but TESOL sells itself. It sells itself on its Mission Statement, its past performance, and its potential—what it can do for its present and future members.

Many now refer to TESOL as TESOL International. But how do we define that word *international?* What does it mean placed in juxtaposition to TESOL? I want to begin by exploring three possible quasi synonyms for *internationalism*: advocacy, multiculturalism, and networking.

ADVOCACY

In 1984 Peter Strevens suggested that a profession possesses six attributes not shared by all occupations. The first four are (a) selective entry, (b) mandatory training, (c) intellectual/practical balance, and (d) standards. But it is the last two that I want to draw

4

your attention to. These are international interdependence and social responsibility, which together suggest that a profession has some responsibility for its members and for those they come in contact with around the world. Social responsibility demands some kind of advocacy; international interdependence demands that this be a global advocacy. Now this creates some problems, as the old League of Nations and the new United Nations organization found out. Nations prize themselves on their independence and do not want others interfering in their internal affairs. So what can an organization like TESOL do? Obviously it cannot write to a head of state and say, "We don't like what you are doing, so change!" No, it can do two things: (a) It can set an example, and (b) It can concern itself with global issues rather than particular issues.

Let us take the first—setting an example. I remember when I was a high school teacher and I worked under a very, very conservative principal. Whenever I suggested a change in the way the school or my department was organized—which was fairly frequently—he would ask if any other school in the district was doing it the way I proposed. If I said yes, he was likely to go along with my idea; if I said no, that was the end of the conversation. I spent time searching for examples, or near examples. Change may come when one group in TESOL is able to point to another group in TESOL and advocate that similar changes be made in their organization, or institution, or community, or region, which places the responsibility on those who are able to act as leaders in various aspects of TESOL—research, working conditions, teacher training, etc.—to do so. In the October 1990 edition of the *TESOL Newsletter*, Rick Orem wrote: "The harsh reality, however, seems to confirm that in order for TESOL to have an impact on employment conditions and sociopolitical concerns worldwide, we must begin to exert ourselves more forcefully in the U.S." (p. 10). As the oldest, largest, and wealthiest member of the TESOL family, the U.S. affiliates (taken as a single group) do have—have always had—a responsibility to set an example, a responsibility which they have accepted and carried out for 25 years with courage and common sense.

And elsewhere in the world non-U.S. affiliates, whether national or regional, are providing excellent examples that others may follow as they advocate improvement in areas that affect ESL/EFL teachers and their clients—but too often we do not know about them in spite of articles in the *TESOL Newsletter*, or the *TESOL Quarterly*, or at sessions at a convention. These examples may be of many kinds: methodology, organization, in-service training, finances. Let me mention an example from Western Canada: TEAL's Charitable Foundation. Five years ago it was a thought in the mind of a past president, Nick Collins. Today it is a fund of $161,000 which provides scholarships, visitorships, and in-service training to the 1000 members of the Association of British Columbia Teachers of English as an Additional Language. As a result, the national organization, TESL Canada, is setting up a national foundation along similar lines, following TEAL's example, and Alberta TESL is considering a foundation. You may not need a fund, and if you do, you may not be able to develop it as TEAL did, but the example is there for those who are interested. Within TESOL are many examples of actions others need to hear about. Later I will be talking about the importance of networking, which provides a medium through which examples that support advocacy can become known.

The second way in which TESOL can act as an advocate is by supporting global rather than particular issues: that is, TESOL will have more impact by seeking to improve literacy worldwide, if that is an issue it considers of value, if it refrains from condemning a particular country for its low literacy rate and telling it what it ought to do. TESOL's task is rather to identify those global issues, about which, because of its specific expertise in second language learning and teaching, it has the right to speak out upon and to act upon in a way that will neither offend nor alarm various authorities, but will help to put right what may be wrong. What might some of those issues be?

Peace

Misunderstandings and miscommunications lie at the root of many quarrels, whether between individuals, communities, or nations. Part of Canada's recent constitutional crisis centred around the current meanings placed upon the words *distinct society* by French- and English-speaking Canadians, and what those words might mean in the future in societal and legal terms. We TESOLers are in the business of communication. We must be aware of those factors in the structure of language, in the effects of translation, and in the process of communication that hinder the coming to reality of a vision—a vision of a better organization, a better society, a better world. Darlene Larson rightly says that we should view peace as a process, not as a state. If we are going to become advocates for peace we must rid ourselves of warlike language; we must advocate the language of mediation, cooperation, and negotiation. There is a lot of material waiting to be researched contained in the language used during the recent Gulf War. What does TESOL have to say about the language of war, the language of peace? What does it have to say about peace education?[1]

Literacy

A world which promotes the development of a sound economy for all, and the appreciation of other cultures and religions, depends to a large degree on literacy. While elementary ideas can be exchanged through the spoken word and pictures, it is the written word, which is carried around the world in books and computers, that provides a permanent record that can be examined time and time again as dreamers try to turn a vision into reality. Literacy opens the door of opportunity—but control of language, first and/ or second, is the pathway to that door. In her 1976 book *The Home of Man*, Barbara Ward, the economist, wrote: "The world's poor increasingly know that their condition is not an act of God but the choice of man [*sic*]" (p. 263). What does TESOL have to say about literacy?

Language Rights

The development of language skills in children, in their first language and, if necessary, in a second or even third language, is their right; without control of language, children will go nowhere. One of Canada's native Members of Parliament was told as a child that he must master the "white man's" speech so that he could talk to him on equal terms. He did and became a very respected and influential member of the Canadian government. Without that control of one of Canada's two official languages, he would probably still be on the reserve. The *Lau v. Nichols* case in the U.S. in 1974 was a landmark case in establishing the right of children in California to assistance in mastering English, the language of instruction in the schools. Should children have the right to begin school in their first language? Should immigrants have the right to maintain their first language in their new country? Should English be the only official language of the U.S. and of parts of Canada? Keith Spicer, Commissioner of Official Languages in Canada in the 1970s, put his finger on part of the problem we have in Canada when he said: "We are the only nation in the world which thinks that learning another language is a pain in the neck instead of an

---

[1] In the wake of the Gulf War, the profession has begun to look seriously at this issue. A pre-session at the 1991 Georgetown Round Table on Languages and Linguistics addressed Language and War. The 26th Annual TESOL Convention in Vancouver, B.C., has scheduled an academic session on Discourse Analysis, Language, and Peace: A Challenge for TESOL.

opportunity" (cited in McLeod, 1979, p. 80). And he went on, mixing his metaphors somewhat: "Maybe all of us who have our snouts in the linguistic trough ought to be doing a lot of missionary work with the general public about the value of languages" (McLeod, 1979, p. 84). What does TESOL have to say about language rights?

Education

No one doubts the importance of education to the well-being of the individual and the community, but any advocacy of the values of education must take into account the political and pedagogical questions that face people in different parts of the world, questions which are not easy to ask, let alone answer, particularly in regions where speech is muzzled. Similarly, the tools of our trade—methodology and materials—cannot be exported from one country to another in the belief that what works in country A will automatically work in country B—it won't. Ideological, attitudinal, and organizational differences between two countries may cause country B to reject methods and materials used successfully elsewhere. A teacher who wrote home to Canada that her students were "freaked out" by her teaching methods had not learned the meaning of cultural imperialism. What does TESOL have to say about the value and process of education?

There are other global issues which may come to your mind such as the environment, but my intention is to focus on those issues which draw on our expertise as second language teachers. So far the resolutions passed at TESOL's Legislative Assembly over the years which have something to do with the international scene have dealt with bilingualism, nuclear disarmament, and refugees. What other issues might TESOL speak out upon? One of our tasks as members of TESOL is to present resolutions in the international sphere, resolutions that will carry out TESOL's mission worldwide.

In his book *The Prime Imperatives*, Wittenberg (1968) wrote: "As far as government is concerned, this is its responsibility to listen. But a government also has a responsibility to speak: to inform, to enlighten, and to a certain extent, to guide public opinion; as well as to make itself accountable to it" (p. 59). Can we insert *TESOL* for *government*? Does TESOL have a responsibility to listen and to speak, to inform, to enlighten, and to a certain extent, to guide public opinion, as well as to make itself accountable to it? Yes, I think it does if it is to fulfil those two attributes of a profession set out by Peter Strevens—international interdependence and social responsibility—but it must be prepared to listen to all its members, those near and those far away, those rich and those poor.

MULTICULTURALISM

I gave as my second synonym of *internationalism* the word *multiculturalism*. It's a big word in Canada—we use it all the time, though few are sure exactly what it means or exactly how it works out in practice. I find somewhat intriguing, perhaps because it is different, a definition of *society* offered by Robert Ardrey (cited in Bullivant, 1981) some twenty years ago: "A society is a group of unequal beings organized to meet common needs. . . . The just society . . . is one in which sufficient order protects members, whatever their diverse endowments, and sufficient disorder provides every individual with full opportunity to develop his genetic endowment, whatever that may be" (p. xii). Perhaps a just multicultural society is one in which there is sufficient order to protect members regardless of their race, religion, or creed and sufficient disorder to give them the opportunity to develop their individuality, whatever they may decide that to be.

I want to break multiculturalism into two parts: multiculturalism in North America and multiculturalism outside North America.

Multiculturalism in North America

The authors of *Megatrends 2000* say, "The world's most taught language (English) is not replacing other languages; it is supplementing them" (Naisbitt & Aburdene, 1990, p. 139). That would suggest that bilingualism is on the increase, but more than that, that the people of the world favour bilingualism. But in the U.S. and Canada there are those who would keep our citizens monolingual. In Canada we have a group called APEC—The Alliance for the Preservation of English in Canada—a silly title, for English is in no danger of being lost. In both the U.S. and Canada there are places declaring themselves "English only" municipalities, and while I can understand their concern if offering services in two languages costs more than the taxpayers can bear (and I question that), I suspect the real reason lies deeper in the inability to recognize that in North America it is possible to be bilingual and bicultural and that this does not constitute a threat to society but rather a benefit.

Our view of internationalism in North America must begin with an appreciation of the wealth of our human resources. Is it true as *Megatrends 2000* states, "It is the habit of Americans [and perhaps Canadians] to brag about previous immigrants and to complain about current ones" (p. 40)? Is it just luck that the U.S. has become one of the most powerful nations of the world—the nation to which others look when they think of democracy and economics? Or is it at least in part due to the richness of the human mix that somehow, by a process which perhaps we do not fully understand, produces the creativity and innovation that has made the U.S. successful? And the authors of *Megatrends 2000* have something to say about that human mix: "The more homogeneous our lifestyles become, the more steadfastly we shall cling to deeper values—religion, language, art, and literature. As our outer worlds grow more similar, we will increasingly treasure the traditions that spring from within" (p. 120). And elsewhere: "The trend toward a global lifestyle and the countertrend toward cultural assertion represent the classic dilemma: how to preserve individuality within the unity of the family or community" (p. 153). Here in TESOL we too must ensure that we preserve the individuality of the cultural and linguistic groups that make up our "strenuous family."

Multiculturalism Outside North America

Megatrends 2000 reports that more than 80% of all information stored in more than 100 million computers around the world is in English; that English is the language of international business; that English prevails in transportation and media; that English is becoming the world's first truly international language; and finally, that one of the greatest appeals of English as a world language is that it is easy to speak badly! (Naisbitt & Aburdene, 1990, pp. 140-141). This would suggest that as the 21st century progresses, more and more people will speak English, that it will become the language in which all the affairs of the world will be conducted. Perhaps, but perhaps not. After watching the incredible changes that have taken place in Eastern Europe recently, forecasting what may happen even a decade ahead is risky. Yet if we in TESOL do not have some sense of where we want to go, we will never build the road that leads there.

Marshall McLuhan (1962), before TESOL was born, coined the phrase the "global village" (p. 31). Just as in a village one person's actions affect others, so in our world today one country's actions can affect many others. The invasion of Kuwait by Iraq is a recent example. TESOL must listen to its non-U.S. affiliates and learn how they view current world changes, learn what their needs are in language training, learn what they can offer to others in TESOL.

Together we must all try to understand the various forces affecting us—industrialization, urbanization, science and technology, economics, political and religious dissension, and always everywhere the struggle for freedom and power. But as *Megatrends*

2000 states: "By identifying the forces pushing the future, rather than those that have contained the past, you possess the power to engage with your reality" (p. 309). Elsewhere the authors comment: "The most exciting breakthroughs of the 21st century will occur not because of technology but because of an expanding concept of what it means to be human" (p. 16). What does it mean to be human in today's world, in a world of rapid change? How do we deal with our international human neighbours? Does "being human" mean interfering with others, or encouraging them to do what we believe to be right, or leaving them alone? How ready are any of us to try to understand other people in their terms? To listen to their voices? To silence our own?

NETWORKING

My last synonym for internationalism was *networking*. I am indebted to Darlene Larson (personal communication, 1990) for a phrase which I hope will stick in your minds. She refers to TESOL as "a global professional network" (p. 21) and that is as fine a definition of internationalism and our strenuous family as you will find—a global professional network.

In September 1990, the Executive Board went on a retreat during which time it decided to draw up a set of objectives for TESOL. You are no doubt aware that TESOL has a Mission Statement and a Long Range Plan in the making. The objectives try to place these in a context, to provide some guidelines which can serve to govern the growth and development of TESOL. The first three objectives deal with professional development, scholarship, and leadership. The fourth reads as follows:

> The Association exists to provide opportunities for networking not only among the members of TESOL but also among the members of the several Affiliates and with the membership of other local, national, and international professional associations with which TESOL shares a common interest.

This conference has given a wonderful opportunity to all of us to network as individuals—that is, for those of us who are here. Not everyone can afford to come, not every affiliate can afford to send a delegate to network with delegates of other affiliates, but TESOL has helped and is planning to continue helping affiliates who lack the funds to send delegates long distances. When Dick Allwright, President of TESOL 1988–1989, asked in the *TESOL Newsletter* of April 1988 how TESOL could become more international, an answer that came through loudly was that many people outside the

U.S. would like to become members but found the fees beyond their capacity to pay. From time to time TESOL's bimonthly general publication (formerly *TESOL Newsletter*, as of February 1991 *TESOL Matters*) publishes the names and addresses of affiliates who have linked or who are seeking to link with other affiliates. Colorado TESOL, for example, has a partnership with an institution in the People's Republic of China by which it pays the institution's membership in TESOL and exchanges information. TESOL itself networks with other like-minded organizations; that is, organizations concerned with language teaching issues such as research, textbook reviews, professional standards, methodology, job opportunities, collaboration between theorists and practitioners; or organizations concerned with global issues that TESOL has identified as important to it. In the spring of 1990 TESOL became officially an NGO (nongovernment organization) of the United Nations Department of Public Information. This will give TESOL easy access to information on the objectives and projects of the United Nations and its agencies. But TESOL is expected to reciprocate by (a) providing a channel through which information concerning the United Nations reaches the public; (b) playing a crucial role in mobilizing public opinion and building understanding for the United Nations, its related agencies and programs; and (c) monitoring and promoting policies of various countries in support of United Nations goals and resolutions. ("TESOL and the United Nations," 1990) If we are serious, that's quite a responsibility!

Darlene Larson, TESOL's liaison to the United Nations, wrote about the importance of TESOL knowing what its message is to other agencies and of timely and efficient information sharing. In her February 1990 article in the *TESOL Newsletter*, she suggests that the various parts that make up TESOL—the standing committees, the affiliates, the interest sections—might each examine what they might give to a TESOL clearinghouse of information, what each might do to build a network to foster global understanding.

We should not minimize the beneficial effect TESOL might have in the world community. Abba Eban (1983) wrote that "international organizations have never been assigned a major role in a world dominated by national sovereign states. Nevertheless, the proliferation of international agencies . . . [is] helping to create a new consciousness of global responsibility and interdependence" (p. 286).

FUTURE

I posed two questions earlier on: (a) What might the future hold for us? and (b) What may be required of us? Let us examine the first question.

Here is where the idealist and the pragmatist meet face to face and must either bang heads or hold hands. Remember Tennyson (1842/1938) who wrote,

> For I dipped into the future, far as human eye
> could see,
> Saw the Vision of the world, and all the wonder
> that would be;

And how he followed this idea of wonder with a terrible verse:

> Heard the heavens fill with shouting, and there
> rained a ghastly dew
> From the nations' airy navies grappling in the
> central blue;

And then brought to these two conflicting viewpoints a breath of optimism:

> Far along the world-wide whisper of the south
> wind rushing warm,
> With the standards of the peoples plunging
> through the thunderstorm;
> Till the war-drum throbbed no longer, and the
> battle-flags were furled
> In the Parliament of man, the Federation of
> the world.
> ("Locksley Hall")

Perhaps the future will continue to hold for us that swing of the pendulum—peace to war and back; compassion to hatred and back; feast to famine and back.

What may be required of us? Perhaps to try to hold on to the pendulum to prevent it swinging towards war, and hatred, and famine, and to do it together as a global profession, as TESOL International.

The authors of *Megatrends 2000* state: "For centuries that monumental, symbolic date [the year 2000] has stood for the future and what we shall make of it. In a few short years that future will be here" (p. 11). When it comes, what shall we have accomplished in the nine years leading up to it? Does TESOL have a role in creating a better world? Without doubt. We cannot rely on world leaders to create a better world. They cannot succeed alone. They do not know by and of themselves the shape of the world that we, the people, envisage. In the corridors of power are many tensions, many irrationalities that we, the people, must reduce and clarify. If violence is not to continue exploding around the world, we must ensure that a strong organic life of nonviolence and rationality is alive and well the world over. Many scientists and scholars are using their sense of responsibility to create and exchange ideas for the betterment of this fragile world. The organization called Educators for Social Responsibility has listed ten themes that might be included in a curriculum: peace and conflict, communication, affirmation, cooperation, negotiation/mediation, handling feelings, celebrating diversity, equity, being peacemakers, and the future (Fine, 1990). Are there themes that ESL/EFL teachers might include in their curricula? George Jacobs (1990) has suggested some that might increase international awareness in ESL classes: change, communication, commonality, diversity, human ability to impact the future, and interdependence. But there are some who condemn the idealist as being impractical. Must that be so? Cannot the ideal and the practical coincide? To quote Abba Eban (1983) again: "The task is, as it always has been, to keep the future open for life and, if possible, for peace. But the understanding of this task requires more complex and strenuous labour by men and women who can see the soil below as well as the vistas ahead" (p. 11).

In *Megatrends 2000* the authors comment: "You possess a front-row seat to the most challenging yet most exciting decade in the history of civilization" (p. 313). But is that enough—"a front row seat," a bystander, a nonparticipant? Not for TESOL, not for this strenuous family—a family that during its first 25 years has shown that it believes in action or, as Robert Louis Stevenson wrote, in "beholding far along the sounding coast its pyramids and tall memorials." I predict that TESOL's next 25 years will see its influence spread around the world.

■

THE AUTHOR

Mary Ashworth is Professor Emerita having trained ESL teachers for many years at the University of British Columbia. She is the author of five books and numerous articles. Now she enjoys gardening, traveling, and meeting old friends.

REFERENCES

Allwright, D. (1988, April). Internationalism in TESOL: Whose problem is it? *TESOL Newsletter*, p. 2.

Bullivant, B. (1981). *The pluralist dilemma in education.* Sydney, Australia: George Allen & Unwin.

Campbell, J. (1988). *The power of myth* (B. J. Flowers, Ed.). NY: Doubleday.

Eban, A. (1983). The new diplomacy. New York: Random House.

Fine, L. (1990, February). Resolving conflict creatively: Peace education concepts in the ESL classroom. *TESOL Newsletter*, p. 19.

Jacobs, G. (1990, February). ESOL and international education. *TESOL Newsletter*, p. 27.

Larson, D. (1990, February). TESOL's role in global understanding: A possible agenda. *TESOL Newsletter*, p. 21.

McLeod, K. A. (1979). *Multiculturalism, bilingualism and Canadian institutions.* Toronto: University of Toronto Press.

McLuhan, M. (1962). *The Gutenberg galaxy.* Toronto: University of Toronto Press.

Naisbitt, J., & Aburdene, P. (1990). *Megatrends 2000.* New York: William Morrow.

Stevenson, R. L. (1918). *Poems.* London: Chatto & Windus.

Strevens, P. (1984, August). The responsibilities of EFL/ESL teachers and their associations. *TESOL Newsletter*, p. 29.

Tennyson, A. (1938). Locksley Hall. In J. W. Bowers & J. L. Brooks (Eds.), *The Victorian age* (p. 90). New York: Appleton-Century-Crofts. (Original work published in 1842)

TESOL and the United Nations: A new partnership. (1990, October). *TESOL Newsletter*, p. 31.

Ward, B. (1976). *The home of man.* Toronto: McClelland & Stewart.

Wittenberg, A. I. (1968). *The prime imperatives.* Toronto: Clark Irwin.

TESOL at Twenty-Five: What are the Issues?

H. DOUGLAS BROWN
San Francisco State University

Four major themes appear to be running through ESOL teaching and research efforts at the present time: (a) In our focus on learners, we are attempting to capitalize on their intrinsic motivation to learn English as a means to their empowerment; (b) sociopolitical issues have us focused on English as an international language and on language policy issues in many countries, including the U.S.; (c) efforts are being made to make curricula more content-centered and task-based, with an emphasis on pressing global issues; (d) our methods are, in turn, increasingly oriented toward cooperative, learner-centered teaching in which learner strategy training plays a significant role.

The occasion of the 25th anniversary of TESOL turns our thoughts to the notion of time. We can be thankful for time. Someone once said, "Time is what keeps everything from happening all at once." While everything does indeed seem to be happening all at once in our profession, we can, I think, look around us and appreciate our current state of the art as a product of the collective wisdom of at least 25 years of research and practice. As we look back over this quarter century of accomplishment, what are some of the major issues and challenges that are currently engaging us, and that, in the course of time, will one day be better resolved?

Several major themes or perspectives run through our teaching and research efforts at the present time. I refer here to issues that cut across many of the topics of these anniversary issues, but which may not be readily identified with any single topic. Four domains will be addressed: (a) Focus on the learner: *Who* are the learners that we are teaching? That is, from the deepest psychological viewpoint, *Why* are they learning English? (b) Focus on sociopolitical and geographical issues: *Where* is English teaching taking place and what effects do geographical differences have on our teaching? (c) Focus on subject matter: *What* are we teaching? Are we teaching structures, functions, and notions, or are we teaching content, tasks, and process? (d) Focus on method: *How* are we teaching English? What methodological approaches characterize our classrooms?

As you read further, I invite you to thumb through the articles that follow in the anniversary issues of the *TESOL Quarterly*. Each paper is an attempt to delve more deeply into our profession. I hope that this article will not so much provide an overview, but rather provide issues to ponder, and some added perspectives.

FOCUS ON THE LEARNER

Our first focus is the learners themselves. For such a viewpoint one might expect a lengthy survey of demographic data on English learners around the world. Such surveys can be useful, but I believe there is a deeper level of the English language learner that forms a prevailing and crucial concern for all teachers and researchers, a level that probes the hearts and minds of students: *Why* are our students learning English? What are their ultimate goals? What can knowledge of the English language do for them?

Two central, related issues presently occupy a good deal of the pedagogical focus on learners. The first is the construct of motivation; the second, a concept associated with Freire (1970) and others, empowerment. In virtually every article in these 25th-anniversary issues, authors have implicitly noted the importance of learners' goals and of the empowering possibilities available through English language competence. Let us look more closely at these two learner issues.

Motivation: From Extrinsic to Intrinsic

Motivation is one of the more complex issues of second language acquisition research and teaching. For two decades, research on motivation has focused on Robert Gardner's (1985; 1988; Gardner & Lambert, 1972) distinction between *integrative* (desire to learn a language stemming from a positive effect toward a community of its speakers) and *instrumental* (desire to learn a language in order to attain certain career, educational, or financial goals) orientations of second language learners. The assumption is that integratively motivated learners will be more successful.

But history has also shown us that motivation to learn a foreign language is far too complex to be explained through just one dichotomy (see Crookes & Schmidt, 1990). It is especially problematic to do so as second languages are increasingly being learned outside of what once were closely allied cultural contexts. In many non-English-speaking countries, for example, English may be learned and used extensively without reference to a particular native culture. Rather, learners become highly proficient in the language in order to carry out specific purposes and/or to communicate almost exclusively with other nonnative speakers of English.

For pedagogical purposes, a more powerful conception of the motivation construct can be found in the contrast between *intrinsic* and *extrinsic* motivation. Intrinsically motivated activities, according to Edward Deci (1975),

> are ones for which there is no apparent reward except the activity itself. People seem to engage in the activities for their own sake and not because they lead to an extrinsic reward. . . . Intrinsically motivated behaviors are aimed at bringing about certain internally rewarding consequences, namely, feelings of *competence* and *self-determination*. (p. 23)

Extrinsically motivated behaviors, on the other hand, are carried out in anticipation of a reward from outside and beyond the self. Typical extrinsic rewards are money, prizes, gold stars, and letter grades. Behaviors initiated solely to avoid punishments are also largely extrinsically motivated.

An overwhelming body of research now shows the superiority of intrinsic motivation in educational settings. Surprisingly, controlled experiments reveal faster learning and greater success by students who perform tasks with no promise of an external reward than those to whom a reward has been promised. Why? First, human beings universally view "incongruity" and "uncertainty," or what Piaget (1985) would call "disequilibrium," as motivating. In other words, we seek out a reasonable challenge. Then we initiate behaviors intended to conquer the challenging situation (Deci, 1975). Incongruity is not itself motivating, but *optimal* incongruity, or what Krashen (1985) calls "*i*+1," presents enough of a possibility of being resolved that we will "go after" that resolution.

The key to the principle of intrinsic motivation is its power to tap into the learner's natural inquisitiveness and then to captivate the learner in a process of a confidence-building, ego-enhancing, quest for competence in some domain of knowledge or skill. While some degree of extrinsic reward will always remain important in the language classroom, virtually all of our successful language teaching efforts today are ultimately attempts to intrinsically motivate our students.

Consider a few activities and approaches that capitalize on intrinsic motivation by appealing to learners' self-determination and autonomy:

- Teaching writing as a thinking process in which learners develop their own ideas freely and openly

- Showing learners reading strategies that enable them to bring their own information to the written word
- Using language experience approaches in which students create their own reading material for others in the class to read
- Doing oral fluency exercises in which learners talk about what interests them and not about a teacher-assigned topic
- Providing an academic lecture in a learner's own field of study to fill an information gap
- Teaching language within a communicative approach (see Savignon, 1990) in which learners accomplish certain specific functions
- Giving grammar lessons, if learners see grammar's potential for increasing their autonomy in the second language

Intrinsic motivation is of course not the only contributor to success for a language learner. Terrell (1990) and others demonstrate convincingly that for some learners, no matter how desperately they want to learn, or how valiantly they try, success may elude them. But if the learners in our classrooms are given an opportunity to "do" language for their own personal reasons of achieving competence and autonomy, surely those learners will have a better chance of success than if they become dependent on external rewards for their motivation.

Empowerment

Closely related to intrinsic motivation is the concept of empowerment. While it is unfortunate that this term has lately become an overused buzzword, it can nevertheless signify an important construct in the language teaching profession. The term was initially popularized by the well-known Brazilian educator Paolo Freire (1970), whose writings and lectures have stirred the souls of many a teacher to embark on the mission of liberating those who are imprisoned by "banking" forms of education that attempt to pour knowledge into the supposedly passive, empty vessels of students' minds. Instead, we are commissioned to empower learners—politically, economically, socially, and morally—to become critical thinkers, equipped with problem-solving strategies, poised to challenge those forces in society that would keep them passive.

Conditions of powerlessness are present in every walk of life and in every corner of the earth. One perspective on this observation can be found in Michael Lerner's (1989) book, *Surplus Powerlessness*. Lerner challenges us to help people everywhere to overcome their sense of powerlessness. According to Lerner, it is not sufficient to win the intellectual battle about what the world must look like. We must help create that world through a social movement capable of making our dreams real. The first step is to understand why most of us participate in making ourselves more powerless than we need to be, and then to build strategies for change (Bahouth, 1990).

Our language classes can begin that process of change. Clarke (1989) defined empowerment as "the process by which individuals gain a measure of control over their lives." Pennycook (1989) has recently reminded us about our mission as teachers to empower learners, to get them intrinsically involved in the process of learning English as a second or foreign language in order to gain a measure of control over their own lives.

English language classes in the 1990s are showing signs of providing such empowerment:

We are moving from:	*and shifting toward:*
a focus only on product	a focus on process
authoritarian structures	egalitarian structures
preplanned, rigid curricula	flexible, open-ended curricula
measuring only performance	gauging competence and potential
praising only "correct" answers	encouraging calculated guessing
championing analysis	valuing synthesis and intuition

The articles that follow in these 25th-anniversary issues bear testimony to our quest as language teachers to work against powerlessness of students. What could be more intrinsically motivating for a learner than to gain strategic linguistic tools for academic success, occupational expertise, political action, personal fulfillment, and communication across international boundaries?

FOCUS ON SOCIOPOLITICAL AND GEOGRAPHICAL ISSUES

The second of four major topics of current professional interchange is the growing importance of such sociolinguistic issues as language policy and language change, international varieties of English, and the politicization of English language issues, especially in the U.S.

English as an International Language

At last count, there were some one billion speakers of English around the globe. (Estimates vary, of course, since census data and other tallies yield only approximate numbers.) The growth of English language use has been staggering, especially in what have been called the *outer* (Kachru, 1988) circle (India, Nigeria, Philippines, etc.) and *expanding* circle (China, Japan, Indonesia, etc.) of countries. Such growth has produced numerous challenges for English teachers; among the more crucial are the following (taken from Kachru, 1988):

1. English is increasingly *not* learned as a tool for interaction with just *native* speakers of the language. This is especially so in countries in the outer and expanding circles.
2. English is *not* always learned as a tool for understanding and teaching U.S. or British cultural values. We have grown accustomed to linking English language instruction with cultural instruction, a linkage which in many cases no longer applies.
3. We are witnessing a trend toward more and more *non*native speakers of English playing a major role in the global teaching of and spread of English. Already most EFL teachers in the world are nonnative speakers.

The recognition of varieties of international English puts a new light on curriculum design and the specific focus of classroom activities, especially in nonnative-English-speaking countries. English is dominant in trade, commerce, banking, tourism, technology, and scientific research. New varieties of English, or "Englishes," in the outer circle have given rise to the internationalization of English, described by Kachru (1988) as "an acculturation in a variety of contexts that has resulted in new contours of the language and the literature—in linguistic innovations, in literary creativity, and in the expansion of the cultural identities of the language" (p. 1).

Even in inner circle countries where English is widely used as a native language, English language programs are changing to keep pace with this new pragmatism. Increasingly, curricula must cater to the immediate and practical needs of learners: English for numerous occupational purposes, for specific academic fields of pursuit, and English in the workplace.

English Plus Versus English Only

In the case of English language teaching in the U.S., the issue of internationalization is curiously juxtaposed with English Only, a movement advocating the exclusive use of the English language for all educational and political contexts, and a movement carrying an implicit assumption that the use of one's "home" language will impede success in learning English. In contrast, the English Plus movement (described in more detail below) rather than devaluing the native languages of U.S. citizens and residents, advocates a perspective in which schools and other institutions promote full use of English while respecting the cognitive, affective, and cultural importance of freely maintaining the use of one's home language.

G. Richard Tucker, Director of the Center for Applied Linguistics, in predicting issues for the 1990s, recently noted that "there will be increasing debate and polarization over the issue of English Only versus English Plus as a guiding principle for U.S. society" (personal communication, 1990). What does not seem to be readily apparent to millions in the U.S. is the fundamental difference between these two sociopolitical viewpoints. English Only proponents across the U.S. fail to articulate the value of the home languages of minorities, and in what I consider a flair of misguided patriotic zeal, tell us how much better it will be for "America" to be unified under one language. Arturo Madrid (1990) provides a cogent commentary of the issue: "The English Only movement taps into and is informed by deeply rooted fears: fear of persons who are different from the majority population and fear of change" (p. 63).

The fear of differentness, sad to say, has historical precedents in the U.S. The late 19th century, a period of reconstruction following the Civil War, brought a flood of immigrants into the country. In 1886 the Statue of Liberty was dedicated. In 1892 Ellis Island was established as a center for the mass processing of thousands of immigrants, many from eastern and southern Europe. Walt Whitman described the U.S. at this time as a "teeming nation of nations" (cited in Calkins, 1975, p. 317). But there was another side of the story, one not so often heard. Newspapers and books reported a growing mood of "Anglo-Saxonism" as more and more immigrants poured into the country. A newspaper editorial of the day noted that "the unique moral qualities of the English speaking race are being threatened by an influx of historically downtrodden, atavistic, and stagnant races" (cited in Calkins, 1975, p. 329). In 1892, Thomas Bailey Aldrich wrote, "Wide open and unguarded stand our gates, and through them presses a wild and motley throng" (cited in Calkins, 1975, p. 330).

It would appear that the late 20th century is witnessing a spreading fear of the current "wild and motley throng." However, responses to the English Only perspective are readily available. Practical solutions lie in various forms of English Plus programs (see Cazden & Snow, 1990), in which home languages and cultures are valued by schools and other institutions, but in which English as a second language is promoted *and* given appropriate funding. The

English Plus principle is currently being practiced, in both the U.S. and Canada, in bilingual education programs, immersion programs, sheltered English, content-centered curricula, and ESL in the workplace. But there remain many political and economic barriers that threaten their success. If this debate is any indication, those of us who teach ESL have a challenging agenda ahead as we strive for cross-cultural understanding and a practical, open-minded English language policy.

FOCUS ON SUBJECT MATTER

The articles that follow in these anniversary issues focus on the subject matter of our teaching, especially on linguistic subcategories. At least two articles deal with some new perspectives on subject matter, as our professional attention is increasingly drawn toward the *purposes* for which learners wish to use their English language skill. In a recent letter, Russell Campbell, a former TESOL President and Professor in the TESL and Applied Linguistics Department at the University of California, Los Angeles, noted that as we look toward the 21st century, "our profession will depend more and more on our ability to provide optimal *conditions* for language acquisition and less and less on language teaching and learning as we traditionally think of it" (personal communication, 1990). As we look around us, already we are seeing rapid growth of content-centered programs, whole language approaches, and task-based classroom activities.

Content-Centered Education

Content-centered instruction, according to Brinton, Snow, and Wesche (1989), is "the integration of content learning with language teaching aims. More specifically, it refers to the concurrent study of language and subject matter, with the form and sequence of language presentation dictated by content material" (p. vii). Tucker and Crandall (1989) point out that such an approach "contrasts sharply with many existing practices of methods in which language skills are taught virtually in isolation from substantive content" (p. 2). When language becomes the medium to convey informational content of interest and relevance to the learner, then learners are pointed toward matters of *intrinsic* concern. Language becomes incidental to and a vehicle for accomplishing a set of content goals.

The rise of language programs in which attention to subject matter is primary has given us new opportunities and challenges. In content-centered classrooms, one hopes for an increase in intrinsic motivation and empowerment. Students are pointed beyond transient extrinsic factors like grades and tests to their own competence and autonomy as intelligent individuals capable of actually doing something with their new language. Challenges range from a demand for a whole new genre of textbooks and other curricular materials to what Jo Ann Crandall (personal communication, 1990) describes as "the requirement that language teachers become much more comfortable with the concepts and skills, as well as the language, of other academic disciplines and of the prospect of working in teams across disciplines."

Whole Language Education and Task-Based Teaching

Other subject-matter issues in our profession include new challenges of presenting "whole language" (see Rigg, 1990) to our students, not language fragmented into "skill areas." Furthermore, the whole language movement now advocates principles of education already referred to above in the section on empowerment. For more on this topic, I invite you to look at Rigg's article in the Autumn 1991 *TESOL Quarterly*.

Yet another subject matter concern is addressed in the present issue of the *Quarterly* by David Nunan, that of task-based learning in the second language classroom. In keeping with current trends toward centering on learners' intrinsic needs for using language, task-based curricula focus on what students can *do* with language. As students resolve ambiguity, find solutions to problems, and accomplish specific tasks with their language, they can more efficiently integrate their linguistic and cognitive competence.

It is essential for all of us to understand that the more recent focus on content, purpose, and task as the primary subject matter in language teaching in no way reduces the importance of the fundamental problem of how to teach language forms. Attention to listening, speaking, reading, and writing, and to grammatical and discourse structures that give rise to the "four skills" has been and always will be a central concern in the profession. In fact, the pedagogical shift from a direct focus on language forms to the creation of "optimal conditions" for language acquisition is a complex linguistic issue (see Long & Crookes, in press). The task-based approach quite simply cannot be viewed as a collective excuse to abandon formal linguistic concerns. Rather, our challenge today is not just how to organize content and task, but also how to ensure the simultaneous, efficient acquisition of essential elements of the language code.

Human Issues: Peace and Environmental Education

Content-centered and task-based language classes have a plethora of subject-matter areas on which to focus a curriculum, a module, or a single activity. We think of topics like English for engineers, English for (various) academic purposes, or "how to buy an airplane ticket" as typical. In our efforts to offer immediately pragmatic, "here and now" material to our students, we can, I believe, also focus learners on some of the more ultimate issues of human survival. It is gratifying to see that at times the content of our language classes have been centered on what I would call human issues, namely, the universal problem of planetary survival—what some (see Fox, 1990) are calling "planethood." Peace education and environmental consciousness-raising comprise a legitimate content-centered focus that can help to empower students.

While we are indeed language teachers, commissioned by our various institutions to enable students to communicate in the English language, I think it is essential to understand that we are also, as Giroux and McLaren (1989) put it (quoted by Pennycook, 1989), "transformative intellectuals." That is, we are

professionals who are able and willing to reflect upon the ideological principles that inform practice, who connect pedagogical theory and practice to wider social issues, and who work together to share ideas, exercise power over the conditions of labor, and embody in teaching a vision of a better and more humane life. (p. 613)

As transformative intellectuals, our commission as teachers most certainly includes the goal of helping learners to become informed about as many issues as possible that intrinsically affect their lives. With conflict, war, and ecological decay as a way of life in what I would call a new world *dis*order, we as Earth's stewards have an urgent mission.

Just in the last few years we have witnessed a global movement of *peace education.* Various books and manuals (see Hicks, 1988; Reardon, 1989) have led the way. The last few TESOL conventions have featured sessions on peace education. Wenden (1990), Ashworth (1990), and others have published articles in the *TESOL Newsletter* calling our attention to ways that ESOL classes can be infused with awareness and action for peace and for conflict resolution. The environment is but one further frontier for Earth's peacemakers (Greig, Pike, & Selby, 1989). So, just as we have had our professional heads turned toward peace education, we must continue to maintain heightened sensitivity to environmental education, an issue that visibly and tangibly touches the lives of every human being on earth (see Brown, in press, for some specific activities for environmental education). The worldwide community of teachers can collectively create an outpouring of tender, loving care for Earth's remaining resources and a deep respect for our fellow stewards on this planet.

FOCUS ON METHOD
Communicative, Cooperative, Student-Centered Teaching

In the last decade, a great deal has been published and spoken about communicative language teaching, cooperative curricula, and student-centered classrooms. Both Savignon's and Nunan's articles in this issue of the *Quarterly* provide current references, problems, and reflections on these topics. Beneath all three trends lies a historical progression of pedagogical efforts to look inside the learner, to ask how that learner can best internalize a second language, and to experiment systematically with classroom approaches to accomplish the learner's communicative goals.

Twenty-five years ago, we were centrally concerned with issues surrounding the linguistic description of languages and their pedagogical applications. We were quite worried about how Chomsky's generative grammar was going to fit into our language classrooms (Lamendella, 1969). We were reluctant to break away from our strong interpretation of the contrastive analysis hypothesis (Wardhaugh, 1970). We were still strongly, if not exclusively, dependent on the discipline of linguistics for our professional and bureaucratic identity. We were only just beginning to question teaching methods that advocated "overlearning" through classroom drill and memorization (Brown, 1972; Rivers, 1964). Insights from children's "natural" means of acquiring their first language were just beginning to be tapped (Cook, 1969). And the description could go on.

Today, we benefit from the victories and defeats of our quarter-century journey. But today the methodological issues are quite different and quite complex. Beyond grammatical and discourse issues, we are probing the nature of social, cultural, and pragmatic features of language. We are exploring pedagogical means for "real-life" communication in the classroom. We are trying to get our learners to develop *fluency*, not just the *accuracy* that has so consumed our historical journey. We are equipping our students with tools for generating unrehearsed language performance "out there" when they leave the womb of our classrooms. We are concerned with how to facilitate lifelong language learning among our students, not just with the immediate classroom task. We are looking at learners as partners in a cooperative venture. And our methods seek to draw on whatever intrinsically sparks learners to explore and to create.

Learner Strategy Training

One of the most powerful methodological principles that is increasingly practiced in our profession is what I like to call the strategic investment of learners in their own linguistic destinies. Teaching methodology can be designed to let students in on some of the "secrets" of successful language learning. Traditionally, students walk into a language classroom and are at the mercy of the teacher, the text, the prescribed curriculum. They usually do not even know what a "strategy" is, and simply assume that language will be learned just like any other subject. We can help students to learn how to learn. We can help them to take some responsibility for their own success by actually providing learners with a sense of what a strategy is and how they can develop some of their own strategies.

Some excellent material on learner strategy training is now available to teachers. Oxford (1989) is a gold mine of information for teachers who wish to see how literally dozens of classroom activities and exercises can train learners to develop successful strategies. O'Malley and Chamot (1990) give an excellent overview of significant research on language learning strategies. Other materials (Carrell, Pharis, & Liberto, 1989; Cohen, 1990; Wenden & Rubin, 1987) combine research reports and practical classroom suggestions. Practical resources are now available to students themselves in the form of learning guidebooks and textbooks. Brown (1989) gives foreign language learners 15 easy-to-read chapters with exercises to heighten awareness and to initiate strategies for their own success. Brown (1991) appeals to former and present language learners to develop some awareness of how they might turn failure into success. Student textbooks like Chamot, O'Malley, and Küpper (1991), and Ellis and Sinclair (1989) offer strategy instruction along with language instruction.

Part of teaching learners how to learn involves helping students simply to become aware of how certain activities in the classroom are designed to develop strategies for success.

When teachers:	*they can help students to be aware:*
play guessing games and other communication games,	that it's important to be a risk taker and to lower inhibitions.
explicitly encourage or direct students to go beyond class-room assignments,	that it's important for them to set their own goals for their own purposes.
use movies or tapes, or have them read passages rapidly, or do skimming and scanning exercises,	of the importance of seeing the "big picture," and of not always focusing on the minute details.
direct students to share their knowledge and ideas, or talk in small groups,	of the importance of socioaffective strategies of cooperative learning.
praise students for good guesses and for trying out the language in novel situations,	that their *intuitions* about the language can be reliable sources of knowledge.
deliberately withhold a direct correction of error, or let stu-dents correct each other's errors,	that they can make their mis-takes work *for* them rather than *against* them.

What could be more intrinsically motivating to students than to develop their own autonomy by utilizing numerous strategies of learning? Their second language becomes their own, and simply the act of accomplishing something in the language is its own reward. Their strategic investment pays off.

We can be proud of this 25-year mark for TESOL. We've come a long way. The problems and issues are complex, but I think increasing numbers of English teachers around the world feel impelled to become better and better transformative intellectuals— agents for change. Language is a tool for overcoming powerless-ness. Our professional commitment intrinsically drives us to help the inhabitants of this planet to communicate with each other and to negotiate the meaning of peace, of goodwill, and of survival on this tender, fragile globe.

■

ACKNOWLEDGMENTS

Some material in this paper was delivered in a featured address, "On Track to the 21st Century: Destinations for the Nineties," at the 24th Annual TESOL Convention, San Francisco, March 1990.

THE AUTHOR

H. Douglas Brown is Professor of English and Director of the American Language Institute at San Francisco State University. His publications include *Principles of Language Learning and Teaching* (Prentice Hall, 1987) and *Breaking the Language Barrier* (Intercultural Press, 1991). He was Editor of *Language Learning* from 1970 to 1979.

REFERENCES

Ashworth, M. (1990, February). TESOL peace education. *TESOL Newsletter*, p. 4.

Bahouth, P. (1990). How can we save it? *Greenpeace, 15*(1), 4-8.

Brinton, D. M., Snow, M. A., & Wesche, M. B. (1989). *Content-based second language instruction.* New York: Newbury House.

Brown, H. D. (1972). Cognitive pruning and second language acquisition. *Modern Language Journal, 56,* 218-222.

Brown, H. D. (1989). *A practical guide to language learning.* New York: McGraw-Hill.

Brown, H. D. (in press). Fifty simple things you can do to teach environmental awareness and action in your English language classroom. *The Language Teacher* (Formerly *JALT Journal: Journal of the Japan Association of Language Teachers*).

Calkins, C. (1975). *The story of America.* Pleasantville, NY: Reader's Digest.

Carrell, P. L., Pharis, B. G., & Liberto, J. C. (1989). Metacognitive strategy training for ESL reading. *TESOL Quarterly, 23*(4), 647-678.

Cazden, C., & Snow, C. (Eds.). (1990). *English Plus: Issues in bilingual education* (Annals of the American Academy of Political and Social Science No. 508). Newbury Park, CA: Sage.

Chamot, A., O'Malley, J., & Küpper, L. (1991). *Building bridges.* New York: Heinle & Heinle.

Clarke, M. (1989, March). *Some thoughts on empowerment.* Paper presented at the 23rd Annual TESOL Convention, San Antonio, TX.

Cohen, A. (1990). *Language learning: Insights for learners, teachers, and researchers.* New York: Newbury House.

Cook, V. (1969). The analogy between first and second language learning. *International Review of Applied Linguistics, 11,* 13-28.

Crookes, G., & Schmidt, R. (1990, March). *Motivation: Reopening the research agenda.* Paper presented at the 24th Annual TESOL Convention, San Francisco, CA.

Deci, E. L. (1975). *Intrinsic motivation*. New York: Plenum Press.

Ellis, G., & Sinclair, B. (1989). *Learning to learn English: A course in learner training*. London: Cambridge University Press.

Fox, L. (1990, April). Planethood: An ESL writing course on global community. *TESOL Newsletter*, p. 19.

Freire, P. (1970). *Pedagogy of the oppressed*. New York: Seabury Press.

Gardner, R. C. (1985). *Social psychology and second language learning*. London: Edward Arnold.

Gardner, R. C. (1988). The socio-educational model of second language learning: Assumptions, findings, and issues. *Language Learning, 38*(1), 101-126.

Gardner, R. C., & Lambert, W. E. (1972). *Attitudes and motivation in second language learning*. Rowley, MA: Newbury House.

Greig, S., Pike, G., & Selby, D. (1989). *Earthrights: Education as if the planet really mattered*. London: World Wildlife Fund.

Hicks, D. (1988). *Education for peace*. London: Routledge.

Kachru, B. B. (1988). Teaching world Englishes. *ERIC/CLL News Bulletin, 12*(1), 1-8.

Krashen, S. D. (1985). *The input hypothesis*. London: Longman.

Lamendella, J. (1969). On the irrelevance of transformational grammar to second language pedagogy. *Language Learning, 19*, 255-270.

Lerner, M. (1989). *Surplus powerlessness*. Washington, DC: Institute for Labor and Mental Health.

Long, M., & Crookes, G. (in press). Three approaches to task-based syllabus design. *TESOL Quarterly*.

Madrid, A. (1990). Official English: A false policy issue. In C. Cazden & C. Snow (Eds.), *English Plus: Issues in bilingual education* (Annals of the American Academy of Political and Social Science No. 508, pp. 32-65). Newbury Park, CA: Sage.

O'Malley, J. M., & Chamot, A. U. (1990). *Learning strategies in second language acquisition*. New York: Cambridge University Press.

Oxford, R. C. (1989). *Language learning strategies: What every teacher ought to know*. New York: Newbury House.

Pennycook, A. (1989). The concept of method, interested knowledge, and the politics of language teaching. *TESOL Quarterly, 23*(4), 589-618.

Piaget, J. (1985). *The equilibrium of cognitive structures*. Chicago: University of Chicago Press.

Reardon, B. (1989). *Educating for global responsibility*. New York: Teachers College Press.

Rigg, P. (1990). Whole language in adult ESL programs. *ERIC/CLL News Bulletin, 13*(2), 1-8.

Rivers, W. (1964). *The psychologist and the foreign language teacher*. Chicago: University of Chicago Press.

Savignon, S. (1990). Communicative language teaching: Definitions and directions. In J. Alatis (Ed.), *Georgetown University Round Table on Languages and Linguistics 1990* (pp. 207-217). Washington, DC: Georgetown University Press.

Terrell, T. D. (1990). Natural versus classroom input: Advantages and disadvantages for beginning language students. In J. Alatis (Ed.), *Georgetown University Round Table on Languages and Linguistics 1990* (pp. 193-206). Washington, DC: Georgetown University Press.

Tucker, G. R., & Crandall, J. (1989). The integration of language and content instruction for language minority and language majority students. In J. Alatis (Ed.), *Georgetown University Round Table on Languages and Linguistics 1989* (pp. 39-50). Washington, DC: Georgetown University Press.

Wardhaugh, R. (1970). The contrastive analysis hypothesis. *TESOL Quarterly, 4*(1), 123-130.

Wenden, A. (1990). Peace education and TESOL: What? How? Why? *TESOL Newsletter, 24*(1), 1.

Wenden, A., & Rubin, J. (Eds.). (1987). *Learner strategies in language learning.* Englewood Cliffs, NJ: Prentice Hall.

PERSPECTIVES ON THE FIELD

Communicative Language Teaching: State of the Art

SANDRA J. SAVIGNON
University of Illinois at Urbana-Champaign

This paper looks briefly at the beginnings of what has come to be known as communicative language teaching (CLT), then discusses current issues and promising avenues of inquiry. The perspective is international. CLT is seen to be not a British, European, or U.S. phenomenon, but rather an international effort to respond to the needs of present-day language learners in many different contexts of learning.

Not long ago, when American structuralist linguistics and behaviorist psychology were the prevailing influences in language teaching methods and materials, second/foreign language teachers talked about communication in terms of language skills, seen to be four: listening, speaking, reading, and writing. These skill categories were widely accepted and provided a ready-made framework for methods manuals, learner course materials, and teacher education programs. They were collectively described as *active* skills, speaking and writing, and *passive* skills, reading and listening.

Today, listeners and readers are no longer regarded as passive. They are seen as active participants in the negotiation of meaning. Schemata, expectancies, and top-down/bottom-up processing are among the terms now used to capture the necessarily complex, interactive nature of this negotiation. Yet full and widespread understanding of communication as negotiation has been hindered by the terms that came to replace the earlier active/passive dichotomy. The skills needed to engage in speaking and writing activities were described subsequently as *productive*, whereas listening and reading skills were said to be *receptive*.

While certainly an improvement over the earlier active/passive representation, the terms productive and receptive fall short of capturing the interactive nature of communication. Lost in this productive/receptive, message sending/message receiving representation is the *collaborative* nature of meaning making. Meaning appears fixed, rather, immutable, to be sent and received, not unlike a football in the hands of a team quarterback. The interest of a football game lies of course not in the football, but in the moves and strategies of the players as they fake, pass, and punt their way along the field. The interest of communication lies similarly in the moves and strategies of the participants. The terms that best represent the collaborative nature of what goes on are *interpretation, expression*, and *negotiation* of meaning. The communicative competence needed for participation includes not only grammatical competence, but pragmatic competence.

The inadequacy of a four skills model of language use is now recognized. And the shortcomings of audiolingual methodology are widely acknowledged. There is general acceptance of the complexity and interrelatedness of skills in both written and oral communication and of the need for learners to have the experience of communication, to participate in the negotiation of meaning. Newer, more comprehensive theories of language and language behavior have replaced those that looked for support to American structuralism and behaviorist psychology. The expanded, interactive view of language behavior they offer presents a number of challenges for teachers. Among them, how should form and function be integrated in an instructional sequence? What is an appropriate norm for learners? How is it determined? What is an error? And what, if anything, should be done when one occurs? How is language learning success to be measured? Acceptance of communicative criteria entails a commitment to address these admittedly complex issues.

Second language acquisition researchers face similar problems. Examination of the learning process from a communicative perspective has meant looking at language in context, analysis of learner expression and negotiation. Contrastive analysis (CA), the prediction of learner difficulties and potential sources of errors based on a contrastive analysis of two or more languages, seemed far more straightforward than do contemporary approaches to error analysis (EA), the analysis of learner language as an evolving, variable system. The focus of this analysis continues to broaden. An initial concern with sentence-level morphosyntactic features has expanded to include pragmatics, taking into account a host of cultural, gender, social, and other contextual variables. Researchers who confront the complexity of their task might well look back with nostalgia to an earlier time when the answers to improved language teaching seemed within reach.

By and large, however, the language teaching profession has responded well to the call for materials and programs to meet learner communicative needs. Theory building continues. Communicative competence has shown itself to be a robust and challenging concept for teachers, researchers, and program developers alike. Communicative language teaching (CLT) has become a term for methods and curricula that embrace both the goals *and* the processes of classroom learning, for teaching practice that views competence in terms of social interaction and looks to further language acquisition research to account for its development. A look in retrospect at the issues which have brought us to our present understanding of CLT will help to identify what appear to be promising avenues of inquiry in the years ahead.

THE BEGINNINGS OF COMMUNICATIVE LANGUAGE TEACHING

From its introduction into discussions of language and language learning in the early 1970s, the term *communicative competence* has prompted reflection. Fortunately for the survival of communicative competence as a useful concept, perhaps, the term has not lent itself to simple reduction, and with it the risk of becoming yet another slogan. Rather, it continues to represent a concept that attracts researchers and curriculum developers, offering a sturdy framework for integrating linguistic theory, research, and teaching practice.

Present understanding of CLT can be traced to concurrent developments on both sides of the Atlantic. In Europe, during the 1970s, the language needs of a rapidly increasing group of immigrants and guest workers, and a rich British linguistic tradition that included social as well as linguistic context in description of language behavior, led to the Council of Europe development of a syllabus for learners based on functional-notional concepts of language use. Derived from neo-Firthian systemic or functional linguistics that views language as meaning potential and maintains the centrality of context of situation in understanding language systems and how they work, a threshold level of language ability was described for each of the languages of Europe in terms of what learners should be able to *do* with the language (van Ek, 1975). Functions were based on assessment of learner needs and specified the end result, the *product* of an instructional program. The term *communicative* was used to describe programs that used a functional-notional syllabus based on needs assessment, and the language for specific purposes (LSP) movement was launched.

Concurrent development in Europe focused on the *process* of communicative classroom language learning. In Germany, for example, against a backdrop of social democratic concerns for individual empowerment, articulated in the writings of contemporary philosopher Jürgen Habermas (1970, 1971), language teaching methodologists Candlin, Edelhoff, and Piepho, took the lead in the development of classroom materials that encouraged learner choice and increasing autonomy (Candlin, 1978). Their systematic collection of exercise types for communicatively oriented English teaching were used in teacher in-service courses and workshops to guide curriculum change. Exercises were designed to exploit the variety of social meanings contained within particular grammatical structures. A system of "chains" encouraged teachers and learners to define their own learning path through principled selection of relevant exercises. Similar exploratory projects were also being initiated by Candlin (1978) at his academic home, the University of Lancaster, England, and by Holec (1979) and his colleagues at the University of Nancy (CRAPEL), France.

Meanwhile, in the United States, Hymes (1971) had reacted to Chomsky's characterization of the linguistic competence of the ideal native speaker and proposed the term communicative competence to represent the use of language in social context, the observance of sociolinguistic norms of appropriacy. His concern with speech communities and the integration of language, communication, and culture was not unlike that of Firth and Halliday in the British linguistic tradition (see Halliday, 1978). Hymes' communicative competence may be seen as the equivalent of Halliday's meaning potential. Similarly, his focus was not language learning but language as social behavior. In subsequent interpretations of the significance of Hymes' views for learners, U.S. methodologists tended to focus on native-speaker cultural norms and the difficulty, if not impossibility, of authentically representing them in a classroom of nonnative speakers. In light of this difficulty, the appropriateness of communicative competence as an instructional goal was questioned (e.g., Paulston, 1974).

At the same time, in a research project at the University of Illinois, Savignon (1972) used the term communicative competence to characterize the ability of language learners to interact with other speakers, to make meaning, as distinct from their ability to perform on discrete-point tests of grammatical knowledge. At a time when pattern practice and error avoidance were the rule in language teaching, this study of adult classroom acquisition of French looked at the effect of practice in the use of communication strategies as part of an instructional program. By encouraging students to ask for information, to seek clarification, to use circumlocution and whatever other linguistic and nonlinguistic resources they could muster to negotiate meaning, to stick to the communicative task at hand, teachers were invariably encouraging learners to take risks, to speak in other than memorized patterns. When test results were compared at the end of the 18-week, 5-hour-per-week program, learners who had practiced communication in lieu of laboratory pattern drills for one hour a week performed with no less accuracy on discrete-point tests of structure. On the other hand, their communicative competence as measured in terms of fluency, comprehensibility, effort, and amount of communication in a series of four unrehearsed communicative tasks significantly surpassed that of learners who had had no such practice. Learner reactions to the test formats lent further support to the view that even beginners respond well to activities that let them focus on meaning as opposed to formal features. (A related finding had to do with learner motivation. Motivation to learn French correlated, not with initial attitudes toward French speakers or the French language, but with success in the instructional program.)

A collection of role plays, games, and other communicative classroom activities were developed subsequently for inclusion in the U.S. adaptation of the French CREDIF materials, *Voix et Visages de la France* (Coulombe, Barré, Fostle, Poulin, & Savignon, 1974). The accompanying guide (Savignon, 1974) described their purpose as that of involving learners in the experience of communication. Teachers were encouraged to provide learners with the French equivalent of expressions like "What's the word for?" "Please repeat," "I don't understand," expressions that would help them to participate in the negotiation of meaning. Not unlike the efforts of Candlin and his colleagues working in a European EFL context, the focus was on classroom process and learner autonomy. The use of games, role plays, pair and other small-group activities has gained acceptance and is now widely recommended for inclusion in language teaching programs.

CLT thus can be seen to derive from a multidisciplinary perspective that includes, at least, linguistics, psychology, philosophy, sociology, and educational research. The focus has been the elaboration and implementation of programs and methodologies that promote the development of functional language ability through learner participation in communicative events. Central to CLT is the understanding of language learning as both an educational and a political issue. Language teaching is inextricably tied to language policy. Viewed from a multicultural intranational as well as international perspective, diverse sociopolitical contexts mandate not only a diverse set of language learning goals, but a diverse set of teaching strategies. Program design and implementation depend on negotiation between policy makers, linguists, researchers, and teachers. And evaluation of program success requires a similar collaborative effort. The selection of methods and materials appropriate to both the goals *and* context of teaching begins with an analysis of both learner needs *and* styles of learning.

IMPLICATIONS FOR EXISTING PROGRAMS

In this connection, the implications of CLT for existing programs merit brief discussion. By definition, CLT puts the focus on the learner. Learner communicative needs provide a framework for elaborating program goals in terms of functional competence. This implies global, qualitative evaluation of learner achievement as opposed to quantitative assessment of discrete linguistic features. Controversy over appropriate language testing persists, and many a curricular innovation has been undone by failure to make corresponding changes in evaluation. The attraction for many of a multiple-choice test with single right answers that a machine can translate into a score is undeniable. Qualitative evaluation of written and oral expression is time-consuming and not so straightforward. Language programs are not alone in this respect. U.S. educators, in particular, continue to feel frustration at the domination of curricula by large-scale, standardized, multiple-choice tests. Teachers, under pressure to make their students do well on such tests, often devote valuable class time to teaching test-taking skills, drilling students on multiple-choice items about writing, for example, rather than allowing them practice in writing. Current efforts at educational reform include the recommendation to return to essay writing and other more holistic assessments of learner ability. Some programs have initiated portfolio assessment, the collection and evaluation of learner poems, reports, stories, and other projects, in an effort to better represent and encourage learner achievement.

Depending upon their own preparation and experience, teachers themselves differ in their reactions to CLT. Some feel understandable frustration at the seeming ambiguity in discussions of communicative ability. Negotiation of meaning is well and good, but this view of language behavior lacks precision and does not provide a universal scale for assessment of individual learners. Ability is viewed, rather, as variable and highly dependent upon context and purpose. Other teachers welcome the opportunity to select and/or develop their own materials, providing learners with a range of communicative tasks. And they are comfortable relying on more global, integrative judgments of learner progress.

An additional source of frustration for some teachers are second language acquisition research findings that show the route, if not the rate, of language acquisition to be largely unaffected by classroom instruction. (For a review of second language acquisition research, see Larsen-Freeman in this issue of the *TESOL Quarterly*.) First language cross-linguistic studies of developmental universals initiated in the 1970s were soon followed by second language studies. Acquisition, assessed on the basis of expression in unrehearsed, oral communicative contexts seemed to follow a similar morphosyntactic sequence regardless of learner age or context of learning. Structural practice of the "skill getting" variety was seen to have little influence on self expression, or "skill using." Although they served to bear out the informal observations of teachers, namely that textbook presentation and drill do not insure learner use of these same structures in their own spontaneous expression, the findings were nonetheless disconcerting. They contradicted both grammar-translation and audiolingual precepts that placed the burden of acquisition on teacher explanation of grammar and controlled practice with insistence on learner accuracy. They were further at odds with textbooks that promise "mastery" of "basic" French, English, Spanish, etc. Teacher rejection of research findings, renewed insistence on standardized tests, and even exclusive reliance on the learners' native or first language, where possible, to be sure they "get the grammar," have been in some cases reactions to the frustration of teaching for communication.

Moreover, the language acquisition research paradigm itself, with its emphasis on sentence-level grammatical features, has served to bolster a structural focus, obscuring pragmatic and sociolinguistic issues in language acquisition. In her discussion of the contexts of competence, Berns (1990) stresses that the definition of a communicative competence appropriate for learners requires an understanding of the sociocultural contexts of language use. In addition, the selection of a methodology appropriate to the attainment of communicative competence requires an understanding of sociocultural differences in styles of learning. Curricular innovation is best advanced by the development of local materials which, in turn, rests on the involvement of classroom teachers.

Numerous such regional projects have been documented. The English language activity types elaborated by Candlin and others for use in German classrooms (Candlin, 1978) are one example. The modular, thematic French units developed for use in Ontario, Canada public schools offer another example; they began with surveys of learners and involved teachers at all stages of revision

(Ullmann, 1987). The task types elaborated by Prabhu for use in teaching English in Bangalore, India (Prabhu, 1987) are a similar example. The national modern language curriculum revision project in Finland (Takala, 1984), and the revision of the English for academic purposes course offerings in the University of Michigan English Language Institute, to better meet the needs of a growing population of international faculty and students (Morley, in press), are but two of many other examples of successful substantive reforms that involved theorists and practitioners working together. These are illustrations not of language for specific purposes in the traditional sense of the term, but, rather, of communicative approaches that have resulted from task-related, project-centered collaboration between researchers, administrators, teachers, and curriculum developers. The benefits have been two-fold: Teams of researchers and practitioners with expertise in both linguistics *and* language teaching have made contributions to both language teaching *and* language acquisition research.

WHAT ABOUT GRAMMAR?

Discussions of CLT not infrequently lead to questions of grammatical or formal accuracy. The perceived displacement of attention to morphosyntactic features in learner expression in favor of a focus on meaning has led in some cases to the impression that grammar is not important, or that proponents of CLT favor learner self-expression without regard for form.

While involvement in communicative events is seen as central to language development, this involvement necessarily requires attention to form. Communication cannot take place in the absence of structure, or grammar, a set of shared assumptions about how language works, along with a willingness of participants to cooperate in the negotiation of meaning. In their carefully researched and widely cited paper proposing components of communicative competence, Canale and Swain (1980) did not suggest that grammar was unimportant. They sought rather to situate grammatical competence within a more broadly defined communicative competence. Similarly, the findings of the Savignon (1972) study did not suggest that teachers forsake the teaching of grammar. Rather, the replacement of language laboratory structure drills with meaning-focused self-expression was found to be a more effective way to develop communicative ability *with no loss of morphosyntactic accuracy*. And learner performance on tests of discrete morphosyntactic features was not a good predictor of their performance on a series of integrative communicative tasks.

The nature of the contribution to language development of both form-focused and meaning-focused classroom activity remains a question in ongoing research. The optimum combination of these activities in any given instructional setting depends no doubt on learner age, nature and length of instructional sequence, opportunities for language contact outside the classroom, teacher preparation, and other factors. However, for the development of communicative ability, research findings overwhelmingly support the *integration* of form-focused exercises with meaning-focused experience. Grammar is important; and learners seem to focus best on grammar when it relates to their communicative needs and experiences. Nor should explicit attention to form be perceived as limited to sentence-level morphosyntactic features. Broader features of discourse, sociolinguistic rules of appropriacy, and communication strategies themselves may be included. (For further discussion and illustration, see Savignon, 1983).

In an effort to represent a distinction between meaning and form in oral expression, some methodologists have made use of the terms *fluency* and *accuracy*. This dichotomy is misleading, however, on at least two counts. It suggests that the form of a message is somehow unrelated to its meaning, and then implicitly proposes an absolute grammatical norm for learners. Accuracy in this instance is measured in terms of discrete features of phonology, morphology, and syntax, and thus fails to take into account the context-relevant, collaborative nature of self-expression. Fluency, on the other hand, suggests speed or ease of self-expression, which may or may not enhance communicative effectiveness.

PROMISING AVENUES OF INQUIRY

Turning now to promising avenues of inquiry in the years ahead, numerous sociolinguistic issues await attention. Variation in the speech community and its relationship to language change are central to sociolinguistic inquiry. Sociolinguistic perspectives on variability and change highlight the folly of describing native-speaker competence, let alone nonnative-speaker competence, in terms of "mastery" or "command" of a system. All language systems show instability and variation. Learner language systems show even greater instability and variability in terms of both the amount and rate of change. Sociolinguistic concerns with identity and accommodation help to explain the construction by bilinguals of a "variation space" which is different from that of a native speaker. It may include retention of any number of features of a previously acquired system of phonology, syntax, discourse, communication strategies, and so on. The phenomenon may be individual or, in those settings where there is a community of learners, general.

In response to a homework question which asked whether retention of a native accent was an example of communicative competence, a native French speaker wrote "Yes. A friend of mine who has been in the U.S. now for several years says he has kept his French accent because he noticed that women like it." His observation parallels those of sociolinguists who have documented the role of noncognitive factors such as motivation and self-identity in first language acquisition (e.g., Hymes, 1971). Self-identity is central to differential competence and the heterogeneity of speech communities. To assume that sheer quantity of exposure shapes children's speech is simplistic. Identification and motivation are what matter. Similarly, in second language acquisition, learner identification and motivation interact with opportunities and contexts of language use to influence the development of competence. In classrooms, which, as social contexts, provide settings for symbolic variation, nonnative-like features may be maintained to exhibit "learner" status (Preston, 1989).

Sociolinguistic perspectives have been important in understanding the implications of norm, appropriacy, and variability for CLT and continue to suggest avenues of inquiry for further research and materials development. Use of authentic language data has underscored the importance of context—setting, roles, genre, etc.—in interpreting the meaning of a text. A range of both oral and written *texts in context* provides learners with a variety of language experiences, experiences they need to construct their own "variation space," to make determinations of appropriacy in their own expression of meaning. *Competent* in this instance is not necessarily synonymous with *native-like*. Negotiation in CLT highlights the need for cross-linguistic, that is, *cross-cultural*, awareness on the part of all involved. Better understanding of the strategies used in the negotiation of meaning offers a potential for improving classroom practice of the needed skills.

Along with other sociolinguistic issues in language acquisition, the classroom itself as a social context for learning has been neglected. Classroom language learning was the focus of a number of research studies in the 1960s and early 1970s (e.g., Scherer & Wertheimer, 1964; Savignon, 1972; Smith, 1970). However, language classrooms were not a major interest of the second language acquisition (SLA) research that rapidly gathered momentum in the years that followed. The full range of variables present in educational settings was an obvious deterrent. Other difficulties included the lack of well-defined classroom processes to serve as variables and lack of agreement as to what constituted learning success. Confusion of form-focused drill with meaning-focused communication persisted in many of the textbook exercises and language test prototypes that directly or indirectly shaped curricula. Not surprisingly, researchers eager to establish SLA as a worthy field of inquiry turned their attention to more narrow, quantitative studies of the acquisition of selected morphosyntactic features.

With the realization that SLA research findings to date, while of value, do not begin to address the larger issues of language development, attention once again has turned to the classroom. The year 1988 alone saw the publication of at least five books on the topic of classroom language learning (Allwright, 1988; Chaudron, 1988; Ellis, 1988; Peck, 1988; van Lier, 1988). A recent initiative, supportive of CLT, is the analysis of activity or task-based curricula. Researchers are looking at classroom language events, breaking them down into units of analysis with a view to establishing a typology of tasks that teachers frequently use. Since tasks determine the opportunities for language use, for the interpretation, expression, and negotiation of meaning, their systematic description constitutes the first step in establishing a relationship between task and learning outcomes. No researcher today would dispute that langauge learning results from participation in communicative events. Despite any claims to the contrary, however, the nature of this learning remains undefined.

An early study of foreign language teacher talk was conducted by Guthrie (1984) who found persistent form/meaning focus confusion even when teachers felt they were providing an optimal classroom acquisition environment by speaking only in the language being learned. Transcriptions of teacher/learner dialogue revealed the unnaturalness, that is, incoherence, of much of the discourse. There have been similar reports with respect to ESL teaching in both the United States and Britain. A 1987 study by Nunan suggests that even when teachers are committed to the concept of a communicative approach, opportunities for genuine communicative interaction may be rare. Even when all lessons ostensibly focus on functional aspects of language use, patterns of classroom interaction provide little genuine communication between teacher and learner or, for that matter, between learner and learner.

A study by Kinginger (1990; see also Kinginger & Savignon, 1991) has examined the nature of learner/learner talk associated with a variety of task types involving small-group or pair work. Conversations representing four distinct task types were observed in two different college-level French programs. The conversations were examined with respect to (a) turn-taking and topic management, with generalizations regarding the degree of learner participation and initiative, and (b) negotiation and repair strategies. Data showed that when learners are constrained by formal considerations or provided with a structure-embedded "text" as a basis for "conversation," their talk had many of the same characteristics as form-focused teacher talk. Analyses of the interactions resulting from other, meaning-focused task types showed them to differ with respect to both quality and quantity of language use. They included examples of ways in which communicative experience can be provided in classroom settings.

Classroom teacher talk and opportunities for learner self-expression are but two features of classroom learning. Broader issues of teacher understanding, preparation, and practice await exploration. Contexts of teaching vary widely. Community attitudes, use and/or perceived usefulness of the language being taught, and differences and similarities with respect to previously learned languages are among the more obvious variables. In these respects, the experience of a teacher of English in San Juan clearly differs from that of a teacher in Osaka, Cairo, or Bonn. And these experiences differ, in turn, from those of teachers in Sydney, Houston, or Bath. But while considerable attention has been directed to *linguistic* variables in contexts of teaching as well as to comparative/contrastive analyses of languages themselves, surprisingly little systematic inquiry has been conducted into the instructional perceptions and practices of teachers themselves. In our efforts to improve language teaching, we have overlooked the language teacher.

A study of Kleinsasser (1989; see also Kleinsasser & Savignon, in press), based on classroom observations and conversations with foreign language teachers in U.S. secondary schools, identified two distinct technical cultures in operation. One technical culture is uncertain and routine. Teachers are uncertain about their ability to promote learning, but routine or predictable in their day-to-day approach to teaching. The other culture is certain and nonroutine. Teachers are confident that learners will learn and tend to support variety and innovation in their instructional practice. Among the other characteristics of certain/nonroutine cultures are discussion and collaboration among teachers. In contrast, heavy reliance on the textbook and nonexistent or infrequent opportunities for spontaneous, communicative language interaction are classroom characteristics of those teachers with an uncertain and routine culture. Discussions with colleagues related to instructional matters are infrequent or nonexistent.

The broader cultural environment is a potential factor in influencing the technical culture of an individual school or other instructional setting. Replication of the Kleinsasser study in other contexts, not only on different levels of instruction within the U.S. but around the world, would serve to clarify and perhaps expand the range of factors that merit inclusion. As new approaches to language teaching are elaborated, exploration of the technical cultures operating in instructional settings, of teachers' perceptions of what they do and why they do it, holds promise for understanding the frequently noted discrepancies between theoretical understanding of second/foreign language acquisition and classroom practice. Innovation in teaching methods and materials is most likely to occur in cultures that are certain and nonroutine.

CONCLUSION

We have much yet to learn about the nature of language and language development. The quest for principles and parameters has only just begun. Yet few would deny that our understanding of the collaborative nature of meaning making is far richer today than it was a quarter of a century ago. The study of language, that is, linguistics, continues to broaden. As questions of situated language use continue to be raised, specially trained ethnographers have come to replace the native speakers who were once the authorities on how language worked. And applied linguistics has emerged as a young and dynamic field of inquiry.

Drawing on current understanding of language use as social behavior, purposeful, and always in context, proponents of communicative language teaching offer a view of the language learner as a partner in learning; they encourage learner participation in communicative events and self-assessment of progress. In keeping with second language acquisition theory, methodologists advise learners to take communicative risks and to focus on the development of learning strategies. A tradition of abstraction in linguistic inquiry has contributed to the neglect of social context in both language teaching and language acquisition research, hindering understanding and acceptance of communicative competence as a goal for learners. When language use is viewed as social behavior, learner identity and motivation are seen to interact with language status, use, and contexts of learning to influence the development of competence. The description and explanation of the differential competence that invariably results must include an account of this interaction.

Valued as are the reasoned proposals of linguists, applied linguists, and second/foreign language teaching methodologists, however, exploration of the potential of communicative language teaching cannot proceed without the involvement of classroom teachers. The constraints of language classrooms are real. Tradition, learner attitudes, teacher preparation and expectations, and the instructional environment in general all contribute to and support teachers' technical cultures. Recommendations for methods and materials must take into account this reality. For them to do so, researchers, curriculum developers, and teachers will have to work together. Teamwork between linguists, methodologists and classroom teachers offers the best hope for the elaboration and diffusion of language teaching methods and materials that work, that encourage and support learners in the development of their communicative competence.

In this connection, the full potential of content-based and task-based curricula remains to be exploited. Through the variety of language activities that they can offer, content-based and task-based programs are ideally suited to a focus on communication, to the development of needed language skills through the interpretation, expression, and negotiation of meaning. As interest in communicative language teaching grows, more traditional programs will undoubtedly find ways to involve both learners and teachers in the definition of goals and the selection of meaning-focused interpretive and expressive tasks designed to meet those goals. Focus on form will then be related to these communicative experiences.

The opportunity for professional growth has never been greater. Current demand around the world for quality programs and language professionals to design and staff them offers unprecedented opportunities for research initiatives. Responding to this demand will require teamwork, a sharing of perspectives and insights. Researchers need to look to teachers to define researchable questions. Teachers, in turn, need to participate in the interpretation of findings for materials and classroom practice. Elaboration of appropriate methods and materials for a particular language teaching program will result only from the cooperation of all concerned.
■

THE AUTHOR

Sandra J. Savignon is Professor of French and of English as an International Language at the University of Illinois at Urbana-Champaign, where she is also director of the multidisciplinary doctoral program in Second Language Acquisition and Teacher Education (SLATE). She is the founding editor of the Addison-Wesley Second Language Professional Library and has served on the editorial boards of *Studies in Second Language Acquisition* and the *Canadian Modern Language Review*. She is currently Vice-President/President Elect of the American Association for Applied Linguistics. Dr. Savignon lectures frequently and has offered seminars for language teachers throughout the U.S., in Canada, South America, Europe, and Asia. She was Distinguished Professor at the 1990 TESOL Summer Institute.

REFERENCES

Allwright, D. (1988). *Observation in the language classroom*. London: Longman.

Berns, M. S. (1990). *Contexts of competence: Social and cultural considerations in communicative language teaching*. New York: Plenum.

Canale, M., & Swain, M. (1980). Theoretical bases of communicative approaches to second language teaching and testing. *Applied Linguistics, 1,* 1-47.

Candlin, C. (1978). *Teaching of English: Principles and an exercise typology*. London: Langenscheidt-Longman.

Chaudron, C. (1988). *Second language classrooms: Research on teaching and learning*. New York: Cambridge University Press.

Coulombe, R., Barré, J., Fostle, C., Poulin, N., & Savignon, S. (1974). *Voix et visages de la France: Level 1*. Chicago: Rand-McNally.

Ellis, R. 1988. *Classroom second language development*. New York: Prentice Hall.

Guthrie, E. (1984). Intake, communication, and second language teaching. In S. J. Savignon & M. S. Berns (Eds.), *Initiatives in communicative language teaching* (pp. 35-54). Reading, MA: Addison-Wesley.

Habermas, J. (1970). Toward a theory of communicative competence. *Inquiry, 13,* 360-375.

Habermas, J. (1971). Vorbereitende Bemerkungen zu einer Theorie der Kommunikative Kompetenz (pp. 101-141). In N. Lishman (Ed.), *Theorie der Gesellschaft oder Sozialtechnologie*. Frankfurt: Suhrkamp. 101-141.

Halliday, M. A. K. (1978). *Language as social semiotic: The social interpretation of language and meaning*. Baltimore: University Park Press.

Holec, H. (1979). *Autonomy and foreign language learning*. Strasbourg: Council of Europe.

Hymes, D. (1971). Competence and performance in linguistic theory. In R. Huxley & E. Ingram (Eds.), *Language acquisition: Models and methods*. London: Academic Press.

Kinginger, C. (1990). *Task variation and classroom learner discourse*. Unpublished doctoral dissertation, University of Illinois at Urbana-Champaign.

Kinginger, C. & Savignon, S. J. (1991). Four conversations: Task variation and learner discourse. In C. Faltis & M. McGroarty (Eds.), *Language in school and society: Policy and pedagogy* (pp. 85-106). New York: Mouton de Gruyter.

Kleinsasser, R. (1989). *Foreign language teaching: A tale of two technical cultures*. Unpublished doctoral dissertation, University of Illinois at Urbana-Champaign.

Kleinsasser, R., & Savignon, S. J. (in press). Linguistics, language pedagogy, and teachers' technical cultures. In J. E. Alatis (Ed.), *Georgetown University Round Table on Languages and Linguistics 1991*. Washington, DC: Georgetown University Press.

Morley, J. (in press). Perspectives on English for academic purposes. In J. E. Alatis (Ed.), *Georgetown University Round Table on Languages and Linguistics 1991*. Washington, DC: Georgetown University Press.

Nunan, D. (1987). Communicative language teaching: Making it work. *ELT Journal, 41*(2), 136-145.

Paulston, C. B. (1974). Linguistic and communicative competence. *TESOL Quarterly, 8*(2), 347-362.

Peck, A. (1988). *Language teachers at work*. New York: Prentice Hall.

Preston, D. R. (1989). *Sociolinguistics and second language acquisition*. Oxford: Basil Blackwell.

Prabhu, N. S. (1987). *Second language pedagogy*. Oxford: Oxford University Press.

Savignon, S. J. (1972). *Communicative competence: An experiment in foreign language teaching*. Philadelphia: Center for Curriculum Development.

Savignon, S. J. (1974). Teaching for communication. In R. Coulombe, R. J. Barré, C. Fostle, N. Poulin, & S. Savignon, *Voix et visages de la France: Level 1* (Teachers' Guide). Chicago: Rand McNally. (Reprinted in *English Teaching Forum, 1978, 16*[2], 2-5, 9)

Savignon, S. J. (1983). *Communicative competence: Theory and classroom practice*. Reading, MA: Addison-Wesley.

Scherer, G., & Wertheimer, M. (1964). *A psycholinguistic experiment in foreign language teaching*. New York: McGraw-Hill.

Smith, P. D. (1970). *A comparison of the cognitive and audiolingual approaches to foreign language instruction: The Pennsylvania foreign language project*. Philadelphia: Center for Curriculum Development.

Takala, S. (1984). Contextual considerations in communicative language teaching. In S. J. Savignon & M. S. Berns (Eds.), *Initiatives in communicative language teaching* (pp. 23-34). Reading, MA: Addison-Wesley.

Ullmann, R. (1987). The Ontario experience: A modular approach to second language teaching and learning. In S. J. Savignon & M. S. Berns (Eds.), *Initiatives in communicative language teaching II* (pp. 57-81). Reading, MA: Addison-Wesley.

van Ek, J., (Ed.). (1975). *Systems development in adult language learning: The threshold level in a European unit credit system for modern language learning by adults.* Strasbourg: Council of Europe.

van Lier, Leo. (1988). *The classroom and the language learner: Ethnography and second language classroom research.* London: Longman.

Communicative Tasks and the Language Curriculum

DAVID NUNAN
Macquarie University

Over the last 25 years the communicative task has emerged as a significant building block in the development of language curricula and also as an element for motivating process-oriented second language acquisition research. This paper reviews the influence of the communicative task on curriculum development and summarizes the research base for task-based language teaching. In the final part of the paper, an agenda for future research is set out.

Over the last 25 years, the communicative task has evolved as an important component within curriculum planning, implementation, and evaluation. In task-based language teaching, syllabus content and instructional processes are selected with reference to the communicative tasks which learners will (either actually or potentially) need to engage in outside the classroom and also with reference to theoretical and empirical insights into those social and psycholinguistic processes which facilitate language acquisition. This approach to language teaching is characterized by the following features:

1. An emphasis on learning to communicate through interaction in the target language

2. The introduction of authentic texts into the learning situation

3. The provision of opportunities for learners to focus, not only on language, but also on the learning process itself

4. An enhancement of the learner's own personal experiences as important contributing elements to classroom learning

5. An attempt to link classroom language learning with language activation outside the classroom

Task-based language teaching has been an important addition to the conceptual and empirical repertoire of the second and foreign language teacher in the eighties, having influenced syllabus design, materials development, and language teaching methodology. In this paper, I shall review the development of task-based language teaching (TBLT). In the first part of the paper, I shall provide an account of the theoretical and empirical basis for TBLT. I shall then discuss the influence of TBLT on curriculum development and classroom practice. In the final part of the paper, I indicate the ways in which I believe that the research agenda should be extended in the nineties.

THE CONCEPTUAL BASIS

Like many other innovations, task-based teaching entered the language field from the educational mainstream. Studies of teachers at work demonstrated that, while teacher education programs taught trainees to plan, implement, and evaluate their programs according to the "rational" model which begins with objectives and moves through tasks to evaluation (Tyler, 1949), the reality was that once they began practicing, teachers tended to focus on pedagogic tasks (Shavelson & Stern, 1981). This insight from research into teachers' professional planning and decision-making processes enhanced the status of task as a curriculum planning tool.

Task-based learning is also linked to mainstream education by its close relationship with experiential learning. This relationship is evident in the following description of experiential learning:

> In experiential learning, immediate personal experience is seen as the focal point for learning, giving "life, texture, and subjective personal meaning to abstract concepts and at the same time providing a concrete, publicly shared reference point for testing the implications and validity of ideas created during the learning process," as pointed out by David Kolb (1984: 21). But experience also needs to be processed consciously by reflecting on it. Learning is thus seen as a cyclical process integrating immediate experience, reflection, abstract conceptualization and action. (Kohonen, in press)

To date, definitions of tasks have been rather programmatic. Long (1985a) suggests that a task is nothing more or less than the things people do in everyday life. He cites as examples buying shoes, making reservations, finding destinations, and writing cheques. The *Longman Dictionary of Applied Linguistics* provides a more pedagogically oriented characterization. Here, it is suggested that a task is

> any activity or action which is carried out as the result of processing or understanding language (i.e., as a response). For example, drawing a

map while listening to a tape, listening to an instruction and performing a command, may be referred to as tasks. (Richards, Platt, & Weber, 1985, p. 289)

The value of tasks, according to the authors, is that they provide a purpose for the activity which goes beyond the practice of language for its own sake.

A similar characterization is offered by Breen (1987) who suggests that a task is

> any structured language learning endeavour which has a particular objective, appropriate content, a specified working procedure, and a range of outcomes for those who undertake the task. 'Task' is therefore assumed to refer to a range of workplans which have the overall purpose of facilitating language learning—from the simple and brief exercise type, to more complex and lengthy activities such as group problem-solving or simulations and decision making. (p. 23)

Elsewhere, I have suggested that tasks can be conceptualized in terms of the curricular goals they are intended to serve, the input data which forms the point of departure for the task, and the activities or procedures which the learners undertake in the completion of the task. Two important additional elements are the roles for teachers and learners implicit in the task, and the settings and conditions under which the task takes place (Nunan, 1989). Later in this paper, I shall use these elements of goals, input data, activities/procedures, roles, and settings as rubrics for synthesizing the considerable amount of research activity which provides an empirical basis for task-based language teaching and learning.

THE CURRICULAR BASIS

Before the development of communicative approaches to language teaching, tasks and exercises were selected as a second order activity, after the specification of the morphosyntactic, phonological, and lexical elements to be taught. Traditionally, curriculum designers and materials writers took as their point of departure the question, What are the grammatical, phonological, and lexical items to be taught? The specification of these items set the parameters for the selection of classroom activities. In other words, selection of classroom activities was driven by curriculum goals specified in phonological, morphosyntactic, and lexical terms. (See, for example, the analysis of content selection and sequencing in a grammar-based syllabus provided by McDonough, 1981, p. 21.)

In a task-based curriculum, the decision-making process is quite different. There are, in fact, two different routes which the curriculum developer/materials writer can take in initiating the design process. The first of these is based on what I have called the rehearsal rationale. Here the question initiating the design process is, What is it that learners potentially or actually need to do with the target language? The second is what I have called the psycholinguistic rationale. Here the initiating question is, What are the psycholinguistic mechanisms underlying second language acquisition, and how can these be activated in the classroom? The linguistic elements to be focused on in the classroom are selected as a second order activity.

Ideally, task selection should occur with reference both to target task rationale and psycholinguistic principles. The way that this might be achieved is illustrated in the procedure set out in Figure 1, adapted from a recently published task-based coursebook (Nunan & Lockwood, 1991). The pedagogic task is selected with reference to the real-world or target task of "giving information in a job interview." Learners are given a model of the target language behaviour, as well as specific practice in manipulating key language items. The actual pedagogic task, a simulation, is also consistent with research on the facilitative effects of classroom interaction (research on language acquisition is reviewed in the next section).

FIGURE 1

Steps Involved in the Development of a Pedagogic Task

Procedure	Example	Rationale
1. Identify target task	Giving personal information in a job interview	To give learners the opportunity to develop language skills relevant to their real world needs
2. Provide model	Students listen to and extract key information from authentic/simulated interview	To provide learners the opportunity to listen to and analyse ways in which native speakers or users of the target language carry out the target task
3. Identify enabling skill	Manipulation drill to practice *wh*-questions with *do*-insertion	To provide learners with explicit instruction and guided practice in those grammatical elements needed to perform the target task
4. Devise pedagogic task	Interview simulation using role cards	To provide learners the opportunity to mobilize their emerging language skills through rehearsal

The growing importance of the pedagogic task as a central element within the curriculum has called into question the conventional distinction between syllabus design and methodology. Traditionally, syllabus design is concerned with the selection and grading of content, while methodology is concerned with the selection and sequencing of tasks, exercises, and related classroom activities. Metaphorically speaking, syllabus design is concerned with the destination, while methodology is concerned with the route. With the development of task-based approaches to language learning and teaching, this distinction has become difficult to sustain. Breen (1984) has neatly captured this change of focus in the following way:

> [TBLT would] prioritize the route itself; a focusing upon the means towards the learning of a new language. Here the designer would give priority to the changing process of learning and the potential of the classroom—to the psychological and social resources applied to a new language by learners in the classroom context. . . . a greater concern with capacity for communication rather than repertoire of communication, with the activity of learning a language viewed as important as the language itself, and with a focus upon means rather than predetermined objectives, all indicate priority of process over content. (pp. 52-53)

Conceptually, then, task-based language teaching has been influenced by developments in mainstream education as well as by major conceptual shifts in our understanding of the nature of language and language learning. It has also been enhanced by a research agenda which has provided an empirical basis upon which curriculum designers, materials writers, and classroom practitioners can draw. The availability of empirical data on tasks has enhanced the status of task-based language teaching at a time when the various "methods" approaches to language teaching have come under increasing criticism for lacking an empirical basis. (See, for example, Long, 1990; Richards, 1990). In the next section, I shall provide a selective review of this research.

THE EMPIRICAL BASIS

One of the strengths of task-based language teaching is that the conceptual basis is supported by a strong empirical tradition. This distinguishes it from most methods approaches to pedagogy, which are relatively data-free. I have already suggested that tasks can be conceptualized in terms of the key elements of goals, input data, activities/procedures, roles, and settings. This conceptual scheme provides a convenient means of synthesising the research on tasks.

Task goals enable the program planner and materials writer to provide explicit links between the task and the broader curriculum it is designed to serve. Without clearly articulated sets of goal statements, there is a risk that task-based teaching programs will lack coherence as Widdowson (1987), among others, has pointed out. Goals are generally referenced against the sorts of things which learners want to do with the language outside the classroom. Typical goal statements include:

1. To develop the skills necessary to take part in academic study
2. To obtain sufficient oral and written skills to obtain a promotion from unskilled worker to site supervisor
3. To communicate socially in the target language
4. To develop the survival skills necessary to obtain goods and services
5. To be able to read the literature of the target culture

Despite its importance for coherent curriculum development, compared to other areas, research on task goals is difficult to find in the literature. One of the few available studies is that by Brindley (1984) who investigated the needs analysis, goal and objective setting practices of teachers of ESL to adults, and the reaction of learners to these practices. Based on an extensive series of interviews, Brindley found that programs in which the goals were explicit and reflected the communicative needs of the learners had greater face validity than those in which the goals were either unstated, inexplicit, or which did not reflect learners' goals. While there was no direct evidence that programs with explicit, relevant goals resulted in more effective learning outcomes, it is not unreasonable to expect that this would be the case, given what we know about the relationship between affective/attitudinal factors and learning outcomes.

Most tasks take as their point of departure input data of some sort. Such data may be linguistic (that is, reading and listening texts of various sorts) or nonlinguistic (for example, diagrams, photographs, picture sequences). This area is considerably better researched than that of goals. A key question underlying research on input tasks is, What factors are implicated in the difficulty of aural and written texts?

In a large-scale investigation of the listening comprehension of secondary students, Brown and Yule (1983) found that two factors significantly affected the difficulty of listening texts. The first factor related to the number of elements in the text and the ease and difficulty of distinguishing between them. The second significant factor was the text type. All other things being equal, descriptions were easier than instructions, which were easier than stories. Arguments or opinion-expressing texts containing abstract concepts and relationships were the most difficult. Follow-up research cited in Anderson and Lynch (1988) identified a number of other factors including the following:

1. The way the information is organized (narrative texts in which the order of events in the texts mirrors the order in which the events actually occurred in real life are easier to comprehend than narratives in which the events are presented out of sequence)
2. The familiarity of the topic
3. The explicitness and sufficiency of the information
4. The type of referring expressions (for young children, pronominal referents are more difficult to comprehend than full noun phrase referents)
5. Text type

In the area of reading comprehension, Nunan (1984) found that similar elements were implicated in the difficulty of school texts for secondary level students. Nunan looked, among other things, at the difficulty of different types of textual relationships as well as at the effect of content familiarity. He found that logical relationships of the type marked by conjunctions were more difficult than referential and lexical relationships. He also found that content familiarity was more significant than grammatical complexity in determining the difficulty of reading texts.

The bulk of task-based research has focused on the activities or procedures which learners carry out in relation to the input data. The key question here has been, What tasks seem to be most helpful in facilitating second language acquisition?

In the first of a series of investigations into learner-learner interaction, Long (1981) found that two-way tasks (in which all students in a group discussion had unique information to contribute) stimulated significantly more modified interactions than one-way tasks (that is, in which one member of the group possessed all the relevant information). Similarly, Doughty and Pica (1986) found that required information-exchange tasks generated significantly more modified interaction than tasks in which the exchange of information was optional. (*Modified interactions* are those instances in which speakers modify their language in order to assure that they have been correctly understood; they result from an indication of noncomprehension, usually on the part of a listener.)

These investigations of modified interaction were theoretically motivated by Krashen's (1981, 1982) hypothesis that comprehensible input was a necessary and sufficient condition for second language acquisition—in other words, that acquisition would occur when learners understood messages in the target language. Long (1985b) advanced the following argument in favor of tasks which promote conversational adjustments or interactional modifications on the part of the learners taking part in the task:

Step 1: Show that (a) linguistic/conversational adjustments promote (b) comprehensible input.

Step 2: Show that (b) comprehensible input promotes (c) acquisition.

Step 3: Deduce that (a) linguistic/conversational adjustments promote (c) acquisition. Satisfactory evidence of the a → b → c relationships would allow the linguistic environment to be posited as an indirect causal variable in SLA. (The relationship would be indirect because of the intervening "comprehension" variable.) (p. 378)

In the last few years the comprehensible input hypothesis has been criticised on theoretical and empirical grounds. For example, Swain (1985) demonstrated that immersion programs in Canada, in which learners received huge amounts of comprehensible input did not lead to the sort of native-like facility in the target language predicted by the input hypothesis. She proposed that in addition to comprehensible input, learners need opportunities that require that their own speech be comprehensible because it is only through such opportunities that learners are pushed to mobilize their emerging grammatical competence. (Such mobilization is precisely what the tasks suggested by Long, 1985b; Doughty & Pica, 1986; and others manage to achieve. In other words, their research may be justified on grounds other than that proposed by the comprehensible input hypothesis.)

More recently, attention has focused on the question of the types of language and discourse patterns stimulated by different task types. Berwick (1988, in press) investigated the different types of language stimulated by transactional and interpersonal tasks. (A transaction task is one in which communication occurs principally to bring about the exchange of goods and services, whereas an interpersonal task is one in which communication occurs largely for social purposes.) He found that the different functional purposes stimulated different morphosyntactic realizations.

In a recent study, I investigated the different interactional patterns stimulated by open and closed tasks. (An open task is one in which there is no single correct answer, while a closed task is one in which there is a single correct answer or a restricted number of correct answers.) It was found that the different task types stimulated very different interactional patterns. This can be seen in the following extracts. In Task A, the relatively closed task, the students are required to sort 20 vocabulary cards into semantic fields. In Task B, having read a text on the topic of habits, the students are required to have an open-ended discussion on the topic of bad habits. (Both extracts are adapted from Nunan, 1991.)

Extract from Task A

Two students, Hilda and Carlos, are studying the following words which have been typed onto pieces of cardboard. Their task is to group the words together in a way which makes sense to them. There is silence for several minutes as the students study the cards:

GEOGRAPHY, ASTRONOMY, AGRICULTURE, ECONOMICS, COMMERCE, ENGLISH, SCIENCE, STATISTICS, BOOK, COMPUTER, PENCIL, DIARY, NEWSPAPER, MAGAZINE, THAILAND, HONG KONG, MELBOURNE, DARWIN, UNITED STATES, ASIAN, DIAGRAM, ILLUSTRATION, PICTURE, CARTOON, VIDEO, COMPETENT, LAZY, INTERESTING, SUPERIOR, UNCOMFORTABLE, REGION.

H: Statistic and diagram—they go together. You know diagram?

C: Yeah.

H: Diagram and statistic are family . . . but maybe, I think, statistic and diagram—you think we can put in science? Or maybe . . .[1]

C: Science, astronomy, [yeah] and er can be agriculture.

H: Agriculture's not a science.

C: Yes, it's similar . . .

H: No. . . . er may be Darwin and science . . .

C: What's the Darwin?

H: Darwin is a man.

C: No, it's one of place in Australia.

H: Yes, but it's a man who discover something, yes, I'm sure.

C: OK.

H: And maybe, look, yes, picture, newspaper, magazine, cartoon, book, illustration

---

[1] Ellipses indicate pauses.

C: [yeah]. Maybe we can put lazy and English together. Er Hong Kong, Thailand together. Asian. Er, United States. Diary with picture, newspaper and so on. . . . Oh, I understand, look, look. Here, it's only adjective—lazy, competent, interesting and comfortable. Er, what is it? Ah yes yes. (She begins to rearrange the cards.)

C: Darwin

Extract from Task B

Maria, Martha, Sylvia, and Sandy are taking part in a small-group discussion on the topic of bad habits.

Maria: My next door neighbour . . . he make eh very noisy, very noisy [yeah].[2] I can't tell him because he's very good people.

(The discussion continues for several minutes.)

Sylvia: . . . you don't want to say anything because you might get upset, of course. Me do the same thing because I've got neighbours in my place and always you know do something I don't like it but I don't like to say bad because I think maybe, you, know make him upset or . . .

Martha: I've got bad neighbour but I feel embarrass . . .

Sylvia: . . . to say something of course, like everyone . . .

Martha: They always come in and see what I'm doing—who's coming. [no good] [yeah, that's no good] They want to check everything. If they see I buy something from the market they expect me to give them some. [oh yeah]. [oh that's not nice] But I . . . it's difficult.

Sylvia: It's a difficult, yeah, but sometime it's difficult . . .,

Martha: They can't understand, I bought them and I gave money . . . . (laughter) [yeah]

Martha: You know sometime difficult to the people because sometime I can't speak the proper, the language, and little bit hard to give to understand . . . and that's—sometime feel embarrass then, I can't say it, you know?

Maria: [turns to the fifth woman, who has not yet spoken] Sarah, you tell [you tell now]

Sarah: My, er, for example, my sister in law she all the time snores in her sleep [oh, yes] And my brother say, "Oh, I'm sorry, we must sleep separate" [separate beds] (laughter). They did. [good idea] A good idea because he couldn't sleep. (Laughter.)

---
[2] Note that it was not possible to identify overlapping speakers.

In addition to the fact that the different task types stimulated different interactional patterns, the research also indicated that some task types might be more appropriate than others for learners at particular levels of proficiency. In the above study, it was found that with lower-intermediate to intermediate learners, the relatively closed tasks stimulate more modified interaction than relatively more open tasks. This is not to say that such students should engage in closed tasks to the exclusion of open tasks. The important thing is that program planners and teachers should select a mix of tasks to reflect the pedagogic goals of the curriculum.

Another element considered within task design is that of teacher/ learner roles. All pedagogic tasks contain roles for teachers and learners, and conflict is likely to occur if there is a misapprehension between teachers and learners about their respective roles. Research related to learner roles has come up with findings which run counter to the folk wisdom of the classroom. For instance, Bruton and Samuda (1980) found that learners are capable of correcting each other successfully. Additionally, according to Porter (1986), learners produce more talk with other learners than with native-speaking partners, and learners do not learn each other's errors. Finally, Gass and Varonis (1985) found that there were advantages, when conducting groupwork, to pairing learners of different proficiency levels as well as from different language backgrounds.

The final element is that of setting, which refers to the learner configuration (either teacher-fronted, small group, pair, or individual), as well as the environment (whether the task takes place in the classroom or outside the classroom). One of the first task studies to be carried out, that by Long, Adams, and Castanos (1976), found that small-group tasks prompt students to use a greater range of language functions than teacher-fronted tasks. In relation to environment, Montgomery and Eisenstein (1985) found that supplementing classroom tasks with community-based experiences resulted in significantly increased language gains.

FUTURE DIRECTIONS: EXTENDING THE RESEARCH AGENDA

Most of the research carried out during the eighties and described in the preceding section was driven by Krashen's input hypothesis, which is based on the belief that opportunities for second language acquisition are maximised when learners are exposed to language which is just a little beyond their current level of competence (Krashen, 1981, 1982). The central research issue here is, What classroom tasks and patterns of interaction provide learners with the greatest amount of comprehensible input? It has been argued that patterns of interaction in which learners are forced to make conversational adjustments promote acquisition. As I have already pointed out, this view represents an indirect rather than direct relationship between environmental factors (for example, types of instruction) and language acquisition. I also referred to research which, while questioning the comprehensible input hypothesis, supported the communicative tasks to which it gave rise.

While the research reviewed in the preceding section represents a healthy state of affairs, the scope needs to be developed and extended both substantively and methodologically. In substantive terms, the research agenda needs to incorporate a greater range of linguistic and psycholinguistic models. Methodologically, the scope of the research needs to be extended by the utilization of a greater range of research tools and techniques. In particular, it would be useful to see the emergence of research which explored the relationships between contextual factors, interpersonal factors, learner proficiency levels; and pedagogic tasks.

In order to indicate the ways in which these principles might influence the shape of future research, I shall briefly review two recent investigations which provide useful indications of the ways in which research on task-based language teaching and learning can be extended both substantively and methodologically.

Berwick (1988; in press) exemplifies the advantages of extending the research agenda on tasks by drawing on insights from a range of theoretical models. Of particular interest is his utilization of functional grammars, specifically the systemic-functional model first articulated by Halliday (see, for example, Halliday, 1985; Halliday & Hasan, 1976; Halliday & Hasan, 1989). This particular model of language attempts to draw explicit links between the functions which language exists to fulfil and its realization at the level of lexicogrammatical choice. In his research, Berwick (1988) explored differences at the level of lexicogrammar attributable to different task types. In classifying tasks, he distinguished between pedagogical and collaborative goals on one hand, and expository and experiential processes on the other. Tasks with pedagogical goals are concerned with the transfer of information through explicit instruction, while collaborative tasks "emphasized cooperative, consensual behaviour and exchange of information about a problem or topic which participants explore freely during the task itself" (Berwick, in press). Tasks based on expository processes are concerned with theoretically based knowledge, whereas experiential processes are concerned with procedural knowledge (in familiar terms, the former is concerned with theoretical knowing [knowing that], while the latter is concerned with practical knowledge [knowing how]). Berwick uses these two dimensions to situate a range of tasks which he used in his study. These are set out in Figure 2. A description of the tasks follows.

Task COM1: This task, residing at the expository end of the process continuum and the pedagogical end of the goal continuum, consisted of a lecture about finding string characters in a text through use of the word-processing program of a personal computer, not physically present in the experimental setting.

Task COM2: This task shared the pedagogical goal of COM1, but was more experiential in that it involved a demonstration of how to find character strings on the laptop computer when it was physically present in front of the participants.

Task LEG1: Participants in this task faced away from each other. One participant had a small Lego toy made of snap-together plastic parts which had to be described so that the second participant was able to assemble a replica of the toy.

Task LEG2: This task was similar to LEG1, except that participants sat face-to-face.

Task DIS: The final task was an informal discussion of any topic of common interest to the participants.

The independent variable in Berwick's study was the task. Dependent variables included a range of discourse features associated with the negotiation of meaning in interaction and utilized in many of the task investigations based on the input hypothesis. Variables included clarification requests, comprehension checks, confirmation checks, definitions, display questions,

FIGURE 2

Goal and Process Dimensions of the Five Tasks Used in the Berwick Study

From "Towards an Educational Framework for Teacher-led Tasks in English as a Foreign Language" by R. Berwick, in press, in *Task-Based Language Teaching* edited by G. Crookes & S. Gass. Copyright Multilingual Matters. Reprinted by permission.

	Processes		
Goals	Expository		Experiential
Pedagogical	COM1		COM2
Collaborative/Social	LEG1	DIS	LEG2

echoes, expressions of lexical uncertainty, referential questions, self-expansions, self-repetitions, and other-repetitions.

Berwick (in press) established through his research that task type is an important determinant of lexicogrammatical exponents. He was also able to relate the tasks and exponents to an educational framework which provides a broad pedagogical rationale for task-based language teaching. I have described his research at some length because it exemplifies the value of drawing on a range of theoretical models in the development of research programs into task-based language teaching and learning.

The second study reviewed in this section is by Duff (in press). Duff carried out a longitudinal case study of a single learner, investigating the extent to which performance on different types of tasks yielded different types of information on the subject's interlanguage. The three tasks investigated included an interview conversation, a picture description, and a Cambodian folktale narration. The dependent measures included the amount of language produced, the range of vocabulary elicited, nominal reference, and negation. Data were collected from a 24-year-old Cambodian male, over a 2-year period.

Duff's study yielded mixed results. While there was some evidence of task-related variability, the subject's performance from one data-collection period to the next also exhibited variability. The study raised five fundamental questions: (a) Are the tasks selected distinct enough to be operationalizable constructs in this type of analysis? (b) Assuming the constructs are valid, are there any meaningful differences across tasks? (c) To what extent can variability be ascribed to other constructs such as genre or topic? (d) Were the features investigated by the researcher the salient ones, or should this line of research be restricted to those features of interlanguage morphology and phonology which have been found to be salient? (e) How is the researcher to account for those differences which were observed?

Duff's study is significant within the current context because it represents a departure from the cross-sectional research which has typified the field since its inception. While the longitudinal case study has been usefully employed in other aspects of SLA research (see, for example, Schmidt, 1983) it is uncommon in research on tasks. In the five fundamental questions she raises as a result of her study, Duff also provides a basis for a substantial research agenda for further research. Finally, she places the issue of interlanguage variability firmly on the research agenda. Looking to the future, I would like to see the issue of variability feature more prominently in research into task-based language learning and teaching.

CONCLUSION

In this paper I have provided a selective overview of the development of task-based language teaching. I have tried to show that, while it had its genesis in mainstream education, task-based teaching has become a powerful influence in language education. At a conceptual level, the approach has been supported by changing conceptions of the nature of language and learning—captured under the rubric of communicative language teaching. Empirically, TBLT is supported by a healthy research agenda which emerged from process-oriented second language acquisition.

In the second part of the paper, I have tried to indicate some of the directions that TBLT might take in the future. In particular, I have suggested that the conceptual and empirical basis needs to be extended both substantively and methodologically, and I described two recent investigations which illustrate the possible shape of research under such an extended agenda.

■

THE AUTHOR

David Nunan is Associate Professor of Linguistics at Macquarie University, Sydney, Australia. His publications include *Syllabus Design* (Oxford University Press, 1988), *The Learner-Centred Curriculum* (Cambridge University Press, 1988), *Designing Tasks for the Communicative Classroom* (Cambridge University Press, 1989), *Second Language Teacher Education* (with J. C. Richards, Cambridge University Press, 1990), *Understanding Language Classrooms* (Prentice Hall, 1989), and *The Australian English Course* (with J. Lockwood, Cambridge University Press, 1991).

REFERENCES

Anderson, A., & Lynch, T. (1988). *Listening*. Oxford: Oxford University Press.

Berwick, R. (1988). *The effect of task variation in teacher-led groups on repair of English as a foreign language*. Unpublished doctoral dissertation, University of British Columbia, Vancouver, Canada.

Berwick, R. (in press). Towards an educational framework for teacher-led tasks in English as a foreign language. In G. Crookes & S. Gass (Eds.), *Task-based language teaching*. Clevedon, Avon, England: Multilingual Matters.

Breen, M. (1984). Process syllabuses for the language classroom. In C. Brumfit (Ed.), *General English syllabus design*. Oxford: Pergamon Press.

Breen, M. (1987). Learner contributions to task design. In C. Candlin & D. Murphy (Eds.), *Language learning tasks*. Englewood Cliffs, NJ: Prentice Hall.

Brindley, G. (1984). *Needs analysis and objective setting in the Adult Migrant Education Service*. Sydney: Adult Migrant Immigration Service.

Brown, G., & Yule, G. (1983). *Teaching the spoken language*. Cambridge: Cambridge University Press.

Bruton, G., & Samuda, G. (1980). Learner and teacher roles in the treatment of oral error in group work. *RELC Journal, 11*(3), 49-63.

Doughty, C., & Pica, T. (1986). "Information gap" tasks: Do they facilitate second language acquisition? *TESOL Quarterly, 20*(3), 305-325.

Duff, P. (in press). Task force on interlanguage performance: An analysis of task as independent variable. In G. Crookes & S. Gass (Eds.), *Task-based language teaching*. Clevedon, Avon, England: Multilingual Matters.

Gass, S., & Varonis, E. (1985). Task variation and nonnative/nonnative negotiation of meaning. In S. Gass and C. Madden (Eds.), *Input in second language acquisition*. Rowley, MA: Newbury House.

Halliday, M. A. K. (1985). *An introduction to functional grammar*. London: Edward Arnold.

Halliday, M. A. K., & Hasan, R. (1976). *Cohesion in English*. London: Longman.

Halliday, M. A. K., & Hasan, R. (1989). *Language, context and text: Aspects of language in a social semiotic perspective*. Oxford: Oxford University Press.

Kohonen, V. (in press). Experiential language learning: Second language learning as cooperative learner education. In D. Nunan (Ed.), *Collaborative language learning and teaching*. Cambridge: Cambridge University Press.

Kolb, D. (1984). *Experiential learning: Experience as the source of learning and development*. Englewood Cliffs, NJ: Prentice Hall.

Krashen, S. (1981). *Second language acquisition and second language learning*. Oxford: Pergamon Press.

Krashen, S. (1982). *Principles and practice in second language acquisition*. Oxford: Pergamon Press.

Larsen-Freeman, D., & Long, M. H. (in press). *An introduction to second language acquisition research*. London: Longman.

Long, M. H. (1981). Input, interaction and second language acquisition. In H. Winitz (Ed.), *Native language and foreign language acquisition* (Annals of the New York Academy of Sciences No. 379, pp. 259-278). New York: New York Academy of Sciences.

Long, M. H. (1985a). A role for instruction in second language acquisition: Task-based language training. In K. Hyltenstam & M. Pienemann (Eds.), *Modelling and assessing second language acquisition*. Clevedon, Avon, England: Multilingual Matters.

Long, M. H. (1985b). Input and second language acquisition theory. In S. Gass & C. Madden (Eds.), *Input in second language acquisition*. Rowley, MA: Newbury House.

Long, M. H. (1990). Task, groups, and task-group interactions. In S. Anivan (Ed.), *Language teaching methodology for the nineties.* Singapore: RELC.

Long, M. H., Adams, L., & Castanos, F. (1976). Doing things with words: Verbal interaction in lockstep and small group classroom situations. In R. Crymes & J. Fanselow (Eds.), *On TESOL '76.* Washington, DC: TESOL.

McDonough, S. (1981). *Psychology in foreign language teaching.* London: Allen & Unwin.

Montgomery, C., & Eisenstein, M. (1985). Real reality revisited: An experimental communicative course in ESL. *TESOL Quarterly, 19*(2), 317-334.

Nunan, D. (1984). *Discourse processing by first language, second phase, and second language learners.* Unpublished doctoral dissertation, Flinders University of South Australia, Adelaide.

Nunan, D. (1989). *Designing tasks for the communicative classroom.* Cambridge: Cambridge University Press.

Nunan, D. (1991). *Language teaching methodology: A textbook for teachers.* London: Prentice Hall.

Nunan, D., & Lockwood, J. (1991). *The Australian English course: Task-based English for post-beginners.* Cambridge: Cambridge University Press.

Porter, P. (1986). How learners talk to each other: Input and interaction in task-centered discussions. In R. Day (Ed.), *Talking to learn: Conversation in second language acquisition.* Rowley, MA: Newbury House.

Richards, J. C. (1990). *The language teaching matrix.* Cambridge: Cambridge University Press.

Richards, J. C., Platt, J., & Weber, H. (1985). *Longman dictionary of applied linguistics.* London: Longman.

Schmidt, R. (1983). Interaction, acculturation, and the acquisition of communicative competence: A case study of an adult. In N. Wolfson & E. Judd (Eds.), *Sociolinguistics and language acquisition.* Rowley, MA: Newbury House.

Shavelson, R. J., & Stern, P. (1981). Research on teachers' pedagogical thoughts, judgments and behaviour, *Review of Educational Research, 51,* 4.

Swain, M. (1985). Communicative competence: Some roles of comprehensible input and comprehensible output in its development. In S. Gass & C. Madden (Eds.), *Input in second language acquisition.* Rowley, MA: Newbury House.

Tyler, R. (1949). *Basic principles of curriculum and instruction.* New York: Harcourt Brace.

Widdowson, H. G. (1987). Aspects of syllabus design. In M. Tickoo (Ed.), *Language syllabuses: State of the art.* Singapore: RELC.

Whole Language in TESOL

PAT RIGG
American Language & Literacy

This paper presents key aspects of the whole language perspective; describes examples of whole language principles in practice in elementary, secondary, and adult ESOL programs; and reviews recent whole language research on second language development.

WHOLE LANGUAGE PRINCIPLES

The term *whole language* has become a popular, even bandwagon term for native speakers of English in elementary education and is beginning to be used in secondary and adult education (Goodman, Bird, & Goodman, 1991; "Special report," 1991). Whole language is both a theoretical perspective and a movement affecting both instruction and research. The movement grew from an original focus on the teaching of reading to native speakers of English; it grew to encompass writing and then the processes of teaching and learning, which in turn involve the roles of teacher and student. What began as a holistic way to teach reading has become a movement for change, key aspects of which are respect for each student as a member of a culture and as a creator of knowledge, and respect for each teacher as a professional. The movement has had its greatest impact in elementary schools and with L1 students and is only beginning to affect secondary and adult education.

In the field of TESOL we are starting to see "whole language" in articles, in book titles, and in convention presentations. Where does the term come from? What does it mean, both to its originators and to us in TESOL? What effect is it having on our teaching of English to speakers of other languages? In this article, I propose to address these questions by summarizing the key points of the whole language perspective; describing some examples of whole language principles in practice in elementary, secondary, and adult ESOL programs; and suggesting how the whole language perspective affects research in L2 development.

Background

The term *whole language* comes not from linguists but from educators—people like Harste and Burke (1977), Ken and Yetta Goodman (1981), and Watson (1989)—who began using it in reference to how English-speaking children become readers. (See "Whole language," 1989, for more detailed descriptions of whole language philosophy and history; see also Y. Goodman, 1989, 1991.) They asserted that language is a whole (hence the name), that any attempt to fragment it into parts—whether these be grammatical patterns, vocabulary lists, or phonics "families"—destroys it. If language isn't kept whole, it isn't language anymore. Harste and Burke (1977) first suggested the term when they described three different theories of reading: phonics, which presumed that reading was basically a process of turning letters into sounds; skills, which presumed that reading was basically a hierarchy of skills, including phonics, word recognition, and comprehension skills; and whole language, which defined reading as a psycholinguistic process (K. S. Goodman, 1967) in which readers interact with texts. Readers predict what comes next; sample cues from the semantic, syntactic, and graphophonic systems; and use their knowledge of the world, of the language, and their purposes for reading to interact with the text and to arrive at meaning (Harste & Burke, 1977).

These early leaders of the movement read the research in composition by Graves (1983), Calkins (1983, 1986), and Atwell (1987), and as a result, they enlarged their focus: Whole language proponents began to think of literacy as including both reading and writing. The researchers in composition were convincing in their focus on the processes of writing instead of on written products. Instead of looking at writing primarily as a means of demonstrating knowledge to a teacher, whole language proponents now viewed writing as a means of discovering for oneself what one thinks. In her address to TESOL in New York, Calkins (1991) moved even further, talking about how we use writing to create and recreate ourselves.

About the same time that the early whole language advocates were incorporating recent research in composition into their view, they began to read Louise Rosenblatt (1938/1976), who described reading as a process of *transacting* with text. In *The Reader, the Text, and the Poem*, Rosenblatt (1978) asserted that, instead of simply interacting, the reader and text "transact" (p. 17), and together create the poem. Rosenblatt also helped explain how individual interpretation of text (private meaning) related to a commonly accepted interpretation (public meaning), and she distinguished between "aesthetic" and "efferent" reading (p. 22)—reading for the experience and reading to find out. For most whole language educators, whose interest had been primarily the reading process, this focus on literature and its interpretation was a significant step. The research into the reading of children whose first language was not English (Goodman & Goodman, 1978) had confirmed that these readers' backgrounds strongly affect the meaning constructed from the page. Rosenblatt was convincing in arguing that we needed to look much more closely at *what* was being read—the text, at *why* it was being read, and at *how* the aesthetic possibilities could be explored. Today's whole language emphasis on literature study (Peterson & Eeds, 1990) and an appreciation of multiple interpretations owes much to the rediscovery of Rosenblatt. As Edelsky (1991) points out, the recognition of the validity of different interpretations promotes pluralism.

Edelsky, Altwerger, & Flores (1991) offer probably the clearest description of what whole language currently is and what it is not; *Whole Language: What's the Difference?* opens with "First and foremost, whole language is a *professional theory*, an explicit theory *in* practice. . . . Whole language weaves together a theoretical view of language, language learning, and learning into a particular stance on education" (p. 7). It is not a method, nor a collection of strategies, techniques, or materials although certain approaches and materials are characteristic of whole language classes.

Principles of Knowledge and of Language

This "professional theory in practice" is based in part on the belief that knowledge is socially constructed, rather than received or discovered. Traditionally, formal education has been viewed as a matter of transferring knowledge from the teacher's head and from textbooks into the students' heads. But if knowledge is constructed, there is no single right answer, either in the text or the teacher. More, the teacher, rather than transmitting knowledge to the students, collaborates with them to create knowledge. This is the foundation for the whole language emphasis on student choice and on collaboration.

A second basic premise is that the major purpose of language is the creation and communication of meaning. We use language to think: In order to discover what we know, we sometimes write, perhaps talk to a friend, or mutter to ourselves silently. We can think in other ways (for example, you can visualize Picasso's *Guernica* or recall the first notes of Beethoven's Fifth Symphony), but language is our primary way of creating meaning. Similarly, language is our primary means of communicating to others. An obvious corollary of this is the assertion that language is always used purposefully. TESOL professionals who are accustomed to functional syllabi easily understand and accept this corollary: They recognize the myriad functions of language and they may use those functions as the basis for organizing the information they present to students learning English as an additional language. An important difference between the whole language and the functional ESL curriculum is that the whole language curriculum demands that language functions always be authentic, always be meaningful. That is, an ESL class might practice some language used in apologies, even though no one in class is really trying to apologize to anyone else. A whole language perspective requires an authentic, "real" situation in which one person truly needs to apologize to another. (See Edelsky, 1987, for a full discussion of authenticity.)

Real is a byword in whole language classes. Notwithstanding the difficulties in defining authenticity, a commitment to real activities is an important component of the whole language perspective. Real activities are defined as those relevant to students' interests, lives, and communities. Activities designed to practice behaviors or skills that will someday be needed are not considered real under this model: Why ask students to engage in practice runs when they could be working on something immediately and directly relevant? Materials too must be real. Too often textbooks used in grades K–12 are written by committees of people who don't teach (and often have never taught), are purchased by other committees of people who may or may not teach, but seldom teach the classes which will use the textbooks, and are read by teachers and students in classrooms far removed from both publisher and textbook selection committee. Textbooks to teach reading, "basals," have come under attack by Goodman, Shannon, Freeman, & Murphy (1988) and Shannon (1989, 1990) and others. These researchers have convinced many teachers and school administrators to use funds allocated for textbooks and consumable workbooks for trade books of children's literature, both fictional and nonfictional. California's decision to replace basals with a literature program in all schools statewide has given strength and support to teachers who want to convince their administration and school boards to try the same. Whole language programs require well-stocked large classroom libraries from which students can select what they want to read, both in free reading time and in literature study. In whole language classrooms students read real books.

Writing too must be real. The students are invited to write for themselves and for others, rather than just for the teacher. Research on the writing of L1 school children (Atwell, 1987; Calkins, 1983; Graves, 1983) has convinced many teachers that it is the processes, not the products, of writing that deserve their attention. As a result, in whole language classes students select their own topics, their own audiences, and write for their own purposes and to their own standards. The writing workshop approach postpones the correction of errors to the prepublication step of editing; this frees both students and teacher to concentrate on matters of content, organization, and style. In a process approach to composing, students and teacher can look at successive drafts with an eye towards increasing clarity, or deepening mood, or using language more vigorously or artfully. Language's "aesthetic qualities . . . the musicality, design and balance and symbolism that give pleasure to language users" (Edelsky et al., 1991, pp. 13-14) allow language users to play with language and to revel in the creative possibilities that range from jump-rope rhymes, through puns and limericks and songs, all the way to *Hamlet*.

Whole language advocates recognize that language is both individual and social. "Who and what we are is determined in great part by our language. Since we are all uniquely individual with an almost infinite number of different life experiences, our oral and written language often reflects those differences" (Kazemek, 1981, p. 1). Both where we grew up and which social class we first belonged to mark our speech; our education and our profession show in both our speech and our writing. One obvious application of this principle is the acceptance (not just tolerance) of nonprestige dialects. When writing teachers support their students in finding and using their own voices, they are putting this principle into practice.

Language is social. It makes a difference who says what to whom, how, and why. What is the social relationship of two people communicating? What are their purposes? What is the situation? The language used by a person on a factory floor expressing anger at perceived incompetence differs, depending on whether the individual is speaking *to* the supervisor or *is* the supervisor. Language use is always in a social context, and this applies to both oral and written language, to both first and second language use. Applying this principle to the whole language class results in paying attention to audience and to context: Both speakers and writers are urged to consider their audience, the person(s) they are addressing; both are reminded to consider the setting in which their messages will be received.

Part of the wholeness of whole language is the inclusion of literacy as a part of language. Because reading and writing are not separate systems from language, in a literate society, using written language is as natural as using conversation, and the uses of written language develop as naturally as do the uses of oral language (Goodman & Goodman, 1981). The four language modes—speaking, writing, listening, and reading—are mutually supportive and are not artificially separated in whole language classes.

Many traditional ESL programs have separated the language modes, offering classes in reading, in writing, in conversation, in pronunciation, in listening. Whole language classes use all four modes, but may offer ESL students the opportunity to zero in on the aspect of language they most need help with. I remember a Yemeni seaman I worked with in Detroit years ago: Ahmed[1] spoke English fluently with near-native pronunciation, but in English he could read only the most common of environmental print signs (STOP, McDonald's) and could write only his name. Ahmed wanted to pass the Seaman First Class test so he could move up in his chosen profession; for him, tutoring in written English seemed the best option. We used his excellent oral English as the base; he dictated his text to me using the language experience approach (Rigg, 1991). Recently a Vietnamese friend of mine, a young woman who writes so beautifully in English that she's been published several times, spoke to an audience of teachers about her language learning experiences; as I listened and watched the puzzled faces of the audience, I wished she had access to a tutor who would use her writing as the basis for work in pronunciation.

Principles of Teaching and Learning

The principles of knowledge and of language lead to principles of teaching and learning. Primary among these is the principle that curriculum and instruction need to be both meaning-centered and student-centered. *Meaning-centered* means that oral and written language experiences must be purposeful, functional, and real. Reading and writing activities must serve real purposes (e.g., to entertain, to convince, to explore, to excuse oneself, and so on). Choice is vital in a whole language class, because without the ability to select activities, materials, and conversational partners, the students cannot use language for their own purposes. So teachers "issue invitations" to students, offering a choice of activities and materials. Authenticity, as defined by Edelsky (1987), is necessary. Whatever the students are doing, whether suggested by themselves or by the teacher, is for their own purposes. If students are writing

---

[1] Student names have been changed.

letters, for example, it is because they want to communicate through writing with the people they are writing to; the letters will be mailed, and (the writers hope) answered. They are not writing pretend letters to practice the form of a friendly or business letter.

Student-centered means building the curriculum in the class with and for the students (Nunan, 1988). A major aspect of the whole language view is respect for each student, with all that that entails in terms of respect for the student's language, home, and culture. This contrasts strongly with the typical traditional class, whether elementary or university level: The standard curriculum in public schools is usually determined by committees of people who have never met the people who actually use the curriculum—the students and teachers. Curriculum committees at the school district level and at the state department of education level do not know any of the students; legislators are even further removed from the people their educational decisions most directly affect.

Related to the principle of respect for the student, and involvement of the students in determining their own curriculum, is the principle of respect for the teacher. A whole language perspective advocates mutual respect among professionals. Typically, in whole language programs, teachers meet as committees to decide on curriculum, on evaluation, and on the management of their school; they choose themselves what books will be on the classroom shelves, deciding themselves how to spend both book and nonbook funds. The training and experience of professional teachers best qualify them to judge what the students in their rooms need and want. Only teachers have close daily contact with the students. Only they are able to determine what materials and activities are appropriate for their students at any time. They know what to offer. Also, their choice is as vital as the students'; if the teachers don't have choices, they cannot offer much choice to their students.

This principle of respect for the teacher, coupled with students' obvious delight in student-centered, meaningful activities, has helped make whole language a large-scale movement in Australia, Canada, and the U.S. Teachers have joined together in peer support groups, often calling their group Teachers Applying Whole Language, or TAWL. These groups are loosely affiliated across Canada and the U.S. through the Whole Language Umbrella, which drew 2,000 to its first conference in the summer of 1990 in St. Louis, MO, and almost that many in August 1991 to Phoenix, AZ. It is not exclusively a grass-roots teachers' movement, since it was started and is still led by teacher educators at various universities. These teachers and teacher educators have held "a whole day of whole language" for the last 2 years at the national conferences of both the International Reading Association (IRA) and the National Council of Teachers of English (NCTE). The movement has become so widespread that it has become a bandwagon: Now a wide variety of publishers and presenters have adopted the label whole language and are using it to market materials and workshops that 10 years ago were labeled back to basics. (See recent issues of IRA's *Reading Today* newsletter for sample ads.)

One more indication of respect for the teacher is that teachers are increasingly recognized as researchers. Bissex and Bullock's (1987) collection of case studies by classroom teachers typifies the sort of research whole language teachers are undertaking and publishing. (Whole language research is discussed later in this paper.)

EVALUATION

Whole language teachers often protest being required to administer standardized tests such as the Iowa Test of Basic Skills (ITBS), arguing that those tests do not accurately describe their students' abilities, nor do they predict their students' performance. Teachers question not only what standardized tests are testing but what they are *teaching* the students. In my state of Arizona, every child must take the ITBS every year, whether the child is a speaker of English, Spanish, Navajo, or any of the several other languages in the state. (English arrived in Arizona about 150 years after Spanish and thousands of years after First Nation languages.) Teachers in several schools report horror stories of children becoming physically ill from the stress of taking the ITBS. They also tell bitterly funny stories of instances in which the ITBS score indicated a child could not do something—simple addition, for example— when the teacher had ample evidence that the child could. My own favorite story came from a member of a local school board who had insisted on basing teachers' and principals' salaries on schools' ITBS scores: This man's daughter received one of the lowest ITBS scores in the district—she had lost her place on the answer sheet.

Evaluation, like curriculum, needs to be meaning-centered and student-centered. Assessment and evaluation of whole language education must itself be holistic (Goodman, Goodman, & Hood, 1989; Harp, 1991). We cannot assess growth by using standardized or criterion-referenced tests which measure isolated, partial, or purposeless language skills (Taylor, 1990). Whole language classrooms typically use student self-evaluation as part of ongoing and informal assessment which allows the instructor and student to document growth and to plan for future instruction. Because students themselves establish their goals, students themselves monitor their progress (Brindley, 1986). Holistic assessment in grades K–12 takes place with teachers keeping narrative records of their "kidwatching" (Y. Goodman, 1985) and portfolios of student writing and reading. Teachers' records are based on

> conferring with the students about their reading and writing, noting difficulties, efficient strategies, personal goals, types of texts they need or want to read and write, and so on; preparing a checklist of specific things that the teacher and the student want to accomplish during a specific time period; collecting samples of a student's reading (perhaps on tape, using some type of miscue analysis) and writing and charting growth over time. (Kazemek, 1989, p. 5)

WHOLE LANGUAGE IN ESOL CONTEXTS

Elementary Education

The preceding discussions have referred to L1 speakers. Do whole language principles hold true in L2 learning? Whole language advocates believe they do, citing two arguments:

1. L2 can develop much as does L1. L2 classes should offer a language-nurturing environment, paying attention to doing things *with* language rather than to language itself (Krashen & Terrell, 1983). This includes literacy as well as oral language.
2. L2, like L1, develops through interaction with peers, rather than through imitation of a teacher's model or through formal study. The holistic ESOL class develops a strong sense of community in the class and school, and uses a variety of collaborative learning activities.

The most obvious place to find whole language in ESOL practice is in elementary classrooms in schools where many of the children speak English as an additional language. Else Hamayan (personal communication, 1988) calls these students "potentially English proficient (PEP)" kids—in contrast to the U.S. government's labeling of them as limited English proficient. I find the terms *LEP* and *limited speakers* derogatory; alternatively, one might label limited English speakers those handicapped by monolingualism, people limited to English.

In elementary schools with PEP students, there are two whole language approaches which do not pull out the PEP students from their grade-level classrooms for ESL instruction. The first approach integrates L2 with L1 students and supplies ESL assistance in the class. McCloskey's (1988) multicultural curriculum for grades K–6,

English Everywhere designed for the Dallas school system, exemplifies this approach. Enright and McCloskey's *Integrating English* (1988) is probably the best-known current text for teachers who want to integrate PEP students into multicultural classes and at the same time integrate content-area subjects into thematic units. An example of a school which puts this into practice is Fair Oaks in Redwood City, California. The teachers who work there have documented the changes of this bilingual school in *Becoming a Whole Language School* (Bird, 1987).

The second major approach offers academic instruction in L1, with ESL taught more implicitly than explicitly. This approach is suitable for bilingual programs in which all nonnative speakers of English share one home language.

Both approaches can be seen at Machan School in Phoenix, Arizona. The school has about 800 students in grades K–6, most of whom qualify as "at-risk" for both state and federal assistance: Ninety percent receive free lunch (an indicator of low income); school scores on the state-required Iowa Test of Basic Skills were lowest in the district in 1989 and 1990; over half of the students speak Spanish as a home language. For the last 3 years, the school has been receiving special state funds for a K–3 bilingual project. As the external evaluator of that project for the past 2 years, I visited Machan School frequently, sitting in on classes, observing and interacting with students, teachers, staff, and community members. I believe it is an excellent example of whole language in an elementary ESOL context.

Machan's principal, Lyn Davey, and the K–3 project director, Kelly Draper, share a whole language view of education, a view which includes staff and community participation in the management of the school. When Dr. Davey became principal 3 years ago, she indicated to the staff that she held a strongly holistic and collaborative view of teaching, learning, and administering, and she invited teachers to join her in implementing this holistic philosophy. As the school begins its 4th year in September 1991, the staff is cohesive, with a strong sense of community and of professionalism. If we could peek into various classrooms, we would see great diversity in teaching styles, but an almost unanimous philosophy of teaching, one that is meaning-centered and student-centered.

A Machan kindergarten class exemplifies the first approach—integration of L1 and L2 students in a multicultural class. Actually, it is two kindergartens; one team of two teachers and an aide collaborate to create one large class in two rooms with two languages in use at all times. The teachers use thematic units, which allow for the integration of different content-area subjects within one theme. The human body was the theme last fall. Early in October, I watched Spanish- and English-speaking students work in pairs to outline each other's body silhouette on black paper. The children cut out their own silhouettes and, throughout the next several days, marked with white chalk the different bones of the human body, looking at a life-size skeleton and feeling their own arms and hands to sense where the bones really were in the flesh. These chalk skeletons on black paper served as wall decorations for the school's celebration of both Halloween, a traditional Anglo-American holiday, and the Day of the Dead, a traditional Mexican holiday celebrated on November 2. This typifies the sorts of activities that these students engage in: Science and art blend together as students study a topic very important to them—in this case their own bodies—with an amazing maturity for 6-year-olds. Throughout an hour, many students move easily from language to language, and the teachers respond in the language selected by the student.

The two teachers believe that it is important to validate and value not only Spanish and English but other languages, so although most of their conversation and reading materials are in these two major languages, the teachers bring in examples of other languages. In both of these rooms, as in almost all the classes at Machan School, students write daily in their journals, on whatever topics they choose, in whichever language is most comfortable (Peyton & Reed, 1990), and their teachers write back. Students read for pleasure daily, selecting from a wide variety of materials, from magazines through children's literature. One of the children who began the class as a monolingual English speaker now offers to translate English expressions into Spanish; Albert is very proud of his new linguistic ability. Fred wrote a story in English about his grandparents, who live in Mexico; he then rewrote the story in Spanish so that his beloved grandparents could read what he had written about them. One of last year's students, now a first grader, has moved from using only Spanish to reading and writing in English, and doing it so well that her classmates say she is the best reader in the room.

The second approach uses the students' home language for instruction. One Machan kindergarten exemplifying the second approach is just beginning to use whole language ideas. All of the instruction in this room is in Spanish. The teacher grew up attending Mexican schools and taught in Mexico until recently, so she knows all the songs, finger games, riddles, stories, and so on, that are appropriate for children of this age from Mexican culture. She began to teach in the U.S. only last year, and only then did she have the opportunity to try any whole language ideas. I remember visiting her room in October: She was helping 20 Spanish-speaking youngsters learn a new song in Spanish. After a few visits, I suggested that perhaps the students could start dictating their stories to her, and could start writing to her in journals, rather than spending over half of their time on drilling of individual letters and letter-sound relationships. The teacher was quite skeptical. "How can they write anything?" she asked me. "They don't know their letters yet." But she tried both the language experience dictation and the dialogue journals, and within the month she was inviting me to return to her class to see the books her children were making. Sure enough, over half of these PEP kids had written stories in Spanish about their families or pets or friends, and were proud to pose for my camera with their very own books. The success of letting the kids write what they wanted to, using whatever invented spelling they created, in whatever handwriting they had at this stage, convinced this teacher of both the efficiency and the joy of this new approach.

In many of Machan's kindergarten and first grades, the students are writing before they are reading. The kids are figuring out how text works by writing their own texts and by hearing literature read to them two to four times a day. The teachers accept the students' texts, and comment on the meaning rather than on the form. One tiny girl who had recently arrived from Mexico filled each page of her journal with a picture of a house underneath which was her emergent writing—lines and circles: ///O/O/O/OOO////. She knew that writing and drawing were different, and she could read what she had written to the teacher: "Mi mamá es en la casa." Later she began to use letters of the alphabet, beginning with M, the first letter of her name.

In this classroom, as in many, theory follows practice. As teachers try some of the techniques or materials recommended by whole language advocates, they want to know why these were so successful, and so go on to learn more of the theoretical foundations.

Secondary Education

The whole language movement has had its least effect in secondary education. Of the 2,000 people attending the first Whole Language Umbrella conference, fewer than 500 represented middle and high school teachers; similarly, fewer than a quarter of those attending the second Umbrella conference came from secondary education. Secondary schools differ from elementary schools in many respects: the most obvious is the number of students each teacher meets daily—easily 150 for secondary teachers, up to 30 for elementary. In part because of the number of students, many secondary teachers focus on teaching subjects, not students.

Secondary teachers typically face rigid curriculum demands: A 10th-grade English class in Virginia, for example, is required to study early American literature, including the novels of J. F. Cooper and the sermons of Cotton Mather and Jonathan Edwards. It demands every last ounce of a teacher's power to drag 30 bored 16-year-olds through 45 minutes of reading and "discussing" "Sinners in the Hands of an Angry God"; in such contexts, there's little energy left among teacher or students to contemplate an alternative text or topic.

Other pressures on secondary teachers to conform quietly are the tests their students must pass to graduate or, in some cases, to participate in extracurricular activities. In elementary school, children who fail an ITBS can still play on the swings at recess, and can often still move into the next grade with their peers, especially in light of research on the harmful effects of retention. But in many high schools, the motto is now No Pass, No Play and, in some cases, Low Test Scores = No Graduation. These pressures, along with the newspaper publication of average SAT scores and articles demanding more from teachers, all pressure secondary teachers into teaching to the test and following state- and district-determined guidelines very closely.

There are pockets of whole language in middle and high schools, especially among teachers of English or foreign languages. Secondary teachers are increasingly finding students from whole language elementary schools in their classes, and these students push for meaningful, relevant activities and materials, creating pressure on their teachers to question the assumption that all of their students should read the same thing at the same time and receive the same message from it. Some of these teachers manage to develop curricula with their students, curricula more relevant than the one developed by the state or district. Some secondary teachers are leaders in the whole language movement: Gilles and her colleagues, for example, wrote *Whole Language Strategies for Secondary Students* (1988) while they were all teaching middle and high school by day and taking classes with Dorothy Watson at the University of Missouri by night.

Wigginton's Foxfire projects (1986), in which L1 high school students interview local elders and write up the elders' special knowledge, have captured the attention and imagination of many English teachers across the United States, but only a few have actually tried using oral history of the local community with their ESOL high school English/language arts students. One middle school in Tucson (Carrillo School) has used oral history: The bilingual students have interviewed the *viejos* in their school's neighborhood, getting the old ones to tell stories of how the neighborhood used to be, and published these stories illustrated by old photographs and by student art. *Our Hispanic Leaders* and *Celebrations in Our Neighborhood* are titles of two of the books the students produced. In Fresno, CA, Waylon Jackson at Yosemite Middle School (D. Freeman, personal communication, 1991) publishes his students' writing and photos, and has the books hard bound; at $7 a book, the volumes are considered bargains by the students' families and friends. Currently, Jackson's students are researching family medical practices and home remedies. This project will culminate in the 1992 class volume.

Sheltered English programs for ESOL students sometimes use holistic techniques. At Fresno High School, David Freeman (personal communication, 1991) consults in setting up courses with teachers from biology and social studies in collaboration with ESL teachers at the local high schools; he says the content-area teachers quickly recognize the fun of working with ESOL students, and they recognize that an experiential approach to concept development will work with all of their students. Freeman says there is a push towards student collaboration on "real" projects and a new tendency to ask discussion questions rather than display questions. Here, too, practice runs ahead of theory.

Adult Education

The term *whole language* is seldom used for adults learning English language and literacy. *Participatory* is the term used by some educators of adults who want their classroom to be a community of learners, and who believe that student choice, student input into curriculum, and self-evaluation are vital. Participatory teachers often cite the teachings of Paulo Freire, from whom they have learned that literacy is much more than decoding someone else's message. Literacy can be empowering and liberating because it opens up to adult students ways to understand and to alter their worlds (Freire, 1970; Freire & Macedo, 1987).

The Bilingual Community Literacy Training Project in Boston is a program in which Haitian Creole speakers become literate in their own dialect and then become the teachers for others of their community (Auerbach, 1990). English literacy thus builds on first language literacy. Two New York City union programs—one at the International Ladies' Garment Workers Union and one at the Amalgamated Clothing and Textile Workers union (Spener, 1991)—use literacy in Spanish and in English to serve the needs of the workers, modeling both the importance of functional aspects of literacy and community involvement.

Gary Pharness' (personal communication, 1991) workplace literacy programs in the Vancouver, B.C., area are based on a writing model of literacy development. Both L1 and L2 speakers of English write personal narratives of their lives. Pharness uses writing rather than reading as the basis for literacy because he believes it is vital for adults to write their own stories and then to discuss these with peers. Through the writing and the discussion, the authors receive both an acceptance of their own histories and a chance to learn how their story is perceived by others. This has the same advantages as dialogue between friends: Ideas can be articulated and then examined. The writers not only become more literate but they become more confident about themselves as people, not just as workers. Increased self-esteem is a major goal of Pharness' programs, and many of the workers in his programs seem to be meeting that goal. One woman student after a year of writing in the literacy class decided to quit her job: "I'm tired of correcting my boss's spelling," she said. Her new job pays better, and the only spelling she corrects is her own.

Mark McCue directs Invergarry Learning Centre's literacy program (Rigg, 1990). Like Pharness, a former colleague of his, McCue uses the writing of personal narrative as the basis for literacy. His students include both L1 and L2 speakers of English. As students enter the literacy class, they receive a black notebook and are instructed to write something, anything, preferably about themselves. Those who cannot do this can dictate something to McCue or an aide, and this language experience text substitutes for the student's own writing and becomes the first reading material. Many of his students publish their writing in the school magazine, *Voices: New Writers for New Readers*,[2] or in *School Daze*, the school newspaper, which is entirely student-run.

The Academy, a union program in the Midwest (Soifer, Young, & Irwin, 1989), publishes student writing, as does the Adult Literacy Resource Institute in Boston. *New Writers' Voices* (not to be confused with *Voices: New Writers for New Readers* from which it derives in conception, name, and layout) are small paperback volumes from Literacy Volunteers of New York City, each telling an adult student's memories. East End Literacy Press[3] in Toronto

---

[2] Available from the Lower Mainland Society for Literacy Education, 9260 140th Street, Surrey, B.C. V3V 5Z4, Canada.

[3] East End Literacy Press publications are available from Pippin Publishing, 150 Telson Road, Markham, Ontario L3R 1E5, Canada.

also publishes student autobiographies, focusing especially on women's stories.

These are but a few of many examples that could be cited of programs using student writing as the basis for student literacy. A. B. Facey (1981) taught himself to write so he could tell his story to his grandchildren; in the course of writing his autobiography he learned to read, but it was the drive to tell his own story, not to read someone else's that propelled his literacy. So too, with many new literates in both L1 and L2. Programs which start with student writing are making statements about whose messages need to be told and need to be read.

By late 1991, Aguirre International is scheduled to have completed its study of model adult education programs in the United States, and may then have a lengthy list of whole language programs for ESOL adults.

RESEARCH

Holistic and naturalistic research into language and learning are part of the whole language movement; the research has been increasingly ethnographic over the last 10 years. The major characteristics of whole language research are:

1. A concern with the people being studied as people, rather than as unnamed subjects as in experimental research. Sometimes in whole language research, the people being studied are co-researchers. Instead of trying to discover how often X occurs in Y situations, whole language researchers want to know what people think and how they go about developing their knowledge.

2. A recognition of contexts as vital factors affecting results; these contexts include physical, social, economic, and political.

3. A willingness to accept the messiness that comes with opening the study to real people living real lives, seeking insights through personal histories and through reflections on those histories.

Illustrative examples are provided by the research of Read (1975); Ferreiro and Teberosky (1982); and Harste, Woodward, and Burke (1984). All interacted with and observed preschool children, trying to discover how these youngsters were thinking about literacy. The research of Read (1975) into youngsters' grasp of alphabetic principles and the research in Spanish of Ferreiro and Teberosky (1982) on youngsters' concepts of print both inform the whole language perspective on how literacy proficiency develops in

L1. The pioneering work of Harste, Woodward, and Burke (1984) with youngsters aged 3 to 6 demonstrated that emergent literacy— the barest beginnings of reading and writing by very young children—differed from the most sophisticated reading and writing of adults only in level of sophistication. The basic process of writing that children go through with their first scribbles is the same process an adult uses; proficiency does not alter the process. Similarly, a child's first reading, perhaps of a McDonald's sign or a brand name on a cereal box, is the same basic process used by sophisticated readers like subscribers to the *TESOL Quarterly*. Again, proficiency does not alter the process; it merely allows one to use the process more efficiently. The basic research procedure of all these was observational, not experimental.

Taylor and Dorsey-Gaines (1988) questioned the assumption that people of color living in extreme poverty were necessarily illiterate. They spent over a year with families living in condemned buildings in New York City and concluded that even under abysmal living conditions, parents and children read and wrote together. Their study typifies recent holistic research in its ethnographic approach and in its myth-debunking conclusion.

Whole language research with L2 populations has a history similar to holistic research with L1 populations: it has moved from an interest in literacy development to a concern with much larger contexts; the research procedures of interviewing and observing continue, but are carried out in more long-term projects. Ethnographic research has strongly affected whole language research, both in its methods and in its broad focus.

The relatively early study by Goodman and Goodman (1978) asked how school children read in English as a second language (the research was carried out in 1972-1975 and reported in Rigg, 1977). A major question of that research was, "Does it make a difference what the student's L1 is?" Speakers of Arabic, Navajo, Samoan, and Spanish read two complete stories aloud, and their reading was subjected to miscue analysis. The conclusion was clear: It doesn't matter which first language an ESL student speaks; the student's ability to read (i.e., understand) material written in English is not determined by that student's home language. The student's background knowledge, on the other hand, does make a difference; if a story is culturally relevant, if it matches what the student knows about the world and about language, it is easier to read.

In 1984, the *TESOL Quarterly* published Hudelson's "Kan Yu Ret an Rayt en Ingles," a landmark study of a few youngsters developing literacy in English as an additional language. That study used repeated observations and interviews over time and showed examples of children's work. Currently Hudelson and Irene Serna, a colleague at Arizona State University, are collaborating on a 3-year study of the Ll literacy development of Spanish-speaking students at Machan School. Both spend at least one day a week at the school, sitting in bilingual classes, observing and interacting with the children whose literacy they have been studying for 2 years now. They tape-record oral reading sessions and conversations with the children and photocopy the children's written work. The case-study approach gives researchers a chance to learn a great deal about a few people, and the insights gained from that knowledge can inform future research, curriculum design, and instruction.

In 1986 TESOL published *Integrating Perspectives* (Rigg & Enright) which explicitly cited teachers as classroom researchers and which demonstrated one way in which researchers could integrate their perspectives. Chapters by Hudelson, Rigg, and Urzúa each focused on one aspect of a small group of Southeast Asian children in a U.S. school: Hudelson analyzed the children's writing; Rigg analyzed their reading; and Urzúa reported on the contexts of school and home in which these children studied and lived. This integration of research was possible because the three shared a whole language view of language development.

In 1987 Edelsky reported 3 years of involvement and observation of a bilingual (Spanish-English) program at an elementary school. The volume is almost alone among research studies in recognizing and discussing the political context affecting educational efforts.

Whole language research with ESOL adults owes a debt to David Nunan (1988), who has carried out studies with thousands of students and hundreds of teachers in the Australian Adult Migrant Education Programme. Nunan uses questionnaires to discover teacher and student experiences and opinions; his insistence that teachers are the real creators of curriculum is based on responses from these surveys.

Nunan's colleague Geoff Brindley (1986) has access to the same population of adult ESOL students and their teachers and has researched various means of assessment, many of which rely on the students themselves to evaluate their progress in language and even to evaluate the sorts of teaching they prefer. This manifests genuine respect for the student.

That respect is carried further in Auerbach's (1991) description of a participatory curriculum, in which teachers become cocreators of curriculum with their students. The topic of this reflective research is student/teacher involvement in curriculum; the methods of research are conversation, observation, and reflection. Throughout, there is respect for the people involved, consideration of the backgrounds each brings and the contexts each currently operates in, and an acceptance of the uncertainty that comes with dealing with real people and real concerns.

WHOLE LANGUAGE IN THE FUTURE?

Pendulums swing. Two forces threaten whole language teaching as it has been described here:

1. As *whole language* becomes a bandwagon term, it is used to mean a great many things, including the very ideas whole language developed in opposition to. Unfortunately, it can no longer always be assumed to refer to a philosophy of education that prizes holistic, natural ideas and respects the individual.

2. The current political situation in the U.S. bodes ill for all educational programs, but particularly for those that can be labeled liberal.

Despite strong pressures on the whole language movement to transform into yet another ineffective attempt at reform, I predict that the teachers who have learned to respect themselves and their colleagues as professionals, and their students as collaborators in building and disseminating knowledge will continue to work in the schools and will continue to demonstrate to their students, their colleagues, their administration, and their community that the best of the whole language perspective makes for the best education. ∎

THE AUTHOR

Pat Rigg has a small consulting firm, American Language & Literacy, in Tucson, AZ. She has a longtime interest in literacy for both L1 and L2 speakers. Rigg edits TESOL's *Adult Education Newsletter* and chairs the NCTE/TESOL Liaison Committee. She is coeditor (with V. G. Allen) of *When They Don't All Speak English* (NCTE, 1989).

REFERENCES

Atwell, N. (1987). *In the middle: Writing, reading, and learning with adolescents.* Upper Montclair, NJ: Boynton/Cook.

Auerbach, E. (1990). Moving on: From learner to teacher. In P. Bossort, C. Monnastes, & G. Malnarich (Eds.), *Literacy 2000: Make the next ten years matter* [Conference summary]. New Westminister, B.C.: Douglas College.

Auerbach, E. (1991). *Making meaning, making change*. Boston, MA: University of Massachusetts, Department of English.

Bird, L. B. (Ed). (1987). *Becoming a whole language school: The Fair Oaks story*. Katonah, NY: Richard C. Owens.

Bissex, G. L., & Bullock, R. H. (Eds.). (1987). *Seeing for ourselves: Case-study research by teachers of writing*. Portsmouth, NH: Heinemann.

Brindley, G. (1986). *The assessment of second language proficiency: Issues and approaches*. Adelaide, Australia: National Curriculum Resource Centre.

Calkins, L. (1983). *Lessons from a child: On the teaching and learning of writing*. Portsmouth, NH: Heinemann.

Calkins, L. (1986). *The art of teaching writing*. Portsmouth, NH: Heinemann.

Calkins, L. (1991). *Living between the lines*. Portsmouth, NH: Heinemann.

Edelsky, C. (1987). *Writing in a bilingual program: Había una vez*. Norwood, NJ: Ablex.

Edelsky, C., Altwerger, B., & Flores, B. (1991). *Whole language: What's the difference?* Portsmouth, NH: Heinemann.

Enright, D. S., & McCloskey, M. L. (1988). *Integrating English: Teaching language in a multicultural classroom*. Addison-Wesley.

Facey, A. B. (1981). *A fortunate life*. Penguin Books Australia.

Ferreiro, E., & Teberosky, A. (1982). *Literacy before schooling*. Portsmouth, NH: Heinemann.

Freire, P. (1970). The adult literacy process as cultural action for freedom. *Harvard Educational Review 40*, 205-221.

Freire, P., & Macedo, D. (1987). *Literacy: Reading the word and the world*. South Hadley, MA: Bergin & Harvey.

Gilles, C., Bixby, M., Crowley, P., Crenshaw, S. R., Henrichs, M., Reynolds, F. E., & Pyle, D. (Eds.). (1988). *Whole language strategies for secondary students*. New York: Richard C. Owens.

Goodman, K. S. (1967). Reading: A psycholinguistic guessing game. *Journal of the Reading Specialist, 6*(4), 126-135. (Reprinted in R. Gollasch [Ed.], *Language and literacy: The collected papers of Kenneth S. Goodman* [Vol. 1, pp. 33-44], 1982, London: Routledge)

Goodman, K. S., Bird, L. B., & Goodman, Y. (Eds.). (1991). *The whole language catalog*. Santa Rosa, CA: American School.

Goodman, K. S., & Goodman, Y. (1978). *The reading of American children whose language is a stable rural dialect of English or a language other than English* (NIE Report No. C-00-3-0087). Washington, DC: U.S. Department of Health, Education, & Welfare.

Goodman, K. S., & Goodman, Y. (1981). *A whole language comprehension-centered view of reading development: A position paper* (Occasional Papers No. 1). Tucson, AZ: University of Arizona, Program in Language & Literacy.

Goodman, K. S., Goodman, Y., & Hood, W. (1989). *The whole language evaluation book.* Portsmouth, NH: Heinemann.

Goodman, K. S., Shannon, P., Freeman, Y. S., & Murphy, S. (1988). *Report card on basal readers.* Katonah, NY: Richard C. Owen.

Goodman, Y. (1985). Kidwatching: Observing children in the classroom. In A. Jaggar & M. T. Smith-Burke (Eds.), *Observing the language learner.* Newark, DE: IRA/NCTE.

Goodman, Y. (1989). Roots of the whole language movement. In Whole language [Special issue]. *Elementary School Journal, 90*(2), 113-127.

Goodman, Y. (1991). History of whole language. In K. S. Goodman, L. B. Bird, & Y. Goodman (Eds.), *The whole language catalog* (p. 386). Santa Rosa, CA: American School.

Graves, D. (1983). *Writing: Teachers and children at work.* Portsmouth, NH: Heinemann.

Harp, B. (Ed.). (1991). *Evaluation and assessment in whole language programs.* Norwood, MA: Christopher-Gordon.

Harste, J. C., & Burke, C. L. (1977). A new hypothesis for reading teacher education research: Both the teaching and learning of reading are theoretically based. In P. D. Pearson (Ed.), *Reading: Research, theory, and practice: Twenty-sixth yearbook of the National Reading Conference.* Chicago: National Reading Conference.

Harste, J. C., Woodward, V., & Burke, C. (1984). *Language stories and literacy lessons.* Portsmouth, NH: Heinemann.

Hudelson, S. (1984). Kan yu ret an rayt en ingles: Children becoming literate in English. *TESOL Quarterly 18*(2), 221-238.

Hudelson, S. (1986). ESL children's writing: What we've learned, what we're learning. In P. Rigg & D. S. Enright (Eds.), *Integrating perspectives: Children in ESL* (pp. 23-54). Washington, DC: TESOL.

Kazemek, F. E. (1989). Whole language and adult literacy education. *Information Update* [Literacy Assistance Center newsletter], 6, 3-5, 7.

Krashen, S., & Terrell, T. (1983). *The natural approach.* Hayward, CA: Alemany Press.

McCloskey, M. L. (1988). *English everywhere: An integrated English as a second language curriculum guide* (Dallas Independent School District Edition). Atlanta, GA: Educo Press.

Nunan, D. (1988). *The learner-centred curriculum: A study in second language teaching.* Cambridge: Cambridge University Press.

Peterson, R., & Eeds, M. A. (1990). *Grand conversations: Literature groups in action.* Richmond Hill, Ontario: Scholastic.

Peyton, J. K., & Reed, L. (1990). *Dialogue journal writing with nonnative English speaking students: A handbook for teachers.* Alexandria, VA: TESOL.

Read, C. (1975). *Children's categorization of speech sounds in English* (Research Rep. No. 17). Urbana, IL: NCTE.

Rigg, P. (1977). The miscue-ESL project. In H. D. Brown, C. A. Yorio, & R. Crymes (Eds.), *On TESOL '77. Teaching and learning ESL: Trends in research and practice* (pp. 206-219). Washington, DC: TESOL.

Rigg, P. (1986). Reading in ESL: Learning from kids. In P. Rigg & D. S. Enright (Eds.), *Integrating perspectives: Children in ESL* (pp. 55-92). Washington, DC: TESOL.

Rigg, P. (1990). Whole language in adult ESL programs. *ERIC/CLL News Bulletin, 13*(2), 1, 3, 7.

Rigg, P. (1991). Using the language experience approach with ESL adults. In J. Bell (Ed.), ESL literacy [Special issue]. *TESL Talk 20*(1), 188-200.

Rigg, P., & Enright, D. S. (Eds.). (1986). *Integrating perspectives: Children and ESL.* Washington, DC: TESOL.

Rosenblatt, L. (1976). *Literature as exploration* (3rd ed.). NY: Noble and Noble. (Original work published 1938)

Rosenblatt, L. (1978). *The reader, the text, and the poem.* Carbondale, IL: Southern Illinois Press.

Shannon, P. (1989). *Broken promises: Reading instruction in 20th century America.* South Hadley, MA: Bergin & Garvey.

Shannon, P. (1990). *The struggle to continue: Progressive reading instruction in America.* Portsmouth, NH: Heinemann.

Soifer, R., Young, D. L., & Irwin, M. (1989). The Academy: A learner-centered workplace literacy education program. In A. Fingeret & P. Jurmo (Eds.), *Participatory literacy education.* San Francisco, CA: Jossey-Bass.

Special report on whole language [Special issue]. (1991, August). *Teacher.*

Spener, D. (Chair). (1991, March). *Participatory practice in workplace ESL: The route to empowerment.* Workshop presented at the 25th Annual TESOL Convention, New York.

Taylor, D. (Ed.). (1990). Assessment in whole language teaching [Special issue]. *English Education, 22*(1).

Taylor, D., & Dorsey-Gaines, C. (1988). *Growing up literate: Learning from inner-city families.* Portsmouth, NH: Heinemann.

Urzúa, C. (1986). A children's story. In P. Rigg & D. S. Enright (Eds.), *Integrating perspectives: Children in ESL* (pp. 93-112). Washington, DC: TESOL.

Watson, D. (1989). Defining and describing whole language. In Whole Language [Special issue]. *Elementary School Journal, 90*(2), 129-141.

Whole language [Special issue]. (1989). *Elementary School Journal, 90*(2).

Wigginton, E. (1986). *Sometimes a shining moment.* NY: Anchor/Doubleday.

From Kindergarten to High School: Teaching and Learning English as a Second Language in the U.S.

CHRISTIAN FALTIS
Arizona State University

The number of non-English-speaking and limited English proficient students in K–12 U.S. public schools is escalating rapidly, and at the same time, fewer of these students are being served by transitional bilingual/ESL programs. Across the nation, schools are responding to these changes by trying new approaches and practices which integrate English language teaching with content learning. Many of these innovations have been successful because of the willingness by all-English classroom teachers to add ESL instructional principles and practices to their repertoire of teaching knowledge and abilities. Also helpful has been the current trend away from ESL methods and toward language-sensitive content teaching. This paper describes (a) contemporary trends in ESL instruction in elementary and secondary schools, (b) the role of second language acquisition research in the new programs and approaches, and (c) ways that bilingual education and TESOL professionals can help all-English teachers who have English learners in their classrooms.

In the United States, the population of school-age children (ages 5–17) during the 1985–1986 academic year considered to be beginning second language speakers of English and thus in need of special language instruction was estimated to be approximately 2.6 million (U.S. General Accounting Office, 1987). In California alone, the population of limited English proficient (LEP) school-age students increased dramatically from 288,427 in 1979 to 861,531 in 1990 (Chang, 1990). Excluding California, nine states have at least 25,000 students with limited English proficiency. In 1988, nearly a quarter of a million such students were enrolled in New York schools. In that same year, more than half a million English learners enrolled in Texas public schools (Olsen, 1988). Without counting the children of undocumented workers from other countries, the population of children for whom English is a second language is conservatively projected to reach 3.5 million by the year 2000 and to approach 6 million by 2020 (Pallas, Natriello, & McDill, 1989).

Although information from the 1990 census is not yet released, a recent report by the U.S. Department of Education (1992) confirms earlier findings that the first language most often spoken by limited English proficient school-age learners is overwhelmingly Spanish. The next two largest groups of school-age children with limited English proficiency are speakers of Western and Eastern European languages (e.g., Armenian, French, Greek, Italian, Polish, and Russian) and speakers of Asian languages (e.g., Chinese, Filipino, Hmong, Khmer, Korean, and Vietnamese).

It is noteworthy to mention that nearly half of all limited English proficient students across the United States are U.S. born (Waggoner, 1987). Moreover, the majority of U.S.-born LEP children speak Spanish as their primary language. Among immigrant children who enroll in U.S. public schools, however, the picture is more complex and often depends on the changing international political and economic conditions (Chang, 1990). For example, in Seattle, Washington, where Asian language (mostly Japanese and Korean) students have comprised the largest number of LEP school-age students for many years, within the last 5 years, a wave of Russian immigrants has changed the LEP school population considerably. Likewise, southern California has also experienced rapid changes in overall language makeup of LEP students in certain school districts. A good example is the situation during the 1989–1990 school year in the Glendale school district. Within that time period, nearly 2,500 Soviet Armenian children enrolled in school, none of them having had any prior experience with English (Chang, 1990).

It is also worthwhile to point out that the nature of the Spanish-speaking immigrant LEP population is changing. Prior to the mid-1980s, most immigrant LEP students from Mexico and Central America were of elementary school age. In recent years, however, a considerable number of the immigrants from Latin America have been adolescents (ages 13–19) of secondary school age (National Council of LaRaza, 1990). Unfortunately, the exact number and country of origin of these newly arrived LEP teenagers are not available. The U.S. census provides information only for ages 5 to 18. Moreover, LEP individuals are not disaggregated from fluent English speakers, and the population is not divided between teenagers and preteens. Consequently, there is no way to discern the actual numbers and language backgrounds or proficiencies of LEP students within the two main school-age groups. (See Olsen, 1989, for an excellent discussion of the problems in making sense of language census survey data.)

A LARGE AUDIENCE WITH DIFFERENT EXPERIENCES AND NEEDS

It should be clear from the information presented above that teachers of English to speakers of other languages are greatly needed in our public schools. But they are needed in different ways, depending on the students' ages, prior schooling experiences and content knowledge, and English language proficiency. Although all school-age students with limited proficiency in English need special instruction to be able to achieve socioacademic success in school, the needs and experiences of LEP students in elementary school differ considerably from those of LEP students in secondary school.

At the elementary level of schooling, LEP students entering school with relatively few mainstream literacy experiences are not as challenging for teachers as they can be for teachers in secondary school, where subject matter content learning depends greatly on proficient literacy abilities and prior subject matter knowledge. Furthermore, teaching English as a second language in the elementary school is often informed by practices of teachers in bilingual education who integrate language acquisition with content learning and who use the students' native languages and English. In contrast, at the secondary level, virtually all of the content areas and ESL are taught almost exclusively in English.

Generally speaking, elementary school–level LEP students enter school in the primary grades (K–3), and a majority of these are fully integrated into the all-English mainstream classroom by the fourth grade (U.S. Department of Education, 1992). More than half of all elementary school LEP students are U.S. born (Waggoner, 1992), and many of those attending urban and suburban public schools participate in either a bilingual education or an ESL program in which they receive some form of English language instruction (U.S. Department of Education, 1992).

Secondary level LEP students, in contrast, are mainly foreign-born immigrants with a variety of educational experiences ranging from no formal schooling to grade-level equivalence (Faltis & Arias, 1992; Lucas, in press). However, the greatest number of secondary level LEP students have at least some English language proficiency, and many are two to three grade levels behind in terms of academic content knowledge and literacy abilities (Minicucci & Olsen, 1991). A small number of secondary LEP students develop fluency in speaking English but are unable to compete in all-English academic classes. These students are often continuing from elementary schools where they were also designated as LEP. Most secondary LEP students are not provided with any kind of special English language instructional support; instead they are left on their own to "sink or swim" in all-English content classrooms.

The purpose of this paper is to examine the evolving role and nature of ESL instruction at the elementary and secondary levels of education. Three main questions are considered for each level of education: (a) What kinds of programs and approaches are currently being used? (b) What is the influence of second language acquisition (SLA) research in these approaches to ESL instruction in bilingual and ESL programs? and (c) How can bilingual education and TESOL professionals help all-English teachers who have English learners in their classrooms? The paper concludes with a discussion of implications for teacher education in the preparation of bilingual, ESL, and mainstream teachers.

TEACHING AND LEARNING ESL IN THE ELEMENTARY SCHOOL

Philosophical Bases

Schools are the major socialization agent outside of the family with a significant role in forming the attitudes, inquiry skills, knowledge, and behaviors of children as they develop socially and academically into adult citizens within a democratic society. Historically as well as currently, most schools are designed to reproduce the cultural ethos and preferred knowledge base of English-speaking European American society. From this perspective, children from nondominant cultural and linguistic backgrounds are resocialized to conform to unfamiliar ways of knowing, communicating, and competing (DeVillar, in press). Some schools reject the conformity model and strive instead to become significant equalizers of social and cultural differences by creating a more cooperative and socially integrative learning environment for all students. Moreover, these schools provide educational opportunities that enable language and ethnic minority children to retain their respective home language and cultural identity as they acquire English and learn to inquire critically about the content they are expected to learn. This latter perspective is a form of cultural pluralism which strives to establish collaborative and equitable power relations among culturally diverse groups (Cummins, in press).

The type and extent of instructional support adopted by schools to enable LEP students to develop English proficiency and critical inquiry skills needed for lifelong learning depends partially on a school's perspective toward cultural pluralism and partially on the language demographics of the students in attendance.

Instructional Support Program Types

In the United States, there are two basic types of programs of recognized instructional support designed for elementary students with limited English proficiency: *bilingual education programs*, in which the students' native language plays anywhere from an integral to a minor role in teaching and learning, and *ESL programs*, in which all instruction takes place in English. Some believe bilingual programs reflect a culturally pluralist perspective because the students' native language is used for instruction. ESL programs, in contrast, are said to reflect a Eurocentric conformity perspective because the students' native language is not used for instruction. However, ESL programs are used in schools that support cultural pluralism in many other ways, for example, in schools that serve students from several different language and ethnic backgrounds and in schools where there are a small number of LEP students. In these two situations, bilingual programs are difficult to implement.

Furthermore, although the two program types may differ in terms of (a) ethnicity and language abilities of the teachers, (b) areas of specialization of the teachers (linguistics vs. curriculum and instruction), and (c) emotional commitment to the role of the home language in the child's educational achievement (Milk, 1985), there is so much within-program variation that it is difficult to say with any certainty that program type alone guarantees a particular philosophical perspective.

Both bilingual and ESL programs are in large measure a result of policies that developed from constitutional, legal, and statutory sources concerned with language issues. In other words, both types of programs came about because of legal interpretations of the Civil Rights Act of 1965, the Equal Educational Opportunities Act (Section 1703[f]), the Supreme Court decision *Lau v. Nichols*, and the Bilingual Education Act of 1968 (Title VII). The collective goal of these political and legal policies is to facilitate access to the learning of English so that students can participate more fully in school and society and thus benefit from such participation.

Although the original Bilingual Education Act of 1968 (which provides funding to school districts for bilingual and ESL programs) did not specifically define the type or nature of programs that schools should use, up until the 1980s, grants were awarded almost exclusively to applicants who developed and operated *transitional bilingual programs* for low income, non-English-speaking students. These programs almost always segregate LEP students from their mainstream English-speaking counterparts while they are participating in the programs.

Another alternative is developmental, two-way bilingual programs, which offer language and content instruction in English along with the native language from kindergarten through 12th grade. In such programs, native English proficient students begin studying content with students for whom the language of instruction is their primary language. English as a language of instruction is introduced gradually to both groups and, depending on the training of the teacher, ESL instruction is similar to that found in transitional bilingual programs.

Since the mid-1980s, the U.S. Department of Education has allowed school districts greater flexibility in their choice of instructional approaches. In particular, Title VII funds have become available for the development of alternative kinds of instructional programs in which the students' home language is not used for teaching. Consequently, in the 1990s increasing numbers of elementary school LEP students are taught English in school through alternatives to transitional bilingual programs, namely, through a variety of ESL programs. Most ESL programs also segregate LEP students from native-English-speaking students for at least part of the day. However, most LEP students must acquire English in school with no special instructional support—a process termed *submersion*. Although LEP students who are submersed into all-English classes are *physically* integrated with native English speakers, they often remain *socially* segregated during instruction (Faltis, 1993).

A study conducted by the National Education Association (Rodríguez, 1990) found that in the 1989–1990 academic year, transitional bilingual education programs served only an estimated 5.6% of all LEP students (K–12) in need of special instructional support. Several years earlier, Stein (1986) reported that only about 10% of all elementary LEP students were being served by bilingual programs. The U.S. Department of Education (1992) reported that in 1987–1988, approximately one third of all public elementary suburban and urban schools across the nation offered ESL programs to LEP students. (This reported figure appears high in light of the fact that Title VII only recently began funding such alternative programs.) In any case, the estimated combined percentages indicate that at least two thirds of all eligible LEP students are submersed in English-only classrooms without special recognized provisions (i.e., native language or ESL instruction) made to help these students gain the English proficiency needed to participate fully in classroom activities. This does not mean that LEP students in English-only classrooms necessarily experience a poor learning environment but rather that they are not being taught by teachers with extensive training in ESL or bilingual methodologies. For example, Freeman and Freeman (1992) describe a number of non-ESL/nonbilingual whole language all-English classrooms in which LEP students participate in a wide variety of meaningful language and literacy activities. Ways of teaching LEP students in the all-English classroom are discussed more fully below.

Transitional Bilingual Programs

These programs use the students' native language for some or all subject-matter instruction while the students are acquiring English as a second language. In other words, the native language is used temporarily as a bridge to English. Transitional bilingual programs are found primarily in schools serving large numbers of LEP students who speak and understand the same minority language. Programs that use the native language for part of the instruction for fewer than 2 years are called *early-exit transitional programs* (Ramírez & Merino, 1990). Students in these programs may continue to have ESL classes even after they no longer receive native language instruction, usually for up to an additional year. Thus, for example, students entering the program in kindergarten would be exited at the end of the first or second grade and placed into an all-English classroom. Bilingual programs that offer various degrees of native language instruction from kindergarten up through the fifth or sixth grade are called *late-exit transitional programs* (Ramírez & Merino, 1990). Students stay in late-exit programs regardless of when full English proficiency is achieved.

ESL instruction in transitional bilingual programs is most often taught as a separate subject and ranges from structured ESL lessons that focus on functional vocabulary development and practical conversational language to more natural language approaches in which students use oral and written language to construct their own understandings of the new language. In the upper elementary grades, structured ESL classes also vary depending on the theoretical perspective of the program and the teachers within it. According to Ramírez and Merino (1990), most structured ESL instruction in elementary bilingual programs relies on whole-group teaching and focus on the learning of sentence-level patterns and vocabulary in isolation. This instructional mode is also widespread in all-English mainstream classrooms (Goodlad, 1984). However, a growing number of bilingual teachers are relying less and less on whole-group teaching and instead are organizing ESL instruction around small-group work which integrates the acquisition of English language and literacy with the purposeful learning of content (see Enright & McCloskey, 1988; Faltis, 1993; Milk, 1990).

ESL Programs

In cases where the number, age range, language background, grade span, and/or demographic location of eligible LEP students make a full-time transitional bilingual program impractical, schools typically implement one or more of the following ESL program types:

ESL pullout. In this type of program, LEP students leave their mainstream classes at certain times during the day to receive structured ESL instruction in a separate classroom location. Instruction typically lasts for 30 to 50 minutes per day and consists of a combination of whole-group and individualized instruction. Emphasis is placed on the development of English vocabulary and structures in the four language skills of listening, speaking, reading, and writing.

There is some feeling that ESL pullout programs may be detrimental to ESL students for several reasons: (a) students are stigmatized as having some kind of problem when they are pulled out of class; (b) students in pullout classes are segregated from their native-English-speaking peers; (c) students miss opportunities for concept development and social interaction that take place during regular classroom instruction.

ESL push in. LEP students remain in the mainstream classroom and receive ESL instruction by an ESL support teacher who visits the classroom on a daily basis for 15 to 50 minutes. Students work in small groups and individually with the teacher. These support teachers function as resource instructors for the regular classroom teacher. Students may practice some of the same kinds of language-oriented content found in pull-out classrooms, but because the ESL teacher works in collaboration with the regular teacher, many of the activities are the same ones being used by the regular teacher. (See McKay & Freedman, 1990, for a description of support teachers in the British educational system. They claim that most U.S. public schools are unfamiliar with the role of support teachers; however, ESL teachers acting as resource instructors go into the mainstream classroom to work with ESL students in many states including New Jersey, Texas, Nevada, and California.)

Structured immersion. LEP students are assigned to self-contained classrooms in which English is the only language of instruction. Structured immersion teachers are often bilingual, but they avoid using the students' native language in class for anything other than emergencies. Students are openly encouraged to use English for classroom interaction. Structured immersion students are taught the same subject matter content as their native English proficient peers in mainstream classrooms, and English is acquired as a by-product of content learning.

A Shift Toward Integrated Language and Content Learning

Milk (1985) was among the first to point out that ESL instruction in bilingual and ESL programs that focuses exclusively on learning language skills does not effectively prepare LEP students for the academic demands of classroom interaction and learning. Milk draws on research from two separate areas to show their special significance for contemporary ESL instruction: (a) exemplary practices in bilingual/ESL classrooms and (b) second language acquisition in classroom settings. In tandem, the findings from these research areas strongly suggest that language is most effectively acquired when it is integrated with meaningful content and when the practice that supports it is relevant to the learner.

Exemplary Teacher Studies

The effectiveness of integrating English language development with content learning was widely heralded in Tikunoff's (1983) "significant bilingual instructional features" study. Tikunoff and a team of researchers studied the teaching behaviors of 58 teachers who were nominated as being exemplary bilingual teachers. One of the many findings Tikunoff reported was that the majority of these teachers integrated ESL into regular subject matter instruction. Moreover, these teachers adjusted instruction to ensure that students understood the language of instruction at the beginning of and during lessons. Students in the classrooms investigated were not pulled out or otherwise separated for structured ESL lessons.

Since the Tikunoff study, several other studies have also found that LEP students in bilingual programs learn English best when language and content are integrated (Faltis & Merino, 1992). For example, Enright (1986); Faltis (1992); Faltis, Merino, and Arias (1992); and Pease-Alvarez, García, and Espinosa (1991) observed and interviewed exemplary classroom teachers in bilingual and ESL settings. Results from these studies confirm Tikunoff's earlier finding that students gain high levels of social and academic proficiency in English when ESL is embedded in subject matter content teaching that is adjusted for second language learners.

All of these post-Tikunoff studies have also shown that the integration of language and content is not enough in itself to bring about successful language learning. These exemplary bilingual/ESL teacher studies show that effective teachers organize their classrooms so that students are able to engage in many kinds of verbal and written interaction with their teacher and their peers. For example, the two bilingual kindergarten teachers studied by Pease-Alvarez, García, and Espinosa (1991) taught in an alternate days bilingual program. On the English days, they organized their classrooms much like their Spanish days, so that students talked and worked together on tasks and activities that required peer cooperation and social interaction. Faltis (1992) observed and interviewed a teacher from an ESL second grade self-contained (immersion) class and from a K-12 ESL pull-out class, both of whom had been nominated on the basis of their reputations and certain other criteria as exemplary ESL teachers (see Faltis, Merino, & Arias, 1992, for a description of the nominating procedure). Both of these teachers used lots of small-group work that required students to use English for meaningful interaction about the content and process involved in the activities. Neither of these teachers "taught ESL" in the sense of presenting students with a curriculum organized around language structures.

Support from SLA Theory

Second language acquisition (SLA) theory supports the shift from structured ESL instruction to the integration of language and content teaching. Research in SLA reveals that in every case of successful SLA, learners had been exposed to regular and substantial amounts of modified language input and had engaged in social interaction where meaning was negotiated among speakers (Scarcella, 1990). Modified language input is more widely known as comprehensible input, language addressed to the learner that has in some way been adjusted to accommodate the learner's needs (Krashen, 1985). According to Krashen, comprehensible input is necessary for SLA because it supplies the learner with meaningful language that is slightly beyond the learner's existing competence.

However, when LEP students engage in social interaction with native speakers or more proficient peers, not only do they receive comprehensible input, they are also encouraged to use precise, coherent, and appropriate language as they negotiate for meaning. As they actively negotiate meaning in order to get ideas across, they are also "pushed" to try out their developing language structures (Swain, 1985). Social interaction allows learners to figure out what is being said, to hear how language is structured, and to see how others use language socially and communicatively. Together, comprehensible input and social interaction which involves the negotiation of meaning provide English learners with two of the most important ingredients for SLA.

The Value of Cooperative Learning

Social interaction involving LEP students and their native-English-speaking peers often occurs in the context of cooperative learning lessons. Many teachers use cooperative learning to involve LEP students because it provides an acquisition-rich learning environment (Faltis, 1989). Student talk that occurs in mixed language cooperative learning lessons gives English learners lots of exposure to contextualized language and thus more opportunities to build comprehension. Input generated from peer communicative exchanges also provides a natural context for greater redundancy and thus for greater understanding (McGroarty, 1989). LEP students are often comfortable talking during cooperative learning and use it as a "practice field" to try out expressions and negotiate meaning without having to worry about making mistakes (Faltis, 1993).

Support from Vygotskian Principles

One of the exemplary ESL teachers observed and interviewed by Faltis (1992) mentioned that her classroom organization is supported not only by SLA theory but by Vygotskian principles as well. The teacher uses lots of small-group work to complement whole-class and individualized teaching and completely integrates ESL instruction with content learning. She says that Vygotsky's (1978) framework for learning supports much of what she does to facilitate language acquisition. According to Vygotsky, students must first experience two-way interaction with an adult or more capable peer and then follow this with individual practice, either alone or in a whole-group setting. Moreover, the assistance that adults or more capable peers provide must be adjusted to the needs of the learner and be temporary so that eventually the learner can take over and perform independently.

Increasing numbers of language educators interested in the schooling of language minority children have turned toward Vygotsky's sociohistorical learning theory to support the integration of language and content learning (see DeVillar & Faltis, 1991; Faltis, 1993; Moll, 1990; Trueba, 1989). Vygotskian learning theory is particularly relevant to integrated ESL instruction because of its requirement that learners necessarily receive assistance about relevant topics through the context of two-way conversations with significant others before individual learning can take place.

Joinfostering: Fully Integrating LEP Students into the All-English Classroom

The dramatic increase in elementary school–age students in need of bilingual and ESL instruction is only part of a much bigger and more complex problem facing our schools. As was pointed out above, many elementary school LEP students spend fewer than 3 years in a bilingual/ESL class setting, and many more receive no special instructional support at all. This means that all-English classroom teachers must be prepared to address the needs of students who come into their classrooms not yet fully proficient in English. A survey by Penfield (1987) showed that a majority of grade-level teachers know very little about the conditions and strategies that benefit second language learners in their classrooms. Many regular classroom teachers fear that LEP students will fare poorly in their classes because teachers are sorely underprepared to address these children's language and cultural needs. These teachers need help from the language teaching profession.

One example of a framework that seeks to address the needs and concerns of regular classrooms by drawing from exemplary practices in bilingual education is *joinfostering* (Faltis, 1993). Joinfostering is the planning and implementation of conditions to promote two-way communication, social integration, and oral and written language acquisition in culturally and linguistically diverse classrooms. Joinfostering provides all-English teachers with strategies to plan for and implement four interrelated social and pedagogical conditions:

1. A high incidence of two-way communicative exchanges between the teacher and students and among students, regardless of their oral English language proficiency
2. The social integration of second language students with native-English-speaking students in all aspects of classroom learning
3. The thoughtful integration of SLA principles with content instruction so that as second language students experience and practice new subject matter knowledge, they develop language as well
4. The involvement and participation of second language students' parents in both classroom- and school-related activities

These joinfostering principles are aimed specifically at helping LEP students join in and participate to the greatest extent possible in the all-English classroom. Importantly, the principles are based on sound first and second language pedagogy found in multicultural classrooms and community settings. To implement these principles, teachers have to be willing to change the existing social organization of the classrooms to create a variety of opportunities for social interaction, social integration, and language learning.

TEACHING AND LEARNING ESL AT THE SECONDARY LEVEL
The Mission of Secondary Schools

Middle schools and high schools have the formidable task of teaching adolescents the skills, problem-solving abilities, and subject matter content that they will need to begin to understand and participate effectively in the adult world. It is generally assumed that secondary students arrive at middle school as literate individuals who are capable of understanding and producing written language, of participating appropriately in the social and academic life of a classroom, and of associating prior subject matter knowledge to new information in math, social studies, science, literature, history, music, and art. Middle and high schools teach students who are in the process of becoming adults, learning responsibility, and understanding the meaning of friendship, groups, gangs, moods, and humor and tragedy. Part of the mission of secondary school, therefore, is also to pay attention to the social, personal, and emotional needs of learners who are very much in transition from childhood to adult reality.

Diversity Among Secondary LEP Students

For more and more secondary schools, their mission is expanding to include the provision of special instruction to students with limited or no English proficiency. Although these students share many of the social, personal, and emotional needs of their native English-speaking counterparts, they may have had completely different childhood and schooling experiences (see Olsen, 1988, for multiple accounts of experiences faced by immigrant adolescent students). Large numbers of secondary level LEP students enter middle and high school weak in academic knowledge and literacy skills in their native languages. Thus, not only are secondary level LEP students in need of special language instruction as well as all of the other adolescent-related needs, but a sizable number require special content-area instruction as well. Minicucci and Olsen (1991) have found that many LEP secondary students are 2 to 3 years behind in academic preparation. Not all secondary LEP students have limited schooling experiences in the native country, however. Some students who are eligible for secondary programs enter school educated up to grade level.

Instructional Support Program Types

Unfortunately, little information is currently available to point to exemplary instructional program models for secondary schools containing large numbers of different types of LEP students. (The one study that discusses exemplary instructional programs for LEP students at the secondary level is Tikunoff et al., 1991. For information on effective linguistically diverse secondary schools, see Lucas, Henze, & Donato, 1990. This study describes six exemplary high schools serving large numbers of different types of LEP students. Also see Freeman, Freeman, & González, 1987, for a description of an effective summer school sheltered program for LEP high school students.) At present, instructional programs at the secondary level are most commonly structured to accommodate LEP students who presumably can read, write, and compute in their native language and who are implicitly as well as explicitly knowledgeable about school culture and school behavior (Minicucci & Olsen, 1991).

Instructional support programs for secondary LEP students vary considerably from school to school, depending on (a) the professional training of the school staff; (b) the size, educational experiences of, and language(s) spoken by the students; (c) the local and regional attitudes toward bilingualism; and (d) the history of special instructional programs already in existence (Lucas, in press). Physically speaking, most secondary instructional programs are located within the walls of the school building, although in most instances, LEP students are socially segregated from native-English-speaking students while they are in these programs. Students attend courses designed especially for them for part of or the entire day until they are deemed ready to move into all-English classes. In some cases, programs for LEP students are situated in buildings that are separate from the school. For example, in geographic locations where large numbers of immigrant students enter school throughout the year, school districts may assign these students to newcomer centers for a short period of time to familiarize them with the school, society, and their own communities (Chang, 1990; Friedlander, 1991). Some secondary schools, mainly high schools, also offer separate ESL vocational programs. Usually students attend newcomer and vocational programs all day for a specific amount of time.

Primary Language Classes

At the secondary level, primary language instruction may not be available to LEP students, and in those states where it is available, it is most likely to be offered to Spanish-speaking students. In some locations, individual primary language instruction in Asian and East Asian languages is offered if teachers are available. Minicucci and Olsen (1991) report that in California, about one third of middle schools offering special instruction use the LEP students' primary language for science, math, and social studies. At the high school level, primary language classes are available mainly to schools populated by Spanish-speaking students with little or no prior schooling experience.

Bilingual Classes

By and large, the most commonplace form of "bilingual" instruction at the secondary level is some form of ESL and/or sheltered English content instruction. These programs are not bilingual in the pedagogical sense, but rather their purpose is to produce bilingual students, particularly students who can function socially and academically first in an all-English content-area classroom (sheltered or unsheltered) and ultimately in an all-English workplace. Less common at the secondary level are bilingual content courses, such as bilingual science, bilingual social studies, and bilingual math. Occasionally, advanced bilingual content-area courses are offered in science, mathematics, and social studies (Minicucci & Olsen, 1991). Bilingual content-area courses are more likely at the middle school level where there are comparable textbooks in math, science, and language arts. At the high school level, few school districts have access to parallel textbooks for the content areas.

English as a Second Language Classes

ESL instruction in the secondary school usually comprises a sequence of three to four levels of ESL classes. More often than not, there are beginning-, intermediate- and advanced-level offerings. In some cases, there is a transitional English class in which students are taught study and learning skills and some academic content. For example, some schools use Chamot and O'Malley's (1986) cognitive academic language learning approach (CALLA). CALLA is a pro- gram designed to enhance English language development through content instruction which incorporates metacognitive, cognitive, and social learning strategies to assist students in the comprehension and recall of key concepts and principles.

The language classes usually present English instruction through sentence-based curricula. Depending on the students' literacy ability, the classes may use written support in the form of textbooks, workbooks, and worksheets. The focus of these classes is on the learning of English grammar and vocabulary and on the four skills of speaking, listening, reading, and writing. Reading and writing activities tend to emphasize accuracy over fluency, and speaking is practiced through pattern drill, role plays, and other context-reduced language activities. Listening is often practiced through Total Physical Response (Asher, 1966) and other structured tasks.

Sheltered English Content Classes

Many secondary schools, especially at the high school level, are moving away from ESL instruction toward sheltered approaches to content-area instruction. There are two alternatives of sheltered English content instruction (SECI): *sheltered English* and *sheltered content teaching*. Although the two terms are used interchangeably, what distinguished them is whether the teacher is certified to teach the content area of the class. Sheltered English teachers are usually ESL-endorsed teachers who teach subject matter content to LEP students; sheltered content teachers, in contrast, are certified content-area teachers with additional preparation in ESL methodology and second language acquisition theory. No research exists on the differences in academic and/or language achievement between the two alternatives. There is some concern, however, among non-ESL secondary and sheltered content teachers that sheltered English teachers may lack knowledge of subject matter pedagogy and thus are inadequately prepared to teach subject matter content.

SECI is a methodology for combining language acquisition strategies with content-area instruction through language-sensitive teachers. SECI has two characteristics that distinguish it from both regular content-area instruction and ESL-oriented instruction: (a) only LEP students are assigned to SECI classes, and (b) the teachers attempt to make their language comprehensible so that regardless of their ESL abilities, all students can participate in class activities. SECI teachers help their students participate in lessons by supporting instructional discourse nonverbally, visually, and through use of prosodic components (e.g., stress, intonation, volume) by tailoring requests for student input to the language abilities of the students, and by frequently checking for comprehension during interactional exchanges.

SECI classes are designed to teach students the same concepts and skills that are covered in a regular classroom for native English speakers. In many cases, there is an emphasis on understanding critical vocabulary, concepts, and skills needed in order to comprehend the key foci of content within any lesson. In whole language-oriented SECI classes, students learn subject matter, content, and vocabulary in the contexts of thematic units involving an assortment of reading and writing activities and student-generated tasks (see, e.g., Hudelson, 1989; Rigg, 1991).

Support from Teen SLA Theory

Just as at the elementary school level there appears to be a move toward the integration of language and content instruction, so too there is a similar trend at the secondary level in the form of SECI. This trend is in large part informed by teen SLA theory, which proposes that adolescents (ages 13–18) are the best (fastest and most efficient) language learners and acquirers of all age groups (Ellis, 1985). According to Krashen (1985), teenagers who have already developed academic and literacy abilities in their native language are especially effective language learners because, not only can they rely on their ability to formally learn about language, they can also fall back on their existing knowledge about language and the world. Many teenage LEP students are very good at using prior experiences to make sense of the input they receive in writing and through conversation. Also, teenage LEP students are already skilled conversationalists who know how to negotiate conversations to sustain interaction. In this manner, teenage LEP students are in a position to receive lots of comprehensible input, to engage in communicative exchanges with more proficient speakers, and to be pushed to elaborate their meaning in a variety of social and academic contexts.

The shift toward SECI is also propelled by reforms that have been taking place in other areas. For example, in the 1980s, high school content teachers began to weave authentic reading and writing activities across the curriculum into all subject matter areas. Classrooms became reading and writing workshops, and literacy was no longer considered a skill separate from speaking and listening, but rather an integral part in whole language learning (Atwell, 1987). From this perspective, literacy is perceived as active learning. Literacy is a way of using language for communicating ideas, for proposing answers, for making sense of the test, and for trying out language. This view of literacy requires that students actively exchange relevant ideas with one another in small- and large-group settings.

Unfortunately, much of what occurs in many SECI classrooms hinders rather than helps teenage LEP students with respect to language as well as content learning. More often than not, instruction in SECI classrooms is teacher centered and predominantly directed at the whole class (Tikunoff, 1989). This means that LEP students are rarely given the opportunity to sustain interaction with peers or the teacher and that the teacher controls the topic and direction of instruction. Moreover, under these circumstances, there are few opportunities for learning through the discussion of written text or through authentic writing activities. The use of whole-group teaching without classroom interaction mirrors what Goodlad (1984) reported about secondary schools in general. Students may be provided lots of comprehensible input during whole-group teaching, but this context for learning severely limits opportunities for oral and written discussion and the negotiation of meaning. Small-group work and real literacy activities are found in some SECI classrooms, mainly in classrooms where the majority of students are members of different primary language backgrounds and among teachers who organize their classrooms around whole language principles (Rigg, 1991).

Help for the All-English Subject Matter Teacher?

Penfield (1987) found that while all the secondary school teachers who responded in her study wanted to facilitate the integration of LEP students into their classrooms, they also viewed this process as extremely problematic. Some teachers believed that LEP students would learn English best by being exposed to native-English-speaking classmates. But at the same time, they feared that the presence of LEP students would make learning more problematic for the native English speakers. Moreover, these same teachers were concerned that their personal teaching styles would have to change as increasing numbers of LEP students entered their classrooms.

At present, very little is being done nationally or locally to help all-English secondary teachers who lack preparation in teaching within a mixed language classroom. However, an exceptional program to help all-English middle school teachers with LEP students in their classrooms is currently being developed in San Bernardino, California, under the direction of Barbara Flores. In this program, ESL teachers team up with content-area teachers and work together to reorganize classroom activities so that LEP students work with native English proficient students. Drawing on Atwell's (1987) work with middle school teachers, the teams organize their classrooms to promote a variety of authentic reading and writing, which in turn facilitate language acquisition during content learning. This approach resembles the push-in model found in elementary schools: LEP students are completely integrated with native English speakers for a majority of learning activities, and the ESL teacher integrates language and literacy instruction across several content areas within extended blocks of time. In fact, a significant feature of the San Bernardino program as well as in other middle school programs is that class periods are restructured to allow teachers longer periods of time to work with students on topics that are thematically related across two or more content areas.

CONCLUSIONS

The teaching and learning of English in U.S. K–12 public schools has come a long way from the days when students were subjected to meaningless pattern drills and other forms of ersatz language practice for 15 to 50 minutes daily. Currently, public schools across the nation are beginning to respond to the needs of LEP students by trying out new approaches and programs and leaving old ones behind. As the number of LEP students increases and the parameters of bilingual education expand to include the all-English classroom, the field of TESOL will need to become even more instrumental in contributing to progress in the ways that schools serve LEP students to facilitate their learning. As the trends now indicate, there is already a move away from methods of language instruction per se to a concern for the learner who will likely acquire language and literacy proficiency in the context of an academic classroom, not in a language classroom.

For bilingual education, the integration of language and content instruction is perhaps the single most important pedagogical advance in recent years. Other important strides within bilingual education are the recognition that language and literacy acquisition are interrelated and that students learn to read and write their first and second languages by interacting with and creating whole, authentic texts (Hudelson, 1989). Research in SLA has also contributed greatly to the advances in what is happening in some K–12 classrooms. The idea that learners need continuous comprehensible input along with opportunities to try out and negotiate meaning has helped fuel the introduction of cooperative and small-group learning into bilingual, ESL, and regular all-English classrooms.

Along with these advances, however, have come all sorts of new problems and issues, all of which are begging for research, particularly at the secondary level. For example, as secondary schools move increasingly toward the use of sheltered English content teaching, the issue of segregation surfaces. SECI is touted as a transitional program designed to prepare students for the all-English classroom. In fact, LEP students who go into SECI programs often never leave them. Instead they spend much of their school day in these classes, totally segregated from native-English-speaking peers. Thus, not only are the students kept from learning in their native language, they are also denied access to interaction with native English speakers, a necessary ingredient for higher levels of SLA. Such linguistic and social segregation is questionable at best.

Another concern that desperately needs to be addressed is the preparation of all-English teachers to work with LEP students. Advances in bilingual education and TESOL must be incorporated into elementary as well as secondary teacher education programs. No longer can LEP students be made the sole responsibility of bilingual and/or ESL teachers. This responsibility must be shared by all teachers. As LEP students exit from bilingual programs or simply enter all-English classrooms, all-English teachers need to be prepared to help these students participate in all activities and understand that LEP students require more time than native English speakers to learn academic concepts. Collier (1987), for example, has shown that both younger (ages 5-7) and older (ages 12-15) LEP students generally take anywhere between 4 and 8 years to perform at the 50th percentile on English language standardized tests in reading, language arts, mathematics, science, and social studies. Mainstream educators and bilingual/TESOL professionals must work together to improve the educational experiences of all children and adolescents in school.
■

THE AUTHOR

Christian Faltis is Associate Professor at Arizona State University, where he teaches courses in the bilingual education graduate program. His recent publications include *Joinfostering: Adapting Teaching Strategies for the Multilingual Classroom* (Merrill, 1993) and *Language Minority Students and Computers* (with R. DeVillar, Haworth Press, 1991). Among his current research interests are language distribution decisions in bilingual instruction, incorporating SLA principles into mainstream teacher education, and critical pedagogy.

REFERENCES

Asher, J. (1966). The total physical response approach to second language learning. *Modern Language Journal, 53*, 3-17.

Atwell, N. (1987). *In the middle: Writing, reading, and learning with adolescents.* Portsmouth, NH: Boynton/Cook.

Chamot, A. U., & O'Malley, J. M. (1986). *A cognitive academic language learning approach: An ESL content-based curriculum.* Wheaton, MD: National Clearinghouse for Bilingual Education.

Chang, H. N. (1990). *Newcomer programs: Innovative efforts to meet the challenges of immigrant students.* San Francisco: California Tomorrow.

Collier, V. (1987). Age and rate of acquisition of second language for academic purposes. *TESOL Quarterly, 21*(4), 617-641.

Cummins, J. (in press). The socioacademic achievement model in the context of coercive and collaborative relations of power. In R. A. DeVillar, C. Faltis, & J. Cummins (Eds.), *Cultural diversity in schools: From rhetoric to practice.* Albany, NY: SUNY Press.

DeVillar, R. A. (in press). The rhetoric and practice of cultural diversity in U.S. schools: Socialization, resocialization, and quality schooling. In R. A. DeVillar, C. Faltis, & J. Cummins (Eds.), *Cultural diversity in schools: From rhetoric to practice.* Albany, NY: SUNY Press.

DeVillar, R. A., & Faltis, C. (1991). *Computers and cultural diversity.* Albany, NY: SUNY Press.

Ellis, R. (1985). *Understanding second language acquisition.* New York: Oxford University Press.

Enright, D. S. (1986). "Use everything you have to teach English": Providing useful input to young language learners. In P. Rigg & D. S. Enright (Eds.), *Children and ESL: Integrating perspectives* (pp. 115-162). Washington, DC: TESOL.

Enright, D. S., & McCloskey, M. L. (1988). *Integrating English: Developing English language and literacy in the multilingual classroom.* Reading, MA: Addison-Wesley.

Faltis, C. (1989). Classroom language use and educational equity: Toward interactive pedagogy. In H. P. Baptiste, H. Waxman, J. Walker de Felix, & J. Anderson (Eds.), *Leadership, equity, and school effectiveness* (pp. 109-126). Newbury Park, CA: Sage.

Faltis, C. (1992). *ESL teachers as experts in integrating language and content.* (Study funded by the Far West Holmes Group). Unpublished manuscript, Arizona State University, Tempe.

Faltis, C. (1993). *Joinfostering: Adapting teaching strategies for the multilingual classroom.* Columbus, OH: Merrill.

Faltis, C., & Arias, M. B. (1992, January). *Issues in bilingual secondary education.* Paper presented at the International Conference of the National Association for Bilingual Education, Albuquerque, NM.

Faltis, C., & Merino, B. (1992). Toward a definition of exemplary teachers in bilingual multicultural school settings. In R. Padilla & A. Benavides (Eds.), *Critical perspectives on bilingual education research* (pp. 277-299). Tempe, AZ: Bilingual Press.

Faltis, C., Merino, B., & Arias, M. B. (1992, April). *Exemplary practices of an expert teacher in a bilingual classroom and community setting: A case study.* Paper presented at the American Educational Research Association Meeting, San Francisco.

Freeman, D., Freeman, Y., & González, R. (1987). Success for LEP students: The Sunnyside sheltered English program. *TESOL Quarterly, 21*(2), 361-367.

Freeman, Y., & Freeman, D. (1992). *Whole language for second language learners.* Portsmouth, NH: Heinemann.

Friedlander, M. (1991). *The newcomer program: Helping immigrant students succeed in U.S. schools.* Wheaton, MD: National Clearinghouse for Bilingual Education.

Goodlad, J. (1984). *A place called school: Prospects for the future.* New York: McGraw-Hill.

Hudelson, S. (1989). "Teaching" English through content-area activities. In P. Rigg & V. Allen (Eds.), *When they don't all speak English: Integrating the ESL student into the regular classroom* (pp. 139-151). Urbana, IL: National Council of Teachers of English.

Krashen, S. (1985). *The input hypothesis: Issues and implications.* London: Longman.

Lucas, T. (in press). Secondary schooling for students becoming bilingual: Issues and practices. In M. B. Arias & U. Casanova (Eds.), *Bilingual education: Politics, research, and practice.* Chicago, IL: National Society for the Study of Education.

Lucas, T., Henze, R., & Donato, R. (1990). Promoting the success of Latino language minority students: An exploratory study of six high schools. *Harvard Educational Review, 60*(3), 315-340.

McGroarty, M. (1989). The benefits of cooperative learning arrangements in second language instruction. *NABE Journal, 12,* 127-143.

McKay, S. L., & Freedman, S. W. (1990). Language minority education in Great Britain: A challenge to current U.S. policy. *TESOL Quarterly, 24*(3), 385-406.

Milk, R. D. (1985). The changing role of ESL in bilingual education. *TESOL Quarterly, 19*(4), 657-672.

Milk, R. D. (1990). Preparing ESL and bilingual teachers for changing roles: Immersion for teachers of LEP children. *TESOL Quarterly, 24*(3), 407-426.

Minicucci, C., & Olsen, L. (1991). *Meeting the challenge of language diversity: An evaluation of programs for pupils with limited proficiency in English, Vol. 5. An exploratory study of secondary LEP programs.* Berkeley, CA: BW Associates.

Moll, L. (Ed.). (1990). *Vygotsky and education: Instructional implication and application of sociohistorical psychology.* New York: Cambridge University Press.

National Council of La Raza. (1990). *Hispanic education: A statistical portrait 1990.* Washington, DC: Author.

Olsen, L. (1988). *Crossing the schoolhouse border: Immigrant students and the California public schools.* San Francisco: California Tomorrow.

Olsen, R. E. W-B. (1989). A survey of limited English proficient student enrollments and identification criteria. *TESOL Quarterly, 23*(3), 469-488.

Pallas, A., Natriello, G., & McDill, E. (1989). The changing nature of the disadvantaged population: Current dimensions and future trends. *Educational Research, 18*, 16-22.

Pease-Alvarez, L., García, E., & Espinosa, P. (1991). Effective instruction for language-minority students: An early childhood case study. *Early Childhood Research Quarterly, 6*, 347-361.

Penfield, J. (1987). ESL: The regular classroom teacher's perspective. *TESOL Quarterly, 21*(1), 21-39.

Ramírez, J. D., & Merino, B. (1990). Classroom talk in English immersion, early-exit and late exit transitional bilingual education programs. In R. Jacobson & C. Faltis (Eds.), *Language distribution issues in bilingual schooling* (pp. 61-103). Clevedon, England: Multilingual Matters.

Rigg, P. (1991). Whole language in TESOL. *TESOL Quarterly, 25*(3), 521-542.

Rodríguez, R. (1990, July). Escasez de maestros bilingües en una etapa crítica [A paucity of bilingual teachers in a critical period]. *La Opinión*, p. 5.

Scarcella, R. (1990). *Teaching language minority students in the multicultural classroom*. Englewood Cliffs, NJ: Prentice Hall.

Stein, C. B. (1986). *Sink or swim: The politics of bilingual education*. New York: Praeger.

Swain, M. (1985). Communicative competence: Some roles of comprehensible input and comprehensible output in its development. In S. Gass & C. Madden (Eds.), *Input in second language acquisition* (pp. 235-253). Rowley, MA: Newbury House.

Tikunoff, W. (1983). Five significant instructional features. In W. Tikunoff (Ed.), *Compatibility of the SBIF features with other research on instruction for LEP students*. San Francisco: Far West Laboratory.

Tikunoff, W. (1989). Providing appropriate opportunities for language minority students in high school academic instruction: The challenge in Arizona. *High School Education Program for Language Minority Students: The Arizona Picture* (pp. 11-19). Los Alamitos, CA: Southwest Regional Educational Laboratory.

Tikunoff, W., Ward, B., van Broekhuizen, D., Romero, M., Castañeda, L., Lucas, T., & Katz, A. (1991). *A descriptive study of significant features of exemplary special alternative instructional programs* (Final Report). Los Alamitos, CA: Southwest Regional Educational Laboratory.

Trueba, H. T. (1989). *Raising silent voices: Educating the linguistic minorities for the 21st century*. New York: Harper & Row.

U.S. Department of Education, National Center for Education Statistics. (1992). *The condition of education, 1992*. Washington, DC: Author.

U.S. General Accounting Office. (1987). *Bilingual education: Information on limited English proficient students*. Washington, DC: Author.

Waggoner, D. (1987). Foreign born children in the United States in the eighties. *NABE Journal, 12*, 23-49.

Waggoner, D. (1992). Numbers of home speakers of non-English languages increasing. *Numbers and Needs, 2*, 2.

Vygotsky, L. S. (1978). *Mind in society*. Cambridge, MA: Harvard University Press.

English for Specific Purposes: International in Scope, Specific in Purpose

ANN M. JOHNS
San Diego State University

TONY DUDLEY-EVANS
The University of Birmingham

Over the past 30 years, English for specific purposes has established itself as a viable and vigorous movement within the field of TEFL/TESL. In this paper, English for specific purposes is defined and its distinguishing features examined. The international nature and scope of the movement are particularly emphasized. Finally, questions and controversies surrounding the movement are discussed.

The study of languages for specific purposes has a long and varied history (Strevens, 1977). In recent years, the focus of research and curriculum development has been upon English, as it has gained ascendancy in international science, technology, and trade. As TESOL enters its second quarter century, the demand for English for specific purposes (e.g., English for science and technology, English for business, vocational ESL) continues to increase and expand throughout the world.

This paper celebrates the modern history of English for specific purposes (ESP), an international movement characterized by a concern with adult students' "wider roles" (Swales, 1988, p. viii; i.e., their roles as English language speakers and writers outside of the classroom) and by its grounding in pedagogy, for ESP "distrusts theories that do not quite work out in the litmus-paper realities of the classroom" (Swales, 1988, p. xvii). We will begin by presenting a standard definition of English for specific purposes, and continue by discussing the distinguishing characteristics of the movement, needs assessment and discourse analysis, that have set it apart from "general purpose English." (For an excellent ESP retrospective, 1962–1981, see Swales, 1988.) Following the discussion of these features, we will focus upon ESP's international scope and influence. Finally, we will address some of the questions and controversies that surround ESP in the 1990s.

A DEFINITION AND DISCUSSION OF PRINCIPAL COMPONENTS

ESP requires the careful research and design of pedagogical materials and activities for an identifiable group of adult learners within a specific learning context. Categories of ESP include various academic Englishes, e.g., English for science and technology, English for graduate teaching assistants, and "general" English for academic purposes, in addition to a number of occupational Englishes, e.g., English for business, and vocational ESL (also called English for the workplace). Peter Strevens (1988), who throughout his life was instrumental in explaining and developing the movement, provided this extended definition and list of claims:

> A definition of ESP needs to distinguish between four absolute and two variable characteristics:
>
> 1) Absolute characteristics:
>   ESP consists of English language teaching which is:
>   —designed to meet specified needs of the learner
>   —related in content (i.e., in its themes and topics) to particular disciplines, occupations and activities
>   —centered on the language appropriate to those activities in syntax, lexis, discourse, semantics, etc., and analysis of this discourse
>   —in contrast with "General English"
> 2) Variable characteristics:
>   ESP may be, but is not necessarily:
>   —restricted as to the language skills to be learned (e.g., reading only)
>   —not taught according to any pre-ordained methodology
>   Claims: the claims for ESP are
>   —being focussed on the learner's need, wastes no time
>   —is relevant to the learner
>   —is successful in imparting learning
>   —is more cost-effective than "General English" (pp. 1-2)

Streven's widely accepted definition will be employed here to discuss two "absolute" components of ESP: needs assessment and discourse analysis.

Needs Assessment

Throughout its history, ESP practitioners have been preoccupied with learner needs, with identifying learner wants and purposes as integral and obligatory elements in materials design.[1] (For more complete discussions of ESP components, see A. M. Johns, 1990a; Robinson, 1980, 1991.) In their early years, needs assessments were fairly simple, precourse procedures (Munby, 1978). Recent needs assessments have grown increasingly sophisticated, however, as materials developers have become aware of the problematic nature of their task. One attempt to capture some of the complexity of the means by which individuals acquire and employ language was made by Jacobson (1986), who observed international students in the process of collecting data for a laboratory report, in order to determine at which points there was communication breakdown. Other assessments have exploited ethnographic principles of "thick description" in an effort to identify the various elements of the target situation in which students will be using English (Ramani, Chacko, Singh, & Glendinning, 1988).

Though the problems involved in assessing learner needs and understanding the situation in which they will be using English are daunting (Coleman, 1988), ESP materials designers and practitioners continue in their efforts to improve and expand their collection and analysis techniques. They argue that all students are enrolled in ESL or EFL classes for particular reasons and that the students' target English situations have identifiable elements; thus, it is the responsibility of teachers to discover these factors and to deliver courses that are suitable for their student populations.

Discourse Analysis

A second, closely related element is discourse analysis, which in ESP refers to the examination of written or oral language, generally for purposes of designing curricular materials. Throughout its recent history (whose beginning Swales, 1988, marks with the Barber, 1962/1988 article), ESP specialists have been concerned with identifying and weighing the importance of features of the authentic, or "genuine" (Widdowson, 1981, p. 4), language of the situations in which students will be using English. In many parts of the world, the focus of this analysis is upon word or item counts, or "lexicostatistics" (Swales, 1988, p. 189). These counts have become

---

[1] One of the most articulate proponents of needs assessment, especially in the EAP reading-writing context, was Dan Horowitz (1986a, 1986b; and A. M. Johns, 1990c). With his death, ESP lost an intelligent and persuasive advocate.

increasingly sophisticated over the years (see, e.g., Gunawardena, 1989). Three promising avenues for modern item counts are the tense/aspect/mood function approaches, "communicative notions," and concordancing. Major contributions to the first approach are found in the work of the "University of Washington School," consisting of a number of well-respected names: Trimble, Selinker, Lackstrom, Huckin, Tarone, and Bley-Vroman (see especially Selinker, Tarone, & Hanzeli, 1981). One of the best publications by this group was devoted to the passive. In this piece, Tarone, Dwyer, Gillette, and Icke (1981) explored the incidence and functions of this feature acknowledged as typical of English for science and technology (EST), within journal articles in a single, well-defined discourse community, astrophysics. In addition to destroying assumptions about the scientific passive in general, the researchers turned to an expert within the astrophysics discourse community to validate their assumptions. The use of experts to suggest and confirm needs and discourse analyses hypotheses has continued since that time. (Huckin & Olsen, 1984; Selinker, 1979)

A second approach, based upon communicative notions, has been inspired by communicative syllabus design. A communicative approach was taken by Kennedy (1987), for example, who employed three different methods (frequency counts from texts, dictionary search, and informant use) to identify nearly 200 different linguistic devices to signal temporal frequency in academic texts.

A third approach in text feature analysis is concordancing (T. F. Johns, 1989). In Stevens' (1991) concordancing program at Sultan Qaboos University (Oman), for example, most of the reading texts assigned to students in their classes in science and technology are on the computer. Students and materials designers use the concordancing system to discover how often and in what contexts words or phrases appear. A similar program has been developed at the University of Zimbabwe (Mparutsa, Love, & Morrison, 1991).

Other text analyses have had more global emphases. Louis Trimble and his colleagues at the University of Washington developed a useful Rhetorical Process Chart, which has assisted researchers and curriculum designers to identify, for example, levels of discourse within texts (Trimble, 1985). Swales (1984, 1990b) has been a leader in encouraging the examination of sections of texts (e.g., introductions) in a number of disciplines in order to determine the required steps. Swales (1990b) defines steps as "elements that make a paper coherent to genre-experienced readers" (p. 190). Most of Swales' work in this area has been devoted to introductions in research papers, in which he has found four prototypical steps: establishment of the field, description of the previous research, gap indication, and introduction of the present research (1990a, p. 192).

Others have chosen to look in depth at one discipline. Dubois (1980, 1985, 1987), for example, has investigated features of spoken and written discourse in biomedicine (e.g., purposes of poster sessions, regulatory language, and citations). Bazerman has examined the language of physics (1984), and Dudley-Evans and Henderson (1990) have devoted a volume to the nature of economics discourse.

Thus far, we have discussed some approaches to analyzing genuine discourse serving real purposes in specified contexts for the development of ESP materials. However, this external view cannot satisfy the many adherents of more process, learner-centered philosophies. Thus, there have begun a number of studies focusing upon learner interaction with discourse, three of which will be mentioned here. Olsen and Huckin (1990) and Daoud (1991) have discovered that many advanced ESL students understand every word in a lecture or in a reading but still fail to grasp the principal arguments or the purposes and audiences for the discourse. These researchers suggest a broader strategy for instruction, based upon the character of the academic community in which the discourse is found. St. John (1987) employed insights from writing process literature to study the efforts of Spanish scientists to produce publishable discourse in English.

In this section, we have focused upon the "absolute" features of ESP identified by Peter Strevens' needs assessment and discourse analysis. We now turn to a contextualized discussion of the international scope of the ESP movement.

INTERNATIONAL SCOPE

There are a number of reasons for the international character of ESP and its importance in EFL environments. As early as the 1970s, the participants at a conference on second language learning and national development in Asia, Africa, and Latin America summed up the need for English as follows:

the language problem in development stems from at least three communication needs which are increasingly being recognized both in developing countries themselves and in other countries aiding in their development: internal communication, transmission of science and technology, and international communication. (Mackay & Mountford, 1978, p. vi)

Countries such as India, Nigeria, Singapore, Fiji, and Kenya require English for internal communication, since this language is shared by educated citizens, and is the most neutral language available. Gueye (1990) argues that in these contexts, ESP, through English for development purposes, should encourage students to understand their roles in the educational and social development of their own nations. Because of the internal English language needs, a number of countries have produced their own ESP textbooks that reflect the norms of local speech and discourse communities rather than any transnational standard. (See, for example, A. M. Johns, 1986.) As economic communities form, the need for English often becomes central to their internal interaction as well. In anticipation of the European Community, for example, Michel Perrin at Bordeaux University, in cooperation with his colleagues at Toulouse and Montpellier, has designed a predoctoral program in ESP for French universities.

Perhaps of greater interest to readers of this volume is another force in the internationalizing of ESP: the explosion of scientific and technical English (EST) especially in professional publications and graduate schools. Baldauf and Jernudd (1983) have found that in chemistry, biology, physics, medicine, and math, more than 65% of all international journals are now English language, a dramatic increase since 1965. To cope with this explosion, conferences and seminars devoted to EST are becoming common. Two recent well-attended Latin American ESP colloquia, held in Brazil and Chile, concentrated principally upon written scientific and technical discourse ("Second Latin American," 1990). A colloquium held in 1990 at the Institute of Agronomy, Rabat, Morocco, included researchers, teachers, and secondary school inspectors interested in technical and scientific English. Yearly, the Chinese association of teachers of English and the British Council cosponsor a conference in which scientific reading and writing play central roles.

A third area of need mentioned by Mackay and Mountford (1978) is for international communication. The language of the airways is English; thus, ESP courses are designed for pilots and other air personnel who must communicate without error with air traffic personnel (Robertson, 1988). The language of the sea is also English; thus maritime workers throughout the world learn SEASPEAK, the International Maritime English (Strevens & Johnson, 1983). There are also many occasions in international business in which English is the chosen or necessary language of communication, even among nonnative-speaking interlocutors (Smith, 1987).

Not surprisingly, international publications voice ESP (and language for specific purposes) concerns: for example, the *ALSED-LSP*

Newsletter (from the Copenhagen School of Economics), published by UNESCO; a number of special issues and publications from the Regional English Language Centre in Singapore; *FACHSPRACHE* (Austria); *ESPMENA* (Sudan); and several others. EFL subscribers to *English for Specific Purposes: An International Journal* far outnumber subscribers from English-speaking nations (this may be partially explained by the fact that ESP is often called something else in English-speaking countries, e.g., "content-based instruction" in the U.S. and English for the workplace (EWP) in Australia; and more than half of the articles are written by authors teaching in EFL contexts. Unfortunately, many of the superior, but localized, ESP projects are not discussed in international publications, a great loss for teachers and materials designers everywhere (Swales, 1988).

ISSUES AND CONTROVERSIES

In the early days, while ESP was establishing itself as a separate and valid activity within the general context of English language teaching, the main controversy centered around the validity of the approach: Was ESP likely to be more successful than general purpose English (GPE) at preparing students for study through the medium of English or working in situations in which communication takes place in English? Early articles, such as those by Higgins (1966) and Allen and Widdowson (1974) argued the case for ESP and were influential in establishing the movement. At that time (late 1960s, early 1970s), ESP activity drew much inspiration from applied linguists such as Barber (1962/1988) and Lackstrom, Selinker, and Trimble (1972). The materials production of ESP practitioners such as Herbert (1965), Swales (1971), and Bates and Dudley-Evans (1976) seemed to parallel the more theoretical work of applied linguists. In the late 1970s and 1980s, theoretical work seemed to lag behind materials development; only recently has theoretically motivated research begun to close the gap.

Now, we find ESP less constrained to argue the case for its own existence. This is partly, we suspect, because the case for ESP has now been accepted internationally, and it is now possible for teachers, especially in EFL contexts, to pursue a career in ESP work. Unfortunately, however, few empirical studies have been conducted to test the effectiveness of ESP courses. Foley's discussion of the ESP program at the University of Petroleum and Minerals (1979) and the report of the evaluation of the Brazil ESP Reading Project (Celani, Holmes, Ramos, & Scott, 1988) are notable exceptions. For the most part, reports on ESP courses consist of what Bowyers (1980) calls "war stories and romances."

Despite its acceptance as an activity central to many English language teaching contexts, controversies and questions within ESP remain. Principal among them are the following:

1. How specific should ESP courses and texts be?
2. Should they focus upon one particular skill, e.g., reading, or should the four skills always be integrated?
3. Can an appropriate ESP methodology be developed?

The question of how specific ESP courses should be was first raised directly by R. Williams (1978) who argued in favor of a "wide-angle" (p. 30) approach in which language and skills are taught through topics that are drawn from a variety of subjects rather than from the students' own discipline or profession. The argument for a wide-angle approach has also been forwarded by Widdowson in his volume *Learning Purpose and Language Use* (1983), as well as by materials writers and teachers of academic writing (Spack, 1988). But the strongest case for this view has been made by Hutchison and Waters. In a number of influential articles, for example, "ESP at the Crossroads" (1980), and in their volume *English for Specific Purposes: A Learner-Centred Approach* (1987), they argue that the narrow-angle approach is demotivating and irrelevant to student needs. In particular, they claim that students should be grouped for ESP classes across broad subject areas with materials drawing from topics that give "access to a number of different specialist areas" (Hutchinson & Waters, 1987, p. 166) thus making students aware of the "lack of specificity of their needs" (1987, p. 167).

We believe that the case made by Hutchinson and Waters is overstated. The seeming suitability of the wide-angle approach to prestudy courses does not mean that it is suitable for all ESP courses, in particular, for graduate students and professionals (Swales, 1990a) and in a number of EFL contexts. The various team-teaching experiments reported in the ESP literature (e.g., de Escorcia, 1984; T. F. Johns & Dudley-Evans, 1980) show that the wide-angle or so-called common core approach needs to be supplemented by some attempt to define students' more specific needs and the actual language difficulties that they face on a day-to-day basis in classes in their disciplines or in their professional lives. The concern with the nature of the discourse community (Joliffe, 1988; Swales, 1990a) and the process of socialization of the "novice" into that community (Ballard, 1984; Berkenkotter, Huckin, & Ackerman, 1991) confirm the need for focus upon the differences among disciplines and professions. Related studies in rhetoric confirm the need for the ESP teacher to take account of the varying epistemological assumptions of different academic disciplines and professional discourse communities. In academic studies, Hansen (1988) shows clearly that rhetorical conventions differ between anthropology and sociology; Benson (1991) demonstrates that values upon which discourses are based vary from discipline to discipline.

The debate about the validity of a focus upon a single skill is conducted along similar lines. In ESP practice, the single skill is usually reading because of its primary importance in many EFL environments. It has been argued (e.g., Chitravelu, 1980; Hutchinson & Waters, 1987) that concentration on one skill is limiting and that some attention to other skills is likely to improve performance in the target skill. Nonetheless, monoskill reading courses have undoubtedly proved popular and successful in many parts of the world, such as China (A. M. Johns, 1986) and some Latin American countries ("Second Latin American," 1990). The exemplary Brazilian ESP project has generated both teaching materials and a number of reports on the relevance of teaching reading alone (Celani, et al., 1988).

Does ESP have its own methodology? It has tended to be a needs- and materials-led movement, historically questioned by only a few (see Phillips & Shettlesworth, 1978). However, with the learner-centered bias of Hutchinson and Waters (1987), interest in methodologies has increased. Courses at the Asian Institute of Technology in Thailand (Hall & Kenny, 1988) and the British Council's English Study Centre in Recife, Brazil, exhibit this influence.

We believe that ESP requires methodologies that are specialized or unique. An English for academic purposes (EAP) class taught collaboratively by a language teacher and a subject-area lecturer (T. F. Johns & Dudley-Evans, 1980), sheltered and adjunct EAP classes (Brinton, Snow, & Wesche, 1989), and special English classes for students in the workplace (Lompers, 1991) require considerably different approaches than those found in general English classes.

Given the importance of the teaching of writing in many ESP situations, it is not surprising that the process/product debate in L1 composition theory (Flower, 1989) has spilled over into ESP. The work of genre analysis (Swales, 1990a) and the increasing influence of the social constructionist view of writing (A. M. Johns, 1990b), however, seem to provide a system of analysis and thereby an approach to the teaching of writing (Weissberg & Buker, 1990) that successfully combines the consideration of end product with the writing process.

FUTURE DEVELOPMENTS

We noted earlier that ESP is now accepted as an important, if idiosyncratic, part of English language teaching, at least in international contexts. It is now increasingly concerned with the "ecological" issue of how to ensure that ESP projects last and continue in local situations (Holliday & Cooke, 1982), and in this, the role of the nonnative-speaker ESP teacher is crucial. As might be predicted, a considerable number of ESP student and teacher preparation programs have arisen in EFL contexts. Two of many examples are the courses for technical students and teaching professionals at Jiao Tong University in Shanghai, China—a country in which there are numerous ESP programs and publications—and at the undergraduate teacher preparation program at the University of Blida, Algeria. Other ESP programs are in the offing, for example, a graduate program at the Catholic University in Santiago, Chile.

It is unfortunate that graduate programs in the United States have not recognized the need for English for specific purposes courses for international students or English-speaking students who desire employment overseas or in specific purpose contexts. Because of this lacuna, it is difficult for agencies such as AMIDEST (American Friends of the Middle East) to place students for graduate studies, and for the United States Information Agency, which provides U.S. consultants for international contexts, to satisfy the requests for English for specific purposes experts (B. Avant, personal communication, 1991).[2] The situation is considerably better in other English-speaking countries. In the United Kingdom, for example, there are a number of ESP teacher training programs, including a Master of Science in Teaching English for Specific Purposes at Aston and a certificate in Teaching ESP at the University of Essex.

For most of its history, ESP has been dominated by English for academic purposes, and under that rubric, by English for science and technology (Swales, 1988); EAP continues to dominate internationally. However, the increased number of immigrants in English-speaking countries and the demand for MBA courses in all parts of the world have increased the demand for professional and business English, vocational English (VESL/EVP in the U.S., EOP in the U.K.), and English in the workplace (WPLT) programs. Again, there is a dilemma about how specific the business and vocational English courses should be and whether these courses are

---

[2] The planned creation of an ESP Special Interest Group in TESOL may improve matters somewhat, though the current SIG membership consists principally of consultants in workplace contexts in the United States, whose needs and interests are considerably different from those of the international student or scholar.

to be considered ESP. It is our contention that all courses in specialized language and practice fall under the English for specific purposes rubric.

As happened in the 1970s in the case of English for academic purposes and English for science and technology, the increasing interest in professional English has resulted in a number of good general business English volumes which have emerged from teaching situations. These include books such as *Business Concepts for English Practice* (Dowling & McDougal, 1982), *Business English* (Wilbert & Lewis, 1990), *In at the Deep End* (Hollett, Carter, Lyon, & Tanner, 1989), and *Ready for Business* (Vaughan & Heyen, 1990) that have clearly benefited from having been piloted and revised in light of teaching experience. However, in the more specific materials on topics such as meeting skills, business negotiation, and case studies, there is the danger of overdependence on the materials writers' intuitions about what is involved in such activities, rather than upon research and analysis of representative discourse. A number of studies have pointed to the mismatch between the textbook view of what happens in, for example, a business meeting and what a detailed analysis reveals (Oertli, 1991; M. Williams, 1988). This is not to suggest that other branches of ESP have not faced the same problems. Research in business-related skills is, however, hampered by the difficulty of obtaining data. Lampi's (1985) work on business negotiation is, unfortunately, a relatively rare example of a business English study based upon authentic data.

As ESP delves deeper into students' needs and extends beyond its traditional EAP base, there will be an increasing need for research into the nature of discourse, written or spoken, that must be produced or understood by those enrolled in ESP courses. The importance to ESP of genre analysis (Swales, 1990a), of the insights of writing scholars such as Bazerman (1988) and Myers (1989), and of the findings of those studying the role of written text in the work situation (Bazerman & Paradis, 1991; Coleman, 1989) will also be of increasing significance. Whether or not this research will take ESP further away from its parent disciplines of TESL/TEFL and applied linguistics, as Swales (1988) suggests, remains to be seen. What is clear is that it will increasingly draw on and work with other disciplines such as rhetoric, the sociology of science, and social psychology.

Interestingly, the converse also seems to be occurring: Other disciplines are now beginning to draw upon the insights of ESP-related research, as can be seen from related work in communication studies (Chukwuma, Obah, Robinson, & St. John, 1991; Love,

1991). A review (Brown, 1991) of *The Language of Economics* (Dudley-Evans & Henderson, 1990) in the *Economic Journal* expresses some impatience with the authors' careful argument for the importance of genre and discourse analysis to an understanding of the nature of communication; the reviewer looked forward to the consideration in a successor volume of "the wider epistemological implication of discourse analysis for the teaching and learning of economics" (p. 1317). ESP may, in fact, begin to expand beyond its classroom role to assume a substantial consultancy role in a wide variety of academic and professional environments.

■

ACKNOWLEDGMENT

The authors would like to thank John Swales for his assistance in shaping the paper and for his valuable comments on its various drafts.

THE AUTHORS

Ann M. Johns is Professor of Academic Skills and Linguistics at San Diego State University in California. She is the author of articles on English for academic purposes and Coeditor (with U. Connor) of *Coherence in Writing: Research and Pedagogical Perspectives* (TESOL, 1990). She is Coeditor (with Tony Dudley-Evans and John Swales) of *English for Specific Purposes: An International Journal*. She has worked cooperatively on curriculum development projects in eight countries. Her research interests include student representation of academic reading and writing tasks, testing academic literacy, and argumentation in the disciplines.

Tony Dudley-Evans is Senior Lecturer and Director of the English for Overseas Students Unit in the School of English at the University of Birmingham. He has coedited international ESP textbooks and has written articles on ESP/EAP. Recently he has coedited *The Language of Economics: The Analysis of Economics Discourse* (with Willie Henderson) (ELT Documents No. 134, 1990). He is Coeditor (with Ann Johns and John Swales) of *English for Specific Purposes: An International Journal*. He has taught and consulted in a variety of environments; his particular interests are ESP, team teaching with subject specialists, and genre analysis.

REFERENCES

Allen, J. P. B., & Widdowson, H. G. (1974). Teaching the communicative use of English. *International Review of Applied Linguistics XII*(1), 1-20.

Baldauf, R. B., & Jernudd, B. H. (1983). Language of publications as a variable in scientific communication. *Australian Review of Applied Linguistics, 6,* 97-108.

Ballard, B. (1984). Improving student writing: An integrated approach to cultural adjustment. In R. Williams, J. M. Swales, & J. Kirkman (Eds.), *Common ground: Shared interests in ESP and communication studies* (ELT Documents No. 117, pp. 43-54). Oxford: Pergamon Press in association with the British Council.

Barber, C. L. (1988). Some measurable characteristics of modern scientific prose. In J. Swales (Ed.), *Episodes in ESP: A source and reference book for the development of English for science and technology.* New York: Prentice Hall. (Reprinted from *Contributions to English syntax and philology* [Gothenberg Studies in English No. 14, 1962, pp. 1-23]. Stockholm: Almquist & Wiksell)

Bates, M., & Dudley-Evans, A. (1976). *Nucleus: English for science and technology.* Harlow, England: Longman.

Bazerman, C. (1984). Modern evolution of the experimental report in physics: Spectroscopic articles in *Physical Review,* 1893-1980. *Social Studies in Science, 14,* 163-196.

Bazerman, C. (1988). *Shaping written knowledge.* Madison: University of Wisconsin Press.

Bazerman, C., & Paradis, J. (1991). *Textual dynamics of the professions.* Madison: University of Wisconsin Press.

Benson, M. J. (1991). University ESL reading: A content analysis. *English for Specific Purposes, 10,* 75-88.

Berkenkotter, C., Huckin, T. M., & Ackerman, J. (1991). Social context and socially-constructed texts: The initiation of a graduate student into a writing research community. In C. Bazerman & J. Paradis, *Textual dynamics of the professions* (pp. 1, 191-216). Madison: University of Wisconsin Press.

Bowyers, R. (1980). War stories and romances. In *Projects in materials design* (ELT Documents Special, pp. 71-82). London: British Council.

Brinton, D., Snow, M.A., & Wesche, M. B. (1989). *Content-based second language instruction.* New York: Newbury House/Harper & Row.

Brown, V. (1991). [Review of *The Language of Economics: The analysis of economics discourse*]. *Economic Journal, 101*(408), 1315-1317.

Cclani, M. A., Holmes, J., Ramos, R. S., & Scott, M. (1988). *The Brazilian ESP project: An evaluation.* Sao Paulo: Universidades Brasileiras.

Chitravelu, N. (1980). Strategies for reading. In *The University of Malaya English for special purposes project* (ELT Documents No. 107, pp. 17-37). London: British Council.

Chukwuma, H., Obah, T., Robinson, P., & St. John, M. J. (1991). *A comparative study of communicative skills projects: Factors affecting success.* Paper presented at the 1991 BALEAP Conference, Southampton University, U.K.

Coleman, H. (1988). Analyzing language needs in large organizations. *English for Specific Purposes, 7,* 155-169.

Coleman, H. (Ed.). (1989). *Working with language: A multidisciplinary consideration of language use in work contexts.* Berlin: Mouton de Gruyter.

Daoud, M. (1991). *The processing of EST discourse: Arabic and French native speakers' recognition of rhetorical relationships in engineering texts.* Unpublished doctoral dissertation, University of California, Los Angeles.

de Escorcia, B. A. (1984). Team teaching for students of economics: A Colombian experience. In R. Williams, J. M. Swales, & J. Kirkman (Eds.), *Common ground: Shared interests in ESP and communication studies* (ELT Documents No. 117, pp. 105-144). Oxford: Pergamon Press and the British Council.

Dowling, B. T., & McDougal, M. (1982). *Business concepts for English practice.* Rowley, MA: Newbury House.

Dubois, B. L. (1980). Genre and structure of biomedical speeches. *Forum Linguisticum, 5,* 140-169.

Dubois, B. L. (1985). Popularization at the highest level: Poster sessions at biomedical meetings. *International Journal of the Sociology of Language, 56,* 67-85.

Dubois, B. L. (1987). Something on the order of around forty to forty-four: Imprecise numerical expressions in biomedical slide talks. *Language in Society, 16,* 527-541.

Dudley-Evans, A., & Henderson, W. (Eds.). (1990). *The language of economics: The analysis of economics discourse* (ELT Documents No. 134). London: Modern English Publications in association with the British Council.

Flower, L. (1989). *Problem-solving strategies for writing* (3rd ed.). San Diego: Harcourt Brace Jovanovich.

Foley, J. (1979). *Problems of understanding science and technological textbooks in English for first year students at the University of Petroleum and Minerals in Saudi Arabia.* Unpublished doctoral dissertation, University of London.

Gueye, M. (1990). One step beyond ESP: English for development purposes. *English Teaching Forum, XXVII*(3), 31-34.

Gunawardena, C. N. (1989). The present perfect in the rhetorical divisions of biology and biochemistry journal articles. *English for Specific Purposes, 8,* 265-274.

Hall, D., & Kenny, B. (1988). An approach to a truly communicative methodology: The AIT pre-sessional course. *English for Specific Purposes, 7,* 19-32.

Hansen, K. (1988). Rhetoric and epistemology in the social sciences: A contrast of two representative texts. In D. A. Joliffe (Ed.), *Writing in academic disciplines: Advances in writing research.* Norwood, NJ: Ablex.

Herbert, A. J. (1965). *The structure of technical English.* London: Longman.

Higgins, J. J. (1966). Hard facts (Notes on teaching English to science students). *English Language Teaching, 21*, 55-60. (Reprinted in J. Swales [Ed.], *Episodes in ESP* [pp. 28-34], 1988, New York: Prentice Hall)

Hollett, V. R., Carter, R., Lyon, L., & Tenner, E. (1989). *In at the deep end.* Oxford: Oxford University Press.

Holliday, A. R., & Cooke, T. (1982). An ecological approach to ESP. In A. Waters (Ed.). *Issues in English for specific purposes* (Lancaster Practical Papers in English Language Education, Vol. 5, pp. 123-143). Oxford: Pergamon Press.

Horowitz, D. M. (1986a). Essay examination prompts and the teaching of academic writing. *English for Specific Purposes, 5*, 197-220.

Horowitz, D. M. (1986b). What professors actually require: Academic tasks for the ESL classroom. *TESOL Quarterly, 20*(3), 445-462.

Huckin, T., & Olsen, L. (1984). On the use of informants in LSP discourse analysis. In A. Pugh & J. Ulijn (Eds.), *Reading for professional purposes* (pp. 120-129). London: Heinemann.

Hutchison, T., & Waters, A. (1980). ESP at the crossroads. *English for specific purposes* (Newsletter), *36*, 1-6. Oregon State University. (Reprinted in J. Swales [Ed.], *Episodes in ESP* [pp. 174-185], 1988, New York: Prentice Hall)

Hutchinson, T., & Waters, A. (1987). *English for specific purposes: A learning-centred approach.* Cambridge: Cambridge University Press.

Jacobson, W. H. (1986). An assessment of the communication needs of non-native speakers of English in an undergraduate physics lab. *English for Specific Purposes, 5*, 173-188.

Johns, A. M. (1986). Some comments on the nature of Chinese ESP coursebooks. In P. Wilcox Peterson (Ed.), *ESP in Practice* (pp. 85-89). Washington, DC: USIA.

Johns, A. M. (1990a). ESP: Its history and contributions. In M. Celce-Murcia (Ed.), *Teaching English as a second or foreign language* (2nd ed., pp. 67-78). New York: Newbury House.

Johns, A. M. (1990b). L1 composition theories: Implications for developing theories of L2 composition. In B. Kroll (Ed.). *Second language writing: Research insights for the classroom* (pp. 24-36). Cambridge: Cambridge University Press.

Johns, A. M. (1990c). Process, literature and academic realities: the contributions of Dan Horowitz. *JALT Journal, 12*, 29-36.

Johns, T. F. (1989). Whence and whither classroom concordancing? In T. Bongaerts, P. de Haan, S. Lobbe, & H. Wekker (Eds.), *Computer applications in language learning* (pp. 9-33). Dordrecht, Netherlands: Foris.

Johns, T. F., & Dudley-Evans, A. (1980). An experiment in team teaching overseas postgraduate students of transportation and plant biology. In *Team teaching in ESP* (ELT Documents No. 106, pp. 6-23). London: British Council. (Reprinted in J. Swales [Ed.], *Episodes in ESP* [pp. 137-156], 1988, New York: Prentice Hall)

Joliffe, D. A. (1988). *Writing in academic disciplines: Advances in writing research*. Norwood, NJ: Ablex.

Kennedy, G. D. (1987). Expressing temporal frequency in academic English. *TESOL Quarterly, 21*(1), 69-86.

Lackstrom, J. E., Selinker, L., & Trimble, L. P. (1972). Grammar and technical English. *English Teaching Forum, X*(5), 58-66.

Lampi, M. (1985). *Linguistic components of strategies in business negotiations*. Unpublished dissertation, University of Jyvaskyla, Finland.

Lompers, A. E. (1991, April). *Critical features in effective workplace language training (WPLT) programs*. Paper presented at the 22nd Annual CATESOL Conference, Santa Clara, CA.

Love, A. (1991). *Communication skills in the ESL African situation*. Paper presented at the 1991 Communication Skills Conference, Nairobi, Kenya.

Mackay, R., & Mountford, A. (1978). *English for specific purposes*. London: Longman.

Mparutsa, C., Love, A., & Morrison, A. (1991). Bringing concord to the ESP classroom. In T. F. Johns & P. King (Eds.). *Classroom concordancing* (ELR Journal, Vol. 4, pp. 115-134). Birmingham: The University of Birmingham, U.K.

Munby, J. (1978). *Communicative syllabus design*. Cambridge: Cambridge University Press.

Myers, G. (1989). *Writing biology: Texts in the social construction of scientific knowledge*. Madison: University of Wisconsin Press.

Oertli, P. (1991). *The language of business meetings: Teaching materials in the light of one reality (An inside-out view)*. Unpublished masters thesis, The University of Birmingham, U.K.

Olsen, L. A., & Huckin, T. N. (1990). Point-driven understanding in engineering lecture comprehension. *English for Specific Purposes, 9*, 33-48.

Phillips, M. K., & Shettlesworth, C. C. (1978). How to arm your students: A consideration of two approaches to providing materials in ESP. In *English for Specific Purposes* (ELT Documents No. 101). London: British Council. (Reprinted in J. Swales [Ed.], *Episodes in ESP* [pp. 104-114], 1988, New York: Prentice Hall)

Ramani, E., Chacko, T., Singh, S. J., & Glendenning, E. H. (1988). An ethnographic approach to syllabus design: A case study of the Indian Institute of Science, Bangalore. *English for Specific Purposes, 7*, 81-90.

Robertson, F. (1988). *Airspeak: Radiotelephony communication for pilots*. New York: Prentice Hall.

Robinson, P. (1980). *ESP: English for specific purposes*. Pergamon Press.

Robinson, P. (1991). *ESP today: A practitioner's guide*. New York: Prentice Hall.

St. John, M. J. (1987). Writing processes of Spanish scientists publishing in English. *English for Specific Purposes, 6*, 113-120.

Second Latin American ESP Colloquium Proceedings. (1990). Santiago: Universidad de Chile.

Selinker, L. (1979). On the use of informants in discourse analysis and language for specialized purposes. *International Review of Applied Linguistics, 17,* 189-215.

Selinker, L., Tarone, E., & Hanzeli, V. (Eds.). (1981). *English for academic and technical purposes: Studies in honor of Louis Trimble.* Rowley, MA: Newbury House.

Smith, L. E. (1987). Language spread and issues of intelligibility. In P. H. Lowenberg (Ed.). *Georgetown University Round Table on Languages and Linguistics 1987: Language spread and issues of language policy: Issues, implications and case studies.* Washington, DC: Georgetown University Press.

Spack, R. (1988). Initiating ESL students into the academic discourse community: How far should we go? *TESOL Quarterly, 22*(1), 29-52.

Stevens, V. (1991). Classroom concordancing: Vocabulary materials derived from relevant, authentic text. *English for Specific Purposes, 10,* 35-46.

Strevens, P. (1977). Special purpose language learning: A perspective. *Language Teaching and Linguistics Abstracts, 10,* 145-163.

Strevens, P. (1988). ESP after twenty years: A re-appraisal. In M. Tickoo (Ed.), *ESP: State of the art* (pp. 1-13). Singapore: SEAMEO Regional Language Centre.

Strevens, P., & Johnson, E. (1983). SEASPEAK: A project in applied linguistics, language engineering and eventually, ESP for sailors. *The ESP Journal* (Now *English for Specific Purposes*), *2,* 123-130.

Swales, J. (1971). *Writing scientific English.* London: Nelson.

Swales, J. (1984). Research into the structure of introductions to journal articles and its application to the teaching of academic writing. In R. Williams & J. Swales (Eds.), *Common ground: Shared interests in ESP and communication studies* (ELT Documents No. 117, pp. 77-86). Oxford: Pergamon Press.

Swales, J. (Ed.). (1988). *Episodes in ESP: A source and reference book for the development of English for science and technology.* New York: Prentice Hall.

Swales, J. M. (1990a). *Genre analysis: English in academic and research settings.* Cambridge: Cambridge University Press.

Swales, J. M. (1990b). Nonnative speaker graduate engineering students and their introductions: Global coherence and local management. In U. Connor & A. M. Johns (Eds.), *Coherence in writing: Research and pedagogical perspectives* (pp. 187-208). Washington, DC: TESOL.

Tarone, E., Dwyer, S., Gillette, S., & Icke, V. (1981).On the use of the passive in two astrophysics journal papers. *The ESP Journal, 1,* 123-140.

Trimble, L. (1985). *English for science and technology: A discourse approach.* Cambridge: Cambridge University Press.

Weissberg, R., & Buker, S. (1990). *Writing up research.* Englewood Cliffs, NJ: Prentice Hall.

Widdowson, H. G. (1981). English for specific purposes: Criteria for course design. In L. Selinker, E. Tarone, & V. Hanzeli (Eds.), *English for academic and technical purposes: Studies in honor of Louis Trimble* (pp. 1-11). Rowley, MA: Newbury House.

Widdowson, H. G. (1983). *Learning purpose and language use.* Oxford: Oxford University Press.

Wilbert, P., & Lewis, M. (1990). *Business English: An individualized learning programme.* Hove, U.K.: Language Teaching Publications.

Williams, M. (1988). Language taught for meetings and language used at meetings: Is there anything in common? *Applied Linguistics, 9,* 45-58.

Williams, R. (1978). EST—Is it on the right track? In C. J. Kennedy (Ed.), English for specific purposes [Special issue]. *MALS Journal* (Midlands Applied Linguistics Association) (pp. 25-31), The University of Birmingham, U.K.

Vaughan, A., & Heyen, N. (1990). *Ready for business.* Harlow, England: Longman.

Second Language Acquisition Research: Staking Out the Territory

DIANE LARSEN-FREEMAN
School for International Training

Since its emergence some 20 years ago, the field of second language acquisition research has focused on two areas: the nature of the language acquisition process and the factors which affect language learners. Initial research was essentially descriptive. More recently, researchers have been attempting to explain how acquisition occurs and how learner factors lead to differential success among learners. The focus has alternately broadened as researchers became more aware of the complexity of the issues and narrowed as greater depth of analysis was required. The paper suggests that the next phase of research will be characterized by a union of these two focal areas: learning and the learner. It also recommends that more research attention be given to tutored acquisition.

One could argue that the launching of the *TESOL Quarterly* 25 years ago predated the emergence of second language acquisition (SLA) research as an identifiable field. Accordingly, my task should have been easier than that of my colleagues writing for these commemorative issues of the *Quarterly*. This was small comfort, however, when faced with the daunting challenge of doing justice to all that has transpired since the early 1970s.[1] What has occurred since then, of course, is a veritable explosion of research focusing first upon the acquisition/learning process and second upon the language learner.[2] This review will be organized around these two foci and around two subthemes: the alternate broadening and

---

[1] Certainly some important studies of language learning were conducted prior to this (see, for example, some of the early studies compiled in Hatch, 1978), but these did not constitute a field of investigation as was to emerge in the 1970s.

[2] It is beyond the scope of this article to treat either of these comprehensively. Interested readers may wish to consult overviews by Ellis (1985), and Larsen-Freeman and Long (1991) for more detail. I have especially drawn upon the latter in writing this review.

I will also be unable to deal with matters concerning research methodology in this article. Interested readers should see J. D. Brown (1988), Hatch and Lazaraton (1991), Kasper and Grotjahn (1991), and Seliger & Shohamy (1989).

narrowing of perspective on the focus of inquiry and the movement from description (or what learners do) to explanation (or how they learn to do it).

THE LEARNING PROCESS: DESCRIPTION

A Broadening of Perspective[3]

Before the emergence of SLA as a field, researchers conducted contrastive analyses between the learners' L1 and L2 in order to anticipate areas of divergence which were likely to cause the learners difficulty and those of convergence where one could expect positive transfer. This practice was consistent with the then prevailing behaviorist view of language acquisition: learning by conditioning. It was thought that if materials could be prepared which would help learners overcome the conditioned habits of their L1 while they were imitating the new patterns of the L2, language acquisition would be facilitated. Errors that might result from interference from the L1 were to be prevented or at least held to a minimum.

Ironically, it was learners' errors, so threatening to behaviorists, which were to lead to the shift in awareness that spawned the SLA field. Overgeneralization errors (*I eated it) typical of first language acquirers were discovered in the oral production of L2 learners. Since such errors could not have resulted from imitation of target language (TL) speech, the errors were taken as support for Chomsky's proposal that the acquisition process was essentially one of rule formation, not habit formation. Learners were seen to play an active role in forming and testing hypotheses in an effort to induce the TL rules from the TL speech to which they were exposed. With the ascribing of an active role to the language learner, the SLA field was born. (See, for example, Oller & Richards, 1973; Schumann & Stenson, 1974).

Learner errors became a major focus of study. Certainly interference errors were detected, but so were errors resulting from overgeneralization, redundancy reduction, and communicative strategies. Errors were also analyzed to see if they reflected the underlying system that Corder (1967) claimed learners used. Error analyses determined this indeed to be the case, and Selinker's (1972) term *interlanguage* (IL) was embraced to signify that learners' approximations of the TL were separate linguistic systems in their own right, not governed by the same rules as either the learners' L1 or L2 (Adjemian, 1976).

---

[3] The sequence described in this section follows from Hakuta and Cancino (1977), and van Els, Bongaerts, Extra, van Os, and Janssen-van Dieten (1984).

While the study of learner errors continued to be illuminating, error analysis alone was deemed an incomplete perspective for a number of reasons (Schachter & Celce-Murcia, 1977). Chief among these was that a focus on errors neglected learners' actual successes. In addition, since learners could sometimes avoid making errors in the L2 by not attempting to produce difficult structures, error analyses did not even account for all sources of learner difficulty (Schachter, 1974). These limitations of error analysis were remedied in a type of analysis which took the learner's performance (errors and well-formed utterances) as the focus of inquiry.

Among the earliest performance analyses were the morpheme studies. In 1974, Dulay and Burt claimed that they had found evidence of an English morpheme order of acquisition based upon ESL learners' relative use of eleven morphemes in obligatory contexts. Furthermore, they asserted, the acquisition order held for both Chinese and Spanish-speaking children, and was therefore thought to be impervious to L1 influence. Dulay, Burt, and Krashen (1982) thus referred to the SLA process as "creative construction: the subconscious process by which language learners gradually organize the language they hear, according to the rules they construct to understand and generate sentences" (p. 276). This and other early morpheme studies excited researchers who welcomed the new view of language acquisition and the empirical support of an innate learner-generated or built-in syllabus (Corder, 1967). These studies also, however, came under attack, mostly for their methodology and claims of minimal L1 interference.

Another type of performance analysis was also being conducted at the time, namely the analysis of the speech data of learners collected at regular intervals for a period of at least several months. Data collected longitudinally enabled researchers to see that learners of all types passed through common developmental stages in their acquisition of certain structures. Developmental sequences were identified for English interrogatives (Cazden, Cancino, Rosansky, & Schumann, 1975; Wode, 1978), negation (Schumann, 1979), German word order (Meisel, Clahsen, & Pienemann, 1981), Swedish relative clauses (Hyltenstam, 1984), English relative clauses (Pavesi, 1986), and a variety of other English structures (Johnston, 1985). Since the intermediate stages in the developmental sequences looked like neither the L1 nor L2, they reinforced the observation that learners were not merely reshaping their L1s to conform to the L2s, but rather that learners were creatively constructing the L2 through a process of gradual complexification. These findings also underscored the need for researchers to examine the learners' IL in its own right in order to understand the acquisition process rather than seeing the IL as an incomplete version of the TL (Bley-Vroman, 1983). This observed acquisition process was not a linear one; often there was backsliding or forgetting when new forms were introduced, resulting in a learning curve that was more U-shaped than smoothly ascending (Kellerman, 1985). Sometimes, too, not all stages in a sequence were traversed, leading to arrested development or fossilized forms. Moreover, learners were freely making use not only of rule-governed utterances, but also of rote-learned formulaic utterances, both routines and patterns (Hakuta, 1976), leading some investigators to suggest that rule-governed language developed from formulaic speech, which was later analyzed by the learner (Wong Fillmore, 1976).

Notwithstanding the insights yielded, a focus on learner performance, as with the error analyses that preceded it, was found to be too narrow. Time and research were required to discover what in hindsight seems obvious: Performance analysis alone could not account for the whole picture. ESL learner Homer's (Wagner-Gough, 1975) utterances such as *what is this is truck* could only be understood by expanding the focus of investigation to include what was being said to Homer prior to his response.

Recognition of the need to examine not only the learner's performance but also the input to the learner, introduced a whole new area of inquiry, namely discourse analysis (Larsen-Freeman, 1980). Hatch has been the SLA researcher who has most promoted the value of examining what learners could be learning when engaged in collaborative discourse. For Hatch, a significant vehicle for acquisition is interaction with other speakers. Rather than the usual view that learners build up to conversational competence after gaining gradual control of lexical items and syntactic structures, Hatch (1978) writes: "One learns how to interact verbally, and out of this interaction, syntactic structures are developed" (p. 409). Since Hatch's observation, much research has been conducted under the rubric of discourse analysis: the study of the acquisition of speech acts (Blum-Kulka & Olshtain, 1984), communicative strategies (Faerch & Kasper, 1983) and classroom discourse analysis (Allwright, 1988; Chaudron, 1988; van Lier, 1988), to name a few.

This brief historical review of the SLA field demonstrates a progressive broadening of perspective. Each type of analysis subsumed without replacing its predecessor. Indeed, each type of analysis continues to be conducted, but with greater awareness of a necessary breadth of inquiry. After the decade of broadening perspective, there came also a recognition of the need for a deeper examination of specific issues raised during the 1970s: specifically,

L1 transfer, input to learners, and IL variation.[4] Thus, the 1980s saw a narrowing of focus so that each of these could be explored more fully. The following is a summary of what was learned.

Narrowing the Perspective: Language Transfer

We have already seen that all errors could no longer be traced to L1 interference. Indeed, the contrastive analysis hypothesis, which stated that those areas of the TL which were most dissimilar to the learners' L1 would cause the most difficulty, was refuted by research that indicated that it was often the similarities between the two languages which caused confusion. In fact, Wode (1978) framed this observation as a principle: "Only if L1 and L2 have structures meeting a crucial similarity measure will there be interference, i.e., reliance on prior L1 knowledge" (p. 116). This principle is significant in two respects. First, it reflects the growing view that transfer could be seen as a cognitive strategy: Learners rely on what they know (Taylor, 1975). Second, it foreshadowed what was to occupy researchers throughout the next decade: specifying precisely when transfer would occur. The fact that four books were published during the 1980s on the theme of transfer in SLA is testament to the vitality of this line of research (Dechert & Raupach, 1989; Gass & Selinker, 1983; Kellerman & Sharwood Smith, 1986; Odlin, 1989).

In addition to Wode's claim that there had to be a "crucial similarity," work by Eckman and by Kellerman contributed to our understanding of when transfer occurs. Eckman (1985) suggested that the markedness difference between the L1 and L2 would play a role. Where the L2 was more marked than the L1, learners would experience more difficulty; furthermore, the relative degree of difficulty would correspond to the relative degree of markedness. Where the two languages were different, but the L2 was not more marked than the L1, difficulty would not arise. Kellerman (1984) noticed that learners' perceptions of the distance between the L1 and L2 would affect the degree to which learners would transfer forms. What was noteworthy here was the extent to which the idea of transfer as a deliberate cognitive strategy had taken hold.

A second question concerning transfer, which stimulated much research during the decade, was precisely what effect transfer had on learners' ILs. We have already seen how it was responsible for errors as well as positive transfer and underproduction or avoidance

---

[4] In fact, each of these areas was the theme of at least one conference. The series of three applied linguistics conferences at the University of Michigan during the decade, for example, addressed language transfer (1982), input (1983), and variation (1987).

of certain structures. Other research demonstrated that transfer manifested itself in the following ways:

1. Overproduction of a particular TL form (Schachter & Rutherford, 1979)
2. Inhibiting or accelerating passage through a developmental sequence (Zobl, 1982)
3. Constraining the nature of hypotheses that language learners make (Schachter, 1983)
4. Prolonging the use of a developmental form when it is similar to an L1 structure (potentially resulting in fossilization) (Zobl, 1983)
5. Substitution (use of L1 form in the L2) (Odlin, 1989)
6. Hypercorrection (overreaction to a particular influence from the L1) (Odlin, 1989)

Clearly, transfer is a much more pervasive phenomenon in SLA than was once thought.

Narrowing the Perspective: Input

Recall that by the end of the 1970s researchers had become aware of the need to examine the raw material or input with which the learners had to work, recognizing, of course, that not all input would become intake (Corder, 1967). Many studies investigated the link between input and output (Gass & Madden, 1985). (I have drawn from Larsen-Freeman, 1985, for a synopsis of these studies.) With regard to the quantity of the input, many, but not all, researchers adduced evidence in support of the hypothesis that learners who have the opportunity to use the L2 regularly or to receive the most input will exhibit the greatest proficiency. Research in the area of input quality searched for a link between certain characteristics of the input (perceptual saliency, frequency of occurrence, syntactic complexity, semantic complexity, instructional sequence) and some aspect of the learners' output. Again, although not without challenge, a recurring finding was the correlation between the frequency of certain forms in the input and their appearance in learners' ILs.

Studies of input also focused on conversations between native (NSs) and nonnative speakers (NNSs) and those between NNSs, comparing both to a baseline of NS-NS interactions (see Day, 1986). Some of the modifications (termed *foreigner talk* [FT]) which NSs make to accommodate NNSs' level of comprehension are slower rate of speech, louder volume (!), fewer false starts, longer pauses, more restricted vocabulary, more concrete lexicon, greater use of gestures, repetition, shorter length, more deliberate enunciation, and simpler syntax (Hatch, 1983). These modifications are not made by all native speakers, nor are they static. The degree of modification of "teacher talk," for example, varies according to the proficiency of the students (Gaies, 1977). Similarly, NSs are continuously readjusting their speech based on their ongoing assessment of their NNS interlocutors' comprehension (Gass & Varonis, 1985).

Long (1980) made an important distinction between the linguistic modifications of FT and those made to the interactional structure of conversations between NSs and NNSs. The latter include such phenomena as comprehension checks, confirmation checks, expansions, requests for clarification, self-repetition, etc., which are the result of the negotiation of meaning between the learners and their conversational partners. It was shown that these interactional or elaborative modifications may enhance NNSs' comprehension even more than linguistic alterations.

Strong proposals have been put forth about the role of input in SLA. For instance, Krashen (1982) called comprehensible input in the presence of a low affective filter the only causal variable in SLA. While most researchers accept the need for learners to comprehend the input (in order for it to become intake and not just noise), few would agree that comprehensible input alone is sufficient. Swain (1985), for example, considered the case of the students in the Canadian French Immersion Program. These students received abundant comprehensible input but had not yet fully acquired grammatical competence in French. Since the learners could understand the input without fully analyzing its syntactic structure, Swain suggested that the learners also needed practice producing comprehensible output. Doing so may force learners to move from semantic to syntactic processing.

Narrowing the Perspective: Variation

As are all natural languages, ILs are variable. It is not surprising, however, that this variability was overlooked in the early days of research given that most attention was focused on the systematicity of IL. Synchronic variability was too obvious to be ignored for long, however. As teachers can readily attest, it is not uncommon for students who appear to have mastered a particular item, to revert to an erroneous form when a new challenge presents itself.

In recent years, the number of books devoted to variation demonstrates the significance of this topic in SLA circles (Adamson,

1988; Burmeister & Rounds, 1990; Eisenstein, 1989; Ellis, 1987; Gass, Madden, Preston, & Selinker, 1989a, 1989b; Preston, 1989; Tarone, 1988). Most of the research has attempted to explain variability, while preserving the notion of an IL system (Huebner, 1985). This has been accomplished by maintaining that variability itself is systematic, i.e., explicable with appeal to certain linguistic and contextual factors, leaving only a portion as nonsystematic free variation. One explanation proffered for the synchronic variability found in learners' performance on tasks has been the sociolinguistic construct of speech style. Tarone (1979) hypothesized that at any point in time a learner's IL is really a continuum of speech styles, where *style* is defined in terms of the amount of attention given to form in the language. With the least attention being given to form, learners rely on a vernacular speech style, a style which shows the greatest systematicity (Labov, 1969). When learners are carefully attending to form, the style they exhibit is at the other end of the continuum. This style is more permeable, i.e., more open to influence from other languages, and is therefore the most variable, or least systematic. (But see Sato, 1985.)

In addition to attention to form as a reason for variable performance, other explanations have been:

1. Learners' monitoring their performance (Krashen, 1977)

2. Sociolinguistic factors (Beebe, 1980)

3. Adjustment of one's speech towards one's interlocutor (convergence) or away from one's interlocutor (divergence) (Beebe & Zuengler, 1983)

4. Linguistic or situational context of use (Ellis, 1985)

5. Discourse domains (Selinker & Douglas, 1985)

6. The amount of planning time learners have (Crookes, 1989)

7. A combination of factors: stage of acquisition, linguistic environment, communicative redundancy (Young, 1988)

8. Learners' use of other-regulated or self-regulated speech (Lantolf & Ahmed, 1989)

What seems to be accepted at the moment is that what appears at first to be random variation can often be accounted for with variable (or probabilistic) rules. The notion of systematicity in IL, therefore, remains intact. What is not clear, however, is just what kind of system it is. What is certain is that being systematic does not mean simply governed by categorical rules.

I shall return to the theme of variation below; before doing so, it should be remembered that a subtheme of this article is the shift from description to explanation. While the early days of SLA research were appropriately consumed by descriptions of what learners do (and still much more is needed at *all* levels of language), by the mid-1980s calls were being made for theory construction and explanations of the acquisition process (see, for example, Long, 1985). (Of course, it should be acknowledged that the questions posed and data collected in describing anything has "the beginning of an explanation embedded in it" (Long, 1990b) and that explanation is a complementary extension of description.)

THE LEARNING PROCESS: EXPLANATION

We have already seen with regard to description how the SLA field has moved from a narrow focus on error analysis to a broader one on discourse analysis and back to a narrow focus on the areas of transfer, input, and variation. Since the latter half of the 1980s, we find a more or less narrow approach being taken with theory construction as well. Following Ellis (1985) and Larsen-Freeman and Long (1991), I will adopt a threefold classification schema for theoretical perspectives in the SLA field: nativist (learning depends upon a significant, specialized innate capacity for language acquisition), behaviorist/environmentalist (the learner's experience is more important than innate capacity), and interactionist (both internal and external processes are responsible). I will illustrate each category with one theoretical perspective in SLA research, recognizing that through my selectivity I will have unavoidably slighted many others.[5]

Nativist: Universal Grammar (UG)

For many years, linguists operating within the tradition of generative grammar have taken as their primary objective a description of the knowledge or competence of the ideal speaker-listener of the language. With the advent of Chomsky's government-binding theory, more attention has been concentrated on the question of how the competence of the native speaker is attained. A major assumption Chomsky makes is that the linguistic input to children acquiring their first language underdetermines or is insufficient to account for language acquisition. Moreover, children

---

[5] Some of the more prominent among these being Krashen's monitor model (1985), Hatch and Hawkins' experiential approach (1985); Bialystok and Ryan's knowledge and control dimensions (1985); McLaughlin's cognitive theory (1987); the multidimensional model (Pienemann & Johnston, 1987; Clahsen, 1987); Andersen's cognitive interactionist model (1988), and the functionalist perspective (Tomlin, 1990).

do not receive negative evidence (they are not told that a given utterance is ungrammatical) and thus must learn from the positive evidence instantiated in the input alone. Since the input is supposedly inadequate, it is assumed that the children possess an innate UG which constrains their grammatical development. The UG consists of a number of fixed abstract principles which predispose children to organize the language they hear in certain ways (White, 1990). The principles, in turn, have parameters associated with them which differ from language to language. One example which has often been cited as a principle in UG is the subjacency principle, which limits movement of constituents within sentences so that, at most, one boundary can be crossed at a time. This principle is held to apply to all languages. What counts as a bounding node, however, is determined by a parametric setting triggered by exposure to a given language. Thus, in English the bounding nodes are S and NP, whereas in Italian and French NP and S' are bounding nodes, but not S (White, 1990).

The impact of Chomsky's theory on SLA can be measured by the number of books that have been published of late dealing with the application of UG to SLA (Flynn, 1987; Flynn & O'Neill, 1988; Gass & Schachter, 1989; Pankhurst, Sharwood Smith, & van Buren, 1988; White, 1988). Some researchers maintain (Felix, 1985; Flynn, 1983; Hilles, 1986; Mazurkewich, 1985; Tomaselli & Schwartz, 1990; White, 1988; Zobl, 1990) that UG is in fact still available to second language learners such that their resulting grammar is shaped by its principles. White points out that the adult second language learner is faced with the same challenge as is a child first language learner: trying to learn a language from degenerate and limited input. (Although just how degenerate the data are is a matter of some debate [cf. Larsen-Freeman & Long, 1991].) Felix adds that sequences of development and paucity of input data suggest that there is good reason to expect that UG may continue to operate even after puberty.

As Schachter (1990) reports, Bley-Vroman (1989), Clahsen and Muysken (1986), and Schachter (1988) (see also Jordens, 1988) have arrived at somewhat different conclusions. These researchers have argued that the results of the SLA process differ so dramatically from first language acquisition (where native speaker competence is always achieved, there are no transfer effects or fossilization, etc.) that it is not likely that UG is present in its entirety in postpubescent learners. It is possible, however, that if language learners do not have direct access to UG, they do through their knowledge of their L1 (Clahsen & Muysken, 1989). Another possibility is that L2 learners initially adopt L1 parameter settings but, if necessary, at certain points in their development, reset the parameters to the values inherent in the L2 (Hulk, 1991).

For now, the question of UG accessibility in SLA is still unresolved. There is evidence that there is at least some accessibility through the learners' L1, although the access may be only partial (Felix & Weigl, 1991).

Environmentalist: Connectionism/Parallel Distributed Processing (PDP)

Although PDP/connectionist models are fairly new to the field, I have chosen to discuss them because of their striking contrast to the UG approach, and because some researchers, at least, believe that they have much to offer the SLA field (Gasser, 1990; Sokolik, 1990; Spolsky, 1988). Sokolik points out that connectionist principles are by no means new; what is new is the attempt to build connectionist models to test their explanatory power in a number of different fields. PDP theorists (Rumelhart, McClelland, & the PDP Research Group, 1986a, 1986b) have built computer models of human cognition based on what is known about the structure of the human brain. PDP theorists assume no innate endowment (although, as Gasser points out, these researchers are increasingly concerned with the initial state of the networks they have constructed). Learning is held to consist of the strengthening of connections in complex neural networks. The strength of their connections or their weight is determined by the frequency of patterns in the input.

As the input is encoded, the computer reorganizes itself to reflect the new statistical relationships present in the input. After being presented with a number of correctly matched input and output patterns, the computer is presented with a novel set of items to see how it generalizes beyond what it has received as input (Sokolik, 1989). Interestingly, what results is performance that looks like rule-governed behavior (some forms are produced correctly, some are incorrect due to overgeneralizations), but which is simply a reflection of the connections formed on the basis of the relative frequency of patterns in the input. It has also been pointed out, however, that some of the computer output is not consonant with the performance of child L1 learners (i.e., some of the errors are not plausible from a human standpoint [Pinker & Prince, 1988]). "One possibility is that L2 learning may be associative in the connectionist sense, whereas L1 acquisition may be more rule driven in the generative sense" (Sokolik, 1989, p. 358). In any event, a model that learns without rules and which will account for at least "some performance without postulating competence" (Spolsky, 1989, p. 227) clearly has the potential to force us to rethink earlier assumptions.

Interactionist: Variable Competence Model

Another theoretical perspective which would require a reexamination of the performance/competence distinction is a model which attempts to account for the external and internal processes responsible for SLA (Ellis, 1985). Recall that Tarone (1979) hypothesized that learners control a continuum of styles ranging from a superordinate style produced when the speaker pays the most attention to form, to a vernacular style produced when the least attention to form is given. Interlanguage data, Tarone (1983) argued, contradict what is called the "homogeneous competence" model of Chomsky, which assumes that there is a homogeneous competence of an ideal speaker-learner available for inspection through intuitional data. Instead, Tarone interprets the IL data to suggest that learners develop heterogeneous capability, which is systematic and which is composed of a range of styles, and Tarone maintains that the proper data for the study of this capability is natural speech.

Ellis (1985) is in substantial agreement with this position. Rather than viewing variability in the data at best as an inconvenience, Ellis places variability at the heart of his model. In the variable competence model, Ellis hypothesizes that free variation is crucial because it serves as the impetus for development. (But see Preston, 1989.) New forms, he believes, first enter the learner's IL in the careful style of speech when learners are attending to form. Tarone (1990) suggests that they may enter the learner's IL due to conversational interactions with native speakers or possibly due to social convergence or Sloblin's (1973) operating principles. Once the learner starts using them, the new forms are in free variation with existing forms, the new and the old coexisting without definably separate functions. Because this state is in violation of the efficiency principle (Ellis, 1990b) or Andersen's (1984) one-to-one principle, a second phase follows. During this replacement phase, learners seek to make maximum communicative use of the L2 resources they have by mapping one form onto one function. Therefore, each form in a pair is gradually restricted in use, i.e., takes on a particular range of target- and nontargetlike forms. In Ellis' model, free variability is the force driving development; systematic variability then comes into play, determining what subsequently happens to newly acquired items.

A Broader View?

The variable competence model rejects the customary distinction between competence and performance that is held to be axiomatic by UG researchers. It is this rejection that has led Gregg (1990) to assert that "variation . . . is not the duty of an acquisition theorist to explain" (p. 379). Gregg insists that a theory of acquisition should explain the acquisition of a speaker's knowledge, not merely describe the speaker's output.

Tarone (1990) rebuts Gregg's criticism, arguing that research on the acquisition of competence has not been particularly elucidating as so much of what is acquired is attributed to an innate capacity. Further, acquisition research from the two perspectives has different objectives, Tarone contends. The variationists seek to explain how knowledge gets realized as use, whereas those who prefer a UG approach take as their objective an explanation of competence or grammatical knowledge, "not the ability to do anything" (Widdowson, 1989, p. 129).

Theoretical perspectives, therefore, need to be assessed in terms of their purpose (Ellis, 1990b). Clearly, at the current, still early stage in SLA research, both perspectives (and others) are welcome.

> The argument as to what kind of explanation, mentalist or functional, best fits the facts is an old one. Doubtlessly, it will continue in the years to come. It is an argument about what needs to be explained and what facts need explaining. Any explanation that ignores what language is primarily for—communication—is incomplete and, therefore, unsatisfactory. But this does not mean that there are no aspects of language that are purely formal. Some undoubtedly are and will need to be explained in terms of abstract linguistic principles. Do we really need to engage in arguments about the relative merits of formal and functional explanations of language? Can we not accept that both are needed? (Ellis, 1990b, p. 390)

Certainly I would concur that multiple perspectives on acquisition are useful, especially since not all theories can be expected to do everything (Bialystok, 1990; Long, 1990b). However, there is reason to be circumspect in this regard: Despite the value of multiple perspectives (see, for example, Beebe, 1988), when we borrow perspective from other fields, we inherit their problems as well. (For example, UG principles keep changing, and within linguistics the theoretical status of variable rules is under debate.) Moreover, extant theories are not always complementary, and we have not yet agreed upon criteria by which to evaluate them (Beretta, in press; Schumann, 1983). I would also, therefore, agree with Gass (1989), who notes that it is important for the vitality of the field that we establish some common ground regarding the intellectual basis and goals of the field. Although we have yet to achieve complete consensus on these, it seems to me that definitional issues are what these past two decades ⊔f research have been about: staking out the territory.

Some have suggested we need a general theory to encompass a wider area than our theories to date (Spolsky, 1989). Others have suggested that we may have to accept that a theory of SLA will be modular, each module explaining different domains of language (Lightbown & White, 1987). Hatch, Shirai, and Fantuzzi (1990) have called for an integrated theory of acquisition. While researchers must of necessity restrict the scope of their investigation and usually do so to one domain (most often it has been morphosyntax, less commonly, phonology; see Ioup & Weinberger, 1987), the dilemma is that everyone recognizes that the domains are interrelated (Eisenstein, Bailey, & Madden, 1982; Nunan, 1987; Pennington, 1990; Sato, 1988). To cite just one example of the problem, Odlin (1989) observes that transfer in one subsystem of language (lexis, syntax, morphology, etc.) will sometimes condition its occurrence in other subsystems. Thus, according to Hatch et al. (1990), a theory must include a much broader scope of research than that centered on two modules—syntax and phonology. It must also include semantics, conversational structure, event scripts and rhetorical organization, but it must do so in a way that integrates the modules on the one hand and also allows them to be viewed separately. It follows, then, "that an attempt to explain acquisition by recourse to a single factor (for example motivation, comprehensible input, or the workings of an innate LAD [language acquisition device]) . . . lacks face validity" (Long, 1990b, p. 661). Indeed, given the complexity of language, why should we expect an explanation of its acquisition to be simple (Larsen-Freeman, 1991)?

We will return to this theme later, but for now we should consider the other major focus in SLA research to date: the focus on the learner.

THE LEARNER: DESCRIPTION

The question of differential success is one of the major conundrums of SLA: Why is it that all individuals with normal faculties successfully acquire their first language but meet with different degrees of success when they attempt to master an L2? A related issue is indeed whether complete success in acquiring an L2 is even possible when study is begun beyond a so-called critical age. In this section I will deal with the matter of age first, followed by a brief look at the other major factors which have been hypothesized to explain the facts of differential success: aptitude, social-psychological variables, personality, cognitive style and learning strategies.

Age

As with so much in the fledgling SLA field, the issue of age-related effects in SLA is a contested one—in fact, even their very existence is controversial. (My sources for this section are primarily Long, 1990a, and Larsen-Freeman & Long, 1991, chapter 6.) The three books published in the last few years which explore the link between age and SLA will serve to illustrate the controversy. The first position is that only children, not adults, can attain native-like pronunciation in the L2 (Scovel, 1988a); the second finds that the data are ambiguous or mixed (Singleton, 1989). The third position holds that older learners enjoy an advantage over younger learners (Harley, 1986, reports evidence showing older learners are faster than younger ones). Opinion also varies about the scope of the alleged effects (only accent or other domains as well?) and the causes of such effects (affective factors, identity, cognitive maturation, input differences, neurological causes?).

Early on, Krashen, Long, and Scarcella (1979) (see also Krashen, Scarcella, & Long, 1982) reviewed the literature on age differences in second language acquisition and came to the conclusion that older learners are initially faster than younger learners when it comes to the acquisition of morphosyntax; however, younger learners outperform older learners in the long run. According to Long (1990a), despite the fact that numerous studies have been conducted since this early conclusion, the generalization seems to hold, "with the exception of some fuzziness in the area of phonology" (p. 260).

Aptitude

Obvious to the casual observer is the fact that individuals learn at different rates. Not so obvious to even the careful observer, however, is whether or not there is a special language learning aptitude which is the source of the difference. Certainly it has long been presumed that there is such a thing as language aptitude, and in fact there are several major tests which are commonly employed to measure it (Carroll, 1981). Some researchers, however, have questioned the existence of an *innate* linguistic aptitude (Neufeld, 1979). A solution to the dispute may lie in the distinction Cummins (1980) makes between cognitive/academic language proficiency (CALP) and basic interpersonal communication skills (BICS). It may be that aptitude tests are a good measure of CALP, or an individual's ability to deal with decontextualized language (Skehan, 1982), which is a learned ability, but not a particularly good measure of BICS, an innate capacity. The fact that so much schoolwork involves CALP could explain the predictive power of aptitude tests on foreign language achievement. This is essentially Krashen's (1981) position when he proposes that aptitude relates only to learning, not to acquisition. In a more recent account of aptitude, however, Skehan (1989) argues that aptitude plays a role in both informal and formal acquisition environments. He also proposes that there are different profiles of language aptitude; some learners possess an analytic aptitude, others are more memory oriented. Wesche (1981) has shown how matching learners' aptitude with methodology can lead to success, while mismatching can have deleterious effects.

Social-Psychological Factors: Attitude and Motivation

Along with aptitude, the social-psychological factors of attitude and motivation have long been thought to have an important bearing on language learning success. In 1959 Gardner and Lambert were able to identify two factors which were responsible for the French proficiency of Anglophone students of French in Montreal: aptitude and a constellation of attitudes towards French Canadians including motivational intensity and integrative motivation. For Gardner and Lambert (cf. Gardner, 1979), there is actually an indirect relationship between attitude and successful SLA. Attitudes affect motivation, which in turn affects SLA.

Since Gardner and Lambert's pioneering research, much work has been done on refining the relationship among the constructs. Just in the area of attitudes alone, for example, learners' parents' attitudes towards speakers of the TL, attitudes of peers, learners' attitudes toward their learning situation, teachers' attitudes towards their students, and one's attitudes towards one's ethnicity were all studied for their influence on SLA.

In the area of motivation, the strength of learners' instrumental (a utilitarian motive for learning an L2) versus integrative (identification with L2 group) motivation has been measured to test predictions of their differential effect on L2 learning outcomes. Different researchers have reached different conclusions about hypothesized correlations depending upon the learner context; perhaps the only reliable finding is that the intensity of the motivation is more important than the type. Clearly more research is needed on the different influences on motivation. For example, in a study conducted by Strong (1984) on the acquisition of English by Spanish-speaking children living in the United States, it was concluded that motivation does not necessarily promote acquisition, but rather stems from it. The children in his study who met with success became more motivated to continue their study than those who were less successful.

Personality

Various personality traits have been thought to facilitate or inhibit SLA: self-esteem (Heyde, 1979), extroversion (Busch, 1982), reaction to anxiety (Bailey, 1983; MacIntyre & Gardner, 1989), risk taking (Ely, 1986), sensitivity to rejection (Naiman, Fröhlich, Stern, & Todesco, 1978), empathy (Guiora, Brannon, & Dull, 1972), inhibition (Guiora et al., 1972), and tolerance of ambiguity (Chapelle & Roberts, 1986). Some of these traits have correlated positively with success in SLA; other findings have been inconclusive.

Two generalizations can be drawn from a review of the literature. First, often it appears that the optimal personality "setting" is a point midway between the two extremes, i.e., moderate anxiety can be facilitating (Scovel, 1978); moderate risk taking is linked with achievement (Beebe, 1983). Second, it is difficult to predict an individual's behavior in a particular situation based on a global trait measurement. Although there no doubt exist some fairly consistent personality traits, more attention must be given to the relation between states and traits.

Cognitive Style

Closely aligned with personality attributes is work on cognitive styles. A cognitive style is the preferred way in which individuals process information or approach a task (Willing, 1988). A few cognitive styles have been investigated for their SLA implications: field independence/dependence, category width, reflectivity/impulsivity, aural/visual, and analytic/gestalt. Cognitive styles are often presented in this fashion—as polarities. In actual fact, humans more commonly exhibit a tendency toward one pole or the other.

Of the cognitive styles which have been studied, field independence has most consistently shown a significant positive correlation with language learning achievement (Chapelle & Roberts, 1986; Hansen & Stansfield, 1981; Tucker, Hamayan, & Genesee, 1976). One puzzling consequence of this finding is that field dependence is often linked with empathy, and empathy has also been found to be correlated with language learning success. H. D. Brown (1977) offers a solution: He observes field independence may be more important to classroom learning, whereas field dependence and empathy may be more beneficial in an untutored language learning situation.

Learning Strategies

The last learner factor to be discussed is one which has stimulated much interest recently. Again, we can look to the number of books that have been published as one sign of the vitality of this area (H. D. Brown, 1991; Cohen, 1990; O'Malley & Chamot, 1990; Oxford, 1990; Stevick, 1989; Wenden & Rubin, 1987).

Rubin (1975) used the term *learning strategies* to refer to "the techniques or devices which a learner may use to acquire knowledge" (p. 43). Rubin compiled a list of strategies employed by good language learners. For example, good language learners are willing to guess when they aren't sure, attend to both form and meaning, and monitor their own and others' speech. Following Rubin's initiative, much of the research has focused upon identifying and classifying learning strategies. A second focus of the research has been on determining the effect of strategy training. As we have seen in other areas, the results are not straightforward. It seems that the performance of students tutored in strategies is superior to the performance of students with no such training; however, the degree to which the training has been effective depends on the task, task difficulty, and the level of support for strategy transfer.

A Broadening of Perspective: Learner Factors

Most of the research just reviewed involves simple correlations between a single individual variable and learner proficiency. This is problematic for the same reason that studying one subsystem of language cannot fully illuminate interrelated acquisition processes. As d'Anglejan and Renaud (1985) point out, learner variables inevitably overlap and interact. Thus, we are likely getting a distorted picture if we study one factor in isolation from others. More powerful multivariate analyses exist and should be employed to examine the relationship among learner factors. (See, for example, Gradman & Hanania, 1991.) Exacerbating the problem is our awareness that some of these variables may affect language proficiency only indirectly as has been postulated by Gardner with respect to attitudes and L2 learning.

As Seliger (1984) contends, "while many characteristics have been related correlationally to language achievement, we have no mechanism for deciding which of the phenomena described or reported to be carried out by the learner are in fact those that lead to language acquisition" (p. 37). Perhaps if our sights were set higher—aspiring to explain how learner factors play a causal role in the acquisition process—we would be able to identify the truly important factors. This is precisely what some theorists like Schumann and Gardner have attempted to do.

LEARNER FACTORS: EXPLANATION

The Acculturation/Pidginization Model

Perhaps the earliest model to award centrality to learner factors was Schumann's acculturation/pidginization model (1978a, 1978b). The model developed from Schumann's observation of the untutored acquisition of English by Alberto, a 33-year-old, working-class Costa Rican living in the Boston area. Alberto lived in a Portuguese-speaking neighborhood and worked in a factory staffed by NNSs of English. Due to his limited contact with English speakers, it is not surprising that Alberto was not a very successful language learner. Schumann explained Alberto's limited acquisition of English by pointing to Alberto's social and psychological distance from speakers of the TL. Social distance comprises eight group-level phenomena: social dominance, integration patterns, enclosure, cohesiveness, size, cultural congruence, attitudes, and intended length of residence. Psychological distance is a construct involving four factors operating at the level of the individual: language shock, culture shock, motivation, and ego permeability.

Noting the similarities which existed between the social and psychological dimensions of Alberto's learning context and the conditions associated with pidginization, Schumann claimed that the processes underlying pidginization and the early stages of naturalistic SLA were analogous. With acculturation (social and psychological proximity), the IL elaborates and develops much as in creolization. Schumann summarized his position by suggesting that SLA is one aspect of acculturation and thus the degree to which the learner acculturates to the TL group will control the degree to which the learner acquires the L2.

The Socioeducational Model

What Schumann labels acculturation is similar in many ways to Gardner's notion of integrativeness, a central feature of Gardner's

(1985) socioeducational model. Gardner's model also confers a high status on learner factors—attitudes and motivation, in particular. Also, like Schumann, Gardner emphasizes the social dimension of language acquisition: "The acquisition of a language involves social adjustment . . . . Languages are acquired in order to facilitate communication, either active or passive, with some cultural community . . . . Emotional adjustments are involved and these are socially based" (p. 125).

Like the other models examined here, the socioeducational model was not intended to explain all of second language learning. It purports to account for a significant and meaningful proportion of the variance in second language achievement. If it withstands the test of time, it will certainly help to broaden our perspective on learner factors.

BROADENING STILL

Despite the broadening in perspective that has occurred within our two foci, further expansion is desirable—and we are beginning to see signs of it in the SLA field. At the Xth University of Michigan Conference on Applied Linguistics in 1983, I said:

> I believe that [questions about learning and the learner] should not be addressed independently as they have been. I think it will not be the case that we will come to some understanding of the SLA process and then introduce learner variables and calculate their effect on the process. Likewise, I think we cannot fully understand what influences the learner apart from his or her engagement in the process of learning. (1985, p. 434)

To cite one example in support of my observation on the interdependence of variables, Scarcella's (1990) review of Young's (1988) work highlights their independence: As L2 proficiency increased, social variables (learner) replaced linguistic ones (learning) as the more powerful influences on variation. The use of plural markers by low-proficiency learners was influenced by the markers' phonological environments. The performance of high-proficiency learners was more likely to be affected by the learners' degree of convergence (adjustment of speech toward) and identification with their interlocutor. We can see how intertwined are social and linguistic factors! (Even UG researchers, who choose to deal with linguistic factors only, will have to account for individual differences in some way. Language acquisition is not only a linguistic phenomenon.) Also implicit in this finding is the dynamic quality of the influential factors; they do not apply continuously, but rather affect learners at different points in their development. Krashen, in his monitor model, recognized the need to take both learning (the acquisition/learning distinction) and learner (the affective filter) factors into account. More recent evidence of this trend is Schumann's (1990) attempt to introduce a cognitive dimension to his acculturation model and Sokolik's (1990) appeal to PDP models to explain learner differences due to age. I predict that increasing numbers of researchers will accept the challenge of integrating these two foci: learning and the learner.

Broadening our perspective to include tutored acquisition would also be desirable. Most of the research to date has dealt with natural or untutored acquisition, as researchers have operated under the tacit assumption that instruction was a variable (see, for example, Schumann, 1978c) which could be factored in after we arrived at some understanding of the natural process. While it is common practice when faced with complex systems to deal with one definable part at a time (Spolsky, 1988), I do not think that instruction can be factored in later, any more than learner factors can be included after we have deciphered the learning process. Thus, researchers should not limit their goals to specifying what is minimally necessary for untutored SLA to occur, but rather, work with teachers in a collaborative manner to help define what is maximally effective in tutored acquisition. Besides, we have reason now to believe that tutored and untutored acquisition are more similar than different, at least in terms of exhibiting common developmental sequences (Ellis, 1989; Pienemann, 1984; Wode, 1981) and some, by no means all, common error types (Felix & Simmet, 1981; Lightbown, 1983; Pica, 1985).

SLA research has not directly answered questions about teaching, which is why a research agenda is needed for pedagogical concerns (Larsen-Freeman, 1990; Lightbown, 1985). Nevertheless, it has, and should, continue to offer enhanced understanding of the learning process and learners (Cohen, Larsen-Freeman, & Tarone, 1991; Cook, 1986; Ellis, 1990a; Hatch, Shirai, & Fantuzzi, 1990) and provide explanatory support for accepted teaching practices (Lightbown, 1985). The next section will distill from the research to date observations which should be relevant to teachers, although I realize that the "relevance resides in the individual" (G. Brown, 1990, p. 156).

ISSUES OF RELEVANCE TO TEACHERS

There are general characteristics of the learning process and of language learners that teachers should be aware of. I list ten here and suggest some pedagogical implications for each.

1. *The learning/acquisition process is complex.* As has been evident throughout this review, simple solutions have evaded researchers for more than 20 years; I would not expect them in the future. There are many complex elements in the SLA puzzle. It is probable that acquisition/learning is not monolithic and that there are multiple subprocesses, multiple routes, and multiple causes. Teachers, therefore, cannot seek simplistic solutions. As Spolsky (1988) has written: "Any intelligent and disinterested observer knows that there are many ways to learn languages and many ways to teach them, and that some ways work with some students in some circumstances and fail with others. (This is why good language teachers are and always have been eclectic . . . .)" (p. 383).

2. *The process is gradual.* Learners do not master forms with their first encounter. Even if they start using the form soon thereafter, the function for which they use it might not coincide with its TL use. Acquisition is a gradual process involving the mapping of form, meaning, and use. Form/functional correspondences do not simply appear in the IL fully formed and error-free. In a pedagogical situation, it makes sense to recycle the presentations of forms (e.g., grammar structures) so that learners will have ample opportunity to work out form-function correspondences. A corollary to this is the acknowledgment that language learning takes time. A conservative estimate of the number of hours young first language learners spend "acquiring" their first language is 12,000–15,000 (Lightbown, 1985); our expectations of second language learning should be realistic.

3. *The process is nonlinear.* Learners do not tackle structures one at a time, first mastering one and then turning to another. Even when learners appear to have mastered a particular form, it is not uncommon to find backsliding occurring when new forms are introduced, presumably due to an underlying restructuring (McLaughlin, 1990) which is taking place. Teachers should not despair when such behavior is exhibited by their students, but should rather expect well-formedness to be restored eventually.

4. *The process is dynamic.* The factors that influence the learner and the cognitive strategies the learner adopts change over time. As Gleick (1987) put it: "The act of playing the game has a way of changing the rules" (quoted in Diller, 1990, p. 238). Teachers should know that what works for learners at one level of proficiency may not do so when learners are at a later stage of proficiency.

5. *Learners learn when they are ready to do so.* What evidence exists suggests that learners will only acquire that for which they are prepared. One empirically supported explanation was offered by Pienemann (1985), who demonstrated that developmental sequences arise from speech processing constraints. The sequences themselves do not appear to be alterable through instruction, so it may not be realistic for teachers to expect students to master aspects of the language which are too far beyond their current stage of development (Brindley, 1987).

6. *Learners rely on the knowledge and experience they have.* Second language learners are active participants in the learning process. They rely on what they know (their L1 or other languages they have mastered, or what they know of the TL) to formulate hypotheses. They then test these against the input to which they are exposed, or at least that part of it that they notice (Schmidt, 1990).

7. *It is not clear from research findings what the role of negative evidence is in helping learners to reject erroneous hypotheses they are currently entertaining (Carroll & Swain, 1991).* It is intuitively appealing, at any rate, to believe that learners can make use of such feedback when it is judicious and they are ready and have time to digest it (Birdsong, 1989; Schachter, 1991). Another tentative conclusion which can be drawn is that a deliberate focus on the formal properties of language or "consciousness raising" (Rutherford & Sharwood Smith, 1988, p. 3) does seem to promote accuracy, at least (Lightbown & Spada, 1990).

8. *For most adult learners, complete mastery of the L2 may be impossible.* Learners can get very good, of course, and a few may even be indistinguishable from native speakers in their command of the L2; however, for most, some aspects of their IL will likely fossilize before acquisition is complete, and for all (nearly all?), there appears to be a physiologically determined critical period for pronunciation. Teachers obviously should encourage learners to go as far as they are capable of going in the L2, but teachers should also be realistic in their expectations.

9. *There is tremendous individual variation among language learners.* Teachers need to take into account these differences and learn to work with them in the classroom—herein lies the interpretive artistry of teaching.

10. *Learning a language is a social phenomenon.* Most (although by no means all) learners seek to acquire a second language in order to communicate with members of the TL group or to participate in their institutions. Much of what happens in the classroom, too, is attributable to the social needs of the participants, both students and teachers (Breen, 1985; Prahbu, 1991).

As I have indicated above, none of these generalizations should be startling to teachers, nor are they precise enough to be prescriptive. They might fit more into the category of expanding awareness or affirming customary practice. What is important is that teachers integrate these and any other generalizations distilled from research into their own experiential framework in guiding their decisions as teachers (Scovel, 1988b).

A FINAL REMARK

In an editorial I wrote for *Language Learning* in 1980, I described the field of SLA in transition from infancy to adolescence. In 1985 I wrote in the same journal that SLA had arrived at older adolescence—surer of itself as a separate discipline while still enjoying the vigor of youth. If I may be permitted to extend the analogy once again, I would have to say that developmentally SLA has entered young adulthood. Matters of identity should no longer be of central concern. As the field enjoys the privileges of adulthood, however, we must also remember the responsibility which accompanies privilege. Forced to adopt a narrow perspective in our research due to practical constraints, we need to acknowledge the limitations of our points of view. What I hope researchers will be able to achieve is what teachers must also accomplish: preserving a detailed focus on the particular or individual, while simultaneously holding the whole.
∎

ACKNOWLEDGMENT

I am grateful to the skillful editing of Sandra Silberstein.

THE AUTHOR

Diane Larsen-Freeman is a Senior Faculty Member in the MAT Program at the School for International Training in Brattleboro, VT. Her books include *Discourse Analysis in Second Language Research* (Newbury House, 1980), *The Grammar Book: An ESL/EFL Teacher's Course* (with M. Celce-Murcia, Newbury House, 1983), *Techniques and Principles in Language Teaching* (Oxford University Press, 1986), and *An Introduction to Second Language Acquisition Research* (with M. Long, Longman, 1991). Dr. Larsen-Freeman was Editor of *Language Learning* from 1980 to 1985.

REFERENCES

Adamson, H. D. (1988). *Variation theory and second language acquisition.* Washington, DC: Georgetown University Press.

Adjemian, C. (1976). On the nature of interlanguage systems. *Language Learning, 26*(2), 297-320.

Allwright, R. (1988). *Observation in the language classroom.* London: Longman.

Andersen, R. (1984). The one to one principle of interlanguage construction. *Language Learning, 34*(4), 77-95.

Andersen, R. (1988). Models, processes, principles, and strategies: Second language acquisition in and out of the classroom. *IDEAL, 3,* 111-138.

Bailey, K. M. (1983). Competitiveness and anxiety in adult second language learning: Looking *at* and *through* the diary studies. In H. Seliger & M. Long (Eds.), *Classroom oriented research in second language acquisition* (pp. 67-103). Rowley, MA: Newbury House.

Beebe, L. (1980). Sociolinguistic variation and style shifting in second language acquisition. *Language Learning, 30*(2), 433-447.

Beebe, L. (1983). Risk-taking and the language learner. In H. Seliger & M. Long (Eds.), *Classroom oriented research in second language acquisition* (pp. 39-66). Rowley, MA: Newbury House.

Beebe, L. (Ed.). (1988). *Issues in second language acquisition: Multiple perspectives.* New York: Newbury House/Harper & Row.

Beebe, L., & Zuengler, J. (1983). Accommodation theory: An explanation for style shifting in second language dialects. In N. Wolfson & E. Judd (Eds.), *Sociolinguistics and second language acquisition* (pp. 195-213). Rowley, MA: Newbury House.

Beretta, A. (in press). Theory construction in SLA: Complementarity and opposition? *Studies in Second Language Acquisition.*

Bialystok, E. (1990). The competence of processing: Classifying theories of second language acquisition. *TESOL Quarterly, 24*(4), 635-648.

Bialystok, E., & Ryan, E. (1985). A metacognitive framework for the development of first and second language skills. In D. L. Forrest-Pressley, G. E. MacKinnon, & T. G. Waller (Eds.), *Metacognition, cognition, and human performance* (pp. 207-249). Orlando, FL: Academic Press.

Birdsong, D. (1989). *Metalinguistic performance and interlinguistic competence*. Berlin: Springer-Verlag.

Bley-Vroman, R. (1983). The comparative fallacy in interlanguage studies: The case of systematicity. *Language Learning, 33*(1), 1-17.

Bley-Vroman, R. (1989). The logical problem of foreign language acquisition. In S. Gass & J. Schachter (Eds.), *Linguistic perspectives on second language acquisition* (pp. 41-68). Cambridge: Cambridge University Press.

Blum-Kulka, S., & Olshtain, E. (Eds.). (1984). Pragmatics and second language learning [Special issue]. *Applied Linguistics, 5*(3).

Breen, M. (1985). The social context for language learning—A neglected situation? *Studies in Second Language Acquisition 7*(2), 135-158.

Brindley, G. (1987). Verb tenses and TESOL. In D. Nunan (Ed.), *Applying second language acquisition research* (pp. 173-204). Adelaide, Australia: National Curriculum Resource Centre.

Brown, G. (1990). Pit Corder: A personal memory. *Second Language Research, 6*(2), 155-158.

Brown, H. D. (1977). Cognitive and affective characteristics of good language learners. In C. Henning (Ed.), *Proceedings of the Los Angeles Second Language Research Forum* (pp. 349-354). Los Angeles: University of California, Department of English.

Brown, H. D. (1991). *Breaking the language barrier: Finding your path to success*. Yarmouth, ME: Intercultural Press.

Brown, J. D. 1988. *Understanding research in second language learning*. Cambridge: Cambridge University Press.

Burmeister, H., & Rounds, P. (Eds.) (1990). *Variability in second language acquisition* (Vols. 1-2). Eugene: University of Oregon, Department of Linguistics.

Busch, D. (1982). Introversion-extroversion and the EFL proficiency of Japanese students. *Language Learning, 32*(1), 109-132.

Carroll, J. (1981). Twenty-five years of research on foreign language aptitude. In K. Diller (Ed.), *Individual differences and universals in language learning aptitude* (pp. 83-118). Rowley, MA: Newbury House.

Carroll, S., & Swain, M. (1991, February–March). *Negative evidence in second language learning*. Paper presented at the 11th Annual Second Language Research Forum, University of Southern California.

Cazden, C., Cancino, H., Rosansky, E., & Schumann, J. (1975). *Second language acquisition sequences in children, adolescents and adults*. (Contract No. NE-6-00-3-0014). Washington, DC: National Institute of Education.

Chapelle, C., & Roberts, C. (1986). Ambiguity tolerance and field independence as predictors of proficiency in English as a second language. *Language Learning, 36*(1), 27-45.

Chaudron, C. (1988). *Second language classrooms: Research on teaching and learning*. Cambridge: Cambridge University Press.

Clahsen, H. (1981). *Spracherwerb in der Kindheit*. Tübingen, Germany: Gunter Narr.

Clahsen, H. (1987). Connecting theory of language processing and (second) language acquisition. In C. Pfaff (Ed.), *First and second language acquisition processes* (pp. 103-116). New York: Newbury House/Harper & Row.

Clahsen, H., & Muysken, P. (1986). The accessibility of universal grammar to adult and child learners: A study of the acquisition of German word order. *Second Language Research, 2,* 93-119.

Clahsen, H., & Muysken, P. (1989). The UG paradox in L2 acquisition. *Second Language Research, 5*(1), 1-29.

Cohen, A. (1990). *Language learning: Insights for learners, teachers and researchers.* New York: Newbury House/HarperCollins.

Cohen, A., Larsen-Freeman, D., & Tarone, E. (1991, April). *The contribution of SLA theories and research to teaching language.* Paper presented at the RELC Regional Seminar.

Cook, V. (Ed.). (1986). *Experimental approaches to second language learning.* Oxford: Pergamon Press.

Corder, S. P. (1967). The significance of learners' errors. *International Review of Applied Linguistics, 5*(4), 161-170.

Crookes, G. (1989). Planning and interlanguage variation. *Studies in Second Language Acquisition, 11*(4), 367-383.

Cummins, J. (1980). The cross-lingual dimensions of language proficiency: Implications for bilingual education and the optimal age issue. *TESOL Quarterly, 14*(2), 175-188.

d'Anglejan, A., & Renaud, C. (1985). Learner characteristics and second language acquisition: A multivariate study of adult immigrants and some thoughts on methodology. *Language Learning, 35*(1), 1-19.

Day, D. (Ed.). (1986). *Talking to learn: Conversations in second language acquisition.* Rowley, MA: Newbury House.

Dechert, H., & Raupach, M. (Eds.). (1989). *Transfer in language production.* Norwood, NJ: Ablex.

Diller, K. (1990). The non-linearity of language-learning and 'post-modern' language teaching methods. In H. Burmeister & P. Rounds (Eds.), *Variability in second language acquisition* (pp. 333-343). Eugene: University of Oregon, Department of Linguistics.

Dulay, H., & Burt, M. (1974). Natural sequences in child second language acquisition. *Language Learning, 24*(1), 37-53.

Dulay, H., Burt, M., & Krashen, S. (1982). *Language two.* New York: Oxford University Press.

Eckman, F. (1985). The markedness differential hypothesis: Theory and applications. In B. Wheatley, A. Hastings, F. Eckman, L. Bell, G. Krukar, & R. Rutkowski (Eds.), *Current approaches to second language acquisition: Proceedings of the 1984 University of Wisconsin–Milwaukee Linguistics Symposium* (pp. 3-21). Bloomington: Indiana University Linguistics Club.

Eisenstein, M. (Ed.). (1989). *The dynamic interlanguage: Empirical studies in second language variation.* New York: Plenum.

Eisenstein, M., Bailey, N., & Madden, C. (1982). It takes two: Contrasting tasks and contrasting structures. *TESOL Quarterly, 16*(3), 381-393.

Ellis, R. (1985). *Understanding second language acquisition.* Oxford: Oxford University Press.

Ellis, R. (Ed.). (1987). *Second language acquisition in context.* Englewood Cliffs, NJ: Prentice-Hall.

Ellis, R. (1989). Are classroom and naturalistic acquisition the same? A study of the classroom acquisition of German word order rules. *Studies in Second Language Acquisition, 11*(3), 305-328.

Ellis, R. (1990a). *Instructed second language acquisition.* Oxford: Basil Blackwell.

Ellis, R. (1990b). A response to Gregg. *Applied Linguistics, 11*(4), 384-391.

Ely, C. (1986). An analysis of discomfort, risktaking, sociability, and motivation in the L2 classroom. *Language Learning, 36*(1), 1-25.

Faerch, C., & Kasper, G. (Eds.). (1983). *Strategies in interlanguage communication.* London: Longman.

Felix, S. (1988). UG-generated knowledge in adult second language acquisition. In S. Flynn & W. O'Neil (Eds.), *Linguistic theory in second language acquisition* (pp. 277-294). Dordrecht, Netherlands: Kluwer Academic.

Felix, S., & Simmet, A. (1981, May). *Natural processes in classroom L2 learning.* Revised version of a paper presented at the IIIème Colloque Group de Recherche sur l'Acquisition des Langues, Paris.

Felix, S., & Weigl, W. (1991). Universal grammar in the classroom: The effects of formal instruction on second language acquisition. *Second Language Research, 7*(2), 162-181.

Flynn, S. (1983). *A study of the effects of principal branching direction in second language acquisition: The generalization of a parameter of universal grammar from first to second language acquisition.* Unpublished doctoral dissertation. Cornell University, Ithaca, NY.

Flynn, S. (1987). *A parameter-setting model of L2 acquisition.* Dordrecht, Netherlands: Reidel.

Flynn, S., & O'Neil, W. (Eds.). (1988). *Linguistic theory and second language acquisition.* Dordrecht, Netherlands: Kluwer Academic.

Gaies, S. (1977). The nature of linguistic input in formal second language learning. In H. Brown, C. Yorio, & R. Crymes (Eds.), *On TESOL '77* (pp. 204-212). Washington, DC: TESOL.

Gardner, R. (1979). Social psychological aspects of second language acquisition. In H. Giles & R. St. Clair (Eds.), *Language and social psychology.* Oxford: Basic Blackwell.

Gardner, R. (1985). *Social psychology and second language learning: The role of attitudes and motivation.* London: Edward Arnold.

Gardner, R., & Lambert, W. (1959). Motivational variables in second language acquisition. *Canadian Journal of Psychology, 13*, 266-272.

Gass, S. (1989). Language universals and second-language acquisition. *Language Learning, 39*(4), 497-534.

Gass, S., & Madden, C. (Eds.). (1985). *Input in second language acquisition*. Rowley, MA: Newbury House.

Gass, S., Madden, C., Preston, D., & Selinker, L. (Eds.) (1989a). *Variation in second language acquisition: Vol. 1. Discourse and pragmatics*. Clevedon, Avon, England: Multilingual Matters.

Gass, S., Madden, C., Preston, D., & Selinker, L. (Eds.). (1989b). *Variation in second language acquisition: Vol. 2. Psycholinguistic issues*. Clevedon, Avon, England: Multilingual Matters.

Gass, S., & Schachter, J. (Eds.). (1989). *Linguistic perspectives on second language acquisition*. Cambridge: Cambridge University Press.

Gass, S., & Selinker, L. (Eds.). (1983). *Language transfer in language learning*. Rowley, MA: Newbury House.

Gass, S., & Varonis, E. (1985). Task variation and nonnative/nonnative negotiation of meaning. In S. Gass & C. Madden (Eds.), *Input in second language acquisition* (pp. 149-161). Rowley, MA: Newbury House.

Gasser, M. (1990). Connectionism and universals of second language acquisition. *Studies in Second Language Acquisition, 12*(2), 179-199.

Gleick, J. (1987). *Chaos: Making a new science*. New York: Viking.

Gradman, H., & Hanania, E. (1991). Language learning background factors and ESL proficiency. *Modern Language Journal, 75*(1), 39-51.

Gregg, K. (1990). The variable competence model of second language acquisition and why it isn't. *Applied Linguistics, 11*(4), 364-383.

Guiora, A., Brannon, R., & Dull, C. (1972). Empathy and second language learning. *Language Learning, 22*(1), 111-130.

Hakuta, K. (1976). A case study of a Japanese child learning English as a second language. *Language Learning, 26*(2), 321-351.

Hakuta, K., & Cancino, H. (1977). Trends in second language acquisition. *Harvard Educational Review, 47*, 294-316.

Hansen, J., & Stansfield, C. (1981). The relationship of field dependent-independent cognitive styles to foreign language achievement. *Language Learning, 31*(2), 349-367.

Harley, B. (1986). *Age in second language acquisition*. Clevedon, Avon, England: Multilingual Matters.

Hatch, E. (1978). Discourse analysis and second language acquisition. In E. Hatch (Ed.), *Second language acquisition: A book of readings* (pp. 402-435). Rowley, MA: Newbury House.

Hatch, E. (1983). *Psycholinguistics: A second language perspective*. Rowley, MA: Newbury House.

Hatch, E., & Hawkins, B. (1985). Second-language acquisition: An experiential approach. In S. Rosenberg (Ed.), *Advances in applied psycholinguistics* (Vol. 2, pp. 241-283). New York: Cambridge University Press.

Hatch, E., & Lazaraton, A. (1991). *The research manual*. New York: Newbury House/HarperCollins.

Hatch, E., Shirai, Y., & Fantuzzi, C. (1990). The need for an integrated theory: Connecting modules. *TESOL Quarterly, 24*(4), 697-716.

Heyde, A. (1979). *The relationship between self-esteem and the oral production of a second language.* Unpublished doctoral dissertation. University of Michigan, Ann Arbor.

Hilles, S. (1986). Interlanguage and the pn-drop parameter. *Second Language Research* 2(1), 33-52.

Huebner, T. (1985). System and variability in interlanguage syntax. *Language Learning, 35*(2), 141-163.

Hulk, A. (1991). Parameter setting and the acquisition of word order in L2 French. *Second Language Research, 7*(1), 1-34.

Hyltenstam, K. (1984). The use of typological markedness conditions as predictors in second language acquisition: The case of pronominal copies in relative clauses. In R. Andersen (Ed.), *Second language: A crosslinguistic perspective* (pp. 39-58). Rowley, MA: Newbury House.

Ioup, G., & Weinberger, S. (Eds.). (1987). *Interlanguage phonology: The acquisition of a second language sound system.* New York: Newbury House.

Johnston, M. (1985). *Syntactic and morphological progressions in learner English* [Research report]. Department of Immigration and Ethnic Affairs, Australia.

Jordens, P. (1988). The acquisition of word order in Dutch and German as L1 and L2. *Second Language Research 4*(1), 41-65.

Kasper, G., & Grotjahn, R. (Eds.). (1991). Methods in second language research. *Studies in Second Language Research, 13*(2).

Kellerman, E. (1984). The empirical evidence for the influence of the L1 in interlanguage. In A. Davies, C. Criper, & A. Howatt (Eds.), *Interlanguage* (pp. 98-122). Edinburgh: Edinburgh University Press.

Kellerman, E. (1985). If at first you do succeed . . . In S. Gass & C. Madden (Eds.), *Input in second language acquisition* (pp. 345-353). Rowley, MA: Newbury House.

Kellerman, E., & Sharwood Smith, M. (Eds.). (1986). *Cross-linguistic influence in second language acquisition.* Oxford: Pergamon Press.

Krashen, S. (1977). Some issues relating to the monitor model. In H. Brown, C. Yorio, & R. Crymes (Eds.), *On TESOL '77* (pp. 144-158). Washington, DC: TESOL.

Krashen, S. (1981). *Second language acquisition and second language learning.* Oxford: Pergamon Press.

Krashen, S. (1982). *Principles and practice in second language acquisition.* Oxford: Pergamon Press.

Krashen, S. (1985). *The input hypothesis: Issues and implications.* New York: Longman.

Krashen, S., Long, M., & Scarcella, R. (1979). Age, rate, and eventual attainment in second language acquisition. *TESOL Quarterly, 13*(4), 573-582.

Krashen, S., Scarcella, R., & Long, M. (Eds.). (1982). *Child-adult differences in second language acquisition.* Rowley, MA: Newbury House.

Labov, W. (1969). Contraction, deletion and inherent variability of the English copula. *Language, 45*(4), 715-762.

Lantolf, J., & Ahmed, M. (1989). Psycholinguistic perspectives on interlanguage variation: A Vygotskyan analysis. In S. Gass, C. Madden, D. Preston, & L. Selinker (Eds.), *Variation in second language acquisition: Psycholinguistic issues.* Clevedon, Avon, England: Multilingual Matters.

Larsen-Freeman, D. (Ed.). (1980). *Discourse analysis in second language research.* Rowley, MA: Newbury House.

Larsen-Freeman, D. (1985). State of the art on input in second language acquisition. In S. Gass & C. Madden (Eds.), *Input in second language acquisition* (pp. 433-444). Rowley, MA: Newbury House.

Larsen-Freeman, D. (1990). On the need for a theory of language teaching. In J. Alatis (Ed.), *Georgetown University Round Table on Languages and Linguistics 1990* (pp. 261-270). Washington, DC: Georgetown University Press.

Larsen-Freeman, D. (1991). Teaching grammar. In M. Celce-Murcia (Ed.), *Teaching English as a second or foreign language* (2nd ed., pp. 279-296). New York: Newbury House/HarperCollins.

Larsen-Freeman, D., & Long, M. (1991). *An introduction to second language acquisition research.* London: Longman.

Lightbown, P. (1983). Exploring relationships between developmental and instructional sequences in L2 acquisition. In H. Seliger & M. Long (Eds.), *Classroom oriented research in second language acquisition* (pp. 217-243). Rowley, MA: Newbury House.

Lightbown, P. (1985). Great expectations: Second language acquisition research and classroom teaching. *Applied Linguistics, 6*(2), 173-189.

Lightbown, P., & Spada, N. (1990). Focus-on-form and corrective feedback in communicative language teaching: Effects on second language learning. *Studies in Second Language acquisition, 12*(4), 429-448.

Lightbown, P., & White, L. (1987). The influence of linguistic theories on language acquisition research. *Language Learning, 37*(4), 483-510.

Long, M. (1980). *Input, interaction and second language acquisition.* Unpublished doctoral dissertation. University of California, Los Angeles.

Long, M. (1985). Input and second language acquisition theory. In S. Gass & C. Madden (Eds.), *Input in second language acquisition* (pp. 377-393). Rowley, MA: Newbury House.

Long, M. (1990a). Maturational constraints on language development. *Studies in Second Language Acquisition, 12*(3), 251-285.

Long, M. (1990b). The least a second language acquisition theory needs to explain. *TESOL Quarterly, 24*(4), 649-666.

MacIntyre, P., & Gardner, R. (1989). Anxiety and second-language learning: Toward a theoretical clarification. *Language Learning, 39*(2), 251-275.

Mazurkewich, I. (1985). Syntactic markedness and language acquisition. *Studies in Second Language Acquisition 7*(1), 15-35.

McLaughlin, B. (1987). *Theories of second-language learning*. London: Edward Arnold.

McLaughlin, B. (1990). Restructuring. *Applied Linguistics, 11*(2), 113-128.

Meisel, J., Clahsen, H., & Pienemann, M. (1981). On determining developmental stages in natural second language acquisition. *Studies in Second Language Acquisition, 3*(1), 109-135.

Naiman, N., Fröhlich, M., Stern, H., & Todesco, A. (1978). *The good language learner* (Research in Education Series No. 7). Toronto: The Ontario Institute for Studies in Education.

Neufeld, G. (1979). Towards a theory of language learning ability. *Language Learning, 29*(2), 227-241.

Nunan, D. (1987). Methodological issues in research. In D. Nunan (Ed.), *Applying second language acquisition research* (pp. 143-171). Adelaide, Australia: National Curriculum Resource Centre.

Odlin, T. (1989). *Language transfer: Cross-linguistic influence in language learning*. Cambridge: Cambridge University Press.

Oller, J. W., & Richards, J. C. (Eds.). (1973). *Focus on the learner: Pragmatic perspectives for the language teacher*. Rowley, MA: Newbury House.

O'Malley, J., & Chamot, A. (1990). *Learning strategies in second language acquisition*. Cambridge: Cambridge University Press.

Oxford, R. (1990). *Language learning strategies: What every teacher should know*. New York: Newbury House/HarperCollins.

Pankhurst, J., Sharwood Smith, M., & van Buren, P. (Eds.). (1988). *Learnability and second languages: A book of readings*. Dordrecht, Netherlands: Foris.

Pavesi, M. (1986). Markedness, discoursal modes, and relative clause formation in a formal and an informal context. *Studies in Second Language Acquisition, 8*(1), 38-55.

Pennington, M. (1990). The context of L2 phonology. In H. Burmeister & P. Rounds (Eds.), *Variability in second language acquisition* (Vol. 2, pp. 541-564). Eugene: University of Oregon, Department of Linguistics.

Pica, T. (1985). The selective impact of classroom instruction on second language acquisition. *Applied Linguistics, 6*(3), 214-222.

Pienemann, M. (1984). Psychological constraints on the teachability of languages. *Studies in Second Language Acquisition, 6*(2), 186-214.

Pienemann, M. (1985). Learnability and syllabus construction. In K. Hyltenstam & M. Pienemann (Eds.,), *Modelling and assessing second language development*. Clevedon, Avon, England: Multilingual Matters.

Pienemann, M., & Johnston, M. (1987). Factors influencing the development of language proficiency. In D. Nunan (Ed.), *Applying second language acquisition research* (pp. 45-141). Adelaide, Australia: National Curriculum Resource Centre.

Pinker, S., & Prince, A. (1988). On language and connectionism: Analysis of a parallel distributed processing model of language acquisition. *Cognition, 28*(1-2), 73-193.

Prahbu, N. S. (1991, March). *The dynamics of the language lesson.* Paper presented at the 25th Annual TESOL Convention, New York City.
Preston, D. (1989). *Sociolinguistics and second language acquisition.* Oxford: Basil Blackwell.
Rubin, J. (1975). What the "good language learner" can teach us. *TESOL Quarterly, 9*(1), 41-51.
Rumelhart, D., McClelland, J., & the PDP Research Group. (1986a). *Parallel distributed processing: Explorations in the microstructures of cognition: Vol. I. Foundations.* Cambridge, MA: MIT Press.
Rumelhart, D., McClelland, J., & the PDP Research Group. (1986b). *Parallel distributed processing: Explorations in the microstructures of cognition: Vol. II. Psychological and biological models.* Cambridge, MA: MIT Press.
Rutherford, W., & Sharwood Smith, M. (Eds.). (1988). *Grammar and second language teaching.* New York: Newbury House/Harper & Row.
Sato, C. (1985). Task variation in interlanguage phonology. In S. Gass & C. Madden (Eds.), *Input in second language acquisition* (pp. 181-196). Rowley, MA: Newbury House.
Sato, C. (1988). Origins of complex syntax in interlanguage development. *Studies in Second Language Acquisition, 10*(3), 371-395.
Scarcella, R. (1990). [Review of *Variation in second language acquisition* (Vols. 1 & 2)]. *Studies in Second Language Acquisition, 12*(4), 458-460.
Schachter, J. (1974). An error in error analysis. *Language Learning, 24*(2), 205-214.
Schachter, J. (1983). A new account of language transfer. In S. Gass & L. Selinker (Eds.), *Language transfer in language learning* (pp. 98-111). Rowley, MA: Newbury House.
Schachter, J. (1988). Second language acquisition and its relationship to universal grammar. *Applied Linguistics, 9*(3), 219-235.
Schachter, J. (1990). On the issue of completeness in second language acquisition. *Second Language Research, 6*(2), 93-124.
Schachter, J. (1991). Corrective feedback in historical perspective. *Second Language Research, 7*(2), 89-102.
Schachter, J., & Celce-Murcia, M. (1977). Some reservations concerning error analysis. *TESOL Quarterly, 11*(4), 441-451.
Schachter, J., & Rutherford, W. (1979). Discourse function and language transfer. *Working Papers on Bilingualism, 19*, 3-12.
Schmidt, R. (1990). The role of consciousness in second language learning. *Applied Linguistics, 11*(2), 129-158.
Schumann, J. (1978a). *The pidginization process: A model for second language acquisition.* Rowley, MA: Newbury House.
Schumann, J. (1978b). The acculturation model for second language acquisition. In R. Gingras (Ed.), *Second language acquisition and foreign language teaching* (pp. 27-50). Washington, DC: Center for Applied Linguistics.
Schumann, J. (1978c). Social and psychological factors in second language acquisition. In J. C. Richards (Ed.), *Understanding second & foreign language learning* (pp. 163-178). Rowley, MA: Newbury House.

Schumann, J. (1979). The acquisition of English negation by speakers of Spanish: A review of the literature. In R. Andersen (Ed.), *The acquisition and use of Spanish and English as first and second languages* (pp. 3-32). Washington, DC: TESOL.

Schumann, J. (1983). Art and science in second language acquisition research. In M. Clark & J. Handscombe (Eds.), *On TESOL '82: Pacific perspectives on language learning and teaching* (pp. 107-124). Washington, DC: TESOL.

Schumann, J. (1990). Extending the scope of the acculturation/pidginization model to include cognition. *TESOL Quarterly, 24*(4), 667-684.

Schumann, J., & Stenson, N. (Eds.). (1974). *New frontiers in second language learning*. Rowley, MA: Newbury House.

Scovel, T. (1978). The effect of affect on foreign language learning: A review of the anxiety research. *Language Learning, 28*(1), 129-142.

Scovel, T. (1988a). *A time to speak: A psycholinguistic inquiry into the critical period for human speech*. New York: Newbury House/Harper & Row.

Scovel, T. (1988b). Multiple perspectives make singular teaching. In L. Beebe (Ed.), *Issues in second language acquisition* (pp. 167-190). New York: Newbury House/Harper & Row.

Seliger, H. (1984). Processing universals in second language acquisition. In F. Eckman, L. Bell, & D. Nelson (Eds.), *Universals of second language acquisition* (pp. 36-47). Rowley, MA: Newbury House.

Seliger, H., & Shohamy, E. (1989). *Second language research methods*. Oxford: Oxford University Press.

Selinker, L. (1972). Interlanguage. *International Review of Applied Linguistics, 10*(3), 209-231.

Selinker, L., & Douglas, D. (1985). Wrestling with "context" in interlanguage theory. *Applied Linguistics, 6*(2), 190-204.

Singleton, D. (1989). *Language acquisition: The age factor*. Clevedon, Avon, England: Multilingual Matters.

Skehan, P. (1982). *Memory and motivation in language aptitude testing*. Unpublished doctoral dissertation, University of London.

Skehan, P. (1989). *Individual differences in second-language learning*. London: Edward Arnold.

Slobin, D. (1973). Cognitive prerequisites for the development of grammar. In C. Ferguson & D. Slobin (Eds.), *Studies of child language development* (pp. 175-208). New York: Appleton-Century-Crofts.

Sokolik, M. (1989). Comments on Bernard Spolsky's "Bridging the gap: A general theory of second language learning." *TESOL Quarterly, 23*(2), 359.

Sokolik, M. (1990). Learning without rules: PDP and a resolution of the adult language learning paradox. *TESOL Quarterly, 24*(4), 685-696.

Spolsky, B. (1988). Bridging the gap: A general theory of second language learning. *TESOL Quarterly, 22*(3), 377-396.

Spolsky, B. (1989). *Conditions for second language learning*. Oxford: Oxford University Press.

Stevick, E. (1989). *Success with foreign languages: Seven who found it and what worked for them*. Hemel Hempstead, England: Prentice Hall.

Strong, M. (1984). Integrative motivation: Cause or result of successful second language acquisition? *Language Learning, 34*(3), 1-14.

Swain, M. (1985). Communicative competence: Some roles of comprehensible input and comprehensible output in its development. In S. Gass & C. Madden (Eds.), *Input in second language acquisition* (pp. 235-253). Rowley, MA: Newbury House.

Tarone, E. (1979). Interlanguage as chameleon. *Language Learning, 29*(1), 181-191.

Tarone, E. (1983). On the variability of interlanguage systems. *Applied Linguistics, 4*(2), 142-163.

Tarone, E. (1988). *Variation in interlanguage*. London: Edward Arnold.

Tarone, E. (1990). On variation in interlanguage: A response to Gregg. *Applied Linguistics, 11*(4), 392-400.

Taylor, B. (1975). The use of overgeneralization and transfer learning strategies by elementary and intermediate students in ESL. *Language Learning, 25*(1), 73-107.

Tomaselli, A., & Schwartz, B. (1990). Analyzing the acquisition stages of negation in L2 German: Support for UG in adult SLA. *Second Language Research, 6*(1), 1-38.

Tomlin, R. (1990). Functionalism in second language acquisition. *Studies in Second Language Acquisition, 12*(2), 155-178.

Tucker, G., Hamayan, E., & Genesee, F. (1976). Affective, cognitive and social factors in second language acquisition. *Canadian Modern Language Review, 32*, 214-226.

van Els, T., Bongaerts, T., Extra, G., van Os, C., & Janssen-van Dieten, A. (1984). *Applied linguistics and the learning and teaching of foreign languages*. London: Edward Arnold.

van Lier, L. (1988). *The classroom and the language learner*. London: Longman.

Wagner-Gough, J. (1975). *Comparative studies in second language learning* (CAL-ERIC/CLL Series on Languages and Linguistics No. 26). Washington, DC: Center for Applied Linguistics.

Wenden, A., & Rubin, J. (Eds.). (1987). *Learning strategies in language learning*. Englewood Cliffs, NJ: Prentice Hall.

Wesche, M. (1981). Language aptitude measures in streaming, matching students with methods, and diagnosis of learning problems. In K. Diller (Ed.), *Individual differences and universals in language learning aptitude* (pp. 119-139). Rowley, MA: Newbury House.

White, L. (1988). Island effects in second language acquisition. In S. Flynn & W. O'Neil (Eds.), *Linguistic theory in second language acquisition* (pp. 144-172). Dordrecht, Netherlands: Kluwer Academic.

White, L. (1989). *Universal grammar and L2 acquisition*. Amsterdam: John Benjamins.

White, L. (1990). Second language acquisition and universal grammar. *Studies in Second Language acquisition, 12*(2), 121-133.

Widdowson, H. (1989). Knowledge of language and ability for use. *Applied Linguistics, 10*(2), 128-137.

Willing, K. (1988). *Learning styles in adult migrant education.* Adelaide, Australia: National Curriculum Resource Centre.

Wode, H. (1978). Developmental sequences in naturalistic L2 acquisition. In E. Hatch (Ed.), *Second language acquisition: A book of readings* (pp. 101-117). Rowley, MA: Newbury House.

Wode, H. (1981). Language-acquisitional universals: A unified view of language acquisition. In H. Winitz (Ed.), *Native language and foreign language acquisition* (Annals of the New York Academy of Sciences No. 379, pp. 218-234). New York: New York Academy of Sciences.

Wong Fillmore, L. (1976). *The second time around: Cognitive and social strategies in second language acquisition.* Unpublished doctoral dissertation, Stanford University, Palo Alto, CA.

Young, R. (1988). Variation and the interlanguage hypothesis. *Studies in Second Language Acquisition, 10*(3), 281-302.

Zobl, H. (1982). A direction for contrastive analysis: The comparative study of developmental sequences. *TESOL Quarterly, 16*(2), 169-183.

Zobl, H. (1983). Markedness and the projection problem. *Language Learning, 33*(3), 293-313.

Zobl, H. (1990). Evidence for parameter-sensitive acquisition: A contribution to the domain-specific versus central processes debate. *Second Language Research, 6*(1), 39-59.

What Does Language Testing Have to Offer?

LYLE F. BACHMAN
University of California, Los Angeles

Advances in language testing in the past decade have occurred in three areas: (a) the development of a theoretical view that considers language ability to be multicomponential and recognizes the influence of the test method and test taker characteristics on test performance, (b) applications of more sophisticated measurement and statistical tools, and (c) the development of "communicative" language tests that incorporate principles of "communicative" language teaching. After reviewing these advances, this paper describes an interactional model of language test performance that includes two components, language ability and test method. Language ability consists of language knowledge and metacognitive strategies, whereas test method includes characteristics of the environment, rubric, input, expected response, and relationship between input and expected response. Two aspects of authenticity are derived from this model. The situational authenticity of a given test task depends on the relationship between its test method characteristics and the features of a specific language use situation, while its interactional authenticity pertains to the degree to which it invokes the test taker's language ability. The application of this definition of authenticity to test development is discussed.

Since 1989, four papers reviewing the state of the art in the field of language testing have appeared (Alderson, 1991; Bachman, 1990a; Skehan, 1988, 1989, 1991). All four have argued that language testing has come of age as a discipline in its own right within applied linguistics and have presented substantial evidence, I believe, in support of this assertion. A common theme in all these articles is that the field of language testing has much to offer in terms of theoretical, methodological, and practical accomplishments to its sister disciplines in applied linguistics. Since these papers provide excellent critical surveys and discussions of the field of language testing, I will simply summarize some of the common themes in these reviews in Part 1 of this paper in order to whet the appetite of readers who may be interested in knowing what are the issues and problems of current interest to language testers. These articles are nontechnical and accessible to those who are not themselves language testing specialists. Furthermore, Skehan (1991) and Alderson (1991) appear in collections of papers from recent conferences that focus on current issues in language testing. These collections include a wide variety of topics of current interest within language testing, discussed from many perspectives, and thus constitute major contributions to the literature on language testing.

The purpose of this paper is to address a question that is, I believe, implicit in all of the review articles mentioned above, What does language testing have to offer to researchers and practitioners in other areas of applied linguistics, particularly in language learning and language teaching? These reviews discuss several specific areas in which valuable contributions can be expected (e.g., program evaluation, second language acquisition, classroom learning, research methodology). Part 2 of this paper focuses on two recent developments in language testing, discussing their potential contributions to language learning and language teaching. I argue first that a theoretical model of second language ability that has emerged on the basis of research in language testing can be useful for both researchers and practitioners in language learning and language teaching. Specifically, I believe it provides a basis for both conceptualizing second language abilities whose acquisition is the object of considerable research and instructional effort, and for designing language tests for use both in instructional settings and for research in language learning and language teaching. Second, I will describe an approach to characterize the authenticity of a language task which I believe can help us to better understand the nature of the tasks we set, either for students in instructional programs or for subjects in language learning research and which can thus aid in the design and development of tasks that are more useful for these purposes.

PART 1: LANGUAGE TESTING IN THE 1990s

In echoing Alderson's (1991) title, I acknowledge the commonalities among the review articles mentioned above in the themes they discuss and the issues they raise. While each review emphasizes specific areas, all approach the task with essentially the same rhetorical organization: a review of the achievements in language testing, or lack thereof, over the past decade; a discussion of areas of likely continued development; and suggestions of areas in need of increased emphasis to assure developments in the future. Both Alderson and Skehan argue that while language testing has made progress in some areas, on the whole "there has been relatively little progress in language testing until recently" (Skehan, 1991, p. 3). Skehan discusses the contextual factors—theory, practical considerations, and human considerations—that have influenced language testing in terms of whether these factors act as "forces for conservatism" or "forces for change" (p. 3). The former, he argues, "all have the consequence of retarding change, reducing openness, and generally justifying inaction in testing" (p. 3), while the latter are "pressures which are likely to bring about more beneficial outcomes" (p. 7). All of the reviews present essentially optimistic views of where language testing is going and what it has to offer other areas of applied linguistics. I will group the common themes of these reviews into the general areas of (a) theoretical issues and their implications for practical application, (b) methodological advances, and (c) language test development.

THEORETICAL ISSUES

One of the major preoccupations of language testers in the past decade has been investigating the nature of language proficiency. In 1980 the "unitary competence hypothesis" (Oller, 1979), which claimed that language proficiency consists of a single, global ability was widely accepted. By 1983 this view of language proficiency had been challenged by several empirical studies and abandoned by its chief proponent (Oller, 1983). The unitary trait view has been replaced, through both empirical research and theorizing, by the view that language proficiency is multicomponential, consisting of a number of interrelated specific abilities as well as a general ability or set of general strategies or procedures. Skehan and Alderson both suggest that the model of language test performance proposed by Bachman (1990b) represents progress in this area, since it includes both components of language ability and characteristics of test methods, thereby making it possible "to make statements about actual performance as well as underlying abilities" (Skehan, 1991, p. 9). At the same time, Skehan correctly points out that as research progresses, this model will be modified and eventually superseded. Both Alderson and Skehan indicate that an area where further progress is needed is in the application of theoretical models of language proficiency to the design and development of language tests. Alderson, for example, states that "we need to be concerned not only with . . . the nature of language proficiency, but also with language learning and the design and researching of achievement tests; not only with testers, and the problems of our professionalism, but also with testees, with students, and their interests, perspectives and insights" (Alderson, 1991, p. 5).

A second area of research and progress is in our understanding of the effects of the method of testing on test performance. A number of empirical studies conducted in the 1980s clearly demonstrated that the kind of test tasks used can affect test performance as much as the abilities we want to measure (e.g., Bachman & Palmer, 1981, 1982, 1988; Clifford, 1981; Shohamy, 1983, 1984). Other studies demonstrated that the topical content of test tasks can affect performance (e.g., Alderson & Urquhart, 1985; Erickson & Molloy, 1983). Results of these studies have stimulated a renewed interest in the investigation of test content. And here the results have been mixed. Alderson and colleagues (Alderson, 1986, 1990; Alderson & Lukmani, 1986; Alderson, Henning, & Lukmani, 1987) have been investigating (a) the extent to which "experts" agree in their judgments about what specific skills EFL reading test items measure, and at what levels, and (b) whether these expert judgments about ability levels are related to the difficulty of items. Their results indicate first, that these experts, who included test designers assessing the content of their own tests, do not agree and, second, that there is virtually no relationship between judgments of the levels of ability tested and empirical item difficulty. Bachman and colleagues, on the other hand (Bachman, Davidson, Lynch, & Ryan, 1989; Bachman, Davidson, & Milanovic, 1991; Bachman, Davidson, Ryan, & Choi, in press) have found that by using a content-rating instrument based on a taxonomy of test method characteristics (Bachman, 1990b) and by training raters, a high degree of agreement among raters can be obtained, and such content ratings are related to item difficulty and item discrimination. In my view, these results are not inconsistent. The research of Alderson and colleagues presents, I believe, a sobering picture of actual practice in the design and development of language tests: Test designers and experts in the field disagree about what language tests measure, and neither the designers nor the experts have a clear sense of the levels of ability measured by their tests. This research uncovers a potentially serious problem in the way language testers practice their trade. Bachman's research, on the other hand, presents what can be accomplished in a highly controlled situation, and provides one approach to solving this problem. Thus, an important area for future research in the years to come will be in the refinement of approaches to the analysis of test method character-istics, of which content is a substantial component, and the inves-tigation of how specific characteristics of test method affect test performance. Progress will be realized in the area of language testing practice when insights from this area of research inform the design and development of language tests. The research on test content analysis that has been conducted by the University of Cambridge Local Examinations Syndicate, and the incorporation of that research into the design and development of EFL tests is illustrative of this kind of integrated approach (Bachman et al., 1991).

The 1980s saw a wealth of research into the characteristics of test takers and how these are related to test performance, generally under the rubric of investigations into potential sources of test bias; I can do little more than list these here. A number of studies have shown differences in test performance across different cultural, linguistic or ethnic groups (e.g., Alderman & Holland, 1981; Chen & Henning, 1985; Politzer & McGroarty, 1985; Swinton & Powers, 1980; Zeidner, 1986), while others have found differential performance between sexes (e.g., Farhady, 1982; Zeidner, 1987). Other studies have found relationships between field dependence and test performance (e.g., Chapelle, 1988; Chapelle & Roberts, 1986; Hansen, 1984; Hansen & Stansfield, 1981; Stansfield & Hansen, 1983). Such studies demonstrate the effects of various test taker characteristics on test performance, and suggest that such characteristics need to be considered in both the design of language tests and in the interpretation of test scores. To date, however, no clear direction has emerged to suggest how such considerations translate into testing practice. Two issues that need to be resolved in this regard are (a) whether and how we assess the specific characteristics of a given group of test takers, and (b) whether and how we can incorporate such information into the way we design language tests. Do we treat these characteristics as sources of test bias and seek ways to somehow "correct" for this in the way we write and select test items, for example? Or, if many of these characteristics are known to also influence language learning, do we reconsider our definition of language ability? The investigation of test taker characteristics and their effects on language test performance also has implications for research in second language acquisition (SLA), and represents what Bachman (1989) has called an "interface" between SLA and language testing research.

METHODOLOGICAL ADVANCES

Many of the developments mentioned above—changes in the way we view language ability, the effects of test method and test taker characteristics—have been facilitated by advances in the tools that are available for test analysis. These advances have been in three areas: psychometrics, statistical analysis, and qualitative approaches to the description of test performance. The 1980s saw the application of several modern psychometric tools to language testing: item response theory (IRT), generalizability theory (G theory), criterion-referenced (CR) measurement, and the Mantel-Haenszel procedure. As these tools are fairly technical, I will simply refer readers to discussions of them: IRT (Henning, 1987), G theory (Bachman, 1990b; Bolus, Hinofotis, & Bailey, 1982), CR measurement (Bachman, 1990b; Hudson & Lynch, 1984), Mantel-Haenszel (Ryan & Bachman, in press). The application of IRT to language tests has brought with it advances in computer-adaptive language testing, which promises to make language tests more efficient and adaptable to individual test takers, and thus potentially more useful in the types of information they provide (e.g., Tung, 1986), but which also presents a challenge not to complacently continue using familiar testing techniques simply because they can be administered easily via computer (Canale, 1986). Alderson (1988a) and the papers in Stansfield (1986) provide extensive discussions of the applications of computers to language testing.

The major advance in the area of statistical analysis has been the application of structural equation modeling to language testing research. (Relatively nontechnical discussions of structural equation modeling can be found in Long, 1983a, 1983b.) The use of confirmatory factor analysis was instrumental in demonstrating the untenability of the unitary trait hypothesis, and this type of analysis, in conjunction with the multitrait/multimethod research design, continues to be a productive approach to the process of construct validation. Structural equation modeling has also facilitated the investigation of relationships between language test performance and test taker characteristics (e.g., Fouly, 1985; Purcell, 1983) and different types of language instruction (e.g., Sang, Schmitz, Vollmer, Baumert, & Roeder, 1986).

A third methodological advance has been in the use of introspection to investigate the processes or strategies that test takers employ in attempting to complete test tasks. Studies using this approach have demonstrated that test takers use a variety of strategies in solving language test tasks (e.g., Alderson, 1988c; Cohen, 1984) and that these strategies are related to test performance (e.g., Anderson, Cohen, Perkins, & Bachman, 1991; Nevo, 1989).

Perhaps the single most important theoretical development in language testing in the 1980s was the realization that a language test score represents a complexity of multiple influences. As both Alderson and Skehan point out, this advance has been spurred on, to a considerable extent, by the application of the methodological tools discussed above. But, as Alderson (1991) notes, "the use of more sophisticated techniques reveals how complex responses to test items can be and therefore how complex a test score can be" (p. 12). Thus, one legacy of the 1980s is that we now know that a language test score cannot be interpreted simplistically as an indicator of the particular language ability we want to measure; it is also affected to some extent by the characteristics and content of the test tasks, the characteristics of the test taker, and the strategies the test taker employs in attempting to complete the test task. What makes the interpretation of test scores particularly difficult is that these factors undoubtedly interact with each other. The particular strategy adopted by a given test taker, for example, is likely to be a function of both the characteristics of the test task and the test taker's personal characteristics. This realization clearly indicates that we need to consider very carefully the interpretations and uses we make of language test scores and thus should sound a note of caution to language testing practitioners. At the same time, our expanded knowledge of the complexity of language test performance, along with the methodological tools now at our disposal, provide a basis for designing and developing language tests that are potentially more suitable for specific groups of test takers and more useful for their intended purposes.

ADVANCES IN LANGUAGE TEST DEVELOPMENT

For language testing, the 1980s could be characterized as the decade of "communicative" testing. Although two strains of communicative approaches to language testing can be traced, as with many innovations in language testing over the years, the major impetus has come from language teaching. One strain of communicative tests, illustrated by the *Ontario Assessment Pool* (Canale & Swain, 1980a) and the *A Vous la Parole* testing unit described by Swain (1985), traces its roots to the Canale/Swain framework of communicative competence (Canale, 1983; Canale & Swain, 1980b). The other, exemplified by the *Test of English for Educational Purposes* (Associated Examining Board, 1987; Weir, 1983), the *Ontario Test of English as a Second Language* (Wesche et al., 1987), and the *International English Language Testing Service* (e.g., Alderson, 1988b; Alderson, Foulkes, Clapham, & Ingram, 1990; Criper & Davies, 1988; Seaton, 1983) has grown out of the English for specific purposes tradition. While a number of lists of characteristics of communicative language tests has been proposed (e.g., Alderson, 1981a; Canale, 1984; Carroll, 1980; Harrison, 1983; Morrow, 1977, 1979), I will mention four characteristics that would appear to distinguish communicative language tests. First, such tests create an "information gap," requiring test takers to process complementary information through the use of multiple sources of input. Test takers, for example, might be required to perform a writing task that is based on input from both a short recorded lecture and a reading passage on the same topic. A second characteristic is that of task dependency, with tasks in one section of the test building upon the content of earlier sections, including the test taker's answers to those sections. Third, communicative tests can be characterized by their integration of test tasks and content within a given domain of discourse. Finally, communicative tests attempt to measure a much broader range of language abilities—including knowledge of cohesion, functions, and sociolinguistic appropriateness—than did earlier tests, which tended to focus on the formal aspects of language—grammar, vocabulary, and pronunciation.

A different approach to language testing that evolved during the 1980s is the adaptation of the FSI oral interview guidelines (Wilds, 1975) to the assessment of the oral language proficiency in contexts outside agencies of the U.S. government. This "AEI" (For American Council for the Teaching of Foreign Languages/Educational Testing Service/Interagency Language Roundtable) approach to language assessment is based on a view of language proficiency as a unitary ability (Lowe, 1988), and thus diverges from the view that has emerged in language testing research and other areas of applied linguistics. This approach to oral language assessment has been criticized by both linguists and applied linguists, including language testers and language teachers, on a number of grounds (e.g., Alderson, 1981b; Bachman, 1988; Bachman & Savignon, 1986; Candlin, 1986; Kramsch, 1986; Lantolf & Frawley, 1985, 1988; Savignon, 1985). Nevertheless, the approach and ability levels defined have been widely accepted as a standard for assessing oral proficiency in a foreign language in the U.S. and have provided the basis for the development of "simulated oral proficiency interviews" in various languages (e.g., Stansfield & Kenyon, 1988, 1989). In addition, the approach has been adapted to the assessment of EFL proficiency in other countries (e.g., Ingram, 1984).

These two approaches to language assessment—communicative and AEI—are based on differing views of the nature of language proficiency, and are thus likely to continue as separate, unrelated approaches in the years to come. Lowe (1988) has explicitly articulated such a separatist view, in stating that the "concept of Communicative Language Proficiency (CLP), renamed Communicative Language Ability (CLA), and AEI proficiency may prove incompatible" (p. 14). Communicative language testing and AEI assessment represent two different approaches to language test design, and each has developed a number of specific manifestations in language tests. As a result, language testing will be enriched in the years to come by the variety of tests and testing techniques that emerge from these approaches.

This summary has focused on common areas among four recent reviews of language testing. In addition to these common areas, each of the reviews mentions specific areas of progress or concern. Skehan (1991) and Alderson (1991) both note that until very recently other areas of applied linguistics have provided very little input into language testing. Skehan, however, is encouraged by the relevance to language testing of recent work in sociolinguistics, second language acquisition, and language teaching, and points out the need for language testing to be aware of and receptive to input from developments in other areas of applied linguistics such as the SLA-based approach to assessing language development of Pienemann, Johnston, & Brindley (1988). Skehan and Alderson both argue that language testing must continue to investigate new avenues to assessment, such as formats that measure communicative abilities more successfully (e.g., Milanovic, 1988); "series tasks," in which specified language interactions are scored in terms of how particular aspects of information are communicated; group testing; self-assessment; and computer-based language testing. Alderson discusses two additional areas to which language testing needs to turn its attention in the years to come: "washback" effects and learner-centered testing. He points out that while we generally assume that tests have an impact on instruction (washback), there is virtually no empirical research into how, if at all, instructional impact functions, under what conditions, and whether deliberate attempts to design tests with positive instructional impact are effective. Alderson also argues persuasively for the greater involvement of learners in the activity of testing, in the design and writing of tests, and in the setting of standards for success. In this regard, I would mention the work of Brindley (1989) in assessing language achievement in learner-centered instructional settings and the papers in de Jong & Stevenson (1990), which address issues in individualizing language testing. A final area of development, mentioned by Bachman (1990b), is the renewed interest in language aptitude and developments in both the definition of the theoretical construct and in approaches to its measurement (Perry & Stansfield, 1990).

As a result of the developments of the 1980s, language testing has emerged as a discipline in its own right within applied linguistics.

Alderson (1991) notes that since 1980 language testing has seen the creation of an internationally respected journal, *Language Testing*, as well as several regular newsletters; five new texts on language testing as well as over a dozen volumes of collected papers have been published; and there are now at least two regular major international conferences each year devoted to language testing. The field of language testing has seen the development of both a model of language test performance that can guide empirical research, and the application of a variety of research approaches and tools to facilitate such research. In sum, language testing can now claim its own research questions and research methodology. As Bachman (1990a) states, "perhaps for the first time in the history of language testing it is possible to see a genuine symbiotic relationship between applied linguistic theory and the tools of empirical research as they are applied to both the development and the examination of a theory of performance on language tests [and to] the development and use of better language tests" (p. 220).

Also as a result of developments in the past decade, language testing is in a better position, I believe, both to make contributions to its sister disciplines in applied linguistics and to be enriched by developments in those disciplines. The next part of this paper briefly describes what I consider two contributions that language testing has to offer to the areas of language learning and language teaching.

PART 2: AN INTERACTIONAL APPROACH TO LANGUAGE TEST DEVELOPMENT

Language tests are used for a variety of purposes; these can be grouped into two broad categories. First, the results of language tests may be used to make inferences about test takers' language abilities or to make predictions about their capacity for using language to perform future tasks in contexts outside the test itself. Second, decisions (e.g., selection, diagnosis, placement, progress, grading, certification, employment) may be made about test takers on the basis of what we infer from test scores about their levels of ability or their capacity for nontest language use. A major consideration in both the design and use of language tests, therefore, is the extent to which the specific test tasks we include elicit instances of language use from which we can make such inferences or predictions. What this implies is that in order to investigate and demonstrate the validity of the uses we make of test scores, we need a theoretical framework within which we can describe language test performance as a specific instance of language use. Specifically, in order to make inferences about levels or profiles of ability, or predictions about capacity for using language to perform future tasks in nontest language use contexts, we need to demonstrate two kinds of correspondences: (a) that the language abilities measured by our language tests correspond in specifiable ways to the language abilities involved in nontest language use, and (b) that the characteristics of the test tasks correspond to the features of a target language use context.

In an instructional setting, for example, in which we may want to use a test to measure learners' degrees of mastery of different components of language ability that have been covered in the curriculum, we need to demonstrate that the content of the test is representative of the content of the course. Specifically, we will want to demonstrate that the components of language ability included in the test correspond to those covered in the course and that the characteristics of the test tasks correspond to the types of classroom learning activities included in the program. Demonstrating correspondences such as these provides some justification for interpreting test scores as evidence of levels of ability in the different components tested.

Another example would be a situation in which we need to select individuals for possible employment in a job which requires a specified level of proficiency in a foreign language. In this case, we need to demonstrate that the tasks included in the test are representative of the language use tasks required by the future job. Demonstrating this correspondence provides some justification for using the test scores to predict future capacity for using the foreign language effectively in the target employment situation.

Demonstrating correspondences between test performance and language use is equally important for justifying the use of language tests in applied linguistics research. For example, if we were interested in investigating the interlanguage development of a specific component of ability in a target language, for example, sensitivity to appropriate register, and wanted to use a test as one of our research instruments, we would need to be sure that the test we used measured this aspect of language ability. Similarly, we would want to specify the characteristics of the tasks included in the test, so as to minimize any variations that may arise between performance on this test and other elicitation procedures we may want to use.

In this part of the paper I will present a framework that I believe provides a basis for relating test performance to nontest language use. This framework includes a model of language ability for describing the abilities involved in language use and test performance and a framework of test method characteristics for relating the characteristics of tests and test tasks to features of the language use context. I will then suggest how this framework can be used to clarify our thinking about the notion of authenticity and for designing test tasks that are authentic.

LANGUAGE ABILITY

The language ability of the language user is one feature of language use. When we design a language test, we hypothesize that the test taker's language ability will be engaged by the test tasks. Thus, in order to relate the abilities we believe are involved in test performance to the abilities involved in language use, we need a model of language ability. The model I will describe here is a refinement of my 1990 model that Adrian Palmer and I are developing (Bachman & Palmer, in press). We define language ability essentially in Widdowson's (1983) terms as the capacity for using the knowledge of language in conjunction with the features of the language use context to create and interpret meaning. Our model of language ability includes two types of components: (a) areas of language knowledge, which we would hypothesize to be unique to language use (as opposed to, for example, mathematical knowledge or musical knowledge), and (b) metacognitive strategies that are probably general to all mental activity.

This view of language ability is consistent with research in applied linguistics that has increasingly come to view language ability as consisting of two components: (a) language knowledge, sometimes referred to as competence, and (b) cognitive processes, or procedures, that implement that knowledge in language use (e.g., Bachman, 1990a; Bialystok, 1990; Spolsky, 1989; Widdowson, 1983). It is also consistent with information-processing, or cognitive, models of mental abilities, which also distinguish processes or heuristics from domains of knowledge (e.g., Sternberg, 1985, 1988).

Language use involves the integration of multiple components and processes, not the least of which are those that constitute language ability. It is unlikely that every language test we develop or use will be intended to measure all the components in our model. Nevertheless, even though we may be interested in focusing on only one or a few of these in a given testing context, we need to be aware of the full range of language abilities as we design and develop language tests and interpret language test scores. For example, even though we may only be interested in measuring an individual's knowledge of vocabulary, the kinds of test items, tasks or texts we use need to be selected with an awareness of what other components of language ability they may evoke. We believe, therefore, that even though a given language test may focus on a narrow range of language abilities, its design must be informed by a broad view of language ability.

Language Knowledge[1]

What we refer to as language knowledge can be regarded as a domain of information that is specific to language ability and that is stored in long-term memory. For our purposes, we do not attempt to characterize how this knowledge is stored. That is, we use the term *knowledge* to refer to both conscious and tacit, analyzed and unanalyzed knowledge. While the importance of such distinctions has been recognized in other areas of applied linguistics, it remains to be seen how relevant they are to the design, development, and use of language tests.

Language knowledge includes two broad areas: organizational knowledge and pragmatic knowledge. These are constantly changing, as new elements are learned or acquired, and existing elements restructured. The learning or acquisition of areas of language knowledge is beyond the scope of my discussion here, and for purposes of describing how they pertain to language use, I will treat them as more or less stable traits or constructs. The areas of language knowledge are given in Figure 1 below.

Discussion of these elements of language knowledge is beyond the scope of this paper. I would simply indicate that this model of language ability has evolved from earlier models, particularly that of Canale & Swain (Canale, 1983; Canale & Swain, 1980b) as a result of both empirical research and review of relevant literature in applied linguistics. The model presented here thus includes a much wider range of elements and provides a more comprehensive view of language ability than have earlier models.

Strategic Competence

The second component of language ability is what I have called strategic competence, and have described as consisting of three sets

---

[1] This description of *language knowledge* is essentially the same as Bachman's (1990b) discussion of *language competence*. The change in terminology from *competence* to *knowledge* reflects the view that the former term now carries with it a great deal of unnecessary semantic baggage that makes it less useful conceptually than it once was. I would note two changes from Bachman's 1990 model: (a) "Vocabulary" has been removed from "organizational competence" and placed within a new area, "propositional knowledge," under "pragmatic knowledge," and (b) "illocutionary competence" has been renamed "functional knowledge."

FIGURE 1

Areas of Language Knowledge

From *Language Testing in Practice* by L. F. Bachman and A. S. Palmer, in press, Oxford, Oxford University Press. Copyright by Oxford University Press. Reprinted by permission.

Organizational knowledge
    (Determines how texts—oral or written—are organized)
    Grammatical knowledge
        (Determines how individual utterances or sentences are organized)
    Textual knowledge
        (Determines how utterances or sentences are organized to form texts)
Pragmatic knowledge
    (Determines how utterances/sentences, intentions and contexts are related to form meaning)
    Propositional knowledge
        (Determines how utterances/sentences are related to propositional content)
    Functional knowledge
        (Determines how utterances/sentences are related to intentions of language users)
    Sociolinguistic knowledge
        (Determines how utterances/sentences are related to features of the language use context)

---

of processes: assessment, planning, and execution (Bachman, 1990b). In applying this model to the practical design and development of language tests, Adrian Palmer and I have refined this view of strategic competence as consisting of three sets of metacognitive strategies: assessment, goal setting, and planning. These are given in Figure 2 below.

Since I will be referring to these in the discussion of interactional authenticity below, I briefly discuss these metacognitive strategies here. First, however, I would point out a dilemma in describing a set of strategies that we hypothesize operate simultaneously and are thus essentially unordered. In situated language use, the metacognitive strategies and areas of language knowledge interact with each other simultaneously. Thus there is no particular ordering or sequencing in the way they operate. Furthermore, the strategies and areas of language knowledge are integrated and interactive, by which I mean that all the components of language ability, although distinct from each other, interact with each other and are fully integrated in any instance of language use. However, since the language used to describe the model is linear, only one strategy can be described at a time; I must begin with one and end with another. This dilemma applies to examples, as well, which must necessarily be described in terms of a sequence of events. However, if the reader will keep in mind that my purpose here is to provide a

FIGURE 2

Metacognitive Strategies

From *Language Testing in Practice* by L. F. Bachman and A. S. Palmer, in press, Oxford, Oxford University Press. Copyright by Oxford University Press. Reprinted by permission.

Assessment	(Taking stock of what you need, what you have to work with, and how well you've done)
1.	Determining the desirability of achieving a particular goal and what is needed to achieve it in a particular context
2.	Determining what knowledge components—language knowledge, schemata, and affective schemata—are available for accomplishing that goal
3.	Determining the extent to which the communicative goal has been achieved by a given utterance
Goal-setting	(Deciding what you're going to do)
1.	Identifying and selecting one or more communicative goals that you want to achieve
2.	Deciding to attempt or not attempt achieving the communicative goal selected
Planning	(Deciding how to use what you have)
1.	Selecting relevant areas of language knowledge for accomplishing the given communicative goal
2.	Formulating a plan for implementing these areas in the production or interpretation of an utterance

general conceptualization for guiding test development and use, rather than to give a detailed description of how language is processed in the mind, I believe that this dilemma in presentation will not be a problem.

Assessment. The strategies of assessment provide a direct link between the context in which language use takes place, the discourse that is used, and the areas of language knowledge that the language user employs in producing or interpreting utterances. Assessment strategies perform three types of functions:

1. Assessing features of the context to determine whether it is feasible to achieve a given goal and if feasible, what is needed to achieve it in a particular context
2. Assessing what areas of language knowledge are available for accomplishing that goal
3. Assessing the extent to which the communicative goal has been achieved

In performing these functions, assessment strategies draw upon and interact with the different areas of language knowledge as well as with real-world knowledge schemata and affective schemata.

Goal setting. From the perspective of the language user, goal setting involves, essentially, deciding what you are going to do, and includes the following functions:

1. Identifying a set of possible communicative goals
2. Choosing one or more goals from this set of possible goals
3. Deciding whether or not to attempt to achieve the goal(s)

Since one of the primary advantages of a language test, as opposed to other ways of obtaining information about an individual's language ability (such as naturalistic observation), is that it is designed to elicit a specific sample of language use, the test taker's flexibility in setting goals for performance on test tasks is necessarily limited. Thus, even though test takers may have some flexibility in setting goals for test performance, this is generally not as much as language users enjoy in nontest language use. As I will argue below, however, one way to increase the degree of interactional authenticity of a language test task is to increase the test taker's involvement in goal setting.

Planning. Strategies of planning involves the following:

1. Selecting the relevant areas of language knowledge for accomplishing the given communicative goal
2. Formulating a plan for implementing these areas in the production or interpretation of an utterance

Strategies in Language Use

Using language involves interpreting or producing utterances with propositional content, functional purpose, and contextual appropriateness. This involves all the strategies and areas of language knowledge simultaneously and interactively. As discussed above, each of the three strategies interacts with all of the areas of language knowledge. In addition, the strategies themselves function interactively. Consider goal setting and assessment: We may modify or abandon a particular goal on the basis of assessment strategies. If, for example, we wanted to invite someone over for dinner, and saw that person at a party, we might decide to speak to them. If, however, we determined that it was inappropriate to extend the invitation in the presence of another person whom we did not want to invite, we would most likely modify our communicative goal and engage in polite conversation until the opportunity to extend the dinner invitation arose.

One implication of this model is that variations in language ability can be attributed to two sources. First, the areas of language knowledge may vary over time and across different language users, so that language knowledge may contain varying combinations of elements from the native language, interlanguage, and the target language. These areas of knowledge may vary both in terms of the presence or absence of different elements and in the nature of the elements that are present. Second, the metacognitive strategies may vary over time and across different language users. Thus these strategies may be used more or less effectively by different individuals in completing a given language test task or by the same individual in completing different test tasks. Furthermore, the strategies may be used in differing proportions and in differing degrees for different language test tasks. This means that test takers' performance on a given test task reflects both their knowledge of the language elements being measured and their capacity for effectively relating this language knowledge to the characteristics of the test task so as to arrive at a successful solution to the problem posed.

TEST METHOD CHARACTERISTICS

So far I have described a model of language ability that consists of areas of language knowledge and metacognitive processes. I have argued that this model can provide a basis for demonstrating the correspondences between the abilities measured by the test and the abilities required for nontest language use.

The second correspondence we need to demonstrate in order to make inferences about abilities or to make predictions about future language use on the basis of language test scores is the correspondence between the characteristics of the test task and the features of a target language use context. It is widely recognized that the features of the language use context, such as the relationship between the language users, the topic, and the purpose, influence the way we use language. It would thus not be surprising to find that characteristics of the method of testing affect the way individuals perform on tests. Indeed, one of the major findings of language testing research over the past decade is that performance on language tests is affected not only by the ability we are trying to measure but also by the method we use to measure it (cf. references in the Theoretical Issues section of Part 1). In a language test, the instances of language use that we elicit are shaped, as it were, by the test tasks we present. Thus, it is the discourse that is included in the test question and the nature of the test task that will determine, to a large extent, how the test taker processes the information presented and responds to the particular task.

Language teachers also realize that the selection of a testing method is important. Frequently one of the first questions asked in testing classes or at conferences is the speaker's opinion of the "best" way to test a particular component of language ability. Teachers are clearly aware that the way they test language ability affects how their students perform on language tests and hence the quality of the information obtained from their tests. These teachers also want to be sure that this test method effect works in ways that will be fair to their students and that will enable them, the teachers, to make inferences about the language abilities they want to measure.

When we consider the different test methods that are commonly used for language tests, we realize that they are not single wholes, but rather collections of characteristics. "Multiple-choice" test items, for example, vary in a number of ways, such as in their length, syntactic complexity, level of vocabulary, topical content, and type of response required, to name but a few. Similarly, the "composition" test method encompasses a wide variety of prompts that can differ in terms of characteristics such as the intended audience, purpose, and specific organizational pattern requested. It is thus clear that we cannot be very precise in our thinking about test methods if we think of them only as holistic types. In order to organize our thinking about test methods, therefore, we first need a way to characterize them. A framework for doing this is presented in Figure 3 below.

Again, given space limitations, I will not discuss these here, but will simply point out that these test method characteristics have been used in several empirical studies to analyze the content of test items and to investigate the relationships between test content and the difficulty and discrimination of test items (Bachman, Kunnan, Vanniarajan, & Lynch, 1988; Bachman et al., 1989; Bachman et al., 1991; Bachman et al., in press).

CHARACTERIZING AUTHENTICITY

I have argued that in order to justify the use of language tests, we need to be able to demonstrate that performance on language tests corresponds in specified ways to nontest language use. I have described a model of language ability that I believe provides a basis for specifying the language ability of the language user as test taker. I have also presented a framework for specifying the characteristics of test tasks in a way that I believe enables us to investigate how these are related to the features of a given target language use context. In the remainder of this paper I will attempt to describe how these models can be used to assess the "authenticity" of a given

FIGURE 3

Test Method Characteristics

From *Fundamental Considerations in Language Testing* (p.119) by L. F. Bachman, 1990, Oxford, Oxford University Press. Copyright 1990 by Oxford University Press. Reprinted by permission.

Characteristics of the testing environment

Characteristics of the test rubric

    Test organization
    Time allocation
    Scoring
    Instructions

Characteristics of the test input

    Format
    Language of input

    Length
    Organizational characteristics
    Pragmatic characteristics

Characteristics of the expected response

    Format
    Language of expected response

    Length
    Organizational characteristics
    Pragmatic characteristics

Relationship between input and response

    Reciprocal
    Nonreciprocal
    Adaptive

---

test task, and suggest some ways this notion of authenticity can be used in the practical design of test tasks.

A number of language testing specialists have discussed the features that characterize an authentic test task (e.g., Alderson, 1981b; Canale, 1984; Carroll, 1980; Harrison, 1983; Morrow, 1977, 1979). When we try to define *authenticity*, however, we notice that it is one of those words like *real* (as in "He's really real") that sounds good but leaves us wondering exactly what it means. In fact, in language testing circles, authenticity has been defined in a number of different ways. One approach, for example has been to define it as direct, in the sense of getting at the ability without going through an intermediate representation of the ability. However, it is impossible to directly observe the neurological programming in the brain that may account for language ability. Thus, all language tests are indirect; they simply permit us to observe behavior from which we can make inferences about language ability.

A second approach has been to define authenticity in terms of similarity to real life. The problem with this definition is that "real life" language use consists of an infinite set of unique and widely varied speech events. Thus, the way in which language is used in real life can vary enormously and includes language use situations as different as announcing a sporting event and keying information from a questionnaire into a computer. Because of the great variation in the language used in real life, we have no basis for knowing what kind of real life language tasks to use as our primary criteria for authenticity.

A third approach to defining authenticity is to appeal to what was once called face validity, which is really nothing more than face appeal. This is just as problematic as the previous two approaches, but in a different way. This definition refers to a purely subjective response on the part of the evaluator and offers us no criteria for use in creating appealing tests. Moreover, there is also the issue, noted by Davies (1977) some years ago, that what is appealing to experts in language testing might be different from what is appealing to teachers, students, or to parents of students.

All three of these approaches to authenticity capture some intuitively useful aspects of authenticity, but they are problematic in many ways. Furthermore, they are not clearly enough defined, I believe, to provide a basis for test development. Adrian Palmer and I (Bachman & Palmer, in press) have attempted to define authenticity in a way that we think still captures the spirit of these approaches but does so in a way that avoids the problems of these approaches and is also specific enough to guide test development. For this purpose, we define two different types of authenticity: situational authenticity and interactional authenticity.

Situational Authenticity

We define situational authenticity as the perceived relevance of the test method characteristics to the features of a specific target language use situation. Thus, for a test task to be perceived as situationally authentic, the characteristics of the test task need to be perceived as corresponding to the features of a target language use situation. For example, one set of test method characteristics relates to certain characteristics of vocabulary (e.g., infrequent, specialized) and topics (e.g., academic, technical) included in the test input. If test takers were specialists in engineering, it is likely that inclusion of technical terms and topics from engineering would tend to increase the situational authenticity of the test. While situational authenticity may appear to be essentially the same as the real-life approach described above, it is fundamentally different in a critical way. The real-life approach assumes that there is a well-defined domain of target language use tasks outside the test itself and that these tasks themselves can be sampled in order to achieve authenticity. In contrast, we define the situational authenticity of a given test task in terms of the distinctive features that characterize a set of target language use tasks. Thus, in designing a situationally authentic test, we do not attempt to sample actual tasks from a domain of nontest language use, but rather try to design tasks that have the same critical features as tasks in that domain.

This definition allows for possibly different perceptions of situational authenticity. Thus, different test takers may have different ideas about their target language use situations. And the perceptions of test takers about the relevance of the characteristics of the test task to their target language use situations may be different from those of the test developers. What this implies is that situational authenticity must be assessed from a number of perspectives and that these all must be taken into consideration in the development and use of language tests.

Language testers and teachers alike are concerned with this kind of authenticity, for we all want to do our best to make our teaching and testing relevant to our students' language use needs. For a reading test, for example, we are likely to choose a passage whose topic and genre (characteristics of the test input) match the topic and genre of material the test user is likely to read outside of the testing situation. Or, if the target language use situation requires reciprocal language use, then we will design a test task in which reciprocity is a characteristic of the relationship between test input and expected response.

Interactional Authenticity

What we call interactional authenticity is essentially Widdowson's (1978) definition of authenticity and is a function of the extent and type of involvement of task takers' language ability in accomplishing a test task. The different areas of language knowledge and the different strategies can be involved to varying degrees in the problem presented by the test task. In contrast to situational authenticity, where the focus is on the relationship between the test task and nontest language use, interactional authenticity resides in interaction between the test taker and the test task.

In order to make these definitions of authenticity useful for test development, we need to be able to specify both the characteristics of the test task and the nature of the involvement of the test taker's language ability. We propose that the situational authenticity of a given test task can be assessed largely in terms of the framework of test method characteristics and that these characteristics can also provide a basis for designing test tasks that are situationally authentic. Assessing interactional authenticity and designing tasks that are interactionally authentic, however, is more complex, since this requires us to consider both the characteristics of the test task and the components of the test taker's language ability. For this reason, I will focus the remainder of the paper on a discussion of the relevance of interactional authenticity to the design of test tasks.

But before I discuss ways of increasing the relative interactional authenticity of test tasks, I present some examples of test tasks that vary in terms of their relative situational and interactional authenticity. This will accomplish a number of objectives, I hope. It will help the reader understand how actual test tasks differ in terms of their authenticity. It will also illustrate what Bachman and Palmer (in press) believe are some fundamental facts about authenticity. First, both situational and interactional authenticity are relative, so that we speak of "low" or "high" authenticity, rather than "authentic" and "inauthentic." Second, we cannot tell how authentic a test task is just by looking at it; we must also consider the characteristics of the test takers and the specific target language use context. Third, certain test tasks may be useful for their intended purposes, even though they are low in either situational or interactional authenticity. Finally, in either designing new tests or analyzing existing tests, estimates of authenticity are only best guesses. We can do our best to design test tasks that will be authentic for a given group of test takers, but we need to realize that different test takers may process the same test task in different ways, often in ways we may not anticipate.

The first example is from an institution abroad where Adrian Palmer and I once worked, in which some of the typists in our department did not understand English very well. Nevertheless they were excellent typists and produced high quality typescripts, even from handwritten documents. These typists had developed a high level of mechanical control of English, and this was all that was required for their job. A screening test for new typists in this situation might involve simply asking job applicants to type from a handwritten document. If the applicants knew that their on-the-job use of English would be limited to exactly this kind of typing, they would probably perceive the typing test as highly relevant to the job. Clearly, however, the test meets very few of the criteria for interactional authenticity. This example illustrates a test task which would be evaluated as highly situationally authentic but low in terms of interactional authenticity. The number *1* in the upper left corner of the diagram in Figure 4 indicates where this example test falls, in terms of authenticity. How useful is this test likely to be for its intended purpose? Probably quite useful.

FIGURE 4

Aspects of Authenticity

Interactional Authenticity

	Low	High
High	1	4
Low	3	2

We can use the same testing situation to invent a second example. Suppose for a moment that these applicants were capable of carrying on a conversation in English, and that we tested them by interviewing them in English. If the topics we talked about in the interview were of interest to them, the interview might actually involve the same types of interactions involved in nontest conversation. If we used the scores from this interview to select individuals whose sole use of English was to type from handwritten documents, how would this example rate with respect to authenticity? I would judge this task to be relatively low in situational authenticity and relatively high in interactional authenticity. The number *2* in the diagram indicates where this example falls. How useful is this test likely to be for predicting applicants' ability to type from handwritten documents? Probably not very useful.

For our third example, suppose we gave international students applying to U.S. universities a test of English vocabulary in which they were required to match words in one column with meanings in a second column. How does this stack up in terms of authenticity?

This task, I would say, is relatively low in both situational and interactional authenticity. The number 3 in the diagram shows where this example falls. How useful is this test likely to be in predicting readiness for academic study in English? Given the generally low predictive utility of language tests for forecasting academic achievement, it is difficult to say how useful this test might be.

One final example: Suppose we used a role play in which a prospective sales person was required to attempt to sell a product. The role play might involve a face-to-face oral conversation with an interlocutor who plays the role of a potential customer. The test taker might be required to engage the hypothetical customer in a conversation, decide what kind of approach to use in the selling task, and carry out the task. How authentic is this test task? I would rate this task as relatively high in both situational and interactional authenticity. The number 4 in the diagram indicates where this test task falls. How useful is this test likely to be in selecting successful sales persons? It could be quite useful, particularly if we included some criteria about successful completion of the task in the scoring.

INCREASING THE INTERACTIONAL AUTHENTICITY OF TEST TASKS

The four examples just given illustrate how test tasks can differ in their relative authenticity, and suggest how authenticity may be useful in evaluating existing tests. I now turn to considerations in designing and developing test tasks that are relatively interactionally authentic.

The two main steps in developing interactionally authentic test tasks are as follows:

1. For a given test task, assess the degree to which the strategies of language ability are involved in successfully completing the test task.

2. Explore ways of increasing the interaction of each strategy.

Assessing Levels of Interactional Authenticity

The involvement of the components of language ability in a given test task can be assessed in a number of ways. We could, for example, imagine ourselves to be typical test takers and then speculate about the levels of involvement of the strategies and areas of language knowledge. What specific areas of language knowledge will be engaged by the test task? Grammatical knowledge?

Sociolinguistic knowledge? What strategies will be evoked—assessment, planning—and to what extent? Another way of assessing interactional authenticity is through observing test takers and asking them to self-report on the strategies they used in attempting a given test task. This method of introspection is being used increasingly by language testing researchers to investigate the strategies used by test takers and how these strategies are related to test performance (e.g., Anderson et al., 1991; Cohen, 1984; Nevo, 1989).

Increasing Interactional Authenticity

Interactional authenticity can be increased, I believe, by increasing the level of involvement of the test taker's language ability. Bachman and Palmer (in press) suggest that this can be done by designing the test method characteristics of the test tasks to provide for the following: (a) requirement, (b) opportunity, (c) feasibility, and (d) interest. In order to assure that the strategies or given areas of language knowledge must be involved for successful completion of the test, one might set up tasks that cannot be done without their involvement. Opportunity for involvement may be provided by allocating adequate time or providing necessary information, tools, references, and so forth. Feasibility of involvement might be increased by adjusting the difficulty of the test task so that the involvement of the strategies and areas of language knowledge will be within the test takers' ability range. Finally, involvement of language ability may be increased by making test tasks interesting to test takers. In this regard, interest may be increased through increased situational authenticity.

Let me offer an example of how one might evaluate interactional authenticity and try to increase it for a specific writing test task. Suppose we want to develop a writing test as a final examination for a composition course. And suppose one procedure that comes to mind involves simply giving the candidates one hour to write a 250-word composition on a prescribed topic. Our initial task specification, or prompt, might simply be: "Write a 250 word composition describing your most frightening experience. You will not be graded on what you say. You will be graded on how well you express your ideas."

Assessment strategies. In this task candidates might assess their experiences with frightening situations and their ability to write about them. This could affect their choice of topics (goal-setting). As they write their essays, they might take some time to assess the correctness of their grammar and spelling. After finishing a draft of their essays, they might spend some time in revision and editing, which involve reassessment of the language produced. Since the instructions indicate that the essay will not be graded on content, however, the candidates might not reassess the information in the essay.

In this task the involvement of assessment is likely to be rather limited. Since the main focus of the task seems to be on how well the candidates express ideas, assessment is likely to be limited primarily to this domain. Moreover, since no detailed grading criteria are provided, the candidates are not prompted to assess what they have written in any particular areas. They might construe "how well you express your ideas" in the prompt to mean correct grammar and spelling. Of course, they may have a much richer set of internal criteria for assessment, both of content and of language, but nothing in the prompt specifically evokes this.

We could increase the involvement of assessment strategies in this task by providing more specific information in the prompt about the criteria for grading. We could also encourage test takers to go back and revise their writing, and provide adequate time for this.

Goal setting. In this example, test takers are assigned a topic, and the involvement of goal setting might be limited to picking a particular frightening experience to describe. They are given no purpose for writing the essay other than to produce something to be graded. And they are given no indication that what they say is of any importance. Their thinking is likely to be limited to "What can I write the best essay about?" Their emotions might be involved in this decision since the topic of the essay is about an emotional experience. On the other hand, the instructions state that the content of what is written will not influence the grade, and this might tend to cause test takers to minimize the importance of what they write, and hence their emotional involvement with it. Also, since the task does not require them to come up with anything new, it might not evoke feelings of interest, concern or excitement.

To increase the involvement of goal setting we might consider allowing the test taker a choice of topics to talk about, the choice to be made on the basis of what the test taker finds interesting. So we might provide the test taker with a list of topics including political, social, educational, and religious issues. We might also give the test taker a choice of purpose or intended audience.

Planning. In our example writing task, no instructions are given as to how to organize the essay or the role that organization plays in the grade the essay will receive. In addition, the task is such that a simple chronological organization would suffice, so the test taker might feel little need to do much planning. Because the task is one that requires little planning, the test taker needs to do very little formal organization of ideas. Thus, the way the task is specified (particularly the lack of indication that the essay needs to be well planned) is likely to result in little involvement of planning.

One way to increase the involvement of planning would be to explicitly state in the prompt that planning is part of the task, and then allowing test takers some time to organize and prepare their thoughts on the topic selected. We might even go so far as to require an outline as part of the test taker's response.

These examples suggest the following principles for increasing interactional authenticity of test tasks:

1. Tasks should consist of multiple, sequential subtasks.
2. Goal setting and planning should be required at the beginning of the task.
3. Request for and provision of feedback should be given at the end of each subtask.
4. Feedback should be used in subsequent subtasks.
5. There should be provision for changing goals and for additional planning.

Clearly, these principles are related to some of the features that have been included in the design of communicative language tests, as discussed in Part 1 above. An information gap can be created by including complementary types of information in different tasks. Information presented aurally via a videotape recording, for example, could be complemented by different information on the same topic presented visually in a reading passage. Another feature of communicative tests is that of task dependency. This can be built into language tests by sequencing tasks so that information generated in completing one task is used to complete subsequent tasks. Answers to listening and reading comprehension questions, for example, could provide the content for a writing task. These principles are consistent with much practice in the development of communicative language tests, and thus cannot be claimed to be original. Nevertheless, it is comforting to find that principles for the design and development of language tests that are derived from theoretical models of language ability and test method characteristics are in keeping with practice that is derived from language teaching.

CONCLUSION

I believe the framework for language testing presented here makes two contributions to the field. First, it grounds practical considerations in test design, development, and use firmly on a theoretical framework of the nature of language ability and test tasks, and thus provides a principled basis for making practical test development decisions. Second, and equally important, this framework enables us to specify and assess the relationship between language test performance and nontest language use, and thus provides a principled basis for addressing issues of validity and authenticity.
■

ACKNOWLEDGMENTS

I would like to thank Adrian Palmer for his useful comments and suggestions in preparing this paper. In particular, the material in Part 2 is largely the result of our collaborative effort to apply a theory of language test performance to the practical design and development of language tests. I also thank Charles Alderson and Peter Skehan for making available their recent reviews of language testing. I am grateful to Kari Sajavaara and Eduardo Cascallar for their valuable comments and suggestions with regard to metacognitive strategies. An earlier version of the second part of this paper was presented at the PennTESOL-East 1991 Spring Conference in Philadelphia, March 1991.

THE AUTHOR

Lyle F. Bachman is Professor of Applied Linguistics at the University of California, Los Angeles. His publications include journal articles in the areas of language testing and program evaluation. His book *Fundamental Considerations in Language Testing* (Oxford University Press) was awarded the 1991 Mildenberger Prize for outstanding research publication in foreign language teaching. His research interests include the development and validation of tests of communicative language ability, the analysis of test content, and the effects of test-taker characteristics on test performance.

REFERENCES

Alderman, D. L., & Holland, P. W. (1981). *Item performance across native language groups on the Test of English as a Foreign Language* (TOEFL Research Report No. 9). Princeton, NJ: Educational Testing Service.

Alderson, J. C. (1981a). Reaction to Morrow paper (3). In J. C. Alderson & A. Hughes (Eds.), *Issues in language testing* (ELT Documents No. 111, pp. 45-54). London: The British Council.

Alderson, J. C. (1981b). Report of the discussion on communicative language testing. In J. C. Alderson & A. Hughes (Eds.), *Issues in language testing* (ELT Documents No. 111, pp. 55-65). London: The British Council.

Alderson, J. C. (1986, January). Levels of reading comprehension: Do they exist? Paper delivered at Salford University, England.

Alderson, J. C. (1988a). *Innovation in language testing: Can the microcomputer help?* (Language Testing Update Special Report No. 1). Lancaster, England: Lancaster University, Institute for English Language Education.

Alderson, J. C. (1988b). New procedures for validating proficiency tests of ESP? Theory and practice. *Language Testing, 5*(2), 220-232.

Alderson, J. C. (1988c, March). Testing reading comprehension skills. In P. L. Carrell, J. Devine, & W. Grabe (Organizers), *Research in reading in a second language.* Colloquium conducted at the 22nd Annual TESOL Convention, Chicago, IL.

Alderson, J. C. (1990, March). *Judgements in language testing.* Paper presented at the 12th Annual Language Testing Research Colloquium, San Francisco, CA.

Alderson, J. C. (1991). Language testing in the 1990s: How far have we come? How much further have we to go? In S. Anivan (Ed.), *Current developments in language testing* (pp. 1-26). Singapore: SEAMEO Regional Language Centre.

Alderson, J. C., Foulkes, J., Clapham, C., & Ingram, D. (1990, March). *International English language testing service (IELTS).* Panel presented at the 12th Annual Language Testing Research Colloquium, San Francisco, CA.

Alderson, J. C., Henning, G., & Lukmani, Y. (1987, April). *Levels of understanding in reading comprehension tests.* Paper presented at the 9th Annual Language Testing Research Colloquium, Miami, FL.

Alderson, J. C., & Lukmani, Y. (1986, March). Reading in a second language. In D. E. Eskey, J. Devine, & P. L. Carrell (Organizers), *Research on reading in a second language.* Colloquium conducted at the 20th Annual TESOL Convention, Anaheim, CA.

Alderson, J. C., & Urquhart, A. H. (1985). The effect of students' academic discipline on their performance on ESP reading tests. *Language Testing, 2*(2), 192-204.

Anderson, N., Cohen, A., Perkins, K., & Bachman, L. (1991). An investigation of the relationships among test-taking strategies, item content, and item difficulty in an EFL reading test. *Language Testing, 8*(1), 41-66.

The Associated Examining Board. (1987). *Test in English for Educational Purposes (TEEP).* Aldershot, England: Author.

Bachman, L. F. (1988). Problems in examining the validity of the ACTFL oral proficiency interview. *Studies in Second Language Acquisition, 10*(2), 149-164.

Bachman, L. F. (1989). Language testing-SLA interfaces. In R. B. Kaplan (Ed.), *Annual Review of Applied Linguistics 1988* (pp. 193-209). New York: Cambridge University Press.

Bachman, L. F. (1990a). Assessment and evaluation. In R. B. Kaplan (Ed.), *Annual Review of Applied Linguistics 1989* (pp. 210-226). New York: Cambridge University Press.

Bachman, L. F. (1990b). *Fundamental considerations in language testing.* Oxford: Oxford University Press.

Bachman, L. F., Davidson, F., Lynch, B., & Ryan, K. (1989, March). *Content analysis and statistical modeling of EFL proficiency tests.* Paper presented at the 11th Annual Language Testing Research Colloquium, San Antonio, TX.

Bachman, L. F., Davidson, F., & Milanovic, M. (1991, March). *The use of test method characteristics in the content analysis and design of EFL proficiency tests.* Paper presented at the 13th Annual Language Testing Research Colloquium, Princeton, NJ.

Bachman, L. F., Davidson, F., Ryan, K., & Choi, I-C. (in press). *An investigation into the comparability of two tests of English as a foreign language: The Cambridge-TOEFL comparability study.* Cambridge: University of Cambridge Local Examinations Syndicate.

Bachman, L. F., Kunnan, A., Vanniarajan, S., & Lynch, B. (1988). Task and ability analysis as a basis for examining content and construct comparability in two EFL proficiency test batteries. *Language Testing,* 5(2), 128-159.

Bachman, L. F., & Palmer, A. S. (1981). The construct validation of the FSI oral interview. *Language Learning, 31*(1), 67-86.

Bachman, L. F., & Palmer, A. S. (1982). The construct validation of some components of communicative proficiency. *TESOL Quarterly, 16*(4), 449-465.

Bachman, L. F., & Palmer, A. S. (1988). The construct validation of self-ratings of communicative language ability. *Language Testing, 5*(2), 260-275.

Bachman, L. F., & Palmer, A. S. (in press). *Language testing in practice.* Oxford: Oxford University Press.

Bachman, L. F., & Savignon, S. (1986). The evaluation of communicative language proficiency: A critique of the ACTFL oral interview. *Modern Language Journal, 70*(4), 380-390.

Bialystok, E. (1990). *Communication strategies: A psychological analysis of second-language use.* Oxford: Basil Blackwell.

Bolus, R. E., Hinofotis, F. B., & Bailey, K. M. (1982). An introduction to generalizability theory in second language research. *Language Learning, 32*(2), 245-258.

Brindley, G. (1989). *Assessing achievement in the learner-centred curriculum.* Sydney, Australia: National Centre for English Language Teaching and Research.

Canale, M. (1983). On some dimensions of language proficiency. In J. W. Oller (Ed.), *Issues in language testing research* (pp. 333-342). Rowley, MA: Newbury House.

Canale, M. (1984). Testing in a communicative approach. In G. A. Jarvis (Ed.), *The challenge for excellence in foreign language education* (pp. 79-92). Middlebury, VT: The Northeast Conference Organization.

Canale, M. (1986). The promise and threat of computerized adaptive assessment of reading comprehension. In C. W. Stansfield (Ed.), *Technology and language testing* (pp. 29-45). Washington, DC: TESOL.

Canale, M., & Swain, M. (1980a). A domain description for core FSL: Communication skills. In *The Ontario assessment instrument pool: French as a second language, junior and intermediate divisions* (pp. 27-39). Toronto, Canada: Ontario Ministry of Education.

Canale, M., & Swain, M. (1980b). Theoretical bases of communicative approaches to second language teaching and testing. *Applied Linguistics, 1*(1), 1-47.

Candlin, C. (1986). Explaining communicative competence limits of testability? In C. W. Stansfield (Ed.), *Toward communicative competence testing: Proceedings of the second TOEFL invitational conference* (pp. 38-57). Princeton, NJ: Educational Testing Service.

Carroll, B. J. (1980). *Testing communicative performance.* London: Pergamon Institute of English.

Chapelle, C. (1988). Field independence: A source of language test variance? *Language Testing, 5*(1), 62-82.

Chapelle, C., & Roberts, C. (1986). Ambiguity tolerance and field dependence as predictors of proficiency in English as a second language. *Language Learning, 36*, 27-45.

Chen, Z., & Henning, G. (1985). Linguistic and cultural bias in language proficiency tests. *Language Testing, 2*(2), 155-163.

Clifford, R. T. (1981). Convergent and discriminant validation of integrated and unitary language skills: The need for a research model. In A. S. Palmer, P. J. M. Groot, & G. A. Trosper (Eds.), *The construct validation of tests of communicative competence* (pp. 62-70). Washington, DC: TESOL.

Cohen, A. D. (1984). On taking tests: What the students report. *Language Testing, 1*(1), 70-81.

Criper, C., & Davies, A. (1988). *ELTS validation project report.* London: The British Council and the University of Cambridge Local Examinations Syndicate.

Davies, A. (1977). The construction of language tests. In J. P. B. Allen & A. Davies (Eds.), *The Edinburgh course in applied linguistics: Vol. 4. Testing and experimental methods* (pp. 38-194). London: Oxford University Press.

de Jong, J. H. A. L., & Stevenson, D. K. (1990). *Individualizing the assessment of language abilities.* Clevedon, England: Multilingual Matters.

Erickson, M., & Molloy, J. (1983). ESP test development for engineering students. In J. W. Oller, Jr. (Ed.), *Issues in language testing research* (pp. 280-288). Rowley, MA: Newbury House.

Farhady, H. (1982). Measures of language proficiency from the learner's perspective. *TESOL Quarterly, 16*(1), 43-59.

Fouly, K. A. (1985). A confirmatory multivariate study of the nature of second language proficiency and its relationship to learner variables. Unpublished doctoral dissertation. University of Illinois at Urbana-Champaign.

Hansen, L. (1984). Field dependence-independence and language testing: Evidence from six Pacific Island cultures. *TESOL Quarterly, 18*(2), 311-324.

Hansen, J., & Stansfield, C. (1981). The relationship between field dependent-independent cognitive styles and foreign language achievement. *Language Learning, 31,* 349-367.

Harrison, A. (1983). Communicative testing: Jam tomorrow? In A. Hughes & D. Porter (Eds.), *Current developments in language testing* (pp. 77-85). London: Academic Press.

Henning, G. (1987). *A guide to language testing.* Cambridge, MA: Newbury House.

Hudson, T., & Lynch, B. (1984). A criterion-referenced measurement approach to ESL. *Language Testing, 1*(2), 171-201.

Ingram, D. E. (1984). *Australian second language proficiency ratings.* Canberra: Department of Immigration and Ethnic Affairs.

Kramsch, C. (1986). From language proficiency to interactional competence. *The Modern Language Journal, 70*(4), 366-372.

Lantolf, J. P., & Frawley, W. (1985). Oral proficiency testing: A critical analysis. *The Modern Language Journal, 69,* 337-345.

Lantolf, J. P., & Frawley, W. (1988). Proficiency: Understanding the construct. *Studies in Second Language Acquisition, 10*(2), 181-195.

Long, J. S. (1983a). *Confirmatory factor analysis.* Beverly Hills, CA: Sage.

Long, J. S. (1983b). *Covariance structure models: An introduction to LISREL.* Beverly Hills, CA: Sage.

Lowe, P., Jr. (1988). The unassimilated history. In P. Lowe, Jr. & C. W. Stansfield (Eds.), *Second language proficiency assessment: Current issues.* Englewood Cliffs, NJ: Prentice Hall.

Milanovic, M. (1988). *The construction and validation of a performance-based battery of English language progress tests.* Unpublished doctoral dissertation, London University, Institute of Education.

Morrow, K. (1977). *Techniques of evaluation for a notional syllabus.* London: Royal Society of Arts.

Morrow, K. (1979). Communicative language testing: Revolution or evolution? In C. J. Brumfit & K. Johnson (Eds.), *The communicative approach to language teaching* (pp. 143-157). Oxford: Oxford University Press.

Nevo, N. (1989). Test-taking strategies on a multiple-choice test of reading comprehension. *Language Testing, 6*(2), 199-215.

Oller, J. W., Jr. (1979). *Language tests at school: A pragmatic approach.* London: Longman.

Oller, J. W., Jr. (1983). A consensus for the eighties? In J. W. Oller, Jr. (Ed.), *Issues in language testing research* (pp. 351-356). Rowley, MA: Newbury House.

Perry, T., & Stansfield, C. W. (Eds.). (1990). *Language aptitude revisited.* Englewood Cliffs, NJ: Prentice Hall.

Pienemann, M., Johnston, M., & Brindley, G. (1988). Constructing an acquisition-based procedure for second language assessment. In A. Valdman (Ed.), *The assessment of foreign language proficiency* [Theme issue]. *Studies in Second Language Acquisition, 10,* 121-243.

Politzer, R. L., & McGroarty, M. (1985). An exploratory study of learning behaviors and their relationship to gains in linguistic and communicative competence. *TESOL Quarterly, 19*(1), 103-123.

Purcell, E. T. (1983). Models of pronunciation accuracy. In J. W. Oller, Jr. (Ed.), *Issues in language testing research* (pp. 133-151). Rowley, MA: Newbury House.

Ryan, K., & Bachman, L. F. (in press). Differential item functioning on two tests of EFL proficiency. *Language Testing.*

Sang, F., Schmitz, B., Vollmer, H. J., Baumert, J., & Roeder, P. M. (1986). Models of second language competence: A structural equation approach. *Language Testing, 3*(1), 54-79.

Savignon, S. J. (1985). Evaluation of communicative competence: The ACTFL provisional proficiency guidelines. *The Modern Language Journal, 69*(2), 129-134.

Seaton, I. (1983). The English Language Testing Service (ELTS): Two issues in the design of the new "non-academic module." In A. Hughes & D. Porter (Eds.), *Current developments in language testing* (pp. 129-139). London: Academic Press.

Shohamy, E. (1983). The stability of oral proficiency assessment on the oral interview testing procedures. *Language Learning, 33,* 527-540.

Shohamy, E. (1984). Does the testing method make a difference? The case of reading comprehension. *Language Testing, 1*(2), 147-170.

Skehan, P. (1988). State of the art article: Language testing I. *Language Teaching, 21*(4), 211-221.

Skehan, P. (1989). State of the art article: Language Testing II. *Language Teaching, 22*(1), 1-13.

Skehan, P. (1991). Progress in language testing: The 1990s. In J. C. Alderson & B. North (Eds.), *Language testing in the 1990s: The communicative legacy* (pp. 3-21). London: Modern English Publications and The British Council.

Spolsky, B. (1989). *Conditions for second language learning.* Oxford: Oxford University Press.

Stansfield, C. W. (Ed.). (1986). *Technology and language testing.* Washington, DC: TESOL.

Stansfield, C. W., & Hansen, J. (1983). Field dependence-independence as a variable in second language cloze test performance. *TESOL Quarterly, 17*(1), 29-38.

Stansfield, C. W., & Kenyon, D. M. (1988). *Development of the Portuguese speaking test.* Washington, DC: Center for Applied Linguistics.

Stansfield, C. W., & Kenyon, D. M. (1989). *Development of the Hausa, Hebrew, and Indonesian speaking tests.* Washington, DC: Center for Applied Linguistics.

Sternberg, R. J. (1985). *Beyond IQ: A triarchic theory of human intelligence*. New York: Cambridge University Press.

Sternberg, R. J. (1988). *The triarchic mind*. New York: Viking.

Swain, M. (1985). Large-scale communicative language testing: A case study. In Y. P. Lee, A. C. Y. Y. Fok, R. Lord, & G. Low (Eds.), *New directions in language testing* (pp. 35-46). Oxford: Pergamon Press.

Swinton, S., & Powers, D. E. (1980). *Factor analysis of the Test of English as a Foreign Language for several language groups* (TOEFL Research Rep. No. 6). Princeton, NJ: Educational Testing Service.

Tung, P. (1986). Computerized adaptive testing: Implications for language test developers. In C. W. Stansfield (Ed.), *Technology and language testing* (pp. 13-28). Washington, DC: TESOL.

Weir, C. J. (1983). The Associated Examining Board's Test of English for academic purposes: An exercise in content validation events. In A. Hughes & D. Porter (Eds.), *Current developments in language testing* (pp. 147-153). London: Academic Press.

Wesche, M., Canale, M., Cray, E., Jones, S., Mendelsohn, D., Tumpane, M., & Tyacke, M. (1987). *The Ontario Test of English as a Second Language (OESL): A report on the research*. Ottawa, Canada: Ontario Ministry of Colleges and Universities.

Widdowson, H. G. (1978). *Teaching language as communication*. Oxford: Oxford University Press.

Widdowson, H. G. (1983). *Learning purpose and language use*. London: Oxford University Press.

Wilds, C. P. (1975). The oral interview test. In R. L. Jones & B. Spolsky (Eds.), *Testing language proficiency* (pp. 29-38). Washington, DC: Center for Applied Linguistics.

Zeidner, M. (1986). Are English language aptitude tests biased towards culturally different minority groups? Some Israeli findings. *Language Testing, 3*(1), 80-95.

Zeidner, M. (1987). A comparison of ethnic, sex and age biases in the predictive validity of English language aptitude tests: Some Israeli data. *Language Testing, 4*(1), 55-71.

THE SKILL AREAS AND BEYOND

Current Developments in Second Language Reading Research

WILLIAM GRABE
Northern Arizona University

Both reading research and practice have undergone numerous changes in the 25 years since TESOL was first established. The last decade, in particular, has been a time of much first and second language research, resulting in many new insights for reading instruction. The purpose of this article is to bring together that research and its implications for the classroom. Current reading research follows from certain assumptions on the nature of the reading process; these assumptions are reviewed and general perspectives on the reading process are presented. Specific attention is then given to interactive approaches to reading, examining research which argues that reading comprehension is a combination of identification and interpretation skills. Reading research in second language contexts, however, must also take into account the many differences between L1 and L2 reading. From the differences reviewed here, it is evident that much more second language reading research is needed. Five important areas of current research which should remain prominent for this decade are reported: schema theory, language skills and automaticity, vocabulary development, comprehension strategy training, and reading-writing relations. Implications from this research for curriculum development are briefly noted.

Research on reading in a second language and efforts to improve second language reading instruction have grown remarkably in the past quarter century, particularly in the last 10 years. It has become difficult to synthesize the array of research and instructional literature in ESL/EFL academic reading, foreign language reading, and second language public school student reading, in addition to the relevant first language reading literature. The efforts to address the needs of many different learner groups has been one cause of this expansion. The recognition that reading is probably the most important skill for second language learners in academic contexts has also been a contributing cause (Carrell, 1989a; Lynch & Hudson,

1991). Finally, the challenge to explore and understand basic comprehension processes has contributed significantly to implications for second language reading instruction. In this article, the primary goal will be to synthesize the reading research which impacts L2 academic reading instruction, recognizing that there are other significant areas of second language reading which require separate discussion (cf. Edelsky, 1986; Edelsky, Altwerger, & Flores, 1991; Gee, 1990; Gunderson, 1991; and Weber, 1991, for discussions of U.S. language-minority students; cf. Bell & Burnaby, 1984; Crandall, in press; and Mickulecky & Newman, 1988, for discussions of adult basic literacy).

A BRIEF HISTORY

Our understanding of reading, both in terms of theory and practice, has changed considerably in the 25 years that the TESOL organization has been in existence. These transitions and changes, both in theory and in practice, are best documented in Silberstein (1987). In the mid- to late 1960s, as Silberstein notes, reading was seen as little more than a reinforcement for oral language instruction. Under the influence of audiolingualism, most efforts to "teach" reading were centered on the use of reading to examine grammar and vocabulary, or to practice pronunciation (Silberstein, 1987). This view of reading was challenged by two major changes, one related to changing ESL institutional needs, the other related to the changing views of reading theory.

In the late 1960s, ESL student enrollment at U.S. and British tertiary institutions increased dramatically. One outcome of this demographic shift was the need to prepare a large number of ESL students with the advanced academic skills required for the university level. The audiolingual method, with its emphasis on oral language skills, was unable to address this need. On a practical level, then, ESL instruction changed in the early 1970s to emphasize advanced reading and writing instruction, albeit without a strong theoretical framework to guide practice (cf. Harris, 1966; Yorkey, 1970). Through the early to mid-1970s, a number of researchers and teacher trainers argued for the greater importance of reading (e.g., Eskey, 1973; Saville-Troike, 1973). By the mid- to late 1970s, many researchers began to argue for a theory of reading based on work by Goodman (1967, 1985) and Smith (1971, 1979, 1982).

The research and persuasive arguments of Goodman and Smith evolved into a "psycholinguistic model of reading." Goodman's research led him to propose that reading is not primarily a process of picking up information from the page in a letter-by-letter, word-by-word manner. Rather, he argued that reading is a selective process. Since it did not seem likely that fluent readers had the time to look at all the words on a page and still read at a rapid rate, it made sense that good readers used knowledge they brought to the reading and then read by predicting information, sampling the text, and confirming the prediction. Smith concurred with Goodman's arguments that reading was an imprecise, hypothesis-driven process. He further argued that sampling was effective because of the extensive redundancy built into natural language as well as the abilities of readers to make the necessary inferences from their background knowledge. In effect, for Smith (and others), the reader contributed more than did the visual symbols on the page.

Two efforts to translate this theory into ESL contexts have been extremely influential on ESL reading theory and instruction from the late 1970s to the present. Clarke and Silberstein (1977) outlined implications for instruction which could be drawn from a psycholinguistic model of reading. Reading was characterized as an active process of comprehending and students needed to be taught strategies to read more efficiently (e.g., guess from context, define expectations, make inferences about the text, skim ahead to fill in the context, etc.). For teachers, the goal of reading instruction was to provide students with a range of effective approaches to texts— including helping students define goals and strategies for reading, to use prereading activities to enhance conceptual readiness, and to provide students strategies to deal with difficult syntax, vocabulary, and organizational structure. It should be noted that many of these instructional implications still remain as important guidelines though no longer motivated by the psycholinguistic model explanation.

Coady (1979) reinterpreted Goodman's psycholinguistic model into a model more specifically suited to second language learners. Coady argued that a conceptualization of the reading process re- quires three components: process strategies, background knowl- edge, and conceptual abilities. Beginning readers focus on process strategies (e.g., word identification), whereas more proficient read- ers shift attention to more abstract conceptual abilities and make better use of background knowledge, using only as much textual in- formation as needed for confirming and predicting the information in the text. His implications for teaching are similar to those of Clarke and Silberstein (1977).

While the 1970s was a time of transition from one dominant view of reading to another, the 1980s was a decade in which much ESL reading theory and practice extended Goodman and Smith's per- spectives on reading (cf. Bernhardt, 1991). At the same time, second language research began to look more closely at other first language reading research for the insights that it could offer. It is with the 1980s, also, that this article will take up the issue of reading theory in first language research.

READING AND THE READING PROCESS

Most of our current views of second language reading are shaped by research on first language learners. This is true in part because first language research has a longer history, first language student populations are much more stable, cognitive psychology has seen comprehension research as a major domain of their field, and considerable cognitive psychology and educational grant funding is available. For these reasons, first language reading research has made impressive progress in learning about the reading process. It makes good sense, then, for second language researchers and teachers to consider what first language research has to say about the nature of the fluent reading process and the development of reading abilities. A primary goal for ESL reading theory and instruction is to understand what fluent L1 readers do, then decide how best to move ESL students in that developmental direction. A reasonable starting point for this discussion is with definitions of reading.

It is well known that simple definitions typically misrepresent complex cognitive processes such as reading. Rather, descriptions of basic knowledge and processes required for fluent reading make a more appropriate starting point. A description of reading has to account for the notions that fluent reading is rapid, purposeful, interactive, comprehending, flexible, and gradually developing (cf. Anderson, Hiebert, Scott, & Wilkinson, 1985; Grabe, 1988b; Hall, White, & Guthrie, 1986; Smith, 1982).

Research has argued that fluent reading is *rapid*; the reader needs to maintain the flow of information at a sufficient rate to make connections and inferences vital to comprehension. Reading is *purposeful*; the reader has a purpose for reading, whether it is for entertainment, information, research, and so on. Reading for a purpose provides motivation—an important aspect of being a good reader. Reading is *interactive*; the reader makes use of information from his/her background knowledge as well as information from the printed page. Reading is also interactive in the sense that many skills work together simultaneously in the process. Reading is *comprehending*; the reader typically expects to understand what s/he is reading. Unlike many ESL students, the fluent reader does not begin to read wondering whether or not s/he will understand the text. Reading is *flexible*; the reader employs a range of strategies to read efficiently. These strategies include adjusting the reading speed, skimming ahead, considering titles, headings, pictures and text structure information, anticipating information to come, and so on. Finally, reading *develops gradually*; the reader does not become fluent suddenly, or immediately following a reading development course. Rather, fluent reading is the product of long-term effort and gradual improvement.

The preceding general description of fluent reading suggests that reading is very complex, that it takes considerable time and resources to develop, and that it cannot simply be taught in one or two courses. This perspective holds equally well for ESL students who are not already fluent readers in English but who need to be for their academic future.

COMPONENT SKILLS IN READING

Because reading is such a complex process, many researchers attempt to understand and explain the fluent reading process by analyzing the process into a set of component skills (e.g., Carpenter & Just, 1986; Carr & Levy, 1990; Haynes & Carr, 1990; Rayner & Pollatsek, 1989). The effort to subdivide into component skills has led researchers to propose at least six general component skills and knowledge areas:

1. Automatic recognition skills
2. Vocabulary and structural knowledge
3. Formal discourse structure knowledge
4. Content/world background knowledge
5. Synthesis and evaluation skills/strategies
6. Metacognitive knowledge and skills monitoring

The development of *automatic perceptual/identification skills* is only beginning to be recognized as important in second language reading (McLaughlin, 1990), but they are widely recognized by cognitive psychologists and educational psychologists as central processes in fluent reading (e.g., Adams, 1990; Carr & Levy, 1990; Rayner & Pollatsek, 1989; Rieben & Perfetti, 1991). In fact, many cognitive psychologists now see the development of automaticity in reading, particularly in word identification skills, as critical to fluent reading (Adams, 1990; Beck & McKeown, 1986; Gough & Juel, 1991; Perfetti, 1991; Stanovich, 1986, 1991).

Automaticity may be defined as occurring when the reader is unaware of the process, not consciously controlling the process, and using little processing capacity (Adams, 1990; Just & Carpenter, 1987; Stanovich, 1990). The primary focus of automaticity research has been at the feature, letter, and word levels, playing a crucial role in descriptions of lexical access skills of fluent readers. Many researchers now believe that automatic lexical access is a necessary skill for fluent readers, and many less-skilled readers lack automaticity in lower-level processing. In fact, cognitive psychologists now argue that the lexical component of fluent readers becomes encapsulated; that is, the process of lexical access during reading does not make use of contextual resources (Stanovich, 1990). The question of whether syntactic structures fall within the notion of automatic recognition is currently being debated (e.g., Flores d'Arcais, 1990; Perfetti, 1990; Rayner & Pollatsek, 1989); Perfetti (1990) has argued that the syntactic parser creates an autonomously driven initial structure which is then open to semantic and discourse contextual effects.

Vocabulary and syntactic knowledge, on a very basic level, are obviously critical to reading. One needs only to pick up a newspaper in an unknown language to verify that background knowledge and predicting are severely constrained by the need to know vocabulary and structure. On a less obvious level, knowledge of structure has an important facilitative effect on reading (Garnham, 1985; Perfetti, 1989; Rayner, 1990; Tannenhaus, 1988). In second language contexts, the role of language structure in comprehension has also been supported (Barnett, 1986; Berman, 1984; Devine, 1988; Eskey, 1988; Swaffar, Arens, & Byrnes, 1991).

Vocabulary knowledge has similarly come to be recognized as a critical feature of reading ability (Koda, 1989; McKeown & Curtis, 1987; Nagy, 1988; Nation & Coady, 1988; Stanovich, 1986; Strother & Ulijn, 1987). In first language reading, researchers have estimated recognition vocabularies of fluent readers to range from 10,000 words to 100,000 words (Anderson & Freebody, 1981; Chall, 1987; Nagy & Herman, 1987). Vocabulary discussions in second language reading argue for far lower total numbers of words, often positing 2,000–7,000 words (Coady, 1983; Kyongho & Nation, 1989; Nation, 1990; Swaffar, 1988). The need to read fluently, in a manner similar to a good L1 reader, would seem to require a knowledge of vocabulary more in line with the larger estimates for first language readers (cf. Beck, McKeown, & Omanson, 1987; Goulden, Nation, & Read, 1990). The consequence of these arguments is that fluent readers need a sound knowledge of language structure and a large recognition vocabulary.

Readers need a good knowledge of *formal discourse structure* (formal schemata). There is considerable evidence that knowing how a text is organized influences the comprehension of the text. For example, good readers appear to make better use of text organization than do poor readers, write better recalls by recognizing and using the same organizational structure as the text studied, and, generally, recall information better from certain types of text organization such as comparison-contrast (Nist & Mealey, 1991; Richgels, McGee, Lomax, & Sheard, 1987). Similar research in second language contexts has replicated the major findings while also revealing interesting specific differences. For example, Carrell (1984a) has shown that more specific logical patterns of organization, such as cause-effect, compare-contrast, and problem-solution, improve recall compared to texts organized loosely around a collection of facts.

Content and background knowledge (content schemata) also has a major influence on reading comprehension. A large body of literature has argued that prior knowledge of text-related information strongly affects reading comprehension (Anderson & Pearson, 1984; Bransford, Stein, & Shelton, 1984; Kintsch & van Dijk, 1978; Wilson & Anderson, 1986). Similarly, cultural knowledge has been shown to influence comprehension (Carrell, 1984b; Pritchard, 1990; Steffenson & Joag-Dev, 1984). Recent efforts to explore the interaction of formal and content knowledge as they influence comprehension has been studied by Roller (1990) and Carrell (1987). In both L1 and L2 contexts, formal and content knowledge play important if somewhat different roles in reading comprehension.

Fluent readers not only seek to comprehend a text when they read, they also evaluate the text information and compare/ synthesize it with other sources of information/knowledge. Thus, *synthesis and evaluation skills and strategies* are critical components of reading abilities. It is also in this context that discussions of "predicting from the text" play a crucial role. Given the real-time constraints of the reading process, fluent readers typically do not use prediction to decide upcoming words in texts or to access words; rather, prediction helps readers anticipate later text development and the author's perspective with respect to the information presented. In this way, predicting information allows us to evaluate the information; take a position with respect to the author's intentions; and decide whether or not the information is useful. Little research actually exists on how readers evaluate texts; that is, how readers might find texts persuasive, interesting, boring, exciting, and so on, and how these evaluations relate to reading comprehension, recall, formal and content schemata, first language background, and readers' prior expectations.

Metacognitive knowledge and skills monitoring is the final important component of fluent reading skills. Metacognitive knowledge may be defined as knowledge about cognition and the self-regulation of cognition (Baker & Brown, 1984; Brown, Armbruster, & Baker, 1986). Knowledge about cognition, including knowledge about language, involves recognizing patterns of structure and organization, and using appropriate strategies to achieve specific goals (e.g., comprehending texts, remembering information). As related to reading, this would include recognizing the more important information in a text; adjusting reading rate; using context to sort out a misunderstood segment; skimming portions of the text; previewing headings, pictures, and summaries; using search strategies for finding specific information; formulating questions about the information; using a dictionary; using word-formation and affix information to guess word meanings; taking notes; underlining; summarizing information; and so on. Monitoring of cognition involves recognizing problems with information presented in texts or an inability to achieve expected goals (e.g., recognizing an illogical summary or awareness of noncomprehension). Self-regulation strategies would include planning ahead, testing self-comprehension, checking effectiveness of strategies being used, revising strategies being used, and so on. N. Anderson (1991), Barnett (1989), and Cohen (1990) have compiled large lists of reading strategies which combine cognitive strategy use and monitoring.

The ability to use metacognitive skills effectively is widely recognized as a critical component of skilled reading. In numerous studies it has been shown that good readers are more effective in using metacognitive skills than less fluent readers. (There is also a developmental factor involved, with older readers making better use of metacognitive skills than younger readers.) In the last 10 years, there has been considerable research on the role of metacognitive strategies in reading and the feasibility of improving these strategies through direct training and instruction (e.g., Lysynchuk, Pressley, & Vye, 1990; Nist & Mealey, 1991; Palincsar & Brown, 1984; Pressley, Johnson, Symons, McGoldrick, & Kurita, 1989). Similarly, second language research has focused attention on the effectiveness of strategy training for improved reading comprehension (e.g., Barnett, 1989; Carrell, Pharis, & Liberto, 1989; Cohen, 1990; Kern, 1989; Swaffar, Arens, & Byrnes, 1991).

A "reading components" perspective is an appropriate research direction to the extent that such an approach leads to important insights into the reading process. In this respect, it is evident that a component skills approach, at least in the broad sense outlined here, is indeed a useful approach. A second basic approach to understanding reading has been to interpret the reading process by means of simple controlling metaphors. The three popular metaphors to dominate reading refer generally to reading processes: bottom-up (primary emphasis on textual decoding), top-down (primary emphasis on reader interpretation and prior knowledge), and interactive processing. There have been a number of overviews of these three perspectives on reading (e.g., Barnett, 1989; Grabe, 1988a; Samuels & Kamil, 1984; Silberstein, 1987; Swaffar, Arens, & Byrnes, 1991). Given the extensive treatment accorded to these issues, this review will focus specifically on interactive approaches to reading—a perspective on reading which seems to generate almost as much confusion as it does insights.

INTERACTIVE APPROACHES TO READING

In general, the term *interactive approaches* can refer to two different conceptions. First, it can refer to the general interaction which takes place between the reader and the text. The basic concept is that the reader (re)constructs the text information based in part on the knowledge drawn from the text and in part from the prior knowledge available to the reader (Barnett, 1989; Carrell & Eisterhold, 1983). Second, the term *interactive approaches* refers to the interaction of many component skills potentially in simultaneous operation; the interaction of these cognitive skills leads to fluent reading comprehension. Simply stated, reading involves both an array of lower-level rapid, automatic identification skills and an array of higher-level comprehension/interpretation skills (Carrell, 1988b, 1989a; Eskey, 1986; Eskey & Grabe, 1988; Rayner & Pollatsek, 1989; Samuels & Kamil, 1984). The two perspectives are complementary, though discussions in the literature tend to stress one perspective over the other, or ignore one of the two perspectives altogether. In fact, most cognitive psychologists and education psychologists stress the interaction-of-skills arrays; in contrast, most second language researchers stress the interaction between the reader and the text. A major factor contributing to this division is the differing degrees of emphasis placed on defining how processes interact and how such processes can be studied through research.

In first language reading research, a major concern involves how to stipulate explicitly the relations among specific skills and how such relations can be examined. One result of this research direction has been to deemphasize explanations which are not explicitly testable or definable within a theory of reading. Thus, cognitive psychologists and psycholinguists such as Adams (1990), Perfetti (1985), and Rayner and Pollatsek (1989) question the explanatory usefulness of top-down inferential and schema-driven explanations for reading ability. Schema theory is a theoretical metaphor for the reader's prior knowledge. Others even question the role of schema theory itself as a research theory explaining memory organization (Garnham, 1985; Iran-Nejad, 1987; Kintsch, 1988; Schacter, 1989). Aside from the fact that we know we can call up prior knowledge from long-term memory, and that information seems to be integrated in efficient ways, it is difficult to know exactly how this prior knowledge is called up and used. The notion that our long-term memory is organized by *stable* schema structures does not appear to be strongly supported by current research. While no one doubts the need to account for the role of prior knowledge and inference making in reading comprehension, many researchers question theories which cannot be explicitly defined.[1] This critique of schema theory has not been a major concern of second language researchers, and the notion of schemata remains a useful metaphorical explanation for many experimental results (e.g., why prereading activities improve reading recall).

An interactive approach clearly has to account for the evidence that has accumulated in the last decade. Most current versions of interactive approaches to reading have taken a strong bottom-up orientation to the processing of lower-level linguistic structure (e.g., Gough, 1985; Perfetti, 1985, 1990; Rayner & Pollatsek, 1989; Stanovich, 1990). The reasons for this orientation follow from extensive research on eye movement as well as from observed minimal context effects on feature, letter, and word recognition, and initial syntactic parsing of sentences. This review will not pursue arguments for a modular approach to lexical access or sentence parsing (cf. Balota, Flores d'Arcais, & Rayner, 1990;

---

[1] A similar skepticism has been leveled at earlier cognitive psychology models which proposed massively interactive connections (e.g., Rumelhart, 1977); that is to say, potentially everything can connect with everything. However, these massively interactive models have continued to be influential due to the advent of computer modeling with recent versions of the interactive-activation model (a parallel distributed processing model) (McClelland, 1987; Taraban & McClelland, 1990). At present, the debate has centered around the notions of modularity of processing components (e.g., lexical access not using external context information) versus strongly interactive connections among processing components (e.g., information from every level assists all processes). Efforts to account for a wider range of the evidence has led to modified views on modularity and connectionism (e.g., Kintsch, 1988; Norris, 1990; Perfetti, 1990; Stanovich, 1990). One interesting extension to the connectionism versus modularity debate has been the current exchange over whether a process such as lexical access exists, or if the lexicon itself even exists as a set of symbolic-level entries (Seidenberg, 1990; Seidenberg & McClelland, 1989, 1990; cf. Besner, 1990; Besner, Twilley, McCann, & Seergobin, 1990; Neumann, 1990). The point of this digression into connectionism and modularity is to recognize that many notions commonly assumed in second language theory are currently being debated quite heatedly in cognitive psychology.

Perfetti & McCutchen, 1987; Stanovich, 1990). Instead, it is sufficient to review evidence which will argue that bottom-up processing contributes importantly to fluent reading.

Recent research on eye movements in reading has demonstrated that fluent readers read most words on a page. These studies show that some 80% of content words and 40% of function words are directly focused on in reading. The point is that we typically do not guess or sample texts, nor is reading an approximative skill. Rather, reading is a very precise and very rapid skill (Adams, 1990; Carpenter & Just, 1986; Rayner & Pollatsek, 1989). The reason readers are so fast is not because they guess well but because they can identify the vast majority of words automatically. As Stanovich (1991) notes,

> It is not that the good reader relies less on visual information, but that the visual analysis mechanisms of the good reader use less capacity. Good readers are efficient processors in every sense: They completely sample the visual array *and* use fewer resources to do so. (p. 21)

Eye movement research has also demonstrated that the visual span in reading is limited; that is, readers are capable of seeing no more than 3-4 letters to the left of fixation point and 10-12 letters to the right (Carpenter & Just, 1986; Mitchell, 1982; Rayner & Pollatsek, 1989). One consequence of this finding is that training notions such as reading broadly (taking in longer segments of text in a single fixation) may have limited usefulness. Learners who do not make use of their full foveal (directly focused) vision may be helped, but only up to the point of 15-16 letter spans. A second consequence of this research is that readers do not see very much beyond the focusing area; thus, readers' eye movements tend to be limited by the need to take in information every 10-15 letter spaces. (This explanation is a simplification; see Rayner & Pollatsek, 1989, for a more accurate explanation.)

Eye movement research has been important in at least two other respects. First, it has shown that most words are recognized before higher-level (nonautomatic) context information can be used to influence lexical access (Just & Carpenter, 1987; Stanovich, 1980, 1981; van Dijk & Kintsch, 1983). Second, it has been shown that eye movement itself, from one fixation point to the next, tends to be automatically controlled in normal fluent reading rather than be under the direct control of some attentional strategy. The eye typically moves to the next longer word rather than sampling words selectively. (See Rayner & Pollatsek, 1989, for a more detailed and accurate explanation.)

Apart from eye movement studies, research on word recognition and lexical access has shown that readers take in letter features of short words simultaneously and that readers seem to recognize all the letters in a word. This conclusion suggests that readers are not only extremely rapid in their recognition skills but they are precise as well. The ability to recognize words rapidly and accurately has been seen as an important predictor of reading ability, particularly with young readers (Adams, 1990; Perfetti, 1985; Stanovich, 1986). While this ability has been characterized as a limited causal factor in reading ability, word recognition accounts for a good share of variance even in the reading abilities of college-level students (Cunningham, Stanovich, & Wilson, 1990; Gough & Tunmer, 1986; Perfetti, 1985).

A review of this research suggests that identification skills are extremely important for fluent readers. Thus, an interactive approach to reading is one that takes into account the critical contributions of both lower-level processing skills (identification) and higher-level comprehension and reasoning skills (interpretation). Exactly how these levels of skills interact is a question which is beyond the scope of this paper, though consistent evidence has been presented which suggests that word and subword identification processes become impervious to context information as these skills become automatized (Rayner & Pollatsek, 1989; Stanovich, 1990).

READING IN A SECOND LANGUAGE

Reading in a second language is influenced by factors which are normally not considered in L1 reading research. These factors may be divided into L2 acquisition and training background differences, language processing differences, and social context differences. *L2 acquisition and training differences* refer to the fact that second language students begin the L2 reading process with very different knowledge from L1 readers. First language learners have already learned somewhere on the order of 5,000 to 7,000 words before they formally begin reading instruction in schools (Singer, 1981). They also have a good intuitive sense of the grammar of the language. L2 learners typically have not already learned a large store of oral language vocabulary; nor do they have a fairly complete sense of the grammar of the language.

Second language students also have certain advantages. Since most academically oriented ESL learners are older than L1 learners, they have a more well-developed conceptual sense of the world; they have considerably more factual knowledge about the world;

and they can make elaborate logical inferences from the text. As a consequence, vocabulary becomes largely a matter of remembering a second label for a well-understood concept. Older ESL students will tend to make more use of metacognitive strategies in their learning as well, making them more efficient learners. ESL students also tend to be motivated by instrumental as well as integrative goals, which improves learning in formal classroom contexts.

Transfer effects from *language processing differences* can also cause difficulties for L2 students. On a very basic level, transfer effects caused by false cognates or near cognates can influence vocabulary recognition. Students' L1 syntactic knowledge can also cause interference. Word order variation, relative clause formation, complex noun phrase structures, and other complex structural differences between languages can mislead the ESL reader, particularly at beginning stages.

Orthographic differences between a student's L1 and English have often been cited as a likely cause of additional difficulties. While this may be true for beginning readers, it is less clear for advanced readers of English. It appears that direction-of-reading differences cause little difficulty, though it is not possible to set up definitive experiments that would isolate this factor (Rayner & Pollatsek, 1989). Punctuation and spacing of written forms also differ across languages but do not seem to disadvantage any linguistic group. Differences between languages with shallow and deep orthographic structure (very regular sound-letter correspondences versus many irregular sound-letter correspondences) have been discussed as a potential source of difficulty for some ESL students. Thus, students from a Spanish language background might have word recognition problems with English, which is less transparently phonemic. Some researchers have suggested that readers of shallow orthographic languages prefer to recode words into sounds before lexical access, arguing that direct lexical access from the orthography would be inefficient (Turvey, Feldman, & Lukatela, 1984). Other researchers have argued that even in languages with shallow orthographies, direct lexical access is an efficient strategy (Besner & Hildebrandt, 1987). Overall, orthographic transparency differences do not appear to lead to different fluent reading strategies (Just & Carpenter, 1987; Rayner & Pollatsek, 1989).

Orthographic influences in reading due to logographic, syllabic, or alphabetic writing systems have also been examined. Logographic writing systems do seem to favor lexical access through direct recognition of word forms, though phonological activation appears to play an important role in word recognition among fluent

L1 readers of Japanese and Chinese (Just & Carpenter, 1987; Rayner & Pollatsek, 1989; cf. discussion of L1 transfer influences in Koda, 1987, 1989). Syllabic systems, such as Hebrew (written without vowels), since they are also less phonemically transparent, tend to favor direct lexical access, though syllabic languages also access words through phonological recoding as well (Bentin, Bargai, & Katz, 1984). Rayner & Pollatsek (1989), summarizing the current research evidence, argue that orthographic differences in languages may have some effect on the preferred route for lexical access, but each language combines direct lexical access with phonological access to words, and fluent readers in all orthographically different languages appear to read texts equally rapidly. (See also Hung & Tzeng, 1981; Just & Carpenter, 1987.)

Linguistic differences at syntactic and discourse levels are more likely to have an influence on reader comprehension, though our ability to test this directly becomes more difficult as issues address higher-level reading processes. Research by Bernhardt (1987), using eye-movement studies of German readers, has found that German readers focus more attention on function words than do fluent readers in English. This may suggest that readers of German need to pay more attention to the syntactic information encoded into functional words. English readers, in contrast, seem to focus more attention on content words. Whether or not such differences would cause problems for ESL readers from a German background is an open question at present. Mitchell, Cuetos, & Zagar (1990) have argued that syntactic parsing strategies may vary according to different languages. They claim that certain strategies for reading will be language-specific rather than universal. (See also Flores d'Arcais, 1990.) It is not clear at present how their findings would affect the second language reader. On the discourse level, Carrell (1984a) found that students from different language backgrounds (Spanish, Asian, Arabic) were able to recall information better depending on different organizational structures of texts. She concludes that different cultures may prefer different ways of organizing information; thus, comprehension of texts may be culturally dependent according to the logical organization of the text.

Differences in reading abilities of ESL students may also be attributed to the *social contexts* of literacy use in students' first languages. A first issue would be the extent of literacy skills students have in their first language. ESL research on reading seldom investigates whether or not students in research studies read equally well in their first languages. Since large differences in reading abilities can be found in contexts in which homogeneous population are assumed, such as in composition courses in U.S. universities, it is not unreasonable to raise this issue in ESL reading research.

Assuming that students have relatively similar reading skills in their first languages, a further question can be posed: To what extent do students use, interpret, or value reading material in their first language? Students who come from cultures where written material represents "truth" might tend not to challenge or reinterpret texts in light of other texts, but will tend to memorize "knowledge." Students who have not had easy access to libraries might be less likely to look for alternative sources of information or question the relative strengths and weaknesses of the texts they encounter. Students who come from communities with limited literacy among the population may downplay the importance of literacy skills and do little extensive reading (Smithies, 1983). In contrast to all of these contexts, literacy in academic settings in developed countries exists within the context of a massive amount of print information. Students come to assume that any source of information can be balanced against alternative sources, and come to expect that challenging a text is a normal academic activity. These students have a distinctly different set of expectations about reading and how texts can be used than do students who have not been socialized in this way. In sum, the social context of students' uses of reading in their first languages, and their access to texts, may have a profound effect on their abilities to develop academic reading skills in English.

Given these differences in second language reading, findings from research with first language students cannot always be applied directly to L2 contexts. (See also Bernhardt, 1991.) Because ESL students are distinct from L1 students (and from each other), research on second language students is essential. In the section to follow, five areas of important and current second language research will be reviewed. Aside from the currency of the research, each area provides important insights for ESL instruction; the improvements in reading instruction resulting from this research demonstrate the importance and vitality of second language reading research.

RECENT RESEARCH IN SECOND LANGUAGE READING

Schema Theory

In spite of the fact that schema theory is not a well-defined framework for the mental representation of knowledge (Garnham, 1985; Kintsch, 1988; Rayner & Pollatsek, 1989), it has been an extremely useful notion for describing how prior knowledge is integrated in memory and used in higher-level comprehension processes (Anderson & Pearson, 1984). Further, implications of schema theory have proven to be very useful in improving reading instruction. This practical insight, along with the intuitive appeal of schema theory, has made it a major focus for research on ESL reading in the 1980s.

Carrell (1984b, 1987) and Carrell and Eisterhold, 1983, have investigated the usefulness of the notion of schema theory for second language reading. This research has found that activating content information plays a major role in students' comprehension and recall of information from a text. Carrell (1987; cf. Barnett, 1989) has also investigated the importance of formal schemata— structures of knowledge about language and textual organization— and has found this to be a significant independent contributor to reading ability. Carrell (1988b) has also argued that a lack of schema activation is one major source of processing difficulty with second language readers. This has been verified not only through culture-specific text comparisons but also in discipline-specific comparisons of readers with familiar and less familiar background knowledge (Alderson & Urquhart, 1988; Strother & Ulijn, 1987).

Schema theory has provided a strong rationale for both prereading activities and comprehension strategy training (Carrell, 1985, 1988a; Floyd & Carrell, 1987). Other research on schema theory has argued that a high degree of background knowledge can overcome linguistic deficiencies (e.g., Hudson, 1982). The major implication to be drawn from this research is that students need to activate prior knowledge of a topic before they begin to read. If students do not have sufficient prior knowledge, they should be given at least minimal background knowledge from which to interpret the text (Barnett, 1989; Carrell, 1988a; Dubin & Bycina, 1991).

"Holding in the Bottom" and Automaticity

One reaction to the overemphasis on top-down models of reading in second language contexts has been a reconsideration of the importance of lower-level processes in reading (e.g., letter, feature, word, and syntactic processing). This view also examines research on reading in L1 contexts which has stressed the importance of lower-level processes in reading (Carpenter & Just, 1986; Perfetti, 1985; Stanovich, 1986).

Eskey (1988), McLaughlin (1990), and Segalowitz (1991) have all stressed the importance of automatic lower-level processing in second language contexts. Less proficient readers often appear to be word-bound, and this phenomenon is often taken as evidence that students are "stuck" on words. Previous perspectives on this language problem argued, in keeping with the psycholinguistic model of reading, that students were not sampling rapidly enough and were afraid to make guesses, to take chances. More current views of this learner problem argue that students are word-bound precisely because they are not yet efficient in bottom-up processing. The problem is that students do not simply recognize the words rapidly and accurately but are consciously attending to the graphic form (and in many second language texts there are often far too many new forms for students to attend to efficiently). No amount of guessing, which many poorer students actually seem to be good at, will overcome this deficiency and lead to automatic word recognition. Thus, while all researchers can agree on the problem, the presumed cause of the problem—and what to do about it—has changed considerably in the last decade (Eskey & Grabe, 1988; Segalowitz, 1991; Stanovich, 1986).

Related to the automaticity issue is the recognition that syntactic and vocabulary knowledge are critical components of reading comprehension (Berman, 1984; Carrell, 1989a; Eskey, 1986; Koda, 1989; Swaffar, 1988). Many researchers refer to the L2 studies which posit a language threshold for second language reading abilities (Clarke, 1980; Devine, 1987; cf. Kern, 1989). From this perspective, below a language proficiency threshold, comprehension processes which are used in students' L1 reading are not used as effectively in their L2 reading; thus, language is seen to play a critical role in second language reading abilities. One possible consequence of this view is to see reading fundamentally as a language process rather than primarily as a thinking process (e.g., Perfetti, 1985; cf. Alderson & Lukmani, 1989). Most second language researchers, however, prefer to propose a balance between language and reasoning processes (e.g., Carrell, 1989a, 1991; Devine, 1988; Eskey, 1986, 1988).

One instructional outcome of this research is the effort to develop automaticity skills in second language readers. Eskey and Grabe (1988) point out a number of instructional options to develop automaticity skills as does Segalowitz (1991; cf. Gatbonton & Segalowitz, 1988, for oral language automaticity development). Reading rate and rapid recognition exercises may improve automaticity (Stoller, 1986) as may repeated readings of texts (Herman, 1985; Samuels, 1979). Nagy and Herman (1987) argue that incidental contact with language through extensive reading is a prime source for automaticity development. Finally, options for teaching structural aspects of texts which may improve automaticity is treated extensively in Grellet (1981). At present, the issue of developing automaticity in word recognition is in need of further research; it is also typically neglected in many current textbook rationales.

Reading and Vocabulary Acquisition

Virtually all second language reading researchers agree that vocabulary development is a critical component of reading comprehension. Barnett (1986) and Strother and Ulijn (1987) have demonstrated that vocabulary is an important predictor of reading ability. Since fluent L1 readers develop such large recognition vocabularies, researchers have asked how such vocabulary growth occurs and whether the same is possible for second language readers. (Note the discrepancy between L1 and L2 estimates of vocabulary development reported above—40,000 words estimated for L1 academic needs, 5,000 to 7,000 words considered adequate for ESL academic coursework.) The issue then becomes how to provide academically oriented second language students with a large recognition vocabulary.

It is important to recognize that the core vocabulary argument, that the 2,000 most frequent vocabulary items account for 80% of all words in texts, may be useful for basic reading instruction (e.g., Nation, 1990); however, it falls far short of the needs of academically oriented ESL students who, in fact, need to know many of the less frequent words (Carter, 1987). A second problematic assumption of the core vocabulary position is that each word form is counted as a single word, though in reality, each word form may represent a number of distinct meanings, some of which depend strongly on the reading context, and some of which are quite different from each other in meaning. The reader needs to know not just a single word form, but the various different meanings which the one word form might represent (cf. Goulden, Nation, & Read, 1990). On the assumption that different word meanings should count as different words, estimates of vocabulary knowledge would need to increase considerably and fall more in the ranges suggested by first language researchers.

Comprehension Strategy Instruction

Research on comprehension strategies took on greater importance in the 1980s. As noted earlier, younger and less proficient students use fewer strategies and use them less effectively in their reading comprehension (Garner, 1987; Nist & Mealey, 1991; Padron

& Waxman, 1988). In second language contexts, better readers have also been shown to be better strategy users (Carrell, 1989b; Devine, 1987). Students who monitor their reading comprehension, adjust their reading rates, consider their objectives, and so on, tend to be better readers.

In L1 contexts, training studies have improved comprehension abilities in students when they are taught to use comprehension strategies (Brown, Armbruster, & Baker, 1986; Caverly & Orlando, 1991; Nist & Mealey, 1991; Lysynchuk, Pressley, & Vye, 1990; Palincsar & Brown, 1984; Pressley, Johnson, et al., 1989). Thus, research has sought to understand better the specific contexts in which comprehension strategies improve comprehension, the specific training procedures which are most effective, and the student variables (e.g., age, need, proficiency, etc.) which influence strategy instruction. This line of research is particularly important because of the promise it holds for reading instruction.[2]

Relatively few strategy training experiments have been done with second language students. Carrell (1985) demonstrated that training students to recognize the organizational structure of texts improved students' abilities to recall information. In a later study, Carrell, Pharis, & Liberto (1989) showed that strategy training with semantic mapping and with the ETR (experience, text, relationship) method both improved reading comprehension scores. Barnett (1988a) reported improvement in reading comprehension from a year-long strategy training experiment in reading. In a related experiment over one semester (Barnett, 1988b), however, she did not see significant improvement in the training group. Kern (1989) reported significant improvement with FL readers of French over a semester of training with emphasis placed on word, sentence, and discourse analysis strategies.

A major problem with strategy training is that there are so many potential training strategies, interactions with student learning styles, and training contexts. Establishing consistent results in second language situations will be difficult until many more strategy training experiments are conducted. Caverly and Orlando (1991), for example, point out that a well-established strategy training

---

[2] However, comprehension strategy instruction has actually proven to be somewhat more complex than indicated here. While many students have trained to perform comprehension strategies successfully, many strategy training experiments have also been unsuccessful. It seems that duration of training, clarity of training procedures, and student responsibility all are important variables in strategy training. There is also a further question of strategy transfer to unrelated reading tasks. Often strategy training does not transfer well to other reading tasks, it seldom creates significant differences in general reading comprehension measures, and it tends not to persist over time. This suggests that optimistic forecasts need to be tempered with the clarification that effective strategy training is not a simple or easy matter (Pressley, Lysynchuk, D'ailly, Smith, & Cake, 1989).

procedure—SQ3R (survey, question, read, recite, review)—has not been shown to be effective in controlled strategy training experiments (for L1). They note, however, that long and intensive training with this procedure does seem to lead to improved performance.

The potential for reading comprehension improvement from comprehension strategy training is enormous. Second language researchers are just beginning to explore the issues in this area, and many research studies claiming success in L1 contexts need to be replicated in L2 contexts to see if such claims can be generalized to second language students. Given the enormous range of research studies that will be needed, this field should remain a major locus of second language reading research for the next decade.

Reading-Writing Relations

In the 1980s, many reading and writing researchers came to the conclusion that reading and writing form important relations with each other: as skills, as cognitive processes, as ways of learning. For some time, L1 researchers have pointed out the high correlation between good writers and good readers and have viewed reading and writing as mutually reinforcing interactive processes (Flood & Lapp, 1987; Kucer, 1987). Stotsky (1983) noted that better writers were better readers, better writers read more, better readers wrote more syntactically mature prose, and reading experiences improved writing more than grammar instruction or further writing exercises (cf. Carson Eisterhold, 1990). At the same time, many researchers have pointed out that reading and writing are not simply reciprocal processes. There are many differences between reading and writing processes (Carson Eisterhold, 1990; Flood & Lapp, 1987; Perfetti & McCutchen, 1987; Purves, 1987; Shanahan, 1984, 1987).

Carson Eisterhold (1990) examined the many arguments for assuming that reading influences writing, that writing influences reading, and that they interactively influence each other. She points out that reading and writing are likely to influence each other reciprocally but not as inverses of the same process. Rather, a bidirectional model states that the reading/writing relationship changes at different stages of language development and aspects of this relationship will be independent of each other (Shanahan, 1984, 1987). Carson, Carrell, Silberstein, Kroll, & Kuehn (1990) examined whether or not reading/writing relationships are closely related in first and second language contexts. Their complex results suggest that the interaction between reading and writing is complex, with certain aspects of each language skill being somewhat independent of the other. This finding supports Shanahan's bidirection theory of reading/writing relationships (cf. Shanahan & Lomax, 1988). Much more research is needed to understand reading/writing relationships, not only as theory but also for its implications for instructional issues.[3]

One implication of this line of research is that reading and writing be taught together in advanced academic preparation. Many cognitive skills are mutually reinforcing, and the integration of literacy skills develops strategic approaches to academic tasks (Tierney, Soter, Flahavan, & McGinley, 1989). It should also be noted that not all good readers are good writers, and not all good writers are good readers (Kucer, 1987; Loban, 1976). Thus, the relationships are anything but simple. While this line of research is new for second language contexts, its importance for improving both reading and writing abilities in ESL students cannot be overemphasized.

There are many other issues and research topics in second language reading which this review will not address (e.g., issues which are related to child second language literacy and adult basic second language literacy). The five research topics treated above are not only current, but also hold strong promise for improved reading instruction. Research is likely to continue in each of these five areas and influence reading curricula and instruction for the next decade.

GUIDELINES FOR READING INSTRUCTION

In a very important way, this article is incomplete. After having reviewed ESL reading research in a fairly comprehensive manner, the next logical step is to interpret this research into curriculum guidelines and effective teaching practices. While a careful treatment of these issues is not possible here, I would like to conclude with a general set of guidelines which can be extrapolated from current reading research as well as from related language teaching sources.

---

[3] It is worth noting that Shanahan and Lomax (1988) found a directional writing-to-reading model of development to be as good a fit of their data as a bidirectional model for beginning learners. (Older learners' performances on reading and writing tasks were better explained by the bidirectional model.) For these beginning learners, the direction of learning to read from learning to write was better than learning to write from learning to read. Thus, the role of beginning writing as a means to improving reading receives strong support (see also Chomsky, 1971; Feitelson, 1988; cf. Krashen, 1984; Smith, 1984). The essential point of early writing is that students learn to make sound-to-letter relations in a natural and motivating way, while they are making meaning. Language experience approaches (LEA) which get students to write their own first drafts of their stories are effective ways of letting students see writing as symbolic representation and learn phonemic-graphic correspondences (Feitelson, 1988).

First, it would seem appropriate that reading instruction be taught in the context of a content-centered, integrated skills curriculum. Content provides learner motivation and purposeful activities; the integration of skills reinforces learning. Second, a reading lab should be used to provide individualized instruction as well as to practice certain skills and strategies (e.g., recognition exercises, timed reading, vocabulary learning strategies) outside of the content-centered course. Third, sustained silent reading should be encouraged to build fluency (automaticity), confidence, and appreciation of reading. Fourth, reading lessons should be planned in a pre-, during-, and postreading framework in order to build background knowledge, practice reading skills within the reading texts themselves, and engage in comprehension instruction. Fifth, specific skills and strategies should be given high priority and practiced consistently. The particular skills and strategies to be stressed depend on the educational contexts, student needs, and teaching objectives. Sixth, group work and cooperative learning should be used regularly to promote discussions of the readings and to work with information from the readings, exploring different solutions for complex activities. Seventh, and finally, students need to read extensively. Longer concentrated periods of silent reading build vocabulary and structural awareness, develop automaticity, enhance background knowledge, improve comprehension skills, and promote confidence and motivation. In short, students learn to read by reading.

ACKNOWLEDGMENTS

I would like to thank Fredricka Stoller and Randi Gilbert for reading earlier drafts of this manuscript and providing helpful comments.

THE AUTHOR

William Grabe is Associate Professor in the English Department at Northern Arizona University. He is Editor of the *Annual Review of Applied Linguistics* and has recently coedited (with Robert B. Kaplan) *Introduction to Applied Linguistics* (Addison-Wesley, 1991). His research interests include the theory and practice of reading and writing development.

REFERENCES

Adams, M. (1990). *Beginning to read.* Cambridge, MA: MIT Press.
Alderson, C., & Lukmani, Y. (1989). Cognition and reading: Cognitive levels as embodied in test questions. *Reading in a Foreign Language, 5,* 253-270.
Alderson, C., & Urquhart, A. (1988). This test is unfair: I'm not an economist. In P. Carrell, J. Devine, & D. Eskey (Eds.). *Interactive approaches to second language reading* (pp. 168-182). New York: Cambridge University Press.
Anderson, N. (1991, March). *Individual differences in second language reading strategies.* Paper presented at the 25th Annual TESOL Convention. New York.
Anderson, R. C., & Freebody, P. (1981). Vocabulary knowledge. In J. Guthrie (Ed.), *Comprehension and teaching: Research reviews* (pp. 77-117). Newark, DE: International Reading Association.
Anderson, R. C., & Pearson, P. D. (1984). A schema-theoretic view of basic processes in reading comprehension. In P. D. Pearson, R. Barr, M. L. Kamil, & P. Mosenthal (Eds.), *The handbook of reading research* (pp. 255-292). New York: Longman.
Anderson, R. C., Hiebert, E., Scott, J., & Wilkinson, I. (1985). *Becoming a nation of readers.* Washington, DC: National Institute of Education.
Baker, L., & Brown, A. (1984). Metacognitive skills and reading. In P. D. Pearson, R. Barr, M. L. Kamil, & P. Mosenthal (Eds.), *The handbook of reading research* (pp. 353-394). New York: Longman.
Balota, D., Flores d'Arcais, G., & Rayner, K. (Eds.). (1990). *Comprehension processes in reading.* Hillsdale, NJ: Lawrence Erlbaum.
Barnett, M. (1986). Syntactic and lexical/semantic skill in foreign language reading: Importance and interaction. *Modern Language Journal, 70,* 343-349.
Barnett, M. (1988a). Teaching reading strategies: How methodology affects language course articulation. *Foreign Language Annals, 21,* 109-119.
Barnett, M. (1988b). Reading through context. *Modern Language Journal, 72,* 150-159.
Barnett, M. (1989). *More than meets the eye: Foreign language reading.* Englewood Cliffs, NJ: Prentice Hall Regents.
Beck, I., & McKeown, M. (1986). Instructional research in reading: A retrospective. In J. Orasanu (Ed.), *Reading comprehension: From research to practice* (pp. 113-134). Hillsdale, NJ: Lawrence Erlbaum.
Beck, I., McKeown, M., & Omanson, R. (1987). The effects and uses of diverse vocabulary instructional techniques. In M. McKeown & M. Curtis (Eds.), *The nature of vocabulary acquisition* (pp. 147-163). Hillsdale, NJ: Lawrence Erlbaum.
Bell, J., & Burnaby, B. (1984). *A handbook for ESL literacy.* Toronto: OISE Press.

Bentin, S., Bargai, N., & Katz, L. (1984). Orthographic and phonemic coding for lexical access: Evidence from Hebrew. *Journal of Experimental Psychology: Learning, Memory, and Cognition, 10*, 353-368.

Berman, R. (1984). Syntactic components of the foreign language reading process. In J. C. Alderson & A. Urquhart (Eds.), *Reading in a foreign language* (pp. 139-156). New York: Longman.

Bernhardt, E. (1987). Cognitive processes in L2: An examination of reading behaviors. In J. Lantolf & A. Labarca (Eds.), *Research on second language acquisition in classroom settings* (Delaware Symposium No. 6, pp. 35-50). Norwood, NJ: Ablex.

Bernhardt, E. (1991). *Reading development in a second language: Theoretical, empirical, and classroom perspectives.* Norwood, NJ: Ablex.

Besner, D. (1990). Does the reading system need a lexicon? In D. Balota, G. Flores d'Arcais, & K. Rayner (Eds.), *Comprehension processes in reading* (pp. 73-99). Hillsdale, NJ: Lawrence Erlbaum.

Besner, D., & Hildebrandt, N. (1987). Orthographic and phonological codes in the oral reading of Japanese Kana. *Journal of Experimental Psychology: Learning, Memory, and Cognition, 13*, 335-343.

Besner, D., Twilley, L., McCann, R., & Seergobin, K. (1990). On the association between connectionism and data: Are a few words necessary? *Psychological Review, 97*, 432-446.

Bransford, J., Stein, B., & Shelton, T. (1984). Learning from the perspective of the comprehender. In C. Alderson & A. Urquhart (Eds.), *Reading in a foreign language* (pp. 28-44). New York: Longman.

Brown, A., Armbruster, B., & Baker, L. (1986). The role of metacognition in reading and studying. In J. Orasanu (Ed.), *Reading comprehension: From research to practice* (pp. 49-75). Hillsdale, NJ: Lawrence Erlbaum.

Carpenter, P., & Just, M. (1986). Cognitive processes in reading. In J. Orasanu (Ed.), *Reading comprehension: From theory to practice* (pp. 11-29). Hillsdale, NJ: Lawrence Erlbaum.

Carr, T., & Levy, B. (Eds.). (1990). *Reading and its development: Component skills approaches.* San Diego: Academic Press.

Carrell, P. L. (1984a). The effects of rhetorical organization on ESL readers. *TESOL Quarterly, 18*(3), 441-469.

Carrell, P. L. (1984b). Schema theory and ESL reading: Classroom implications and applications. *Modern Language Journal, 68*, 332-343.

Carrell, P. L. (1985). Facilitating ESL reading by teaching text structure. *TESOL Quarterly, 19*(4), 727-752.

Carrell, P. L. (1987). Content and formal schemata in ESL reading. *TESOL Quarterly, 21*(3), 461-481.

Carrell, P. L. (1988a). Interactive text processing: Implications for ESL/second language reading classrooms. In P. Carrell, J. Devine, & D. Eskey (Eds.), *Interactive approaches to second language reading* (pp. 239-259). New York: Cambridge University Press.

Carrell, P. L. (1988b). Some causes of text-boundedness and schema-interference in ESL reading. In P. Carrell, J. Devine, & D. Eskey (Eds.), *Interactive approaches to second language reading* (pp. 101-113). New York: Cambridge University Press.

Carrell, P. L. (1989a). SLA and classroom instruction: Reading. *Annual Review of Applied Linguistics 1988, 9*, 233-242.

Carrell, P. L. (1989b). Metacognitive awareness and second language reading. *Modern Language Journal, 73*, 121-134.

Carrell, P. L. (1991). Second language reading: Reading ability or language proficiency. *Applied Linguistics, 12*, 159-179.

Carrell, P. L., & Eisterhold, J. (1983). Schema theory and ESL reading pedagogy. *TESOL Quarterly, 17*, 553-573.

Carrell, P. L., Pharis, B., & Liberto, J. (1989). Metacognitive strategy training for ESL reading. *TESOL Quarterly, 23*(4), 647-678.

Carson Eisterhold, J. (1990). Reading-writing connections: Toward a description for second language learners. In B. Kroll (Ed.), *Second language writing: Research insights for the classroom* (pp. 88-101). New York: Cambridge University Press.

Carson, J., Carrell, P. L., Silberstein, S., Kroll, B., & Kuehn, P. (1990). Reading-writing relationships in first and second language. *TESOL Quarterly, 24*(2), 245-266.

Carter, R. (1987). *Vocabulary: Applied linguistic perspectives.* Boston: Allyn & Unwin.

Caverly, D., & Orlando, V. (1991). Textbook study strategies. In R. Flippo & D. Caverly (Eds.), *Teaching reading and study strategies* (pp. 86-165). Newark, DE: International Reading Association.

Chall, J. (1987). Two vocabularies for reading: Recognition and meaning. In M. McKeown & M. Curtis (Eds.), *The nature of vocabulary acquisition* (pp. 7-17). Hillsdale, NJ: Lawrence Erlbaum.

Chomsky, C. (1971). Write first, read later. *Childhood Education, 47*, 296-299.

Clarke, M. (1980). The short circuit hypothesis of ESL reading—Or when language competence interferes with reading performance. *Modern Language Journal, 64*, 203-209.

Clarke, M., & Silberstein, S. (1977). Toward a realization of psycholinguistic principles for the ESL reading class. *Language Learning, 27*, 135-154.

Coady, J. (1979). A psycholinguistic model of the ESL reader. In R. Mackay, B. Barkman, & R. R. Jordan (Eds.), *Reading in a second language* (pp. 5-12). Rowley, MA: Newbury House.

Coady, J. (1988, March). *Research on L2 vocabulary acquisition: Putting it in context.* Paper presented at the 22nd Annual TESOL Convention, Chicago, IL.

Cohen, A. (1990). *Language learning.* New York: Newbury House.

Crandall, J. (in press). Adult literacy. *Annual Review of Applied Linguistics 1991, 12*.

Cunningham, A., Stanovich, K., & Wilson, M. (1990). Cognitive variation in adult college students differing in reading ability. In T. Carr & B. Levy (Eds.), *Reading and its development: Component skills approaches* (pp. 129-159). San Diego: Academic Press.

Devine, J. (1987). General language competence and adult second language reading. In J. Devine, P. Carrell, & D. Eskey (Eds.), *Research in reading in English as a second language* (pp. 73-86). Washington, DC: TESOL.

Devine, J. (1988). The relationship between general language competence and second language reading proficiency: Implications for teaching. In P. Carrell, J. Devine, & D. Eskey (Eds.), *Interactive approaches to second language reading* (pp. 260-277). New York: Cambridge University Press.

Dubin, F., & Bycina, D. (1991). Academic reading and the ESL/EFL teacher. In M. Celce-Murcia (Ed.), *Teaching English as a second or foreign language* (2nd ed., pp. 195-215). New York: Newbury House.

Edelsky, C. (1986). *Writing in a bilingual program: Habia una vez.* Norwood, NJ: Ablex.

Edelsky, C., Altwerger, B., & Flores, B. (1991). *Whole language: What's the difference?* Portsmouth, NH: Heinemann Educational Books.

Eskey, D. (1973). A model program for teaching advanced reading to students of English as a foreign language. *Language Learning, 23,* 169-184.

Eskey, D. (1986). Theoretical foundations. In F. Dubin, D. Eskey, & W. Grabe (Eds.), *Teaching second language reading for academic purposes* (pp. 3-23). Reading, MA: Addison-Wesley.

Eskey, D. (1988). Holding in the bottom: An interactive approach to the language problems of second language readers. In P. Carrell, J. Devine, & D. Eskey (Eds.), *Interactive approaches to second language reading* (pp. 93-100). New York: Cambridge University Press.

Eskey, D., & Grabe, W. (1988). Interactive models for second language reading: Perspectives on instruction. In P. Carrell, J. Devine, & D. Eskey (Eds.), *Interactive approaches to second language reading* (pp. 223-238). New York: Cambridge University Press.

Feitelson, D. (1988). *Facts and fads in beginning reading.* Norwood, NJ: Ablex.

Flood, J., & Lapp, D. (1987). Reading and writing relationships: Assumptions and directions. In J. Squire (Ed.), *The dynamics of language learning* (pp. 9-26). Urbana, IL: National Conference on Research in English.

Flores d'Arcais, G. (1990). Parsing principles and language comprehension during reading. In D. Balota, G. Flores d'Arcais, & K. Rayner (Eds.), *Comprehension processes in reading* (pp. 345-357). Hillsdale, NJ: Lawrence Erlbaum.

Floyd, P., & Carrell, P. (1987). Effects on ESL reading of teaching cultural content schemata. *Language Learning, 37,* 89-108.

Garner, R. (1987). *Metacognition and reading comprehension.* Norwood, NJ: Ablex.

Garnham, A. (1985). *Psycholinguistics: Central topics.* New York: Methuen.

Gatbonton, E., & Segalowitz, N. (1988). Creative automatization: Principles for promoting fluency within a communicative framework. *TESOL Quarterly, 22*(3), 473-492.

Gee, J. (1990). *Social linguistics and literacies: Ideologies in discourse.* New York: The Falmer Press.

Goodman, K. (1967). Reading: A psycholinguistic guessing game. *Journal of the Reading Specialist, 6,* 126-135.

Goodman, K. (1985). Unity in reading. In H. Singer & R. Ruddell (Eds.), *Theoretical models and processes of reading* (3rd ed., pp. 813-840). Newark, DE: International Reading Association.

Gough, P. (1985). One second of reading: Postscript. In H. Singer & R. Ruddell (Eds.), *Theoretical models and processes of reading* (3rd ed., pp. 687-688). Newark, DE: International Reading Association.

Gough, P., & Juel, C. (1991). The first stages of word recognition. In L. Rieben & C. Perfetti (Eds.), *Learning to read: Basic research and its implications* (pp. 47-56). Hillsdale, NJ: Lawrence Erlbaum.

Gough, P., & Tunmer, W. (1986). Decoding, reading, and reading disability. *Remedial and Special Education, 7,* 6-10.

Goulden, R., Nation, P., & Read, J. (1990). How large can a receptive vocabulary be? *Applied Linguistics, 11,* 341-363.

Grabe, W. (1988a). Reassessing the term "interactive." In P. Carrell, J. Devine, & D. Eskey (Eds.), *Interactive approaches to second language reading* (pp. 56-70). New York: Cambridge University Press.

Grabe, W. (1988b). What every EFL teacher should know about reading in English. *Anglo-American Journal, 7,* 177-200.

Grellet, F. (1981). *Developing reading skills.* New York: Cambridge University Press.

Gunderson, L. (1991). *ESL literacy instruction: A guidebook to theory and practice.* Englewood Cliffs, NJ: Prentice Hall Regents.

Hall, W., White, T., & Guthrie, L. (1986). Skilled reading and language development: Some key issues. In J. Orasanu (Ed.), *Reading comprehension: From research to practice* (pp. 89-111). Hillsdale, NJ: Lawrence Erlbaum.

Harris, D. (1966). *Reading improvement exercises for students of English as a second language.* Englewood Clitts, NJ: Prentice Hall.

Haynes, M., & Carr, T. (1990). Writing system background and second language reading: A component skills analysis of English reading by native speaker-readers of Chinese. In T. Carr & B. Levy (Eds.), *Reading and its development: Component skills approaches* (pp. 375-421). San Diego: Academic Press.

Herman, P. (1985). The effect of repeated readings on reading rate, speech pauses and word recognition accuracy. *Reading Research Quarterly, 20,* 553-565.

Hudson, T. (1982). The effects of induced schemata on the "short circuit" in L2 reading: Non-decoding factors in L2 reading performance. *Language Learning, 32,* 1-31.

Hung, D., & Tzeng, O. (1981). Orthographic variations and visual information processing. *Psychological Bulletin, 90*, 377-414.

Iran-Nejad, A. (1987). The schema: A long-term memory structure or a transient structural phenomena. In R. Tierney, P. Anders, & J. Mitchell (Eds.), *Understanding readers' understanding* (pp. 109-127). Hillsdale, NJ: Lawrence Erlbaum.

Just, M., & Carpenter, P. (1987). *The psychology of reading and language comprehension*. Boston: Allyn & Bacon.

Kern, R. (1989). Second language reading strategy instruction: Its effects on comprehension and word inference ability. *Modern Language Journal, 73*, 135-149.

Kintsch, W. (1988). The role of knowledge in discourse comprehension: A construction-integration model. *Psychological Review, 95*, 163-182.

Kintsch, W., & van Dijk, T. (1978). Toward a model of discourse comprehension and production. *Psychological Review, 85*, 363-394.

Koda, K. (1987). Cognitive strategy transfer in second language reading. In J. Devine, P. Carrell, & D. Eskey (Eds.), *Research in reading in English as a second language* (pp. 125-144). Washington, DC: TESOL.

Koda, K. (1989). The effects of transferred vocabulary knowledge on the development of L2 reading proficiency. *Foreign Language Annals, 22*, 529-540.

Krashen, S. (1984). *Writing: Research, theory, and application*. New York: Pergamon Press.

Kucer, S. (1987). The cognitive base of reading and writing. In J. Squire (Ed.), *The dynamics of language learning* (pp. 27-51). Urbana, IL: National Conference on Research in English.

Kyongho, H., & Nation, P. (1989). Reducing the vocabulary load and encouraging vocabulary learning through reading newspapers. *Reading in a Foreign Language, 6*, 323-335.

Loban, W. (1976). *Language development: Kindergarten through grade twelve* (Research Report No. 18). Urbana, IL: National Council of Teachers of English.

Lynch, B., & Hudson, T. (1991). EST Reading. In M. Celce-Murcia (Ed.), *Teaching English as a second or foreign language* (2nd ed., pp. 216-232). New York: Newbury House.

Lysynchuk, L., Pressley, M., & Vye, N. (1990). Reciprocal teaching improves standardized reading-comprehension performance in poor comprehenders. *The Elementary School Journal, 90*, 469-484.

McKeown, M., & Curtis, M. (Eds.). (1987). *The nature of vocabulary acquisition*. Hillsdale, NJ: Lawrence Erlbaum.

McLaughlin, B. (1990). Restructuring. *Applied Linguistics, 11*, 113-128.

McClelland, J. (1987). The case for interactionism in language processing. In M. Coltheart (Ed.), *Attention and performance XII: The psychology of reading* (pp. 3-36). Hillsdale, NJ: Lawrence Erlbaum.

Mickulecky, L., & Newman, A. (Eds.). (1988). Adult literacy [Special issue]. *Journal of Reading, 31*, 588-694.

Mitchell, D. (1982). *The process of reading*. New York: John Wiley & Sons.

Mitchell, D., Cuetos, F., & Zagar, D. (1990). Reading in different languages: Is there a universal mechanism for parsing sentences? In D. Balota, G. Flores d'Arcais, & K. Rayner (Eds.), *Comprehension processes in reading* (pp. 285-302). Hillsdale, NJ: Lawrence Erlbaum.

Nagy, W. (1988). *Teaching vocabulary to improve reading comprehension.* Urbana, IL: National Council of Teachers of English.

Nagy, W., & Herman, P. (1987). Breadth and depth of vocabulary knowledge: Implications for acquisition and instruction. In M. McKeown & M. Curtis (Eds.), *The nature of vocabulary acquisition* (pp. 19-35). Hillsdale, NJ: Lawrence Erlbaum.

Nation, P. (1990). *Teaching and learning vocabulary.* New York: Newbury House.

Nation, P., & Coady, J. (1988). Vocabulary and reading. In R. Carter & M. McCarthy (Eds.), *Vocabulary and language teaching* (pp. 97-110). New York: Longman.

Neumann, O. (1990). Lexical access: Some comments on models and metaphors. In D. Balota, G. Flores d'Arcais, & K. Rayner (Eds.), *Comprehension processes in reading* (pp. 165-185). Hillsdale, NJ: Lawrence Erlbaum.

Nist, S., & Mealey, D. (1991). Teacher-directed comprehension strategies. In R. Flippo & D. Caverly (Eds.), *Teaching reading and study strategies* (pp. 42-85). Newark, DE: International Reading Association.

Norris, D. (1990). Connectionism: A case for modularity. In D. Balota, G. Flores d'Arcais, & K. Rayner (Eds.), *Comprehension processes in reading* (pp. 331-343). Hillsdale, NJ: Lawrence Erlbaum.

Padron, Y., & Waxman, H. (1988). The effect of ESL students' perceptions of their cognitive strategies on reading achievement, *TESOL Quarterly, 22*(1), 146-150.

Palincsar, A., & Brown, A. (1984). Reciprocal teaching of comprehension fostering and comprehension-monitoring activities. *Cognition and Instruction, 1,* 117-175.

Perfetti, C. (1985). *Reading ability.* New York: Oxford University Press.

Perfetti, C. (1989). There are generalized abilities and one of them is reading. In L. Resnick (Ed.), *Knowing, learning and instruction: Essays in honor of Robert Glazer* (pp. 307-334). Hillsdale, NJ: Lawrence Erlbaum.

Perfetti, C. (1990). The cooperative language processors: Semantic influences in an autonomous syntax. In D. Balota, G. Flores d'Arcais, & K. Rayner (Eds.), *Comprehension processes in reading* (pp. 205-230). Hillsdale, NJ: Lawrence Erlbaum.

Perfetti, C. (1991). Representations and awareness in the acquisition of reading competence. *Learning to read: Basic research and its implications* (pp. 33-44). Hillsdale, NJ: Lawrence Erlbaum.

Perfetti, C., & McCutchen, D. (1987). Schooled language competence: Linguistic abilities in reading and writing. In S. Rosenberg (Ed.), *Advances in applied psycholinguistics: Vol. 2. Reading, writing, and language learning* (pp. 105-141). New York: Cambridge University Press.

Pressley, M., Johnson, C., Symons, S., McGoldrick, J., & Kurita, J. (1989). Strategies that improve children's memory and comprehension of text. *The Elementary School Journal, 90,* 3-32.

Pressley, M., Lysynchuk, L., D'ailly, H., Smith, M., & Cake, H. (1989). A methodological analysis of experimental studies of comprehension strategy instruction. *Reading Research Quarterly, 24,* 458-470.

Pritchard, R. (1990). The effects of cultural schemata on reading processing strategies. *Reading Research Quarterly, 25,* 273-295.

Purves, A. (1987). Commentary. In J. Squire (Ed.), *The dynamics of language learning* (pp. 52-54). Urbana, IL: National Conference on Research in English.

Rayner, K. (1990). Comprehension process: An introduction. In D. Balota, G. Flores d'Arcais, & K. Rayner (Eds.), *Comprehension processes in reading* (pp. 1-6). Hillsdale, NJ: Lawrence Erlbaum.

Rayner, K., & Pollatsek, A. (1989). *The psychology of reading.* Englewood Cliffs, NJ: Prentice Hall.

Richgels, D., McGee, L., Lomax, R., & Sheard, C. (1987). Awareness of four text structures: Effects on recall of expository text. *Reading Research Quarterly, 22,* 177-196.

Rieben, L., & Perfetti, C. (Eds.). (1991). *Learning to read: Basic research and its implications.* Hillsdale, NJ: Lawrence Erlbaum.

Roller, C. (1990). The interaction between knowledge and structure variables in the processing of expository prose. *Reading Research Quarterly, 25,* 79-89.

Rumelhart, D. (1977). Toward an interactive model of reading. In S. Dornic (Ed.), *Attention and Performance IV* (pp. 573-603). New York: Academic Press.

Samuels, J. (1979). The method of repeated readings. *The Reading Teacher, 32,* 403-408.

Samuels, J., & Kamil, M. (1984). Models of the reading process. In P. D. Pearson, R. Barr, M. L. Kamil, & P. Mosenthal (Eds.), *The handbook of reading research* (pp. 185-224). New York: Longman.

Saville-Troike, M. (1973). Reading and the audiolingual method. *TESOL Quarterly, 7(2),* 395-405.

Schacter, D. (1989). Memory. In M. Posner (Ed.), *Foundations of cognitive science* (pp. 683-725). Cambridge, MA: MIT Press.

Segalowitz, D. (1991). Does advanced skill in a second language reduce automaticity in the first language? *Language Learning, 41,* 59-83.

Seidenberg, M. (1990). Lexical access: Another theoretical soupstone? In D. Balota, G. Flores d'Arcais, & K. Rayner (Eds.), *Comprehension processes in reading* (pp. 33-71). Hillsdale, NJ: Lawrence Erlbaum.

Seidenberg, M., & McClelland, J. (1989). A distributed, developmental model of visual word recognition and naming. *Psychological Review, 96,* 523-568.

Seidenberg, M., & McClelland, J. (1990). More words but still no lexicon: Reply to Besner, et al. (1990). *Psychological Review, 97,* 447-452.

Shanahan, T. (1984). Nature of the reading-writing relation: An exploratory multivariate analysis. *Journal of Educational Psychology, 76,* 466-477.

Shanahan, T. (1987). The shared knowledge of reading and writing. *Reading Psychology, 8,* 93-102.

Shanahan, T., & Lomax, R. (1988). A developmental comparison of three theoretical models of the reading-writing relationship. *Research in the Teaching of English, 22,* 196-212.

Silberstein, S. (1987). Let's take another look at reading: Twenty-five years of reading instruction. *English Teaching Forum, 25,* 28-35.

Singer, H. (1981). Instruction in reading acquisition. In O. Tzeng & H. Singer (Eds.), *Perception of print* (pp. 291-311). Hillsdale, NJ: Lawrence Erlbaum.

Smith, F. (1971). *Understanding reading.* New York: Holt, Rinehart & Winston.

Smith, F. (1979). *Reading without nonsense.* New York: Teachers College Press.

Smith, F. (1982). *Understanding reading* (3rd ed.). New York: Holt, Rinehart & Winston.

Smith, F. (1984). The promise and threat of microcomputers for language learning. In J. Handscombe, R. Orem, & B. Taylor (Eds.), *On TESOL '83: The question of control* (pp. 1-18). Washington, DC: TESOL.

Smithies, M. (1983). Reading habits at a third world technological university. *Reading in a Foreign Language, 1,* 111-118.

Stanovich, K. (1980). Toward an interactive-compensatory model of individual differences in the development of reading fluency. *Reading Research Quarterly, 16,* 32-71.

Stanovich, K. (1981). Attentional and automatic context effects in reading. In A. Lesgold & C. Perfetti (Eds.), *Interactive processes in reading* (pp. 241-267). Hillsdale, NJ: Lawrence Erlbaum.

Stanovich, K. (1986). Matthew effects in reading: Some consequences of individual differences in the acquisition of literacy. *Reading Research Quarterly, 21,* 360-407.

Stanovich, K. (1990). Concepts of developmental theories of reading skill: Cognitive resources, automaticity, and modularity. *Developmental Review, 10,* 72-100.

Stanovich, K. (1991). Changing models of reading and reading acquisition. In L. Rieben & C. Perfetti (Eds.), *Learning to read: Basic research and its implications* (pp. 19-31). Hillsdale, NJ: Lawrence Erlbaum.

Steffensen, M., & Joag-Dev, C. (1984). Cultural knowledge and reading. In C. Alderson & A. Urquhart (Eds.), *Reading in a foreign language* (pp. 48-61). New York: Longman.

Stoller, F. (1986). Reading lab: Developing low-level reading skills. In F. Dubin, D. Eskey, & W. Grabe (Eds.), *Teaching second language reading for academic purposes* (pp. 51-76). Reading, MA: Addison-Wesley.

Stotsky, S. (1983). Research on reading/writing relationships: A synthesis and suggested directions. *Language Arts, 60,* 627-642.

Strother, J., & Ulijn, J. (1987). Does syntactic rewriting affect English for Science and Technology (EST) text comprehension? In J. Devine, P. Carrell, & D. Eskey (Eds.), *Research in reading in English as a second language* (pp. 89-101). Washington, DC: TESOL.

Swaffar, J. (1988). Readers, texts, and second languages: The interactive processes. *Modern Language Journal, 72,* 123-149.

Swaffar, J., Arens, K., & Byrnes, H. (1991). *Reading for meaning: An integrated approach to language learning.* Englewood Cliffs, NJ: Prentice Hall.

Tannenhaus, M. (1988). Psycholinguistics: An overview. In F. Newmeyer (Ed.), *Linguistics: The Cambridge survey: Vol. 3. Language: Psychological and biological aspects* (pp. 1-37). New York: Cambridge University Press.

Taraban, R., & McClelland, J. (1990). Parsing and comprehension: A multiple-constraint view. In D. Balota, G. Flores d'Arcais, & K. Rayner (Eds.), *Comprehension processes in reading* (pp. 231-263). Hillsdale, NJ: Lawrence Erlbaum.

Tierney, R., Soter, A., O'Flahavan, J., & McGinley, W. (1989). The effects of reading and writing on thinking critically. *Reading Research Quarterly, 24,* 134-173.

Turvey, M., Feidman, L., & Lukatela, G. (1984). The Serbo-Croatian orthography constrains the reader to a phonologically analytic strategy. In L. Henderson (Ed.), *Orthographies and reading* (pp. 81-89). Hillsdale, NJ: Lawrence Erlbaum.

van Dijk, T., & Kintsch, W. (1983). *Strategies of discourse comprehension.* New York: Academic Press.

Weber, R. (1991). Linguistic diversity and reading in an American society. In R. Barr, M. Kamil, P. Mosenthal, & P. D. Pearson (Eds.), *Handbook of reading research (Vol. 2,* pp. 97-119). New York: Longman.

Wilson, P., & Anderson, R. C. (1986). What they don't know will hurt them: The role of prior knowledge in comprehension. In J. Orasanu (Ed.), *Reading comprehension: From research to practice* (pp. 31-48). Hillsdale, NJ: Lawrence Erlbaum.

Yorkey, R. (1970). *Study skills for students of English as a second language.* New York: McGraw-Hill.

Out of the Woods:
Emerging Traditions in the
Teaching of Writing

ANN RAIMES
Hunter College, City University of New York

Twenty-five years ago, writing instruction was characterized by an approach that focused on linguistic and rhetorical form. Since then, we have gone into the woods in search of new approaches, focusing in turn on the writer and the writer's processes, on academic content, and on the reader's expectations. In our search for a new approach, we have come up against some thorny issues, five of which are described in detail: the topics for writing, the issue of "real" writing, the nature of the academic discourse community, contrastive rhetoric, and responding to writing. The difficulty of negotiating our way also makes us susceptible to false trails. The paper ends with a discussion of emerging traditions that reflect shared recognitions rather than provide new methodologies.

Most good fairy tales, at least the ones that delight us and make us or our children beg for more, begin with looking back to "once upon a time." Since the TESOL organization has now reached its 25th anniversary, this seems a good way to begin looking at the story of how the teaching of writing to adult (secondary and higher education) nonnative speakers of English has developed since 1966; we can follow it up with an account of the thickets and thorny problems we face as we journey into the woods. Despite false trails, we might still, true to the best endings of fairy tales, be able to find a way out of the woods and live happily ever after. But that last is only speculation. Let's begin by looking back at the trails we've followed up to now, keeping in mind that we might not all have met the same witches, wizards, wolves, or good fairies along the way. Readers should be aware that the author of this article has been teaching ESL for more than 25 years, and so her telling of the story is inevitably influenced by the paths she chose to follow.

ONCE UPON A TIME: WRITING INSTRUCTION AND RESEARCH 1966–1991

This brief historical survey delineates four approaches to L2 writing instruction that have been evident in the last 25 years. Each approach, at least as it emerges in the literature, has a distinctive focus, highlighting in one case the rhetorical and linguistic *form* of the text itself; in another, the *writer* and the cognitive processes used in the act of writing; in another, the *content* for writing; and in the last, the demands made by the *reader*. The dates given mark the approximate time when each focus first appeared consistently in our literature; no final dates are given, since all the approaches are still, in varying degrees, subscribed to in theory and certainly in practice.

Focus on Form, 1966–

Once upon a time, when the TESOL organization first was founded in 1966, the audiolingual method was the dominant mode of instruction. The view that speech was primary meant that writing served a subservient role: to reinforce oral patterns of the language. So in language instruction, writing took the form of sentence drills— fill-ins, substitutions, transformations, and completions. The content was supplied. The writing reinforced or tested the accurate application of grammatical rules. In the 1970s, the use of sentence combining (O'Hare, 1973; Pack & Henrichsen, 1980), while still focusing on the manipulation of given sentences and thus, according to Zamel (1980), ignoring "the enormous complexity of writing" (p. 89), provided students with the opportunity to explore available syntactic options.

In the early 1970s, too, passages of connected discourse began to be used more often as classroom materials in the teaching of writing. Controlled composition tasks, still widely used today, provide the text and ask the student to manipulate linguistic forms within that text (see, for example, Byrd & Gallingane, 1990; Kunz, 1972; Paulston & Dykstra, 1973). However, the fact that students are using passages of connected discourse does not necessarily guarantee that the students view them as authentic. If the students are concentrating on a grammatical transformation, such as changing verbs from present to past, they "need pay no attention whatever to what the sentences mean or the manner in which they relate to each other" (Widdowson, 1978, p. 116).

It was not only grammatical form that was emphasized in the 1960s and early 1970s. Concern for rhetorical form was the impetus for Kaplan's influential 1966 article that introduced the concept of contrastive rhetoric. His "doodles article," as he calls it (Kaplan, 1987, p. 9), represents the "thought pattern" of English as "dominantly linear in its development" (Kaplan, 1966, p. 4) in contrast to the paragraph patterns of other languages and cultures. It has led to compensatory exercises that offer training in recognizing and using topic sentences, examples, and illustrations. These exercises often stress imitation of paragraph or essay form, using writing from an outline, paragraph completion, identification of topic and support, and scrambled paragraphs to reorder (see, for example, Kaplan & Shaw, 1983; Reid & Lindstrom, 1985).

Formal considerations are also the basis for a great deal of current L2 writing research. Textual features, such as the number of passives or the number of pronouns, are counted and compared for users of different cultures (Reid, 1990). Researchers examine the structure of such features as introductory paragraphs (Scarcella, 1984), the form of essays in various languages (Eggington, 1987; Hinds, 1987; Tsao, 1983), cohesion and coherence (Connor, 1984; Johns, 1984), and topical structure (Lautamatti, 1987). A large-scale study of written composition across 14 countries established to codify tasks and describe the state of writing instruction has provided a rich data base for cross-cultural discourse analyses (Purves, 1988). (For a summary of text-based research, see Connor, 1990.) A form-dominated approach has the largest body of research to inform and support it; it has been with us for a long time, and lends itself to empirical research design.

Focus on the Writer 1976–

The 1970s saw the development of more than sentence combining and controlled composition. Influenced by L1 writing research on composing processes (Emig, 1971; Zamel, 1976), teachers and researchers reacted against a form-dominated approach by developing an interest in what L2 writers actually do as they write. New concerns replaced the old. In place of "accuracy" and "patterns" came "process," "making meaning," "invention," and "multiple drafts." The attention to the writer as language learner and creator of text has led to a "process approach," with a new range of classroom tasks characterized by the use of journals (Peyton, 1990; Spack & Sadow, 1983), invention (Spack, 1984), peer collaboration (Bruffee, 1984; Long & Porter, 1985), revision (Hall, 1990), and attention to content before form (Raimes, 1983a; Zamel, 1976, 1982, 1983). Zamel (1983) has recommended that teachers not present instruction in the use of thesis sentences and outlines before the students have begun to explore ideas. In response to theory and research on writers' processes, teachers have begun to allow their students time and opportunity for selecting topics, generating ideas, writing drafts and revisions, and providing feedback. Where linguistic accuracy was formerly emphasized from the start, it is now often downplayed, at least at the beginning of the process, delayed until writers have grappled with ideas and organization. Some practitioners even entirely omit attention to grammar, as in ESL writing textbooks that contain no grammar reference or instructional component (e.g., Benesch & Rorschach, 1989; Cramer, 1985).

Research publications on L2 writing processes grew rapidly in the 1980s to inform and support the new trends in instruction (e.g., Cumming, 1989; Friedlander, 1990; Hall, 1990; Jones, 1982, 1985; Jones & Tetroe, 1987; Raimes, 1985, 1987; Zamel, 1982, 1983; for a summary, see Krapels, 1990). However, although we are beginning to discover much about the writing process, the small number of subjects in case study research limits generalizations, and we are rightly warned that the "lack of comparability across studies impedes the growth of knowledge in the field" (Krapels, 1990, p. 51).

Despite the rapid growth in research and classroom applications in this area, and despite the enthusiastic acceptance of a shift in our discipline to a view of language as communication and to an understanding of the process of learning, teachers did not all strike out along this new path. The radical changes that were called for in instructional approach seemed to provoke a swift reaction, a return to the safety of the well-worn trail where texts and teachers have priority.

Focus on Content 1986–

Some teachers and theorists, alienated by the enthusiasm with which a process approach was often adopted and promulgated (Horowitz, 1986a), interpreted the focus on the writer's making of personal meaning as an "almost total obsession" (Horowitz, 1986c, p. 788) with "the cognitive relationship between the writer and the writer's internal world" (Swales, 1987, p. 63). Those who perceived the new approach as an obsession inappropriate for academic demands and for the expectations of academic readers shifted their focus from the processes of the writer to content and to the demands of the academy. By 1986, a process approach was being included among "traditional" (Shih, 1986, p. 624) approaches and in its place was proposed what Mohan had already proposed in 1979— a content-based approach. In content-based instruction, an ESL course might be attached to a content course in the adjunct model (Brinton, Snow, & Wesche, 1989; Snow & Brinton, 1988) or language courses might be grouped with courses in other disciplines (Benesch, 1988). With a content focus, learners are said to get help with "the language of the thinking processes and the structure or shape of content" (Mohan, 1986, p. 18). It is interesting to note here that the content specific to English courses—language, culture, and literature—is largely rejected (see Horowitz, 1990) in favor of the subject matter of the other fields the ESL students are studying.

The research studies that inform this approach include analysis of the rhetorical organization of technical writing (Selinker, Todd-Trimble, & Trimble, 1978; Weissberg, 1984), studies of student writing in content areas (Jenkins & Hinds, 1987; Selzer, 1983), and surveys of the content and tasks L2 students can expect to encounter in their academic careers (Bridgeman & Carlson, 1983; Canseco & Byrd, 1989; Horowitz, 1986b). While classroom methodology might take on some of the features of a writer-focused approach, such as prewriting tasks and the opportunity for revision, the main emphasis is on the instructor's determination of what academic content is most appropriate, in order to build whole courses or modules of reading and writing tasks around that content.

This content-based approach has more repercussions on the shape of the curriculum than the two approaches previously described, for here the autonomous ESL class is often replaced by team teaching, linked courses, "topic-centered modules or mini-courses," sheltered (i.e., "field specific") instruction, and "composition or multiskill English for academic purposes (EAP) courses/tutorials as adjuncts to designated university content courses" (Shih, 1986, p. 632–633). With an autonomous ESL class, a teacher can—and indeed often does—move back and forth among approaches. With ESL attached in the curriculum to a content course, such flexibility is less likely. There is always the danger that institutional changes in course structure will lock us into an approach that we want to modify or abandon.

Focus on the Reader 1986–

Simultaneously with content-based approaches came another academically oriented approach, English for academic purposes, which focuses on the expectations of academic readers (Horowitz, 1986a, 1986b, 1986c; Reid, 1987, 1989). This approach, in which the ESL teacher runs a theme-based class, not necessarily linked to a content course, is also characterized by its strong opposition to a position within a writer-dominated process approach that favors personal writing. A reader-dominated approach perceives language teaching "as socialization into the academic community—not as humanistic therapy" (Horowitz, 1986c, p. 789).

The audience-dominated approach, focusing on the expectations of readers outside the language classroom, is characterized by the use of terms like *academic demands* and *academic discourse community*. Attention to audience was, in fact, first brought to the fore as a feature of the process approach, but the focus was on known readers inside the language classroom, as peers and teachers responded to the ideas in a text. An English for academic purposes approach focuses on the reader, too—not as a specific individual but as the representative of a discourse community, for example, a specific discipline or academia in general. The reader is an initiated expert who represents a faculty audience. This reader, "particularly omniscient" and "all-powerful" (Johns, 1990a, p. 31), is likely to be an abstract representation, a generalized construct, one reified from an examination of academic assignments and texts.

Once the concept of a powerful outside reader is established, it is a short step to generalizing about the forms of writing that a reader will expect, and then an even shorter step to teaching those forms as prescriptive patterns. Recommendations such as the following: "Teachers must gather assignments from across the curriculum, assess the purposes and audience expectations in the assignments, and present them to the class" (Reid, 1987, p. 34) indicate a return to a form-dominated approach, the difference being that now rhetorical forms, rather than grammatical forms, are presented as paradigms.

A reader-dominated approach, like the other approaches, has generated its own body of research: mostly surveys of the expectations and reactions of faculty members (Johns, 1981; Santos, 1988), studies of the expectations of academic readers with regard to genres (Swales, 1990), and identifications of the basic skills of writing transferable across various disciplines (Johns, 1988).

These four approaches are all widely used and by no means discrete and sequential. Certainly the last three appear to operate more on a principle of critical reaction to a previous approach than on cumulative development. In all, our path through the woods of writing instruction is less clearly defined now in 1991 than it was in 1966. Then there was one approach, form-dominated, clearly defined, and relatively easy to follow in the classroom. Now teachers have to consider a variety of approaches, their underlying assumptions, and the practices that each philosophy generates.

Thus, leaving the security of what Clarke and Silberstein call the "explicitly mandated reality" (1988, p. 692) of one clear approach, we have gone in search of a new theoretical approach or approaches to L2 writing instruction.

INTO THE WOODS:
THICKETS AND THORNY ISSUES

Once we have left the relative safety of a traditional form-dominated approach and set off into the woods in search of new theories, our progress is hampered by many thickets and thorny issues. These we have to confront and negotiate before we can continue our journey. Particularly thorny are five classroom-oriented issues that arise in our literature and in teachers' discussions frequently enough to trouble L2 writing instructors, issues that in my more than 25 years of teaching have provided cause for reflection and uncertainty: the topics for writing; the issue of "real" writing; the nature of the academic discourse community; the role of contrastive rhetoric in the writing classroom; and ways of responding to writing. These areas, difficult to negotiate, will be described as discrete items, each posing its own set of problems. A word of caution is in order, though: Readers should not expect to find here miracle solutions or magic charms to lead the way past these thickets and out of the woods.

The Topics for Writing

One of the major problems teachers face is what students should write about. Topics for writing are an integral part of any writing course, and the four approaches outlined above lead to what can be a bewildering array of topics for teachers. In a form-dominated approach, topics are assigned by the teacher; since the interest is in how sentences and paragraphs are written rather than in what ideas are expressed, each piece of writing serves as a vehicle for practicing and displaying grammatical, syntactic, and rhetorical forms. For this purpose, almost any topic will serve. In a writer-dominated approach (usually called a process approach), the students themselves frequently choose the topics, using personal experience to write about what concerns them, or responding to a shared classroom experience, often a piece of expository writing or a work of literature (Spack, 1985). In a content-dominated approach, topics will be drawn from the subject matter of either a particular discipline or a particular course, supplied either by the content teacher when content and writing course are linked in the adjunct model (Snow & Brinton, 1988) or by the language teacher in theme-based EAP courses. And in a reader-dominated approach, the model is one of the writing-across-the-curriculum movement, with language teachers examining what other disciplines assign and training students how to respond to those assignments by "deconstructing" (Johns, 1986a, p. 253) the essay prompt and by following a model of the appropriate form of academic writing.

The problem of whether to teach personal or academic writing has surfaced frequently in recent years (Mlynarczyk, in press) and has no easy solution. Approaches that focus on rhetorical form and on the reader's expectations look to the larger community for guidance. ESL instruction is seen as a service "to prepare students to handle writing assignments in academic courses" (Shih, 1986, p. 617). For EFL students and for international students in the U.S., who will probably only write in English as part of their educational requirement and not at all thereafter, this might be suitable. However, the purposes are different for the many ESL immigrant and refugee nonnative speakers in secondary and college classrooms. This last group, a rapidly growing one, Leki (1990) equates with native speakers of English, who, she says, are "more likely to write for many different contexts in the course of their professional lives" (p. 14). For native speakers—and, by extension, certain large groups of ESL students—Hairston (1991) rejects the idea that writing courses should be "service courses" taught for the benefit of academic disciplines, since "writing courses taught by properly trained teachers do have important content: learning how to use language to express ideas effectively" (p. B1).

"Real" Writing

A great deal of the recent controversy about the teaching of writing has centered not only around the topics students write about but also around the dichotomy of process and product. Horowitz initiated lengthy debate (see Braine, 1988; Hamp-Lyons, 1986; Horowitz, 1986a, 1986b, 1986c; Liebman-Kleine, 1986; Lyons, 1986; Reid, 1984; Spack, 1988; Zamel, 1983) by questioning the effectiveness of the process approach with its focus on the writer. In particular, Horowitz (1986) criticized what he termed the "cavalier view" (p. 141) of a process proponent (this author) who said at the 1985 TESOL Convention that examination writing was not "'real'" (p. 141) writing. Horowitz is not alone in his complaint. Cited as a major flaw in a process approach is the fact that "the Process Approach fails to give students an accurate picture of university writing" (Johns, 1990b). The issue of what university writing is and what kind of writing ESL students should be doing is a thorny one, and the use of the term *real* relates to this issue in practice as well as in theory.

In practice, I and many of my colleagues teach two types of writing in our classes: writing for learning (with prewriting, drafts, revisions, and editing) and writing for display (i.e., examination writing). Our students are aware of the different purposes and different strategies. They recognize that these are distinct. The use of the term *real* in this context was initiated by Searle (1969), who makes a clear distinction between real questions and exam questions. In real questions, the speaker wants to know the answer; in exam questions, the speaker wants to know if the hearer knows. Similar distinctions can be made with writing. In a writing class, students need to be taught both how to use the process to their advantage as language learners and writers, and also how to produce an acceptable product upon demand. A shortcoming of the debate around these issues is that process and product have been seen as *either/or* rather than *both/and* entities. However, while students certainly need to learn how to pass exams, they also need to perceive writing as a tool for learning, a tool that can be useful to them throughout their professional and personal lives.

As evidence of the difficulty of defining authentic writing, it is interesting to note that even Horowitz (1986b) has used the designation *real* to describe writing. He suggests ways to simulate "the essential characteristics of *real* university writing assignments" (p. 449) and discusses the context of "a *real* academic task" [italics added] (p. 459). Here, too, the use of the term *real* could be questioned. However, we should not assume that the implication is necessarily that the topics and tasks that come from ESL teachers' own repertoire are somehow unreal; it is, rather, that Horowitz and others find them less appropriate in certain settings. In any case, the L2 debate provides a great deal of evidence for what Harris (1989) has observed in L1 writing: "One seems asked to defend either the power of the discourse community or the imagination of the individual writer" (p. 2). Obviously, the whole area of the types of writing students are expected to do and the types of writing we should teach is one surrounded by controversy.

The Nature of the Academic Discourse Community

Frequently cited as important in determining the nature of "real" writing and the topics we should assign are the demands of the "academic discourse community." These demands provide a set of standards that readers of academic prose, teachers in academic settings, expect. So some L2 writing teachers look to other disciplines to determine their course content, their readings, their models, and their instruction of rhetorical form. One thorny issue here is whether we should put our trust in this community, or whether we shouldn't rather be attempting to influence and change the academic community for the benefit of our students, while teaching our students how to interpret the community values and transform them (for discussion of similar issues, see Auerbach, 1986, 1990; Peirce, 1989).

According to Johns (1990a), teachers who emphasize the conventions of the discourse community will begin with "the *rules* [italics added] of discourse in the community" (p. 32), since academic faculty "insist that students learn to 'talk like engineers', for example, *surrendering their own language and mode of thought* [italics added] to the requirements of the target community (p. 33). The language used here—"rules" and "surrender"—reveals perceptions regarding who exercises power in the community and the value of that power. In contrast, Patricia Bizzell (cited in Enos, 1987) sees the academic community as synonymous with "dominant social classes" and has recommended that we not direct our students towards assimilation but rather find ways to give them "critical distance" on academic cultural literacy, so that eventually "elements from students' native discourse communities can be granted legitimacy in the academic community" (p. vi).

Another thorny problem is whether we view the academic discourse community as benign, open, and beneficial to our students or whether we see discourse communities as powerful and controlling, and, as Giroux (cited in Faigley, 1986) puts it, "often more concerned with ways of excluding new members than with ways of admitting them" (p. 537). These opposing views point to the validity of Berlin's (1988) statement that every pedagogy implies "a set of tacit assumptions about what is real, what is good, what is possible, and how power ought to be distributed" (p. 492). Teaching writing is inherently political, and how we perceive the purposes of writing vis-a-vis the academic community will reflect our political stance.

Reflecting our stance, too, is how we interpret the information that comes to us from members of the academic community. In a survey of 200 faculty members' opinions in response to the question, "Which is more important for success in your classes, a general knowledge of English or a knowledge of English specific to the discipline?", (Johns, 1981, p. 57) most faculty members ranked general English above specific purposes English. This result was interpreted in the following way:

There could be a number of reasons for the general English preferences, the most compelling of which is that most faculty do not understand the nature and breadth of ESP. They tend to think of it as an aspect of the discipline that has to do with vocabulary alone. (p. 54)

The mix of signals perhaps reflects a more generalized ambivalence of TESOL practitioners: Subject-area faculty are viewed as a valuable resource; however, when they do not support what ESL teachers and researchers expect, it is tempting to discount their perceptions.

A focus on the academic discourse community also raises issues as to whether academic writing is good writing, whether academic discourse "often masks a lack of genuine understanding" (Elbow, 1991, p. 137) of how a principle works, and indeed whether there is a fixed and stable construct of academic writing even in one discipline. Elbow goes so far as to say that we can't teach academic discourse "because there's no such thing to teach" (p. 138). This issue of the nature, requirements, even the existence of, an academic discourse community is a thicket in which we could be entangled for a long time.

Contrastive Rhetoric

Although it has been 25 years since contrastive rhetoric research was introduced (Kaplan, 1966, Leki, 1991) and the concept is frequently mentioned in discussions of theory and research, its applications to classroom instruction have not developed correspondingly. Published research informs teachers about the different ways in which the written products of other languages are structured (e.g., Eggington, 1987; Hinds, 1987; Tsao, 1983), but the nature of transfer in L2 writing remains under debate (see Mohan & Lo, 1985) and transfer has been found not to be significant in certain types of task, such as paraphrase (Connor & McCagg, 1983). The declared intention of contrastive rhetoric research is, however, "not to provide pedagogic method" but rather to provide teachers and students with knowledge about how the links between culture and writing are reflected in written products (Grabe & Kaplan, 1989, p. 271).

Rather than abstracting a principle of the "linear" development of English prose (Kaplan, 1966) as a pedagogic principle, contrastive rhetoric is more useful as a consciousness-raising device for students; teachers can discuss what they have observed about texts in different cultures and have students discover whether research findings hold true in their experience of their L1 texts.

The thicket that contrastive rhetoric presents for teachers as they wander into the woods of theory is the question of the value of prescribing one form of text—English form—not just as an alternative, but as the one privileged form of text, presented as the most logical and desirable, with which other learned systems interfere. Land and Whitley (1989), in discussing how readers read and judge ESL students' essays, found that nonnative speaker readers could "accommodate to more kinds of rhetorical patterns" (p. 287) than could native-speaker readers. If we are to move away from courses that are "as retributive as they are instructive" and away from "composition as colonization," we need, they say, to "recognize, value, and foster the alternative rhetorics that the ESL student brings to our language" (p. 286), not treat them only as features that interfere with language learning. Land and Whitley fear that "in teaching Standard Written English rhetorical conventions, we are teaching students to reproduce in a mechanical fashion our preferred vehicle of understanding" (p. 285).

In the same way that multiple "literacies" (Street, 1984) are posed against the idea of one dominant cultural literacy (Hirsch, 1987), so a broad use of contrastive rhetoric as a classroom consciousness-raising tool can point to linguistic variety and rhetorical choices; a narrow use would emphasize only prescriptions aimed at counteracting L1 interference. An extensive research study (Cumming, 1989) of the factors of writing expertise and second-language proficiency of L2 writers revealed in the qualities of their texts and their writing behaviors warns against such a narrow use of contrastive rhetoric: "Pedagogical prescriptions about the interference of learners' mother tongue in second-language performance—espoused in audiolingual methodologies and theories of linguistic transfer or contrastive rhetoric—appear misdirected" (pp. 127-128) since students' L1 is shown to be an important resource rather than a hindrance in decision making in writing.

Responding to Writing

With a number of approaches to teaching writing to choose from, teachers are faced with a similar variety of ways to respond to students' writing. Since a response on a student's paper is potentially one of the most influential texts in a writing class (Raimes, 1988), teachers are always concerned about the best approach. Some of the options follow, illustrating the variety at our disposal. We can correct errors; code errors; locate errors; indicate the number of errors (see Robb, Ross, & Shortreed, 1986, for a discussion of these); comment on form; make generalized comments about content, e.g., "good description" or "add details" (Fathman & Whalley, 1990, p. 182); make text-specific comments, e.g., "I'm wondering here what Carver tells the readers about the children"; ask questions; make suggestions; emote with comments like "Nice!" or "I'm bored" (Lees, 1979, p. 264); praise; ask students to comment on the source of the error (Raimes, 1990); or ask L1 peers to reformulate the students' texts (Cohen, 1983). Given the range of choices, it's hardly surprising that responding is a thorny issue. It is, in fact, so problematic that much of our written response to students' texts is inconsistent, arbitrary, and often contradictory (Zamel, 1985).

In an effort to understand more about teachers' responses, researchers are looking at students' responses to feedback (Cohen, 1987; Cohen & Cavalcanti, 1990; Radecki & Swales, 1988), finding mainly that students simply "make a mental note" of a teacher's response. The fact that little of the research examines activities that occur after the act of responding seems to get at the heart of the problem. If teachers see their response as the end of the interaction, then students will stop there. If, however, the response includes specific directions on what to do next, an "assignment" (Lees, 1979, p. 265), there is a chance for application of principles.

FALSE TRAILS

The five thorny issues just discussed are ones that trouble teachers and concern theorists and researchers. There are many others, too, rendering our journey into the woods exciting, even hazardous. As teachers read the theories and research and try to figure out what approach to adopt in a writing classroom, they will sometimes confront a false trail that seems to promise a quick way out of the woods, an easy solution. We have seen evidence of false trails in the rise and demise of various methods (Clarke, 1982, 1984; Richards, 1984). Similarly, prescriptions of one approach for our whole profession and all our students can be seen as false trails, too, since they actually lead back to another "explicitly mandated reality" (Clarke & Silberstein, 1988) to replace the mandate of form-focused instruction. Such a prescription in the teaching of writing appears in proposals for the widespread adoption of content-based language teaching as "the dominant approach to teaching ESL at all levels" (Celce-Murcia, 1989, p. 14).

I regard proposals like this as false trails because they perpetuate one of the errors that has been at the heart of many of our thorny problems about writing. That problem, alluded to earlier, is that we tend to discuss ESL/EFL students as if they are one or at the most two groups. Much of the dissension and controversy that has surfaced at conferences and in our literature would, I submit, simply cease to exist if we defined our terms. Our field is too diverse for us to recommend ways of teaching ESL in general. There is no such thing as a generalized ESL student. Before making pedagogical recommendations, we need to determine the following: the type of institution (high school, two-year college, four-year college, research university?) and the ESL student (undergraduate or graduate? freshman or junior? international student [returning to country of origin] or immigrant/refugee? with writing expertise in L1 or not? with what level of language proficiency?) If we are to prescribe content, we need to ask, Whose content? For the nonnative-speaking first-year students in my university, to offer modules of marketing, accounting, and nursing is to depart from the very tradition of a liberal arts education. On the other hand, for very specialized international graduate students, a content approach might be the most appropriate. When Johns and Connor (1989, reported in Leki, 1990) maintain that no such thing as general English exists, they are referring to international students, but immigrant students need general English; that is, they need more than ways to adapt to course requirements for a few years. They need to be able to write in English for the rest of their working and earning lives. They need to learn not only what academia expects but how to forge their place in it, and how to change it. Indeed, on many campuses now, a diverse student body is urging the replacement of the male Eurocentric curriculum model with one emphasizing gender representation and cultural diversity. Adopting a content-based approach for all ESL students would be succumbing to what I have called "the butler's stance" (Raimes, in press), one that over-values service to other disciplines and prescribes content at the expense of writer, reader, and form.

Being lost in the woods might be uncomfortable, but we have to beware of taking an easy path that might, in fact, lead us back to where we started, to a reliance on form and prescription.

OUT OF THE WOODS: EMERGING TRADITIONS IN THE TEACHING OF WRITING

What is the story now after a 25-year journey, beset by thickets, thorns, and false trails? Are new traditions emerging?

I am reminded of an article I wrote for this journal 8 years ago (Raimes, 1983b), in which I argued that in spite of the thrust towards communicative competence, there had been no real revolution in our field. While there were then signs of some shifts in the assumptions about what we do, we were still enmeshed in tradition but were beginning to raise important questions. At that time Kuhn's (1970) description of a paradigm shift seemed apt for the field of ESL/EFL in general: "the proliferation of competing articulations, the willingness to try anything, the expression of explicit discontent, the recourse to philosophy and to debate over fundamentals" (p. 91). That description seems still to be apt for the teaching of writing, where there is certainly evidence of competition, discontent, and debate, and where now, given the plurality of approaches, designs, and procedures, it seems more appropriate to talk of *traditions* rather than of one *tradition*.

If any clear traditions are emerging, they have more to do with recognition of where we are now rather than delineation of exactly where we are going. I see five such emerging traditions of recognition: recognition of the complexity of composing, of student diversity, of learners' processes, of the politics of pedagogy, and of the value of practice as well as theory. I end with a brief discussion of each.

Recognition of the Complexity of Composing

Despite all the false trails and some theorists' desire to offer one approach as the answer to our problems, what seems to be emerging is a recognition that the complexity of the writing process and the writing context means that when we teach writing we have to balance the four elements of form, the writer, content, and the reader. These are not discrete entities. Rather,

> writers are readers as they read their own texts. Readers are writers as they make responses on a written text. Content and subject matter do not exist without language. The form of a text is determined by the interaction of writer, reader, and content. Language inevitably reflects subject matter, the writer, and the writer's view of the reader's background knowledge and expectations. (Raimes, in press)

This complexity may mean that no one single theory of writing can be developed (Johns, 1990a) or it may mean that a variety of theories need to be developed to support and inform diverse approaches (Silva, 1990). In either case, recognition of complexity is a necessary basis for principled model building.

Recognition of Student Diversity

While there is still a tendency to discuss our field as if it were the easily definable entity it was 25 years ago, there are signs that we are beginning to recognize the diversity of our students and our mission, and to realize that not all approaches and procedures might apply to all ESL/EFL students. Reid (1984) notes this when she reminds Zamel of the differences between advanced students and novice writers, particularly with regard to cognitive development; Horowitz (1990) notes this when he lists the questions that we need to ask about our students before we decide to use literature or any other content. For heterogeneous classes, a "balanced" stance is recommended (Booth, 1963; Raimes, in press), one that presents a governing philosophy but pays attention within that philosophy to all four elements involved in writing: form, writer, content, and reader. The combination of complexity and diversity makes it imperative for us not to seek universal prescriptions, but instead to "strive to validate other, local forms of knowledge about language and teaching" (Pennycook, 1989, p. 613).

Recognition of Learners' Processes

Amidst all the winding and intersecting paths and false trails, one trail seems to be consistently well marked and well traveled. While there is controversy about what a process approach to teaching writing actually comprises and to what extent it can take academic demands into account, there is widespread acceptance of the notion that language teachers need to know about and to take into account the process of how learners learn a language and how writers produce a written product. Such a notion of process underlies a great deal of current communicative, task-based, and collaborative instruction and curriculum development (Nunan, 1989a, 1989b). Even writing theorists who are identified with content-based and reader-based approaches frequently acknowledge the important role that the writer's processes play in the writing class (Johns, 1986b; Shih, 1986; Swales, 1987). The process approach more than any other seems to be providing unifying theoretical and method-ological principles.

Recognition of the Politics of Pedagogy

Along with the recognition of the complexity of composing and the diversity of our students and their processes has come a more explicitly political understanding: The approach we take to the academic discourse community and the culturally diverse students in our classrooms will inevitably reflect "interested knowledge," which is likely to be "a positivist, progressivist, and patriarchal" view presented as "a method" (Pennycook, 1989, p. 589). All approaches should, therefore, be examined with a set of questions in mind: Who learns to do what? Why? Who benefits? (See

Auerbach, 1986, 1990). Recognizing the power of literacy, we need to ask "what kind of literacy we want to support: literacy to serve which purposes and on behalf of whose interests" (Lunsford, Moglen, & Slevin, 1990, p. 2) and to keep in mind that "to propose a pedagogy is to propose a political vision" (Simon, 1987, p. 371).

Recognition of the Value of Practice

Both in L1 and in L2 instruction, the power that theory, or method, has held over instruction is being challenged by what Shulman (1987) calls "the wisdom of practice" (p. 11). North (1987) argues that in L1 writing instruction we need to give credit to "practitioners' lore" as well as to research; teachers need to use their knowledge "to argue for the value of what they know and how they come to know it" (p. 55). Before we heed our theorists and adopt their views, it will help us if we first discover how often they teach writing to ESL students, where they teach it, how they teach it, and who their students are. We need to establish a context. We need to know the environment in which they have developed what Prabhu (1990, p. 172) calls "a teacher's sense of plausibility about teaching," which is the development of a "concept (or theory, or in a more dormant state, pedagogic intuition), of how learning takes place and how teaching causes and supports it." But better than putting the research into a teaching context is for teachers to become researchers themselves. Classroom-based research and action research is increasingly recommended to decrease teachers' reliance on theorists and researchers (Richards & Nunan, 1990). Teachers can keep sight of the forest as well as the trees.

These recognitions characterize our position at the end of our 25-year journey from "once upon a time," journeying into the woods, facing the tangle of thickets and thorny problems to trying to recognize—and avoid—false trails. Our own telling of the story might also include having taken some false trails or having met and vanquished a few big bad wolves in our travels. The fact that we are beginning to emerge from the woods with new recognitions but not a single new approach is perhaps the happiest 1991 ending that we can expect, given the diversity and complexity of our students and of learning and teaching writing. But by the turn of the century, we could well be reading (and writing) a different story.
■

ACKNOWLEDGMENTS

Many thanks to Kate Parry, Ruth Spack, and Vivian Zamel, who read earlier drafts of this paper and offered perceptive and helpful advice. Thanks also go to the graduate students in my course, Rhetoric and Composition, who steered me away from the idea of using "Little Red Writing Hood" as a subtitle for this paper.

THE AUTHOR

Ann Raimes is the author of many articles on writing research, theory, and teaching, and on ESL methodology. Her books include *Techniques in Teaching Writing* (Oxford University Press, 1983), *Exploring Through Writing* (St. Martin's Press, 1987), and *How English Works: A Grammar Handbook with Readings* (St. Martin's Press, 1990). She has taught ESL for more than 25 years.

REFERENCES

Auerbach, E. R. (1986). Competency-based ESL: One step forward or two steps back? *TESOL Quarterly, 20*(3), 411-429.

Auerbach, E. R. (1990). Review of *Alien winds: The reeducation of America's Indochinese refugees. TESOL Quarterly, 24*(1), 85-91.

Benesch, S. (Ed.). (1988). *Ending remediation: ESL and content in higher education.* Washington, DC: TESOL.

Benesch, S., & Rorschach, B. (1989). *Academic writing workshop II.* Belmont, CA: Wadsworth.

Berlin, J. A. (1988). Rhetoric and ideology in the writing class. *College English, 50*(5), 477-494.

Booth, W. C. (1963). The rhetorical stance. *College Composition and Communication, 14*(2), 139-145.

Braine, G. (1988). Comments on Ruth Spack's "Initiating ESL students into the academic discourse community: How far should we go?" *TESOL Quarterly, 22*(4), 700-702.

Bridgeman, B., & Carlson, S. B. (1983). *Survey of academic writing tasks required of graduate and undergraduate foreign students* (TOEFL Research Rep. No. 15). Princeton, NJ: Educational Testing Service.

Brinton, D., Snow, M. A., & Wesche, M. (1989). *Content-based second language instruction.* New York: Newbury House.

Bruffee, K. (1984). Collaborative learning and the "conversation of mankind." *College English, 46*(7), 635-652.

Byrd, D. R. H., & Gallingane, G. (1990). *Write away 2.* New York: Newbury House.

Canseco, G., & Byrd, P. (1989). Writing required in graduate courses in business administration. *TESOL Quarterly, 23*(2), 305-316.

Celce-Murcia, M. (1989). Models for content-based curricula for ESL. *CATESOL Journal, 2*(1), 5-16.

Clarke, M. A. (1982). On bandwagons, tyranny, and common sense. *TESOL Quarterly, 16*(4), 437-448.

Clarke, M. A. (1984). On the nature of technique: What do we owe the gurus? *TESOL Quarterly, 18*(4), 577-594.

Clarke, M. A., & Silberstein, S. (1988). Problems, prescriptions and paradoxes in second language teaching. *TESOL Quarterly, 22*(4), 685-700.

Cohen, A. D. (1983, December). Reformulating compositions. *TESOL Newsletter*, p. 1, 4-5.

Cohen, A. D. (1987). Student processing of feedback on their compositions. In A. Wenden & J. Rubin (Eds.), *Learner strategies in language learning* (pp. 57-68). Englewood Cliffs, NJ: Prentice Hall.

Cohen, A. D., & Cavalcanti, M. C. (1990). Feedback on compositions: Teacher and student verbal reports. In B. Kroll (Ed.), *Second language writing: Research insights for the classroom* (pp. 155-177). New York: Cambridge University Press.

Connor, U. (1984). A study of cohesion and coherence in English as a second language students' writing. *Papers in Linguistics: International Journal of Human Communication, 17*, 301-316.

Connor, U. M. (1990). Discourse analysis and writing/reading instruction. *Annual Review of Applied Linguistics, 11*, 164-180.

Connor, U., & McCagg, P. (1983). Cross-cultural differences and perceived quality in written paraphrases of English expository prose. *Applied Linguistics, 4*, 259-268.

Cramer, N. A. (1985). *The writing process: 20 projects for group work.* Rowley, MA: Newbury House.

Cumming, A. (1989). Writing expertise and second language proficiency. *Language Learning, 39*(1), 81-141.

Eggington, W. G. (1987). Written academic discourse in Korean: Implications for effective communication. In U. Connor & R. B. Kaplan (Eds.), *Writing across languages: Analysis of L2 text* (pp. 153-168). Reading, MA: Addison-Wesley.

Elbow, P. (1991). Reflections on academic discourse: How it relates to freshmen and colleagues. *College English, 53*(2), 135-155.

Emig, J. (1971). *The composing processes of twelfth graders.* Urbana, IL: National Council of Teachers of English.

Enos, T. (1987). *A sourcebook for basic writing teachers.* New York: Random House.

Faigley, L. (1986). Competing theories of process: A critique and a proposal. *College English, 48*(6), 527-542.

Fathman, A. K., & Whalley, E. (1990). Teacher response to student writing: Focus on form versus content. In B. Kroll (Ed.), *Second language writing: Research insights for the classroom* (pp. 178-190). New York: Cambridge University Press.

Friedlander, A. (1990). Composing in English: Effects of a first language on writing in English as a second language. In B. Kroll (Ed.), *Second language writing: Research insights for the classroom* (pp. 109-125). New York: Cambridge University Press.

Grabe, W., & Kaplan, R. B. (1989). Writing in a second language: Contrastive rhetoric. In D. M. Johnson & D. H. Roen (Eds.), *Richness in writing: Empowering ESL students* (pp. 263-283). New York: Longman.

Hairston, M. (1991, January 23). Required writing courses should not focus on politically charged social issues. *Chronicle of Higher Education,* pp. B1-B3.

Hall, C. (1990). Managing the complexity of revising across languages. *TESOL Quarterly, 24*(1), 43-60.

Hamp-Lyons, L. (1986). No new lamps for old yet, please. *TESOL Quarterly, 20*(4), 790-796.

Harris, J. (1989). The idea of community in the study of writing. *College Composition and Communication, 40*(1), 11-22.

Hinds, J. (1987). Reader versus writer responsibility: A new typology. In U. Connor & R. B. Kaplan (Eds.), *Writing across languages: Analysis of L2 text* (pp. 141-152). Reading, MA: Addison-Wesley.

Hirsch, E. D., Jr. (1987). *Cultural literacy: What every American needs to know.* Boston: Houghton Mifflin.

Horowitz, D. M. (1986a). Process, not product: Less than meets the eye. *TESOL Quarterly, 20*(1), 141-144.

Horowitz, D. M. (1986b). What professors actually require: Academic tasks for the ESL classroom. *TESOL Quarterly, 20*(3), 445-462.

Horowitz, D. M. (1986c). The author responds to Liebman-Kleine. *TESOL Quarterly, 20*(4), 788-790.

Horowitz, D. M. (1990). Fiction and nonfiction in the ESL/EFL classroom: Does the difference make a difference? *English for Specific Purposes, 9,* 161-168.

Jenkins, S., & Hinds, J. (1987). Business letter writing: English, French, and Japanese. *TESOL Quarterly, 21*(2), 327-349.

Johns, A. M. (1981). Necessary English: A faculty survey. *TESOL Quarterly, 15*(1), 51-57.

Johns, A. M. (1984). Textual cohesion and the Chinese speaker of English. *Language Learning and Communication, 3,* 69-74.

Johns, A. M. (1986a). Coherence and academic writing: Some definitions and suggestions for teaching. *TESOL Quarterly, 20*(2), 247-265.

Johns, A. M. (1986b). The ESL student and the revision process: Some insights from schema theory. *Journal of Basic Writing, 5*(2), 70-80.

Johns, A. M. (1988). The discourse communities dilemma: Identifying transferable skills for the academic milieu. *English for Specific Purposes, 7,* 55-60.

Johns, A. M. (1990a). L1 composition theories: Implications for developing theories of L2 composition. In B. Kroll (Ed.), *Second language writing: Research insights for the classroom* (pp. 24-36). New York: Cambridge University Press.

Johns, A. M. (1990b, March). *Process, literature, and academic realities: Dan Horowitz and beyond.* Handout for paper presented at the 24th Annual TESOL Convention, San Francisco, CA.

Jones, C. S. (1982). Attention to rhetorical form while composing in a second language. In C. Campbell, V. Flashner, T. Hudson, & J. Lubin (Eds.), *Proceedings of the Los Angeles Second Language Research Forum* (Vol. 2, pp. 130-143). Los Angeles: University of California, Los Angeles.

Jones, C. S. (1985). Problems with monitor use in second language composing. In M. Rose (Ed.), *Studies in writer's block and other composing process problems* (pp. 96-118). New York: Guilford Press.

Jones, C. S., & Tetroe, J. (1987). Composing in a second language. In A. Matsuhashi (Ed.), *Writing in real time: Modeling production processes* (pp. 34-57). Norwood, NJ: Ablex.

Kaplan, R. B. (1966). Cultural thought patterns in intercultural education. *Language Learning, 16*(1), 1-20.

Kaplan, R. B. (1987). Cultural thought patterns revisited. In U. Connor & R. B. Kaplan (Eds.), *Writing across languages: Analysis of L2 text* (pp. 9-20). Reading, MA: Addison-Wesley.

Kaplan, R. B., & Shaw, P. A. (1983). *Exploring academic discourse.* Rowley, MA: Newbury House.

Krapels, A. (1990). An overview of second language writing process research. In B. Kroll (Ed.), *Second language writing: Research insights for the classroom* (pp. 37-56). New York: Cambridge University Press.

Kuhn, T. S. (1970). *The structure of scientific revolutions* (2nd ed.). Chicago: University of Chicago Press.

Kunz, L. (1972). *26 steps: A course in controlled composition for intermediate and advanced ESL students.* New York: Language Innovations.

Land, R. E., & Whitley, C. (1989). Evaluating second language essays in regular composition classes: Toward a pluralistic U.S. rhetoric. In D. M. Johnson & D. H. Roen (Eds.), *Richness in writing: Empowering ESL students* (pp. 284-293). New York: Longman.

Lautamatti, L. (1987). Observations in the development of the topic in simplified discourse. In U. Connor & R. B. Kaplan (Eds.), *Writing across languages: Analysis of L2 text* (pp. 87-114). Reading, MA: Addison-Wesley.

Lees, E. O. (1979). Evaluating student writing. *College Composition and Communication, 30*(4), 370-374.

Leki, I. (1990). Potential problems with peer responding in ESL writing classes. *CATESOL Journal, 3*(1), 5-19.

Leki, I. (1991). Twenty-five years of contrastive rhetoric: Text analysis and writing pedagogies. *TESOL Quarterly, 25*(1), 123-143.

Liebman-Kleine, J. (1986). In defense of teaching process in ESL composition. *TESOL Quarterly, 20*(4), 783-788.

Long, M. H., & Porter, P. A. (1985). Group work, interlanguage talk, and second language acquisition. *TESOL Quarterly, 19*(2), 207-228.

Lunsford, A., Moglen, H., & Slevin, J. (Eds.). (1990). *The right to literacy.* New York: Modern Language Association.

Mlynarczyk, R. (in press). Personal and academic writing: A false dichotomy? *TESOL Journal.*

Mohan, B. A. (1979). Relating language teaching and content teaching. *TESOL Quarterly, 13*(2), 171-182.

Mohan, B. A. (1986). *Language and content.* Reading, MA: Addison-Wesley.

Mohan, B. A., & Lo, W. A. (1985). Academic writing and Chinese students: Transfer and developmental factors. *TESOL Quarterly, 19*(3), 515-534.

North, S. M. (1987). *The making of knowledge in composition: Portrait of an emerging field*. Portsmouth, NH: Boynton/Cook, Heinemann.

Nunan, D. (1989a). *Designing tasks for the communicative classroom*. Cambridge: Cambridge University Press.

Nunan, D. (1989b). Toward a collaborative approach to curriculum development: A case study. *TESOL Quarterly, 23*(1), 9-25.

O'Hare, F. (1973). *Sentence combining: Improving student writing without formal grammar instruction*. Urbana, IL: National Council of Teachers of English.

Pack, A. C., & Henrichsen, L. E. (1980). *Sentence combination*. Rowley, MA: Newbury House.

Paulston, C. B., & Dykstra, G. (1973). *Controlled composition in English as a second language*. New York: Regents.

Peirce, B. N. (1989). Toward a pedagogy of possibility in the teaching of English internationally: People's English in South Africa. *TESOL Quarterly, 23*(3), 401-420.

Pennycook, A. (1989). The concept of method, interested knowledge, and the politics of language teaching. *TESOL Quarterly, 23*(4), 589-618.

Peyton, J. K. (Ed.). (1990). *Students and teachers writing together: Perspectives on journal writing*. Alexandria, VA: TESOL.

Prabhu, N. S. (1990). There is no best method—Why? *TESOL Quarterly, 24*(2), 161-176.

Purves, A. C. (Ed.). (1988). *Writing across languages and cultures*. Newbury Park, CA: Sage.

Radecki, P. M., & Swales, J. M. (1988). ESL student reaction to written comments on their written work. *System, 16*, 355-365.

Raimes, A. (1983a). Anguish as a second language? Remedies for composition teachers. In A. Freedman, I. Pringle, & J. Yalden (Eds.), *Learning to write: First language/second language* (pp. 258-272). Harlow, England: Longman.

Raimes, A. (1983b). Tradition and revolution in ESL teaching. *TESOL Quarterly, 17*(4), 535-552.

Raimes, A. (1985). What unskilled ESL students do as they write: A classroom study of composing. *TESOL Quarterly, 19*(2), 229-258.

Raimes, A. (1987). Language proficiency, writing ability, and composing strategies: A study of ESL college student writers. *Language Learning, 37*(3), 439-468.

Raimes, A. (1988). The texts for teaching writing. In B. K. Das (Ed.), *Materials for language learning and teaching* (pp. 41-58). Singapore: SEAMEO Regional Language Centre.

Raimes, A. (1990). *How English works: A grammar handbook with readings*. (Instructor's Manual). New York: St. Martin's Press.

Raimes, A. (in press). Instructional balance: From theories to practices in teaching writing. *Georgetown University Round Table on Languages and Linguistics 1991*.

Reid, J. (1984). Comments on Vivian Zamel's "The composing processes of advanced ESL students: Six case studies." *TESOL Quarterly, 18*(1), 149-159.

Reid, J. (1987, April). ESL composition: The expectations of the academic audience. *TESOL Newsletter*, p. 34.

Reid, J. (1989). English as a second language composition in higher education: The expectations of the academic audience. In D. M. Johnson & D. H. Roen (Eds.), *Richness in writing: Empowering ESL students* (pp. 220-234). New York: Longman.

Reid, J. (1990). Responding to different topic types: A quantitative analysis from a contrastive rhetoric perspective. In B. Kroll (Ed.), *Second language writing: Research insights for the classroom* (pp. 191-210). New York: Cambridge University Press.

Reid, J., & Lindstrom, M. (1985). *The process of paragraph writing.* Englewood Cliffs, NJ: Prentice Hall.

Richards, J. C. (1984). The secret life of methods. *TESOL Quarterly, 18*(1), 7-23.

Richards, J. C., & Nunan, D. (Eds.). 1990. *Second language teacher education.* Cambridge: Cambridge University Press.

Robb, T., Ross, S., & Shortreed, I. (1986). Salience of feedback on error and its effect on EFL writing quality. *TESOL Quarterly, 20*(1), 83-93.

Santos, T. (1988). Professors' reactions to the academic writing of nonnative-speaking students. *TESOL Quarterly, 22*(1), 69-90.

Scarcella, R. C. (1984). How writers orient their readers in expository essays: A comparative study of native and nonnative English writers. *TESOL Quarterly, 18*(4), 671-688.

Searle, J. R. (1969). *Speech acts: An essay in the philosophy of language.* Cambridge: Cambridge University Press.

Selinker, L., Todd-Trimble, M., & Trimble, L. (1978). Rhetorical function shifts in EST discourse. *TESOL Quarterly, 12*(3), 311-320.

Selzer, J. (1983). The composing processes of an engineer. *College Composition and Communication, 34*(2), 178-187.

Shih, M. (1986). Content-based approaches to teaching academic writing. *TESOL Quarterly, 20*(4), 617-648.

Shulman, L. S. (1987). Knowledge and teaching: Foundations of the new reform. *Harvard Educational Review, 57*(1), 1-22.

Silva, T. (1990). Second language composition instruction: Developments, issues, and directions in ESL. In B. Kroll (Ed.), *Second language writing: Research insights for the classroom* (pp. 11-23). New York: Cambridge University Press.

Simon, R. (1987). Empowerment as a pedagogy of possibility. *Language Arts, 64*(4), 370-382.

Snow, M. A., & Brinton, D. M. (1988). The adjunct model of language instruction: An ideal EAP framework. In S. Benesch (Ed.), *Ending remediation: ESL and content in higher education* (pp. 33-52). Washington, DC: TESOL.

Spack, R. (1984). Invention strategies and the ESL college composition student. *TESOL Quarterly, 18*(4), 649-670.

Spack, R. (1985). Literature, reading, writing, and ESL: Bridging the gaps. *TESOL Quarterly, 19*(4), 703-725.

Spack, R. (1988). Initiating ESL students into the academic discourse community: How far should we go? *TESOL Quarterly, 22*(1), 29-51.

Spack, R., & Sadow, C. (1983). Student-teacher working journals in ESL freshman composition. *TESOL Quarterly, 17*(4), 575-593.

Street, B. V. (1984). *Literacy in theory and practice.* Cambridge, England: Cambridge University Press.

Swales, J. (1987). Utilizing the literatures in teaching the research paper. *TESOL Quarterly, 21*(1), 41-68.

Swales, J. M. (1990). *Genre analysis: English in academic and research settings.* Cambridge: Cambridge University Press.

Tsao, F-F. (1983). Linguistics and written discourse in English and Mandarin. In R. B. Kaplan (Ed.), *Annual review of applied linguistics 1982* (pp. 99-117). Rowley, MA: Newbury House.

Weissberg, R. C. (1984). Given and new: Paragraph development models from scientific English. *TESOL Quarterly, 18*(3), 485-499.

Widdowson, H. G. (1978). *Teaching language as communication.* Oxford: Oxford University Press.

Zamel, V. (1976). Teaching composition in the ESL classroom: What we can learn from research in the teaching of English. *TESOL Quarterly, 10*(1), 67-76.

Zamel, V. (1980). Re-evaluating sentence-combining practice. *TESOL Quarterly, 14*(1), 81-90.

Zamel, V. (1982). Writing: The process of discovering meaning. *TESOL Quarterly, 16*(2), 195-210.

Zamel, V. (1983). The composing processes of advanced ESL students: Six case studies. *TESOL Quarterly, 17*(2), 165-187.

Zamel, V. (1985). Responding to student writing. *TESOL Quarterly, 19*(1), 79-101.

Listening in the Native and Second/Foreign Language: Toward an Integration of Research and Practice

PATRICIA DUNKEL
The Pennsylvania State University

After reviewing research on native language (NL) listening, the article discusses (a) the importance of listening in second language acquisition, (b) factors that influence success or failure of comprehension of first or second language messages, (c) the role of listening in the L2 curriculum, (d) posited models of NL and L2 listening comprehension, and (e) proposed taxonomies of listening skills and pedagogical activities. The essay argues that researchers and practitioners working together can foster greater understanding of L2 listening comprehension; it is hoped that such collaborations will lead to better preparation of nonnative speakers of English who must function effectively in a contemporary industrialized society that appears to be shifting increasingly toward the use of English, and simultaneously to be shifting away from literacy toward orality.

LISTENING IN THE NATIVE LANGUAGE: PROBLEMS OF DEFINITION AND OPERATIONALIZATION

To make Words serviceable to the end of Communication, it is necessary . . . that they excite in the Hearer, exactly the same *Idea*, they stand for in the mind of the Speaker. Without this, Men fill one another's Heads with noise and sounds; but convey not thereby their Thoughts, and lay not before one another their Ideas, which is the end of Discourse and Language (Locke, 1689/1988, p. 478).

John Locke's conception of the nature of verbal communication and listening comprehension may seem both perceptive and contemporary to today's second language acquisition (SLA) researchers and teachers, but such a view of human understanding was neither original to Locke nor novel to his time. As Taylor (1986) notes, the telementational conception of human understanding can be found "lurking in the linguistic reflections of Aristotle, St. Augustine, and the Modistae, the Port Royal grammarians,

Hobbes, and many others" (p. 17). Thus, the endeavor of today's communication scholars and SLA researchers to penetrate and illuminate the mental processes involved in comprehending discourse spoken in one's native language (NL) or second/foreign language (L2) is a quest that has engrossed philosophers since ancient times, has absorbed psychologists and speech communication scholars since the early part of the 20th century, and, more recently, has captured the attention of SLA researchers and practitioners of English as a second language as well as English as a foreign language. The study of listening comprehension has, in fact, become a polestar of second language acquisition theory building, research, and pedagogy (see Anderson & Lynch, 1988; Bernhardt & James, 1987; Brown, 1987; Byrnes, 1984; Dunkel, Chaudron & Henning, 1990; Galvin, 1985; Joiner, 1986; Krashen, 1977, 1981; Lund, 1990; Morley, 1991; Nagle & Sanders, 1986; Richards, 1983, 1985, 1990; Rost, 1990; Underwood, 1989; Ur, 1984).

Although epistemologists such as Locke and Aristotle long ago attempted to fathom the origin, modes, and scope of "human understanding," conduct of empirical investigations of native-language listening processes by speech communication scholars, speech scientists, and psychologists began to burgeon in the latter half of the 20th century, and a number of bibliographies and reviews of NL listening research give evidence of an increasing interest in listening (see Carroll, 1971; Coakley & Wolvin, 1986; Devine, 1967, 1978; Duker, 1964, 1968, 1969; Keller, 1960; Wilkinson, 1970; Witkin, 1990).

In his synthesis of NL reading and listening comprehension research, Carroll (1971) noted the increase in the quantity of empirical research on native language listening during the 1950s and 1960s, although he found few of the investigations to be "sufficiently penetrating and analytical" (p. 130). He observed that much of the research conducted in the 1950s and 1960s seemed focused on establishing "listening ability as a valid objective for the educational program, without determining its nature and parameters in a precise manner" (p. 130) and bemoaned the fact that even in the seventh decade of the 20th century, "there did not seem to exist any comprehensive theory of listening behavior in relation to language behavior in general or to other modes of language reception" (e.g., reading comprehension) (p. 130).

Twenty years after Carroll presented his synthesis of the central foci and basic quality of the NL listening research conducted during the first seven decades of this century, Witkin (1990) examined the state of the art of NL listening theory and research and pronounced it to be in a perilous state. According to Witkin, one of the chief problems facing the field of NL listening research is the lack of a generally agreed upon definition of listening. She notes that the vocabulary used to discuss NL listening is diffuse, with "some terms being on a highly abstract level, and some describing quite specific physiological or neurological processes" (p. 9).[1] Wolvin and Coakley (1988) have also expressed their concern about the disaccord concerning definitions and operationalizations of the construct of listening comprehension in the native language.[2]

In an extension of Wolvin and Coakley's examination of the listening definitions given by 16 communication scholars between 1925 and 1985, Glenn (1989) analyzed an additional 34 definitions of listening appearing in speech communication scholarly books and instructional texts. She concurred that there indeed appears to be no universally accepted definition of the construct of native language listening. Glen contends that the problem of definition limits communication research in listening and lessens the chance of finding effective methods of training individuals to be effective listeners (and speakers) of their native language (English). It also highlights the difficulty of generating "a universal conceptual definition of listening from which operational guidelines may be established" (Glen, 1989, p. 29).[3]

In addition to pointing out the "definition and operationalization" problem, Witkin (1990) identified several other problems endemic in theory building and research on NL listening comprehension: Most research on listening is *not* based on theory; the extant

---

[1] Barber and Fitch Hauser (cited in Witkin, 1990) identified 315 variables used in studying NL listening comprehension, some of which were defined in broad terms (e.g., listening, memory, perception, and attention); some in more precise terms (e.g., selectivity, channel, feedback, and decoding), and others in highly specific terms (e.g., electrochemical impulses, auditory discrimination, and dichotic/diotic listening).

[2] Wolvin and Coakley (1988) found the following numerous and varied differences in the meaning of the term *listening*. Researchers perceive NL listening to involve the hearer's "analyzing, concentrating, understanding, registering, converting meaning to the mind, engaging in further mental activity, responding, reacting, interpreting, relating to past experiences and future expectancies, assimilating, acting upon, selecting, receiving, apprehending, hearing, remembering, identifying, recognizing, comprehending, sensing, evaluating, emphasizing, and organizing" (p. 57). Many of the terms used by some researchers to describe listening are synonyms for expressions used by others. There is much verbal confusion and overlap of meaning as well as general disagreement concerning the psycholinguistic process of listening, according to Wolvin and Coakley.

[3] A similar assertion could be made with respect to the construct of second/foreign language listening. Definitions range from the simple and reductive (e.g., "listening is the activity of paying attention to and trying to get meaning from something we hear" [Underwood, 1989, p. 1]), to the more expansive and encompassing notion that listening needs to be defined in terms of the various *types* of listening: critical, global, intensive, interactional, transactional, recreational, and selective listening (Rost, 1990).

research is often contradictory; and almost no studies have been done to replicate or verify previous research. The problematic state of research may partially be due to the fact that there exists "a serious question among scholars as to whether there is an 'art' to listening research, and whether indeed the processes can be observed and studied" (Witkin, 1990, p. 7). This perception needs to be altered if we are to increase the quantity and quality of the empirical research base on listening, as well as the quality of listening training.

Although there is a growing interest in and concern for NL listening research and training due to the central role listening plays in language development, human relations (as well as international relations), and academic and business success, there seems to be very little genuine agreement about what listening entails, and how it operates. It is remarkable that there is so little understanding of a process that is so vitally important for an individual's survival and prosperity in interpersonal relationships, and in the academic and corporate environments.[4]

Even as NL communication scholars have begun to recognize the critical role listening skills play in the effective functioning of an individual in academic environments and business organizations, second language acquisition scholars have begun to apprehend the critical role listening plays in second language acquisition and learning. As a result, today's SLA researchers and L2 classroom teachers are endeavoring to (a) understand the *causative role* participatory and nonparticipatory listening plays in second language acquisition (both in naturalistic environments and in formal contexts such as classrooms;[5] (b) determine the role listening comprehension skill development does or should play in the L2

---

[4] Wolvin and Coakley's (1991) review of some Fortune 500 corporations' perceptions of the importance of listening in corporate settings indicates that listening is the most necessary and important communication skill for the following: entry-level employment; job success (DiSalvo, 1980; Larsen, & Seiler, 1976; Murphy & Jenks, 1982); general career competence (Muchmore & Galvin, 1983; Painter, 1985) and managerial competency ("The 20% Activities," 1978); and the effectiveness of subordinates (Downs & Conrad, 1982) and supervisors or middle management personnel (Harris & Thomlison, 1983). Citations are from Wolvin and Coakley, 1991, p. 153.

[5] Phillips and Omaggio (cited in Dunkel, 1991a) make a distinction between participatory and nonparticipatory listening. Participatory listening is characterized by the listener having the opportunity to seek clarification or modification of the discourse from the speaker. (Pica, Young, & Doughty, 1987, have investigated the impact of participatory or interactive listening on comprehension and intake of the input.) Nonparticipatory listening comprehension, on the other hand, does not allow for aural-oral interaction during input (e.g., when a learner listens to a conversation played via audiotape, or when listening to a lecture in a large lecture hall, or to a computerized test of L2 listening comprehension; see, for example, Dunkel, 1991a).

curriculum, especially in the beginning stages of learning; (c) pinpoint the factors "inside and outside the head" that enhance or depress comprehension of L2 input; (d) identify the components (subskills) of listening and to deduce the dynamic process(es) involved in L2 listening comprehension; and (e) deduce specific instructional tasks and classroom activities that enhance listening skill development for L2 learners. The remainder of this article discusses these five issues in the context of pedagogical theory, research, and instruction in both native language and L2 listening comprehension, and it raises issues that researchers and practitioners need to consider in the coming years when designing listening studies as well as instructional materials and classroom activities.

THE ROLE OF LISTENING IN SECOND LANGUAGE ACQUISITION AND ITS PLACE IN THE L2 CURRICULUM: OF THE INFLUENCE OF RESEARCH ON PRACTICE

A major catalyst for the relatively recent and intense interest in listening comprehension research has been the realization and accumulating evidence that input plays a critical role in second language acquisition. M. Long (1985) points out that current theories of second language acquisition, such as the information processing model (McLaughlin, Rossman, & McLeod, 1983), monitor model (Krashen, 1977), the intake model (Chaudron, 1985), the interaction model (Hatch, 1983), all emphasize the key role listening plays in the development of a learner's second/foreign language, particularly at the beginning stages of language development. Byrnes (1984) and Dunkel (1986) have also highlighted the valuable insights gained from studies of child language acquisition that suggest the pivotal role listening comprehension plays in native language development.

As a result of current theory that proposes and empirical research that indicates the importance of prespeaking in language development, it has become increasingly commonplace for L2 teachers to deemphasize speaking and to emphasize listening in the early stages of L2 instruction. Synthesizing findings of recent and not so recent research on second language acquisition and pedagogical theory that tend to support the beneficial aspects of providing beginning-level learners with a "silent" or "prespeaking" period of L2 instruction, Daniels, Pringle, and Wood (1986) articulate the theoretical rationale and obtained evidence for the benefits of delayed oral practice in early-stage learning:

(1) A tendency toward better all-round performance has been noted in learners who have experienced a silent period than in those who have not (Asher et al., 1974; Postovsky, 1974; Thiele and Scheibner-Herzig, 1983).[6]

(2) Learners who are required at too early a stage to speak are likely to suffer from a phenomenon known as "task overload" which probably inhibits language acquisition and the exercise and development of discriminatory skills, creates anxiety and encourages interference from L1 (Ingram et al., 1975; Nord, 1975; Krakowian, 1981). Understanding or misunderstanding goes on in the intimacy of our own heads. If not called upon to perform, learners can come to grips with the new foreign language, under cover, without having to expose their sometimes vulnerable "language ego" to the censure of teachers or peers (Gary and Gary, 1981; Marton, 1983; Daniels and Wood, 1984).

(3) In natural circumstances both child and adult acquirers of foreign languages typically go through a "silent period" (Hakuta, 1974; Huang and Hatch, 1978; Dulay et al., 1982, pp. 22-24).

(4) The audio-lingual approach has laid great emphasis on the importance of speaking as a foreign language learning goal, to the extent that many language learners are able to "vocalize" (which presumably does not have the same status or manifest the same complexity of creativeness as "speaking" while remaining, in the words of Belasco [1981] cited in Nord [1981]), "virtually incompetent in understanding the spoken language." Understanding competence is very possibly of more use to most learners of foreign languages than is speaking competence. It would therefore seem logical, given the impossibility of doing everything at once, to give priority to training in listening comprehension (Nord, 1974; Davies, 1980). (pp. 47-48)

Gary and Gary (1981) stress the cognitive, affective, and utilitarian advantages of delaying oral exercise and increasing listening practice for L2 learning: (a) The *cognitive advantage:* As Postovsky (1974; cited in Gary & Gary, 1981) argues, "requiring learners to produce material that they have not yet stored in their memory will lead to language interference and overload of short-term memory" (p. 4); (b) The *affective advantage:* Forcing learners to produce language before they are cognitively, emotionally, and linguistically ready is traumatic. "Both first and second language learners generally prefer not to speak a language which they only

---

[6] In an experiment in which two fifth form classes of beginning level students of English as a foreign language were taught for 6 weeks with an emphasis on early or delayed oral production plus total physical response approaches, Thiele and Scheibner-Herzig (1983) found that those receiving training in listening comprehension combined with an initial delay of oral practice surpassed those taught by conventional methods both in their listening and their overall command of English. The delayed production method was also found to have a positive effect on subjects' attitudes toward studying English, and it created a classroom atmosphere "devoid of anxiety" (p. 285).

imperfectly perceive (see, e.g., Ervin-Tripp, 1974; Sorensen, 1967; Asher, 1979)" (p. 5); and (c) The *utilitarian advantage:* Comprehension-oriented instruction uses classroom time more efficiently than production-oriented instruction since all the students can be listening and responding individually rather than in unison in choral drill. According to Gary and Gary (1981), "language learners who have been taught to capitalize on the advantages of a receptive approach to language learning are more likely to be inclined to continue their language study alone, independently of a particular language program. This can be carried out, for example, by their listening to the radio, watching TV, or going to foreign language films" (p. 6–7).

Although it has become generally accepted practice to provide beginning-level learners with a considerable amount of comprehensible input (Krashen, 1981), Rickerson (1984) stresses the need to provide foreign/second language students with opportunity to produce the language to enhance the motivation during language learning. He reports that when the Defense Language Institute, following Postovsky's lead,

> tried to become more cost-effective and efficient by limiting courses *solely* to learning listening comprehension, it was discovered that the absence of speaking was detrimental to learning to listen. Learner motivation was probably the reason. For instance, students wanted enough German to travel to the country, to order a *Bier* in a *Gasthaus*, and to converse with the population. Eliminating speaking was counterproductive. As a result, speaking has been reinstated as a part of all basic courses regardless of the student's future assignment. It seems that for acquisition to take place fully, a balance in both skills is required. (p. 214)

Not only is listening comprehension important at the beginning stages of SLA, it appears to be crucially important for advanced-level learners (e.g., those with TOEFL scores > 500) as well (Powers, 1985). When asked to indicate the relative importance of listening, reading, speaking and writing for international students' success in their academic departments, U.S. and Canadian professors of engineering, psychology, chemistry, computer science, English and business, for example, gave the receptive skills of listening and reading the highest ratings. (Reading comprehension was seen as the most important of the four abilities in all disciplines surveyed except English.) Listening was rated the second most important in four of the six disciplines (engineering, psychology, chemistry, and computer science).

Issues for L2 Researchers and Practitioners

Until the 1980s, much of the language teaching field took listening for granted, according to Morley (1991), who attributes the trivial treatment listening has received from L2 practitioners to the "elusiveness" (p. 82) of our listening awareness. As Weaver (cited in Morley, 1991) remarks, "after all, listening is neither so dramatic nor so noisy as talking. The talker is the center of attention for all listeners. His [sic] behavior is overt and vocal, and he hears and notices his own behavior, whereas listening activity often seems like merely being there—doing nothing" (p. 82). Morley (1991) maintains that we need to realize that listening is anything but a passive activity, and she urges practitioners not to dismiss listening in a cavalier manner. "The importance of listening cannot be underestimated; it is imperative that it not be treated trivially in second and foreign language curricula" (p. 82). Neither should it receive cavalier treatment from SLA researchers. Listening research should be fostered to advance the state of SLA theory building, and to expand the knowledge base about the process of L2 comprehension and the effective methods of teaching L2 listening comprehension to beginning-, intermediate-, and advanced-level learners. Some of the investigations should be directed toward probing the impact that specific factors, internal and external to the listener, have on the success or failure of L2 comprehension in order to provide guidance to L2 curriculum designers and classroom teachers as well as to L2 listening materials writers.

FACTORS AFFECTING NL AND L2 LISTENING COMPREHENSION: OF FUNDAMENTAL INFLUENCES "INSIDE AND OUTSIDE THE HEAD" OF THE LISTENER

NL researchers have sought to identify the factors "inside the head" and "outside the head" that influence comprehension of oral communication in positive and negative ways. Communication scholars Watson and Smeltzer (1984), for example, highlight several internal or "inside the head" (i.e., receiver) factors that can hinder NL listening comprehension: (a) personal internal distractions (e.g., hunger, headaches, emotional disturbance); (b) personal disinterest in the topic of the message; (c) inattentiveness (e.g., daydreaming); (d) positive and/or negative emotional responses toward the speakers, topic, or occasion; (e) detouring (what the speaker says makes you think of something else which is off the topic); (f) jumping to conclusions about what a person is going to say before it is said; (g) over-reacting to the language of the speaker (e.g., her/his use of slang, cursing); (h) over-reacting to the message of the speaker (reacting to the political implications of the message); (i) tending toward rebuttal (developing a counter argument before the speaker is finished); and (j) rehearsing a response (thinking about what you have to say rather than what is being said). (It is interesting to note that none of these learner traits has been examined in an L2 empirical investigation, to my knowledge. Any one would prove of interest, particularly to teachers of advanced-level learners of ESL/EFL.)

Samuels (1984) discusses the impact of several additional factors internal to NL listeners, two of which are intelligence and language facility. Some questions to be considered with respect to these factors are the following: (a) Intelligence: Does the listener have the requisite intelligence to comprehend the discourse? and (b) Language facility:

> Is the listener accurate and automatic in the ability to segment and parse the speech stream into morpheme and syntactic units? . . . Does the listener have an extensive vocabulary? Does the listener know the variety of ways in which a word can be used? . . . Can the listener take embedded sentences and parse them into understandable units? . . . Can the listener identify the referent for the anaphoric terms used? . . . Is the listener able to make inferences necessary to comprehend the elliptical sentences commonly used in casual conversation? (p. 184)

(While the questions raised are directed toward NL listeners, they seem equally appropriate for L2 listeners as well.)

With respect to the inferential process, Rost (1990) claims that "understanding spoken language is essentially an inferential process based on a perception of cues rather than straightforward matching of sound to meaning" (p. 33). Rost suggests that the L2 listener must perform the following inferential processes while listening:

(1) estimating the sense of lexical references;

(2) constructing propositional meaning through supplying case-relational links;

(3) assigning a "base (conceptual) meaning" in the discourse;

(4) assigning underlying links in the discourse;

(5) assuming a plausible intention for the speaker's utterances. (pp. 62-63)

Carroll (1977) has identified several affective and cognitive variables that affect NL listening comprehension, including the listener's (a) degree of motivation to comprehend and learn the information contained in the message and the amount of interest in the topic of discussion; (b) ability to perceive relations among elements of the discourse, and ability to focus attention on the discourse and ignore distractions in the environment. Goss (1982) posits that essentially NL listening comprehension is a function of the receiver's basic information-processing ability and level of cognitive complexity, the latter being operationalized as an ability to hold in focus and compare alternative perceptions on an issue.

Not only do internal factors affect NL comprehension, external factors also influence the success or failure of the comprehension or learning process. Carroll (1977) relates the ability to learn from being told to factors *external* to the native language listener: the rate at which material is presented, and the conceptual difficulty and organization of the information presented. He notes that although research studies have shown that presentation rates may vary rather widely without seriously affecting comprehension (Fairbanks, Guttman, & Miron, 1957; Foulke, Amster, Nolan, & Bixler, 1962; Goldstein, 1940), the listening materials for these studies involved well-organized, readily understood materials. As soon as the materials become less well organized or conceptually more difficult, native language comprehension suffers.

Carroll also points out the inverse relationship between comprehension and length of the material; he claims that the presentation of a long series of sentences (even for native speakers) becomes somewhat analogous to the presentation of a long series of arbitrary associations:

> To the extent that subject-predicate relations in sentences or various base structures contained in sentences can be regarded as arbitrary associations, the learning of a series of sentences becomes analogous to paired associate learning, and some of the same considerations that apply to paired associate learning might apply to this case. . . . For example, inter-sentence similarity might have the same effect as inter-pair similarity in paired associate learning of nonsense pairs. (p. 507-508)

Finally, Carroll (1977) suggests that learning from aurally received input is enhanced by repetition of the material heard (repetition on the part of both the speaker and the listener). To Carroll's thinking, just as a list of arbitrary associations becomes better learned by presenting them over a series of trials, continuous discourse is better learned by rehearing, repeating, or rereading it.

Watson and Smeltzer (1984) cite three additional text, environmental, and speaker variables that can confound successful NL listening comprehension: (a) ambiguity of the message; (b) environmental distractions (e.g., phones ringing, other voices); and (c) distracting mannerisms of the speaker (e.g., stuttering, nervous or incomprehensible gestures).

Wolvin and Coakley (1988) mention the influence of culture and self-concept on the listener's participation in the communication process. They note that a listener's culture "essentially serves to define who he or she is and how he or she will communicate through his or her perceptual filter" (p. 121). In addition, they note that for most of us, even our native-language listening self-concept is not always a positive one, due in part to sensitivity developed as a result of parental commands and cajoles related to listening that were administered during childhood (e.g., a parent's or teacher's barb, "You're not *listening* to me!"). L2 listeners can also suffer the effect of a negative listening self-concept if they feel inadequate to the task of understanding the English spoken by native speakers, and this lack of confidence may influence their listening comprehension in adverse ways. "The fear of misinterpreting, inadequately processing and/or not being able to adjust psychologically to messages sent by others" (Preiss & Wheeless, 1989, p. 72) plays a meaningful role in suppressing comprehension of a message delivered in the listener's native language and in his or her second/foreign language as well.

For L2 listeners, all of the internal and external barriers mentioned above undoubtedly serve also to confound comprehension of L2 messages, and SLA researchers are beginning to theorize about and investigate many of these factors as well as a number of additional factors that serve either to detract from or to support a receiver's L2 comprehension. Faerch and Kasper (1986), for example, discuss several inside-the-L2-head factors of a psycholinguistic/sociolinguistic and experiential nature that impact comprehension, including L2 listeners' (a) knowledge of the L2 linguistic code; (b) degree of sociocultural competence (i.e., their degree of familiarity with the sociocultural content of the message conveyed by the speaker); (c) and strategic competence (i.e., their ability to guess meanings of unfamiliar terms heard and to use verbal and nonverbal strategies to compensate for gaps in their knowledge of the linguistic code).

Oxford (1990) also speculates about the importance of the L2 listener's ability to employ cognitive strategies involving deductive reasoning and compensation strategies (e.g., guessing intelligently about the meaning of what is heard) as well as indirect strategies of a metacognitive nature (e.g., delaying speech production to focus on listening), of an affective type (e.g., getting the general meaning without knowing every word), and of a social character (e.g., asking for clarification or repetition of what was heard). Many of these contentions, however, remain empirical questions and call for research that will affirm or disconfirm the hypotheses put forth (as well as all the hypotheses put forth concerning the interactive effect of the various factors internal to the listener).

In a survey of 30 Chinese teachers and 60 students, Boyle (1984) identified the factors perceived to be most salient influences on EFL listening comprehension, in terms of (a) speaker factors, such as the language ability of the speaker (native speaker vs. beginning-level speaker, etc.), the quality of the speech signal (the degree of accent, speed, etc.), and the prestige and personality of the speaker (a consideration not typically mentioned in the NL listening literature); (b) factors in the oral text, such as the complexity of the lexis and syntax, the amount of cohesion and organization evident in the text; and (c) listener factors (e.g., intelligence; memory, gender, motivation, and background knowledge). In a discussion of the application of schema theory to L2 listening comprehension research and practice, D. Long (1989) highlights the critical role both the inside-the-head factor, background knowledge (*content schemata*) as well as the outside-the-head factor (*textual schemata*) play in L2 listening comprehension.[7] She notes that Mueller (1980) determined that listeners more proficient in German needed less help from visual contextual cues to activate appropriate scripts (see Footnote 7), whereas the less proficient learners (who were not able to rely on linguistic cues to activate appropriate schemata) had greater need of verbal contextual organizers. Weissenreider's (1987) research on listening to Spanish-language newscasts also demonstrates that knowledge about the newscast process (textual schemata) and the specific themes of the news reports (content schemata) augmented comprehension of the news information. In a study of the effect of speech modification, prior knowledge, and listening proficiency on the lecture learning of students of English as a foreign language, Chiang (1990) provides additional evidence that knowledge of the content schemata enhances the comprehension for EFL listeners. The supportive effect of prior knowledge has been well documented in the reading comprehension literature but rarely examined in the listening comprehension literature (see also Chiang & Dunkel, in press).

---

[7] According to Anderson and his colleagues (cited in D. Long, 1989), *textual schemata* involves knowledge of the discourse-level conventions of text. "For example, when making an operator-assisted long distance telephone call, the caller expects to be asked for specific types of information such as type of assistance required, billing number, and name. *Content schemata*, on the other hand, are derived from the individual's life experiences: checking out library books, purchasing license plates, going to the dentist's office" (p. 33).
According to Schank and Abelson's definition (cited in Long, 1989, p. 33), *scripts* are "predetermined, stereotyped sequences of action that define well-known situations"; scripts aid the listener to comprehend "input relating to commonplace situations." Long notes, for example, the script for ordering at a drive-through window of a fast-food restaurant would aid comprehension of spoken discourse about this particular activity at a McDonald's (or similar) restaurant.

Sheils (1988) also considers familiarity with the content schemata of a talk to be vitally important for listeners and highlights several additional factors that are thought to affect the difficulty of processing oral discourse (i.e., to make it easier or harder). They are related to the content, structural, and linguistic features of the oral text, and to the speaker's style of delivery and speech: (a) the density and degree of predictability and explicitness of information contained in the speech; (b) the degree of linguistic complexity; (c) length and conceptual difficulty of the text; (d) amount of time allowed to process the text; (e) the speed of delivery and comprehensibility of the accent; (f) the transparency of the organization and the inclusion of evident discourse signals marking the structure and organization of the information. With regard to the precise functional effect of discourse markers on L2 listeners' comprehension of academic discourse, Chaudron and Richards (1986) empirically demonstrated that a speaker's use of discourse signals facilitates comprehension of lecture information. More specifically, they found that lecturers who included clearly signaled macromarkers (e.g., *"What I'm going to talk about today; you probably know something about already"; This is how it came about"* [p. 127]) made the task of understanding a lecture easier for the L2 listener. (Rather interestingly, they found that inclusion of micromarkers, for example, *OK, all right, after this*) did not aid the learners' retention of the lecture content.)

Materials writers Anderson and Lynch (1988) illustrate the ease-difficulty continuum of L2 comprehension. They note that listening to a radio broadcast of a parliamentary debate is relatively demanding of the listener, whereas listening to a child read from a book of fairy tales is much less demanding. The factors influencing the ease or difficulty of these tasks for the L2 listener are a function of (a) the type of language heard; (b) the context in which listening occurs; and (c) the task or purpose of the listening. In Anderson and Lynch's estimation, the parliamentary debate input may be hard to follow because of the unpredictability, complexity, and possible abstractness of the content, the crosstalk and overlap of voices, and the involved linguistic form and different accents. Anderson and Lynch do, however, point out that the effect of the complexity of input interacts with the listener's purpose in listening. They note that if the listener

has switched on the radio simply to determine whether the parliamentary debate has finished or whether today's instalment of our favorite radio serial has started yet, then the listening experience—despite that long list of difficult input features—is not a demanding one. For some listeners, however, the broadcast debate from Westminster will involve a much more difficult task or set of tasks. A business executive, for example, will be paying close attention to what is said in the annual Budget debate because she needs to remember it, either to pass the information on to her colleagues straight away, or to use it at a later stage. (p. 46)

Anderson and Lynch make the point that what makes the executive's task so difficult is the attempt to remember the details of the debate and the fact of trying to interpret what is implied in the debate rather than what is simply and clearly stated. The listener was, in other words, required to synthesize, interpret, and analyze the information heard.

It is clear that internal and external factors may interact in a variety of ways to make the L2 listener's task easier or more complex, but what is not quite clear is exactly how each functions to affect the comprehension of listeners from various cultural backgrounds and of different levels of language proficiency and possessing different learner traits.

Issues for L2 Researchers and Practitioners

Since the 1950s, we have gained some important and potentially useful insights about the numerous factors inside and outside the head of the listener that impact comprehension of the message; however, the speculations concerning the influence of these factors have rarely been derived from empirical investigations. More often, they have sprung from logico-deductive speculation, fueled by professional intuition garnered as a result of years of classroom teaching. We are, as a result, in dire need of empirical investigations that assess the validity of our assumptions regarding the interactive effects certain factors have on L2 listening comprehension. Several L2 researchers have, indeed, conducted studies examining the effects of *factors internal to the listener* (see Call's 1985 study on auditory short-term memory and listening comprehension, and Dunkel, Mishra, & Berliner's 1989 study of the effects of memory and language proficiency on NL and L2 lecture learning), *factors external to the listener* (see Chaudron & Richards's 1986 study of the effect of discourse markers on the comprehension of L2 lectures, and Pica, Doughty, & Young's 1987 examination of the impact of communicative interaction on L2 comprehension), and *listener strategies* (see O'Malley, Chamot, & Küpper's 1989 study of the mental processes L2 listeners use to comprehend L2 information and Benson's 1989 case study of the note-taking habits of an EFL listener).

We need, however, to increase vastly the number of empirical studies that investigate the ways in which factors inside and outside the L2 head affect comprehension of L2 discourse for beginning-, intermediate- and advanced-level L2 listeners from various sociocultural backgrounds. We can look to the NL listening research literature for help in identifying some of the factors that seem to influence comprehension of L2 discourse, but we need to create our own expansive corpus of research on the subject. The L2 research base is still in its infancy. Instructors who teach L2 listening need to work hand in hand with researchers to ensure the quality, quantity and utility of experimental and ethnographic studies of L2 listening. Teachers can, for example, help frame research questions that need to be addressed by researchers. (Joiner, 1986, notes that "listening is a young field and, as such, one with not only many unanswered questions, but also many questions that have yet to be raised" [p. 68]). Teachers can also help the research effort by making their students available as subjects for experimental or ethnographic research, and by conducting action research in their classrooms. In addition, researchers who conduct empirical investigations of L2 listening have the responsibility of ensuring that their findings are made available and *accessible* to classroom listening teachers who may not necessarily be schooled in the interpretation of statistical analyses. Working hand in hand, teachers and researchers can expand the L2 research base and guarantee that research impacts on practice, and vice versa.

THE COMPONENTS AND DYNAMICS OF LISTENING COMPREHENSION AND PEDAGOGY: OF COMPREHENSION MODELS AND TAXONOMIES OF LISTENING SKILLS AND PEDAGOGICAL EXERCISES

As mentioned previously, communication scholars and second language acquisition researchers have attempted to capture the essence of the construct of listening comprehension in succinct definitions (although they have rarely succeeded in their attempts) as well as in simple-to-elaborate models of L1/L2 comprehension (Goss, 1982; Nagle & Sanders, 1986; Rost, 1990; Wolvin, 1990). Wolvin (cited in Witkin, 1990), for example, described 12 speech communication models of NL listening proposed between 1956 and 1986 that ranged from

> simple diagrams or hierarchical ordering of listening components to Barker's 1971 complex model of listening in the context of the total communication process, including auditory and visual elements of

reception, perception, discrimination, and response, and both cognitive and affective elements; and Lundsteen's (1979) flow chart model of the processes taken by an effective listeners, incorporating responding and organizing, getting meaning, and thinking beyond listening. (p. 11)

Faerch and Kasper (1986) make reference to the Jarvella and Nelson psycholinguistic model of NL comprehension which assumes that "language understanding is usually a product of several cognitive subsystems working together in a harmonious way" (p. 264). Faerch and Kasper contend that Jarvella and Nelson's model compartmentalizes study of the comprehension of verbal input into speech perception,

investigating the intake, segmentation, and identification of strings of sounds (or letters); the understanding of individual sentences, with an emphasis on the parsing of syntactic structure, the construction of propositions or on elaborating implied (semantic and pragmatic) meaning; and finally the comprehension of spoken and written discourse, e.g., reconstructing the recipients' "story grammars." (p. 264)

The emphasis in this NL model of verbal comprehension is on "higher-level processes" of meaning construction, according to Faerch and Kasper. In Nagle and Sanders' (1986) L2 comprehension model, comprehension and learning are viewed as interrelated, interdependent, but distinctive cognitive phenomena. They distinguish between automatic and controlled decoding processes that interact with and affect implicit and explicit linguistic knowledge as well as other types of nonlinguistic knowledge. The researchers posit that "comprehension becomes more efficient as knowledge increases, processes become automatic, and experience confirms the reliability of the learner's decoding, inferring, and predicting" (p. 22).

Rost (1990) points out that "although some models of verbal understanding have been attempted, they are for the most part broad descriptions of linguistic and pragmatic competence or narrow descriptions of verbal processes" (p. 7).[8] Model building, however, forms the foundation of theory development and should be vigorously pursued in the coming decades if we are to advance the knowledge base about the process of listening comprehension, in general, and L2 comprehension in particular.

---

[8] The central aspects of Dunkel, Chaudron, and Henning's (1990) narrow model of L2 listening comprehension, which was designed with computer-adaptive testing purposes in mind, involve the specification of a range of listening processes and performances, or cognitive operations, referred to as "tasks," which are coupled with a range of general "text types" and specific "text elements" as well as several dimensions of response formats, combinations of all of which lead to a large (open-ended) set of "test task frames."

Not only have various models of NL and L2 listening comprehension been proposed, but researchers have also constructed a number of taxonomies delineating the microskills needed for effective listening and the various listener tasks and functions related to these microskills. In addition, manifold pedagogical exercises incorporating many of the identified microskills have been designed by materials writers for use by ESL/EFL classroom teachers. The taxonomies serve to highlight some of the abilities that listeners need to develop if they are to function as skillful listeners. Richards's 1985 taxonomy, for example, lists 33 individual microskills of L2 participatory or conversational listening (e.g., the ability to recognize the communicative functions of utterances, according to situations, participants, and goals), and 18 specific microskills involved in nonparticipatory, academic listening (e.g., the ability to identify relationships among units within discourse, such as major ideas, generalizations, hypotheses, supporting ideas, examples).

Lund's 1990 taxonomy of "real-world listening behaviors" (p. 106) identifies six listener functions that define the part(s) of the text that the listener will attend to and process (pp. 107-109): (a) *identification* of some "aspect of the linguistic code or content of the message" (e.g., at the lowest level of proficiency, discriminating between minimal phonemic pairs; or at the advanced level, writing down all the adjectives used in a radio commercial); (b) *orientation*, which involves "determining essential facts about the text, including the roles of the participants, the general topic and genre of the discourse" (e.g., "determining that one is hearing a news broadcast and that the news involves sports"); (c) *main idea comprehension* of the message (e.g., "understanding a lecture well enough to summarize the main points or complete a basic outline"); (d) *detail comprehension* (e.g., "getting the departure times and the platform numbers for several trains to a destination"); (e) *full comprehension*, which involves understanding the main idea plus the details (e.g., "understanding a lecture so that one can take detailed notes or make a detailed outline").

Lund (1990) also distinguishes several overt listener responses that can be used to check that one of the six functions has been performed successfully: (a) *doing* (the listener responds physically to a command); (b) *choosing* (the listener selects from alternatives such as pictures, objects, texts); (c) *transferring* (the listener draws a picture of what is heard); (d) *answering* (the listener answers questions about the message); (e) *condensing* (the listener outlines or takes notes on a lecture); (f) *extending* (the listener provides the ending to a story heard); (g) *duplicating* (the listener translates the messages into the native language or repeats it verbatim); (h) *modeling* (the listener orders a meal after listening to a model order); (i) *conversing* (the listener engages in a conversation or "'talks back' to a particularly silly or offensive ad on the radio" (p. 111).

Many of the activities suggested in Lund's function-response matrix of listening activities build upon those identified by Ur (1984) in her pragmatic and useful work on teaching listening comprehension. Ur (1984) describes and illustrates the process of L2 listening in terms of focused and task-based activities in which L2 listeners participate (e.g., they listen to the news, weather, or sports; hear a speech or lecture; obtain professional advice from a doctor), and she categorizes listening into two types: (a) listening for perception (they hear and group sounds at the phoneme, word, and sentence levels), and (b) listening for comprehension in which listeners make no response (e.g., they follow a familiar text), a shorter response (e.g., they detect mistakes in an aural description), or a longer response (e.g., they paraphrase, translate, answer questions on a text, or summarize information heard).

In discussing the design of instructional materials and classroom activities, Richards (1990) exhorts materials and classroom teachers to incorporate (and model) the two main purposes of communication—to convey factual or propositional information (a transactional purpose) and to further social relationships and/or to express personal attitudes (an interactional purpose)—as well as the two different types of information processes: "top-down" listening (learners read information about a topic, then listen to a minitalk on the topic and check whether or not the information was mentioned in the talk) and "bottom-up" listening (learners identify the referents of pronouns used in a conversation). Richards decries the fact that too often commercially produced materials set goals that are incompatible with the communicative intent of the message used as the stimulus, and he further also criticizes the fact that published listening texts require students to adopt a single approach to listening, one that often demands a detailed understanding of the content of a discourse and the recognition of every word and structure that occurred in a text. He emphasizes that students should not be required to respond to interactional discourse as if it were being used for transactional purposes, nor should they be expected to use a bottom-up approach to an aural text if a top-down approach would be more appropriate. Richards also makes the case that "in developing classroom activities and materials for teaching listening comprehension, a clear understanding is needed of the nature of top-down and bottom-up approaches to listening and how these processes relate to different kinds of listening purposes" (p. 65).

Peterson (1991) incorporates Richards's notion of bottom-up and top-down processing into her proposals for various types of listening exercises specifically geared toward developing the L2 listening comprehension of beginning-, intermediate-, and advanced-level listeners. Examples of the exercise types include the following: (a) bottom-up processing for beginning-level listeners (they discriminate between intonation contours in a message), for intermediate-level listeners (they recognize unstressed function words in the speech stream), and for advanced-level listeners (they use the lecturer's volume and stress to identify important information for note taking); top-down processing goals for beginning-level listeners (they identify the emotional state of the speaker), for intermediate-level listeners (they identify registers of speech as formal/informal, polite/impolite), and for advanced-level listeners (they listen to a statement and indicate what further meaning can be inferred from the statement). Peterson also sets her exercise types within the framework of interactional and transactional language (see Peterson, 1991).[9]

Issues for L2 Researchers and Practitioners

The various models of listening comprehension, as well as the sundry taxonomies of listening skills and pedagogical activities, have largely been derived from insights gained as a result of classroom experience and perusal of the NL and L2 listening literature.[10] Both the assumptions concerning the accuracy and utility of the models as well as claims of effectiveness for suggested pedagogical activities are legion; the empirical evidence supporting these contentions is scant, at best. It is, therefore, expedient that researchers and classroom teachers make every effort to ascertain to what degree psychological reality and instructional value are indeed embodied and reflected in the various theoretical models of listening comprehension (see, for example, Nagle & Sanders, 1986), the taxonomies of component subskills (see, for example, Richards, 1990), the dynamic processes involved in L2 listening comprehension (see, for example, Dunkel, 1986; Rost, 1990), the sundry

---

[9] Anderson and Lynch (1988), Rost (1990), Underwood (1989), and Ur (1984) identify a plethora of task-based activities, listening goals, and types of texts that can be used to help learners develop L2 listening proficiency.

[10] D. Long (1989) expressed concern that most of our current knowledge about comprehension has been borrowed from the NL cognitive psychological literature. "Some danger of 'lack of fit' always exists when applying borrowed theories to second language acquisition" (p. 33). Caution should be exercised when attempting to siphon NL-related findings into L2 practices.

enumerations of pedagogical activities and instructional approaches (see, for example, Lund, 1990; Peterson, 1991). We also need to determine which internal and external factors impact favorably or negatively on L2 listening comprehension (as well as to what degree, and in which ways) given certain levels of language proficiency and specific types of instructional environments (ESL vs. EFL settings, for example).

We need to achieve these research goals so that more valid and effective instructional approaches and listening materials can be devised and used. Let us hope that by the year 2000, a more expansive and higher quality base of research will be available to guide and enlighten second/foreign language teachers and second language acquisition researchers. These goals will not be achieved, however, unless L2 researchers aggressively search out sources of funding within their home institutions (e.g., from those interested in the retention of minority and international undergraduate and graduate students), and outside (e.g., from the United States Department of Education for U.S. researchers) that will allow them to conduct more empirical studies of the dynamic processes involved in L2 listening. A comprehensive understanding of L2 listening comprehension will prove elusive unless classroom teachers work hand in hand with researchers to promote research and to test the internal and external validity of researchers' speculations and empirical findings about the construct of L2 listening comprehension.

THE IMPORTANCE OF LISTENING IN CONTEMPORARY POSTLITERATE SOCIETY

In reflecting on contemporary life, and orality and literacy from antiquity to the present, the renowned classicist Eric Havelock (1986) concluded that as a result of the proliferation of electronic media, the presence of orality has become an accepted fact in contemporary society. Electronic media may even have effected a shift from literacy to orality in modern life; speaking of the U.S., Freedman (1982) asserts that "we have slowly but emphatically shifted our means of communication from the printed word to images and sounds, from books to television, movies, radio, and recordings. Instead of reading today, most of us prefer to look and listen" (p. A-15).[11] Wolvin and Coakley (1988) maintain that the

[11] The shift toward a postliterate society may be having an especially profound impact on the younger generation in the industrialized world. Based on statistics published in a 1985 A. C. Nielsen Company survey, Wolvin and Coakley (1988) calculate that in the United States, young people, from ages two to eighteen, spend more than 20,000 hours before television sets, which is over 7,000 hours more than they spend in school from kindergarten through 12th grade.

United States, like many other nations in the industrial world, has become a nation of listeners, and those coming to live, work, and study in the English-speaking industrial nations of the world will need to become highly proficient listeners of English. As disturbing as the shift from literacy to orality in modern society may be to many, the electronic communication revolution has focused attention on the need to gain more detailed knowledge of what promotes and hinders the understanding of messages communicated in the native and second/foreign language. The challenge has been with us from, and before, the time of John Locke and will, no doubt, accompany us into the next century. In the coming years, it is likely that the use of computer-mediated technologies for foreign/second language instruction will become commonplace, especially in the industrialized nations of the world, and their use in the service of second/foreign language instruction will doubtlessly increase.

In a discussion of trends and issues involving use of technology in L2 learning and instruction, Garrett (1991) describes the kinds of technological resources that are available to support language learning in the closing decade of the 20th century (e.g., traditional audiotape/videotape materials) and the various approaches to using them. She also describes the emerging technologies that will become more available in the not-too-distant future as a result of advances in speech digitization and synthesis. In the coming century, the use of computer-generated speech promises to make the teaching of listening comprehension a more interactive, illustrative, and dynamic experience than it had been in the environment of the noninteractive, audiotape laboratory of the mid- to late 20th century (see Dunkel, 1991b for a discussion of the use of computerized educational simulations and games for L2 instruction). Garrett (1991), for example, notes that

> learners often experience a difficult transition from hearing pedagogical audio to understanding natural spoken language; the computer and interactive technologies will allow teachers to select materials of all kinds, support them as learners' needs dictate, and use the visual options of screen presentation or the interactive capabilities of computer control to help students develop good . . . listening techniques. (p. 95)

The use of speech technology also holds promise for advancing the efficiency, reliability, and validity of assessing L2 listening comprehension proficiency (see Dunkel, 1991a, for a discussion of the advantages and prototype design of a computerized test of listening comprehension in English as a second language). For many, it may not be clear how technology will affect the teaching of listening comprehension in the coming decades, but it is quite clear that it will play a greater role in the future as emerging technology becomes more available as well as less expensive and difficult to use. It is not just visionary, but wise, to remain appraised of developments in instructional technology as they relate to the teaching of listening comprehension to the generations of ESL/EFL students who will be born into the postliterate societies of the 21st century.

■

ACKNOWLEDGMENTS

I would like to thank colleagues Dennis Gouran (The Pennsylvania State University), Joyce Neu (Emory University), J. D. Brown (University of Hawaii), and Donna Johnson (University of Arizona) for helpful comments on early drafts of the essay. I would, however, especially like to acknowledge the critical role Sandra Silberstein, Editor of the *TESOL Quarterly*, played in helping bring the paper into its final form. Her meticulous editing of the paper is appreciated and admired.

THE AUTHOR

Patricia Dunkel is Associate Professor of Speech Communication and Director of the MATESL Program at The Pennsylvania State University. Her publications include three listening comprehension textbooks (*Advanced Listening Comprehension* [with F. Pialorsi], Newbury House, 1982; *Intermediate Listening Comprehension* [with P. Lim], Newbury House, 1986; and *Start with Listening* [with C. Gorder], Newbury House, 1987) as well as articles concerning instruction and research in L2 listening comprehension and computer-adaptive testing of L2 listening proficiency.

REFERENCES

Anderson, A., & Lynch, T. (1988). *Listening.* New York: Oxford University Press.

Asher, J. (1979). *Learning another language through actions: The complete teacher's guidebook.* Los Gatos, CA: Sky Oaks Productions.

Asher, J. J., Kusudo, J. A., & De La Torre, R. (1974). Learning a second language through commands: The second field test. *Modern Language Journal, 58,* 24-32.

Beatty, M., & Payne, S. (1984). Listening comprehension as a function of cognitive complexity: A research note. *Communication Monographs, 51,* 85-89.

Benson, M. (1989). The academic listening task: A case study. *TESOL Quarterly, 23*(3), 421-445.

Bernhardt, E., & James, C. (1987). The teaching and testing of comprehension in foreign language learning. In D. W. Birckbichler (Ed.), *Proficiency, policy, and professionalism in foreign language education* (pp. 65-81). Lincolnwood, IL: National Textbook Company.

Boyles, J. (1984). Factors affecting listening comprehension. *ELT Journal, 38*, 34-38.

Brown, G. (1987). Twenty-five years of teaching listening comprehension. *English Teaching Forum, 25*, 11-15.

Byrnes, H. (1984). The role of listening comprehension: A theoretical base. *Foreign Language Annals, 17*, 317-329.

Call, M. (1985). Auditory short-term memory, listening comprehension, and the input hypothesis. *TESOL Quarterly, 19*(4), 765-781.

Carroll, J. B. (1971). *Learning from verbal discourse in educational media: A review of the literature* (Contract No. 1-7-071069-4243). Princeton, NJ: Educational Testing Service.

Carroll, J. B. (1977). On learning from being told. In M. C. Wittrock (Ed.), *Learning and instruction* (2nd ed., pp. 496-512). Berkeley, CA: McCutchan.

Chaudron, C. (1985). Intake: On models and methods for disco·'ering learners' processing of input. *Studies in Second Language Acquisition, 7*, 1-14.

Chaudron, C., & Richards, J. C. (1986). The effect of discourse markers on the comprehension of lectures. *Applied Linguistics, 7*, 113-127.

Chiang, C. (1990). *Effects of speech modification, prior knowledge, and listening proficiency on the lecture listening comprehension of Chinese EFL (English as a foreign language) students.* Unpublished doctoral dissertation. The Pennsylvania State University, University Park.

Chiang, C., & Dunkel, P. (in press). The effects of speech modification, prior knowledge, and listening proficiency on EFL lecture learning. *TESOL Quarterly.*

Coakley, C., & Wolvin, A. (1986). Listening in the native language. In B. H. Wing (Ed.), *Listening, reading, and writing: Analysis and application* (pp. 11-42). Middlebury, VT: Northeast Conference on the Teaching of Foreign Languages.

Daniels, H. R., Pringle, P., & Wood, D. (1986). Playing it by ear: Things that happen inside a silent period. *System, 14*, 47-57.

Daniels, H. R., & Wood, D. (1984). The silent period, or what to do with language learners who are seen and not heard. *TESOL France News, 4*, 25-30.

Davies, N. F. (1980). Putting receptive skills first: An experiment in sequencing. *Canadian Modern Language Review, 36*, 461-467.

Devine, T. G. (1967). Listening. *Review of Educational Research, 37*, 152-158.

Devine, T. G. (1978). Listening: What do we know about fifty years of research and theorizing? *Journal of Reading, 21*, 296-304.

DiSalvo, V. S. (1980). A summary of current research identifying communication skills in various organizational contexts. *Communication Education, 29,* 283-290.

DiSalvo, V. S., Larsen, D., & Seiler, W. J. (1976). Communication skills needed by persons in business organizations. *Communication Education, 25,* 269-275.

Downs, C. W., & Conrad, C. (1982). Effective subordinancy. *Journal of Business Communication, 19,* 27-37.

Duker, S. (1964). Listening. *Review of Educational Research, 34,* 156-163.

Duker, S. (1968). *Listening bibliography* (2nd ed.). Metuchen, NJ: Scarecrow Press.

Duker, S. (1969). Listening. In R. L. Ebel (Ed.), *Encyclopedia of educational research* (4th ed., pp. 747-753). New York: Macmillan.

Dulay, H., Burt, M., & Krashen, S. (1982). *Language two.* New York: Oxford University Press.

Dunkel, P. (1986). Developing listening fluency in L2: Theoretical principles and pedagogical considerations. *Modern Language Journal, 70,* 99-106.

Dunkel, P. (1988). The content of L1 and L2 students' lecture notes and its relation to test performance. *TESOL Quarterly, 22*(2), 259-281.

Dunkel, P. (1991a). Computerized testing of nonparticipatory L2 listening comprehension proficiency: An ESL prototype development effort. *Modern Language Journal, 75,* 64-73.

Dunkel, P. (1991b). Noncomputerized and computerized simulations and games in L2 learning. *CAELL Journal, 2,* 2-12.

Dunkel, P., Chaudron, C., & Henning, G. (1990, January). *A collaborative research endeavor to design a tentative model of L2 developmental listening proficiency compatible with technological testing applications* (Final report, Collaborative Research Fellowship). Washington, DC: The Johns Hopkins University, National Foreign Language Center.

Dunkel, P., Mishra, S., & Berliner, D. (1989). Effects of note taking, memory, and language proficiency on lecture learning for native and nonnative speakers of English. *TESOL Quarterly, 23*(3), 543-549.

Ervin-Tripp, S. (1974). Is second language learning like the first? *TESOL Quarterly, 8*(1), 111-128.

Faerch, C., & Kasper, G. (1986). The role of comprehension in second language learning. *Applied Linguistics, 7,* 257-274.

Fairbanks, G., Guttman, N., & Miron, M. S. (1957). Auditory comprehension: The relation to listening rate and selective verbal redundancy. *Journal of Speech and Hearing Disorders, 22,* 23-32.

Foulke, E., Amster, C. H., Nolan, C. Y., Bixler, R. H. (1962). The comprehension of rapid speech by the blind. *Exceptional Children, 29,* 134-141.

Freedman, M. (1982, 7 April). Not so; It's a communications revolution. *The Evening Sun,* p. A-15.

Galvin, K. (1985). *Listening by doing—Developing effective listening skills.* Lincolnwood, IL: National Textbook Co.

Garrett, N. (1991). Technology in the service of language learning: Trends and issues. *Modern Language Journal, 75,* 74-101.

Gary, J. O., & Gary, N. (1981). Caution: Talking may be dangerous to your linguistic health. *IRAL, 19,* 1-14.

Glen, E. (1989). A content analysis of fifty definitions of listening. *Journal of the International Listening Association, 3,* 21-31.

Goldstein, H. (1940). *Reading and listening comprehension at various controlled rates* (College Contributions to Education, No. 821). New York: Teachers College, Columbia University, Bureau of Publications.

Goss, B. (1982). *Processing communication.* Belmont, CA: Wadsworth.

Hakuta, K. (1974). Prefabricated patterns and the emergence of structure in second language acquisition. *Language Learning, 24,* 287-297.

Harris, T. E., & Thomlison, T. D. (1983). Career-bound communication education: A needs analysis. *Central States Speech Journal, 34,* 260-267.

Hatch, E. (1983). Simplified input and second language acquisition. In Roger Andersen (Ed.), *Pidginization and creolization as language acquisition* (pp. 64-86). Rowley, MA: Newbury House.

Havelock, E. (1986). *The muse learns to write: Reflections on orality and literacy from antiquity to the present.* New Haven: Yale University Press.

Huang, J., & Hatch, E. (1978). A Chinese child's acquisition of English. In E. Hatch (Ed.), *Second language acquisition* (pp. 118-131). Rowley, MA: Newbury House.

Ingram, F., Nord, J., & Draft, D. (1975). A program for listening comprehension. *Slavic and East European Journal, 19,* 1-10.

Joiner, E. (1986). Listening in the foreign language. In B. H. Wing (Ed.) *Listening, reading, writing: Analysis and application* (pp. 43-70). Middlebury, VT: Northeast Conference on the Teaching of Foreign Languages.

Keller, P. (1960). Major findings in listening in the past ten years. *Journal of Communication, 10,* 29-38.

Krakowian, B. (1981). Techniques of teaching in the "pre-speaking" period. *System, 9,* 133-139.

Krashen, S. (1977). The monitor model for adult second language performance. In M. Burt, C. Dulay, & M. Finocchiari (Eds.), *Viewpoints on English as a second language* (pp. 152-161). New York: Regents.

Krashen, S. (1981). *Second language acquisition and second language learning.* Oxford: Pergamon Press.

Locke, J. (1689/1988). *An essay concerning human understanding.* New York: Oxford University Press.

Long, D. (1989). Second language listening comprehension: A schema-theoretic perspective. *Modern Language Journal, 73,* 32-40.

Long, M. (1985). Input and second language acquisition theory. In S. Gass & C. Madden (Eds.), *Input in second language acquisition* (pp. 377-393). Rowley, MA: Newbury House.

Lund, R. (1990). A taxonomy for teaching second language listening. *Foreign Language Annals, 23,* 105-115.

Lundsteen, S. W. (1979). *Listening: Its impact at all levels on reading and the other language arts.* Urbana, IL: ERIC Clearinghouse on Reading and Communication Skills Arts.

Marton, W. (1983). Second language acquisition tactics and language pedagogy. *System, 11,* 313-323.

McLaughlin, B., Rossman, T., & McLeod, B. (1983). Second language learning: An information processing perspective. *Language Learning, 33,* 135-158.

Morley, J. (1991). Listening comprehension in second/foreign language instruction. In M. Celce-Murcia (Ed.), *Teaching English as a second or foreign language* (2nd ed., pp. 81-106). New York: Newbury House.

Mueller, G. (1980). Visual contextual cues and listening comprehension: An experiment. *Modern Language Journal, 64,* 335-340.

Muchmore, J., & Galvin, K. (1983). A report of the task force on career competencies in oral communication skills for community college students seeking immediate entry into the work force. *Communication Education, 32,* 207-220.

Murphy, C., & Jenks, L. (1982). Getting a job after college—What skills are needed? San Francisco: Far West Laboratory for Educational Research and Development. *Journal of Career Education, 10,* 80-93.

Nagle, S., & Sanders, S. (1986). Comprehension theory and second language pedagogy. *TESOL Quarterly, 20*(1), 9-26.

Nord, J. R. (1974). Why can't I just learn to listen? *American Foreign Language Teacher, 4,* 4-6.

Nord, J. R. (1975). The importance of listening. *The English Teacher's Magazine, 24,* 34-39.

Nord, J. R. (1980). Developing listening fluency before speaking: An alternative paradigm. *System, 8,* 1-22.

Nord, J. R. (1981). Three steps leading to listening fluency: A beginning. In H. Winitz (Ed.), *The comprehension approach to foreign language instruction.* Rowley, MA: Newbury House.

O'Malley, M., Chamot, A., & Küpper, L. (1989). Listening comprehension strategies in second language acquisition. *Applied Linguistics, 10,* 418-437.

Oxford, R. (1990). *Language learning strategies: What every teacher should know.* New York: Newbury House.

Painter, C. M. (1985). A survey of communication skills needed on-the-job by technical students. *Journal of Studies in Technical Careers, 7,* 135-160.

Peterson, P. (1991). A synthesis of methods for interactive listening. In M. Celce-Murcia (Ed.), *Teaching English as a second or foreign language* (2nd ed., pp. 106-122). New York: Newbury House.

Pica, T., Doughty, C., & Young, R. (1986). Making input comprehensible: Do interactional modifications help? *IRAL, 72,* 1-25.

Pica, T., Young, R., & Doughty, C. (1987). The impact of interaction on comprehension. *TESOL Quarterly, 21*(4), 737-758.

Postovsky, V. A. (1974). Effects of delay in oral practice at the beginning of second language learning. *Modern Language Journal, 58,* 229-239.

Powers, D. (1985, December). *A survey of academic demands related to listening skills* (TOEFL Res. Rep. No. 20). Princeton, NJ: Educational Testing Service.

Preiss, R., & Wheeless, L. (1989). Affective responses in listening: A meta-analysis of receiver apprehension outcomes. *Journal of the International Listening Association, 3,* 72-102.

Richards, J. C. (1983). Listening comprehension: Approach, design, and procedure. *TESOL Quarterly, 17*(2), 219-240.

Richards, J. C. (1985). Listening comprehension: Approach, design, and procedure. In J. C. Richards, *The context of language teaching* (pp. 189-207). New York: Cambridge University Press.

Richards, J. C. (1990). *The language teaching matrix.* New York: Cambridge University Press.

Rickerson, E. (1984). Curriculum for proficiency: Concepts to build on. *Die Unterrichtspraxis, 17,* 207-224.

Rost, M. (1990). *Listening in language learning.* New York: Longman.

Samuels, S. (1984). Factors influencing listening: Inside and outside the head. *Theory into Practice, 23,* 183-189.

Sheils, J. (1988). *Communication in the modern languages classroom.* Strasbourg, France: The Council of Europe. (Available from Manhattan Publishing Company, 1 Croton Pt. Avenue, Box 650, Croton, NY 10520)

Sorensen, A. (1967). Multilingualism in the northwest Amazon. *American Anthropologist, 69,* 670-684.

Taylor, T. (1986). Do you understand? Criteria of understanding in verbal interaction. *Language & Communication, 6,* 171-180.

Thiele, A., & Scheibner-Herzig, G. (1983). Listening comprehension training in teaching English to beginners. *System, 11,* 277-286.

The 20% activities that bring 80% payoff. (1978, June). *Training,* p. 6.

Underwood, M. (1989). *Teaching listening.* New York: Longman.

Ur, P. (1984). *Teaching listening comprehension.* Cambridge: Cambridge University Press.

Watson, K., & Smeltzer, L. (1984). Barriers to listening: Comparison between students and practitioners. *Communication Research Reports, 1,* 82-87.

Weaver, C. (1972). *Human listening: Process and behavior.* New York: Bobbs-Merrill.

Weissenreider, M. (1987). Listening to the news in Spanish. *Modern Language Journal, 71,* 18-27.

Wilkinson, A. (1970). Research in listening comprehension. *Educational Research, 12,* 140-144.

Witkin, B. R. (1990). Listening theory and research: The state of the art. *Journal of the International Listening Association, 4,* 7-32.

Wolvin, A. (1990). Listening pedagogy and andragogy: The state of the art. *Journal of the International Listening Association, 4,* 33-61.

Wolvin, A., & Coakley, C. (1988). *Listening* (3rd ed.). Dubuque, IA: Wm. C. Brown.

Wolvin, A., & Coakley, C. (1991). A survey of the status of listening training in some Fortune 500 corporations. *Communication Education, 40,* 152-164.

Grammar Pedagogy in Second and Foreign Language Teaching

MARIANNE CELCE-MURCIA
University of California, Los Angeles

To provide some perspective on current issues and challenges concerning the role of grammar in language teaching, the article reviews some methodological trends of the past 25 years. When, and to what extent, one should teach grammar to language learners is a controversial issue. The paper proposes a decision-making strategy for resolving this controversy, based on learner and instructional variables. Then taking Canale and Swain's (1980) model of communicative competence, which views grammatical competence as one component of communicative competence, the paper argues that grammar instruction is part of language teaching. In this new role, grammar interacts with meaning, social function, or discourse—or a combination of these—rather than standing alone as an autonomous system to be learned for its own sake. After addressing feedback and correction in terms of research and pedagogical techniques, the article concludes with a survey of options for integrating grammar instruction into a communicative curriculum and with a reformulation of the role of grammar in language teaching.

When the *TESOL Quarterly* first began publication in 1967, the teaching of grammar (i.e., the teaching of morphological inflections, function words, and syntactic word order) was a central concern in English language teaching. In fact, as Rutherford (1987) points out, for 2,500 years the teaching of grammar had often been synonymous with foreign language teaching.

In 1967 the audiolingual approach had dominated language teaching in the U.S. for over two decades; its followers held that language learning occurred largely through habit formation. This view of language learning was about to be challenged by proponents of the cognitive code approach who, countering audiolingualism's adherence to habit formation, argued that language learning was rule-governed behavior.

Prior to 1967 and for several years thereafter, however, no one challenged the centrality of grammar either as content for language teaching or as the organizing principle for curriculum or materials development. Such a challenge emerged in the mid-1970s, and in the section below, entitled "Integrating Grammar Into a Communicative Curriculum," we shall consider the major changes that have taken place since 1967 in terms of content and curriculum in language teaching and the implications for teaching grammar.

Since the differences between the way we viewed grammar in 1967 and the way we view it today are yet to be fully appreciated, this article will begin with an historical overview followed by a discussion of relevant issues and research. This discussion will serve as background for a reformulation of the role of grammar in language teaching.

HISTORICAL BACKGROUND

During the past 25 years, the major methodological approaches to language teaching have differed regarding whether explicit grammar instruction has a role to play in the second or foreign language classroom. The four methodological approaches I shall survey are the (a) audiolingual approach, (b) cognitive code approach, (c) comprehension approach, and (d) communicative approach. (For a broader historical survey that treats several additional approaches, see Celce-Murcia, 1991.)

The audiolingual approach (e.g., Fries, 1945; Lado, 1964) represents the first attempt by U.S. structural linguists to influence the teaching of modern foreign languages. Grammatical structures were very carefully sequenced from basic to more complex (based on linguistic description), and vocabulary was strictly limited in the early stages of learning. Consonant with the then-current behavioral school of psychology, audiolingual proponents assumed that language learning was habit formation and overlearning; thus, mimicry of forms and memorization of certain sentence patterns were used extensively to present rules inductively. A variety of manipulative drill types was practiced with the objective of minimizing (or preventing altogether) learners' errors, which were viewed as bad habits that would be hard to break if they became established. Errors were the result of interference from the first language. Teachers were told that they should correct all errors that they were not able to prevent. The focus of instruction rarely moved beyond the sentence level.

The cognitive code approach (Jakobovits, 1968, 1970), largely a reaction to the behaviorist features of audiolingualism, was influenced by the work of linguists like Chomsky (1959) and psycholinguists like Miller (e.g., Miller & Buckhout, 1973). Language learning was viewed as hypothesis formation and rule acquisition, rather than habit formation. Grammar was considered important, and rules were presented either deductively or inductively depending on the preferences of the learners. Errors were viewed as inevitable by-products of language learning and as something that the teacher and learner could use constructively in the learning process. Error analysis and correction were seen as appropriate classroom activities, with the teacher facilitating peer and self-correction as much as possible. The source of errors was seen not only as transfer from the first language but also as normal language development (errors similar to early L1 errors) and/or the internal complexities of the target language. The focus was still largely sentence-oriented, and materials writers often drew on Chomsky's early work in generative grammar (1957, 1965).

The comprehension approach (Winitz, 1981) represents attempts by many language methodologists working in the U.S. during the 1970s and 1980s to recreate the first language acquisition experience for the second/foreign language learner. The notion that comprehension is primary and that it should thus precede any production epitomizes this approach; a pedagogical offshoot is the view that comprehension can best be taught initially by delaying production in the target language while encouraging the learner to use meaningful nonverbal responses to demonstrate comprehension. Some practitioners of the comprehension approach carefully sequence grammatical structures and lexical items in their instructional programs (Asher, 1977; Winitz, no date); they thus present grammar inductively. Others propose that a semantically based syllabus be followed instead and that all grammar instruction be excluded from the classroom since they feel that it does not facilitate language acquisition; at best it merely helps learners to monitor or become aware of the forms they use (Krashen & Terrell, 1983). Proponents of this latter philosophy also believe that error correction is unnecessary, perhaps even counterproductive, since they feel that errors will gradually self-correct as learners are exposed to ever more complex, rich, and meaningful input in the target language.

The communicative approach, which came to the fore in the mid-1970s, originates in the work of anthropological linguists in the U.S. (Hymes, 1972) and functional linguists in Britain (Halliday, 1973), all of whom view language as an instrument of communication. Those who have applied this philosophy to language teaching (e.g., Widdowson, 1978; Wilkins, 1976), claim that communication is the goal of second or foreign language instruction and that the syllabus of a language course should not be organized around grammar but around subject matter, tasks/projects, or semantic notions and/or pragmatic functions. In other words, language instruction should be content-based, meaningful, contextualized, and discourse-based (rather than sentence-based). The teacher's role is primarily to facilitate language use and communication; it is only secondarily to provide feedback and correct learner errors. Among the proponents of this approach, there is currently some debate regarding the nature, extent, and type of grammar instruction or grammar awareness activities appropriate for second or foreign language as well as a certain ambivalence about issues such as whether, when, and how teachers should correct grammatical errors.

THE CURRENT CHALLENGE

Given the preceding historical survey, it is obvious that TESOL methodologists have not offered consistent advice to teachers about the role of grammar in language teaching over the past 25 years. Even today the situation is far from clear. Teachers who want to know what, if anything, they should do about their ESL/EFL students' errors are understandably frustrated because of the many conflicting positions taken at professional conferences and in the methodological literature.

Existing research, while not conclusive, strongly suggests that some focus on form may well be necessary for many learners to achieve accuracy as well as fluency in their acquisition of a second or foreign language (see, for example, Long, 1983; Rutherford & Sharwood Smith, 1988). Indeed as Richards (1985) points out, there is no actual empirical evidence that proves "communicative" language classrooms—especially those that preclude any learner focus on form—produce better language learners than do more traditional classrooms. In spite of the intuitive appeal and the anecdotal evidence supporting proposals for exclusively commu- nicative language teaching, there is equally appealing and convincing anecdotal evidence (Higgs & Clifford, 1982) that a grammarless approach—whether comprehension-based or commu- nicative—can lead to the development of a broken, ungrammatical, pidginized form of the target language beyond which students rarely progress. Following Selinker (1972), such learners are often said to have "fossilized" (i.e., prematurely plateaued) in their acquisition of the target language.

Thus, while we await a more satisfactory conclusion to this debate regarding when and how to teach grammar, it is clear that no one should dismiss grammar instruction altogether, for there is at present no convincing evidence that to do so would ultimately be beneficial to second or foreign language learners, especially those who need to achieve a high level of proficiency and accuracy.

A PEDAGOGICAL STRATEGY

A strategy proposed by Celce-Murcia (1985) provides guidelines to assist teachers in deciding to what degree they ought to deal with grammar in their own classes.

Learner Variables

An observant ESL/EFL teacher knows that individuals learn in different ways (Hartnett, 1985). Some learners, consciously or unconsciously, have an analytic style and learn best by formulating and testing hypotheses or "rules." Other learners have a holistic style and learn best by experiencing, gathering, and restructuring relevant data but doing little or no apparent analysis.

Young children, for example, are by necessity more holistic in their approach to learning than adults. This suggests that age is an important learner variable in helping ESL/EFL teachers decide the extent to which they should focus on form. If the ESL learners concerned are young children, it is most likely that little explicit grammar instruction is needed. If the students are adolescents or adults, however, their learning may well be facilitated by some explicit focus on form.

Proficiency level is also a factor. If the ESL students are beginners (regardless of age), there is little justification in focusing on form, beyond presenting and practicing the obvious form-meaning correspondences in context. This is because when one is beginning to learn something completely new and different, one tends to initially approach the new "object" holistically for a time before feeling ready to do any meaningful analysis. However, if the learners are at the intermediate or advanced level, it may well be necessary for the teacher to provide some form-related feedback and correction in order for the learners to progress.

The educational background of the students is another learner variable. If students are preliterate with little formal education, then it is probably not very productive to focus extensively on form. Even this population (i.e., preliterate or semiliterate adults with little formal education) may demand some grammar because of cultural expectations regarding what constitutes language instruction. While they may not benefit linguistically from grammar instruction, the teacher who satisfies their cultural expectations with some grammar may then do other things that will be beneficial and which the students will accept. On the other hand, if the students are literate and well educated, they may become frustrated and annoyed if the teacher does not provide adequate opportunity for them to focus on the formal aspects of the target language, which would, of course, include correction of their errors and answers to their questions.

Instructional Variables

The need to focus on form also changes according to the educational objectives that the ESL teacher must address. When one is teaching a receptive skill such as listening or reading, it is distracting and irrelevant to emphasize grammar unduly since these receptive skills require competence primarily in the areas of word recognition and semantic processing. (Even listening and reading may involve some focus on form. For example, better understanding and awareness of logical connectors can enhance both reading and listening comprehension.) However, if the teacher is focusing on productive skills (i.e., speaking and, in particular, writing), then formal accuracy can become an important concern because rules of pedagogical grammar are essentially rules of production.

Furthermore, for the productive skills, register and medium are additional factors to consider. If the teacher is offering a conversation class, then accuracy of form is much less an issue than it is if the class is dealing with formal expository writing.

Finally, what does the learner need to be able to do in the target language? If the learner's immediate goal is survival communication, formal accuracy is of marginal value; on the other hand, if the learner wants to function as an academic, a diplomat, or a business executive, then a high degree of formal accuracy is essential.

Judging the Importance of Grammar for a Given Class

Given the six variables discussed above, it is somewhat complicated but not impossible for ESL/EFL instructors to decide the degree to which it is appropriate to focus on form with a given group of students. I have found that a grid such as the following is a useful visual aid to help teachers arrive at a sound decision.

The more factors the teacher identifies on the left side of the grid, the less important it is to focus on form; the more factors the teacher identifies on the right, the more important the grammatical focus. Such a grid helps the teacher decide, for example, when teaching

FIGURE 1

Variables that Determine the Importance of Grammar

From "Making Informed Decisions About the Role of Grammar in Language Teaching" by M. Celce-Murcia, 1985, February, *TESOL Newsletter*, p. 4. Copyright 1985. Adapted by permission.

	Less Important	——— Focus on Form ———	More Important
Learner variables			
Age	Children	Adolescents	Adults
Proficiency level	Beginning	Intermediate	Advanced
Educational background	Preliterate, no formal education	Semiliterate, some formal education	Literate, well educated
Instructional variables			
Skill	Listening, reading	Speaking	Writing
Register	Informal	Consultative[a]	Formal
Need/use	Survival communication	Vocational	Professional

[a] Joos (1962) defines the consultative register as the language we use with people we deal with frequently—perhaps every day—but with whom we are not close on a personal level. This register is between formal (the language for public lectures or academic articles) and informal (the language used among peers who know each other well). For purposes of this paper, I have ignored the two extreme registers described by Joos: frozen and intimate.

beginning-level adults who are preliterate and in need of survival communication skills, that focus on form is not a top priority. On the other hand, the grid suggests that when teaching literate young adults who are in college and at the high-intermediate proficiency level, some focus on form is essential if the teacher wants to help the students successfully complete their composition requirement.

The importance of a reasonable degree of grammatical accuracy in academic or professional writing cannot be overstated. McGirt (1984), for example, found that 40% of the university-level ESL writers in his study were judged to have produced fully acceptable writing after he corrected their essays for surface-level morphological and syntactic errors. Without McGirt's grammatical corrections, the same essays were rated unacceptable (nonpassing) by experienced composition teachers. Of the remaining ESL writers in McGirt's study, 20% produced essays that were judged acceptable even without the grammatical errors corrected (but this 20% committed only 3.1 errors per 100 words); 40% wrote essays that were rated unacceptable with or without the errors corrected. It should also be noted that the ESL writers in McGirt's study committed an average of 7.2 grammatical errors per 100 words, which one can assume is too many errors for the context described.

Given that under certain circumstances grammar instruction is absolutely necessary and given that there are classes in which it is imperative that ESL teachers use effective techniques to remediate errors, the next two sections of this paper will deal with grammar instruction and error correction.

GRAMMAR INSTRUCTION

As a result of the communicative revolution in language teaching, it has become increasingly clear that grammar is a tool or resource to be used in the comprehension and creation of oral and written discourse rather than something to be learned as an end in itself. When learned as a decontextualized sentence-level system, grammar is not very useful to learners as they listen, read, speak, and write in their second or foreign language. Indeed, as Canale and Swain (1980) have posited, communicative competence consists of four components, only one of which—Item 3 below—involves grammar:

1. Sociolinguistic competence (i.e., appropriacy): The speaker/writer knows how to express the message in terms of the person being addressed and the overall circumstances and purpose of the communication.

2. Discourse competence: The selection, sequence, and arrangement of words and structures are clear and effective means of expressing the speaker/writer's intended message.

3. Linguistic competence (i.e., accuracy): The forms, inflections, and sequences used to express the message are grammatically correct.

4. Strategic competence: The speaker/writer has effective and unobtrusive strategies to compensate for any weaknesses s/he has in the above three areas.

Certainly, in many person-to-person communications, sociolinguistic appropriacy and discourse competence are more important than grammatical accuracy, provided that the grammar used is not inaccurate to the point of miscommunicating the intended message; communication is the overriding concern. However, there are situations where a reasonable degree of accuracy is also critical, and this is our current focus.

In order for ESL/EFL teachers to consistently present grammar as serving some higher-order objective, Celce-Murcia and Hilles (1988) suggest that grammar should never be taught as an end in itself but always with reference to meaning, social factors, or discourse—or a combination of these factors. Larsen-Freeman's (1991) position is similar: She sees form, meaning, and function as three interacting dimensions of language; the classroom teacher must decide in which dimension the students are experiencing the greatest learning challenge at any given moment and respond with appropriate instruction.

Teaching Grammar as Meaning

As an example, teaching the different spatial meanings signaled by the prepositions *in* and *on* is best viewed as grammar in the service of meaning. If learners are presented with many fully illustrated and well-demonstrated examples such as the following and then asked to describe other similar situations, they have a basis for understanding and practicing the correct use of these two prepositions:

1a. Bob put the book *in* the box./The book is *in* the box.
 b. Bob put the book *on* the table./The book is *on* the table.

2a. Ann threw the ball *in* the basket./The ball is *in* the basket.
 b. Ann threw the ball *on* the floor./The ball is *on* the floor.

A sufficient number of good, clear examples will be enough for some learners; others will also find it useful to know quite explicitly that *in* favors the placement of objects in three-dimensional containers and *on* favors the placement of objects on two-dimensional flat surfaces.

Teaching Grammar as Social Function

An example of grammar used in the service of socially appropriate messages is the use of certain modal auxiliaries to express politeness when one is requesting a favor. When they make requests, ESL/EFL learners need to know that *would* is more polite than *will* and that *could* is more polite than *can*:

3. (*Will/Would*) you open the door?

4. (*Can/Could*) I talk to you for a minute?

Learners must become aware of the possible consequences of using the wrong modal form in a request: The addressee may conclude that the nonnative speaker is being inappropriately abrupt, familiar, or rude even when this is not at all the social message intended. Sufficient practice with intended social messages in dialogues, role plays, and simulations (as well as careful observations of native-speaker behavior and/or elicitation of native-speaker preferences with reference to specific request situations) will help establish the link between grammar and socially appropriate behavior.

Teaching Grammar as Discourse

The link between grammar and discourse is especially crucial for ESL composition students. They will have to learn that definitions, for example, make heavy use of adjectivals such as relative clauses:

5. A thermometer is an instrument that measures temperature.
6. A relative clause is an embedded sentence that modifies a noun.

In addition, students need to realize that such definitions can easily be reversed with the functional definition preceding the name of the device being defined:

7. An instrument that measures temperature is a thermometer.
8. An embedded sentence that modifies a noun is a relative clause.

Learners must also recognize that these structures are used for a variety of communicative purposes, for example:

1. Vocabulary elicitation

   What do you call an instrument that measures temperature?

   A thermometer.

2. Extended definition

   A relative clause is an embedded sentence that modifies a noun. It consists of a relative pronoun, a word that refers to the noun being modified, along with the other elements needed to complete the modifying proposition. For example, in the sentence *I read the article that John wrote*, *that John wrote* is the relative clause modifying the noun *article*. The relative pronoun *that* refers to the same thing as the noun *article*. In fact, we can paraphrase the relative clause with the sentence *John wrote the article*. A relative clause is thus a useful stylistic option that allows speakers and writers to combine into one sentence two propositions, both of which contain a noun referring to the same person or thing.

Not only does the paragraph above define the notion of a relative clause, it also contains several relative clauses as well as some other adjectivals that students can examine at the discourse level to appreciate not only how different types of relative clauses are formed but also how they are used. My colleagues and I have found that after comprehension and analysis of two or three similar example texts defining other objects or concepts, ESL composition students are better prepared to write their own extended definition on some object or concept that is familiar to them and useful in their major field of study.

Almost as important as developing a sense of when to use certain structures in discourse depending on topic or genre is the need to master the conventions of discourse that cross sentence boundaries and help the writer create text. Halliday and Hasan (1976) refer to these features of text structure as cohesion. According to them, cohesion involves the principled use of (a) referential forms (e.g., pronouns, demonstratives, the definite article); (b) substitute expressions such as *one(s)*, *do*, and *so*; (c) ellipsis; (d) conjunction; and (e) lexical chaining to create texture in discourse.

FEEDBACK AND CORRECTION

Error Gravity

Burt and Kiparsky (1974), in an analysis of error gravity, noted that there are local errors produced by second language learners such as an omitted article or a superfluous preposition:

9. °Let us consider Stevenson's invention of the steam engine as ∅ starting point.
10. °It was dark as we approached *to* the house.

They claimed that such local errors do not usually cause problems with communication, and they contrasted such relatively innocuous local errors with global errors such as faulty word order (Example 11) or the use of the wrong logical connector (*conjunction* in Halliday and Hasan's terms) (Example 12):

11. °The English language use many people.
12. °I didn't question his decision *yet* [instead of *because*] I trusted him completely.

Burt and Kiparsky concluded that global errors contribute to miscommunication and thus require correction much more than local errors do, a hypothesis subsequently confirmed by Tomiyama's (1990) research.

Virtually all the errors that Burt and Kiparsky cited—whether local or global—were discussed and exemplified at the sentence level. Today, however, it is useful to reinterpret their notion of local errors as sentence-level errors and global errors as discourse-level errors.[1] This leads us to conclude that discourse-level errors deserve our closest attention because they are more likely to be a source of miscommunication or confusion than sentence-level errors, a conclusion which has been confirmed by Frodesen's (1991) study of unacceptable ESL compositions. Thus familiarity with the cohesive devices of English (i.e., the grammatical and lexical "glue" of discourse) and careful observation of how these and other discourse conventions are employed by effective writers will give nonnative learners of English tools for creating more accurate and coherent text. As Carrell (1982, 1987) reminds us, however, skill in using cohesive devices will not guarantee that ESL writers will produce effective and coherent prose since higher-order discourse principles such as content-schemata and formal-schemata also come into play.

Stages for Error Correction

There are times during an ESL lesson when the teacher may reasonably ask the students whether a sentence is grammatically correct and, if not, why. Chaudron (1983) cautions us, however, that learners become better at this type of exercise as they become more proficient and that beginners are typically weak at making grammaticality judgments in a second language. Chaudron's review of the research also reminds us that while intermediate-level learners can begin to recognize and correct their own errors, more advanced learners are able to correct the errors of other learners as well.

Thus ESL teachers with low-intermediate learners may want to facilitate their students' ability to recognize and locate errors, since these skills precede the ability to accurately correct an error. How can this be done? The teacher might begin by asking students to identify the incorrect—instead of the correct—sentences in sets of two or three sentences:

13a. *I enjoy to take photographs.
  b. I enjoy taking photographs.

14a. *The professor which wrote the book gave the lecture.
  b. *The professor wrote the book gave the lecture.
  c. The professor who wrote the book gave the lecture.

---

[1] *Word order* is of course a notion that applies to both the syntactic level and the discourse level. Some word-order errors such as *The English language use many people* are syntactic in that at the sentence-level one may say either *Many people use the English language* or *The English language is used by many people* but not *The English language use many people*. At the discourse level, one of the two syntactically permitted strings will be more appropriate than the other depending on discourse factors such as topic continuity, speaker's intention, and so on.

If students have difficulty with somewhat analytical discussions of grammaticality and correctness, the teacher may want to begin to raise their awareness of form more indirectly. For example, Sentences A and B below are on the board or visible via the overhead projector:

T: Okay, many of you say Sentence A, while I say Sentence B. What's the difference?
A. We have done that exercise yesterday.
B. We did that exercise yesterday.

For a more complex and demanding activity, students at higher proficiency levels can be asked to judge each sentence in a connected series, and if judged ungrammatical, to correct it, as in Figure 2.

FIGURE 2

Error Detection and Correction Exercise

Sentence/Clause	Grammatical?	Correction if needed
If I won the lottery,		
I would to buy a new car.		
I'd buy my mother a house,		
and my sister some furnitures.		

Teaching Exceptions to Rules

Teaching grammar normally involves helping learners internalize rules and patterns that they can then apply more generally in their language use; however, most rules or patterns have exceptions, a problem that requires a different type of learning. In an interesting study, Tomasello and Herron (1988) compared two methods for teaching grammatical exceptions to two groups of U.S. learners of French (the technique reported, however, is very likely also applicable to learners of ESL/EFL). In one method, students induced the rule after receiving several regular examples, and then the teacher stated the exceptions. In the other method, referred to as the garden path condition, the teacher presented regular examples to induce the rule, and then asked the class to apply the rule to an exception. This elicited an erroneous overgeneralization, which the teacher then immediately corrected. Eight structures with exceptions were targeted for treatment—four for each method (the two groups of students received the opposite treatment).

Subsequent formal testing revealed that students learned the exceptions better when the garden path condition had been the treatment. This advantage persisted for the entire semester. The researchers hypothesized that by inducing an overgeneralization and then immediately correcting it, the teacher helped the learners focus their attention on both the rule and the special features of a given item that marked it as an exception.

Holistic Correction Techniques

Most holistic error correction techniques involve getting students to work with their own texts. For example, if students tape-record a narrative about a frightening experience, they can then be instructed to transcribe the story exactly as they related it on tape. Later they can rewrite the narrative as written text, trying to avoid the grammatical errors they made when speaking as well as making other appropriate adjustments as they generate the written version. (Such adjustments would include getting rid of fragments, false starts, using fewer initial *ands*, etc.) With the tape recordings and the written versions in hand, the teacher can verify the accuracy of each transcription and the subsequent changes and corrections the learner made in the written text.

Another holistic correction technique is *reformulation*, which has been explored by Cohen (1983, 1985), among others. In reformulation the teacher or tutor takes a paragraph or short essay written by the learner and instead of correcting the learner's mistakes, the teacher/tutor rewrites the passage on another sheet in his or her own words, which means that vocabulary and overall organization may change as well as grammar. The learner then compares the original with the reformulated version to see if the intended message is preserved and, in consultation with the teacher/tutor, the learner comes to understand why the changes were made. This process can be very useful but also time-consuming; fortunately, there are some less demanding adaptations such as the teacher's attaching a sheet to the original with several reworded phrases and clauses that the learner might want to consider when s/he revises the paper.

For those intermediate learners interested primarily in correction of oral production, Wechsler (1987) developed and tested "interview analysis," a holistic technique where spontaneous speech is elicited, recorded, and transcribed at intervals. The teacher/tutor reviews the transcripts with the learner and trains him/her to correct the transcript with a brightly colored pen. After several months of doing the interview analysis procedure with two intermediate-level French speakers, Wechsler was able to reduce significantly the frequency of errors in their spontaneous English speech with regard to regular and irregular past-tense forms, plurals, possessives, and *for-to* purpose constructions. Errors in the use of the third-person singular, present tense, however, did not decrease significantly for Wechsler's two learners.

Correction in Written Work

Returning to ESL writing, which is where much if not most error correction is done, there are many traditional feedback techniques that teachers have long used with a degree of success. These include underlining but not correcting errors, indicating error types on a checklist attached to the essay (Knapp, 1972), and indicating error type and frequency on a note returned with the essay (e.g., find three verbs that are missing the third-person singular, present inflection and correct them). Some teachers have used peer-correction activities with good success (Witbeck, 1976), while others prefer to prepare composite essays for class/group correction that illustrate common errors from several students' written work in order to prevent the embarrassment students may experience when their peers publicly correct their written work. Finally, some teachers advocate the use of audiocassettes to correct ESL compositions (Bracy Farnsworth, 1974), claiming that it is more useful to the students than either checklists or written notes in the margin and that it is less time-consuming than individual conferences with students, which is yet another feedback technique that some teachers use.

Intervention

Sometimes feedback and correction must be accomplished quickly and spontaneously. Such a need arises in the course of an ESL/EFL lesson when it becomes clear that a particular aspect of grammar is troubling many students in the class. A fully professional ESL/EFL teacher should be able to intervene, and in a few minutes, get students to focus on the problem, to become aware of both the error and the correct form, and to practice the correct form briefly.

Celce-Murcia and Hilles (1988) refer to such interventions as "minigrammar lessons" (p. 145) and illustrate this procedure for errors such as the following: *You should to speak louder.* In a minigrammar lesson the teacher presents relevant data to the class and without lecturing gets the students to detect and correct the targeted error. The teacher then helps the students generate a rule or paradigm and gives them a contextualized exercise so they can immediately practice the problematic structure and produce the correct form.

After such an intervention, the class returns to the lesson at hand, and if necessary the teacher presents more elaborate follow-up practice in a subsequent lesson.

Answering Questions

Another form of feedback that many students seek is the teacher's answers to questions they have about aspects of English that puzzle them. When a student asks "What's a relative clause?" often an example sentence on the board with the relative clause underlined is faster and more effective than a definition. When a student asks why *ten dollars* is correct in *This book costs ten dollars* but incorrect in *°This is a ten dollars book*, the teacher should be able to explain quickly and concisely that a measure phrase like *ten dollar(s)* consists of a cardinal number followed by a unit of measure; when the measure phrase does not precede and modify a noun, the unit word is plural if the number is greater than one:

15. The house has one bath.
16. The car has four doors.
17. The magazine costs one dollar.
18. The book costs ten dollars.

However, when the measure phrase functions as a modifier and occurs before a noun, then the measure word is never plural:

19. °This is a ten dollars book.
20. This is a ten dollar book.
21. °John has a two bedrooms house.
22. John has a two bedroom house.

The teacher might consider giving the student who asked the question follow-up exercises to ensure that the explanation has been understood.

INTEGRATING GRAMMAR INSTRUCTION INTO A COMMUNICATIVE CURRICULUM

Prior to the advent of communicative language teaching, the content of a language course typically consisted of the grammatical structures and words that would be covered in the course. At best, the structures and words were organized around situations or topics (e.g., the post office, going to the movies). Strongly influenced by the English for specific purposes movement (see Johns, 1991; Johns & Dudley-Evans, 1991), communicative language teaching often starts with a determination of the purposes or objectives that the learner has. This is followed by an examination of the content the learner must understand and the tasks the learner will need to perform as well as the oral and/or written discourse the learner will be expected to comprehend and produce in the target language in the course of performing the tasks previously identified.

For any language learner with a definable learning purpose, the question of what grammar to teach does not become relevant until an adequate corpus of purposeful task-based discourse samples has been compiled. A discourse analysis can then be performed to identify discourse-level and sentence-level structures (as well as vocabulary items) that are especially useful and frequent for a given topic (i.e., content) and/or task or genre (e.g., writing a report). The language course ideally will be organized around the relevant content, or tasks, or both. And the discourse-level and sentence-level grammar, vocabulary, and other aspects of language form will be presented and practiced in the context of texts like the ones that were compiled and organized for the course.

For the general purpose language learner, the beginning-level course can develop a base by dealing first with grammar-meaning correspondences (e.g., *in* vs. *on*; present tense vs. present progressive, etc.) and then with grammar-function correspondences (e.g., *could* is more polite than *can* in requests; *well* at the beginning of a conversational response often signals that the speaker is about to express a disagreement, etc.). As soon as a basic threshold level (van Ek, 1976) has been established, the course must also begin to deal with discourse-level grammar (e.g., use of articles, use of active vs. passive voice, etc.).

A related issue is the kind of content and tasks that the language teacher can use to organize language courses. Many options exist for integrating form, meaning, and content. Brinton, Snow, and Wesche (1989) show how academic subject matter from areas such as psychology or history can be organized in various ways to complement and facilitate language instruction. Stern (1991), among others, shows how literature can be used as content for language instruction in ways that include but go far beyond traditional literary appreciation. Fried-Booth (1986) shows the teacher how projects of different scope and type can provide a focus for language development; and while Eyring (1991) adds insights about using project work with academic learners, she also suggests that the learners' past and ongoing life experiences constitute appropriate content for more general language classes.

The greatest potential—and also the greatest challenge—in these new and innovative language curricula lies in integrating focus on form with content-based and/or task-based language teaching. Teachers and learners alike must come to appreciate that dealing with such content and tasks requires both top-down and bottom-up language skills. The top-down skills represent understanding the content and the tasks, specifically what the meaningful task components are and how they are organized and sequenced in relation to each other. The bottom-up skills involve accurately using the words and structures needed to accomplish the tasks in relation to the content. Thus grammar instruction comes in when bottom-up skills are inadequate. If learners do not have the words and structures needed to carry out the tasks or to understand the content, then relevant discourse samples must be presented. Language features must be practiced in the context of the content and tasks with the help of the language teacher, who in effect will be teaching the learners to do a type of discourse analysis which focuses on grammar and many other things as well.[2]

Alternatively, if the learners are able to produce a rough approximation of the task, then the learners' performance can be used as the starting point. A careful analysis of and presentation of appropriate and inappropriate—and correct and incorrect—performance features will raise learner awareness and set the stage for discourse-based remedial activities, some of which will include correction of faulty grammatical structures along the lines suggested above in the sections on grammar instruction and error correction.

CONCLUSION

During the past 25 years we have seen grammar move from a position of central importance in language teaching, to pariah status, and back to a position of renewed importance, but with some diminution when compared with the primacy it enjoyed 25 years ago and had enjoyed for so long before then. Grammar is now viewed as but one component in a model of communicative competence (Canale & Swain, 1980; Hymes, 1972), and thus it can no longer be viewed as a central, autonomous system to be taught and learned independent of meaning, social function, and discourse

---

[2] Going well beyond the sentence level, discourse analysis is concerned with how language users produce and interpret language in context. It examines how lexicogrammar and discourse systematically vary across social situations and, at the same time, help to define those situations. Analysts attend to the form, meaning, and function of language whether they begin with discourse-level segments and work down to forms or begin with forms and work up to the discourse level.

structure. Nor can the grammar of adolescent and adult second and foreign language learners be viewed as a system that will simply emerge on its own given sufficient input and practice. Grammar, along with lexis—and also phonology for spoken discourse—are resources for creating meaning through text and for negotiating socially motivated communication. These resources need to be learned and sometimes they also need to be taught; however, when taught, they must be taught in a manner that is consonant with grammar's new role. Finding effective ways to do this is the current challenge.
■

ACKNOWLEDGMENTS

I owe an enormous debt to Diane Larsen-Freeman and Sharon Hilles, with both of whom I have coauthored books related to the teaching of grammar. Many of my ideas are a direct result of these collaborations. With specific reference to this paper, I sincerely thank Diane, Sharon, and also Bill Rutherford for their very helpful comments on an earlier draft. Responsibility for all errors and omissions in the paper are mine alone, however.

THE AUTHOR

Marianne Celce-Murcia is Professor of TESL and Applied Linguistics at the University of California, Los Angeles. She has served as member-at-large on the TESOL Executive Board and also as a member of the *TESOL Quarterly*'s Editorial Advisory Board. She is coauthor with Diane Larsen-Freeman of *The Grammar Book: An ESL/EFL Teacher's Course* (Newbury House, 1983) and with Sharon Hilles of *Techniques and Resources in Teaching Grammar* (Oxford University Press, 1988).

REFERENCES

Asher, J. J. (1977). *Learning another language through actions: The complete teacher's guidebook*. Los Gatos, CA: Sky Oaks.

Bracy Farnsworth, M. (1974). The cassette tape recorder: A bonus or a bother in ESL composition correction. *TESOL Quarterly* 8(3), 285-291.

Brinton, D., Snow, M. A., & Wesche, M. B. (1989). *Content-based second language instruction*. New York: Newbury House.

Burt, M., & Kiparsky, C. (1974). Global and local mistakes. In J. Schumann & N. Stenson (Eds.), *New frontiers in second language learning* (pp. 71-80). Rowley, MA: Newbury House.

Canale, M., & Swain, M. (1980). Theoretical bases of communicative approaches to second language teaching and testing. *Applied Linguistics, 1*(1), 1-47.

Carrell, P. L. (1982). Cohesion is not coherence. *TESOL Quarterly 16*(4), 479-488.

Carrell, P. L. (1987). Content and formal schemata in ESL reading. *TESOL Quarterly, 21*(3), 461-482.

Celce-Murcia, M. (1985, February). Making informed decisions about the role of grammar in language teaching. *TESOL Newsletter*, pp. 1, 4-5.

Celce-Murcia, M. (1991). Language teaching approaches: An overview. In M. Celce-Murcia (Ed.), *Teaching English as a second or foreign language* (2nd ed., pp. 3-11). New York: Newbury House.

Celce-Murcia, M., & Hilles, S. (1988). *Techniques and resources in teaching grammar.* New York: Oxford University Press.

Chaudron, C. (1983). Research on metalinguistic judgments: A review of theory, methods, and results. *Language Learning, 33*(3), 343-377.

Chomsky, N. (1957). *Syntactic structures.* The Hague: Mouton.

Chomsky, N. (1959). [Review of *Verbal Behavior*]. *Language, 35*(1), 26-58.

Chomsky, N. (1965). *Aspects of the theory of syntax.* Cambridge, MA: MIT Press.

Cohen, A. D. (1983, December). Reformulating compositions. *TESOL Newsletter*, pp. 1, 4-5.

Cohen, A. D. (1985). Reformulation: Another way to get feedback. *The Writing Lab Newsletter, 10*(2), 6-10.

Eyring, J. L. (1991). Experiential language learning. In M. Celce-Murcia (Ed.), *Teaching English as a second or foreign language* (2nd ed., pp. 346-359). New York: Newbury House.

Fried-Booth, D. (1986). *Project work.* Oxford: Oxford University Press.

Fries, C. C. (1945). *Teaching and learning English as a foreign language.* Ann Arbor, MI: University of Michigan Press.

Frodesen, J. (1991). *Aspects of coherence in a writing assessment context: Linguistic and rhetorical features of native and non-native English essays.* Unpublished doctoral dissertation, University of California, Los Angeles.

Halliday, M. A. K. (1973). *Explorations in the functions of language.* London: Edward Arnold.

Halliday, M. A. K., & Hasan, R. (1976). *Cohesion in English.* London: Longman.

Hartnett, D. (1985). Cognitive style and second language learning. In M. Celce-Murcia (Ed.), *Beyond basics: Issues and research in TESOL* (pp. 16-33). New York: Newbury House.

Higgs, T. V., & Clifford, R. (1982). The push towards communication. In T. V. Higgs (Ed.), *Curriculum, competence, and the foreign language teacher* (pp. 57-79). Lincolnwood, IL: National Textbook.

Hymes, D. (1972). On communicative competence. In J. B. Pride & J. Holmes (Eds.), *Sociolinguistics: Selected readings* (pp. 269-293). Harmondsworth, England: Penguin.

Jakobovits, L. (1968). Implication of recent psycholinguistic developments for the teaching of a second language. *Language Learning, 18*(1&2), 89-109.

Jakobovits, L. (1970). *Foreign language learning: A psycholinguistic analysis of the issues.* Rowley, MA: Newbury House.

Johns, A. M. (1991). English for specific purposes (ESP): Its history and contributions. In M. Celce-Murcia (Ed.), *Teaching English as a second or foreign language* (2nd ed., pp. 67-77). New York: Newbury House.

Johns, A. M., & Dudley-Evans, T. (1991). English for specific purposes: International in scope, specific in purpose. *TESOL Quarterly, 25*(2), 297-314.

Joos, M. (1962). *The five clocks: A linguistic excursion in the five styles of English usage.* New York: Harcourt, Brace, and World.

Knapp, D. (1972). A focused, efficient method to relate composition correction to teaching aims. In H. B. Allen & R. N. Campbell (Eds.), *Teaching English as a second language* (2nd ed., pp. 213-221). New York: McGraw-Hill.

Krashen, S., & Terrell, T. (1983). *The natural approach.* Hayward, CA: Alemany Press.

Lado, R. (1964). *Language teaching: A scientific approach.* New York: McGraw-Hill.

Larsen-Freeman, D. (1991). Teaching grammar. In M. Celce-Murcia (Ed.), *Teaching English as a second or foreign language* (2nd ed., pp. 279-296). New York: Newbury House.

Long, M. (1983). Does second language instruction make a difference? A review of research. *TESOL Quarterly 17*(3), 359-382.

McGirt, J. D. (1984). *The effect of morphological and syntactic errors on the holistic scores of native and non-native compositions.* Unpublished master's thesis, University of California, Los Angeles.

Miller, G., & Buckhout, R. (1973). *Psychology: The science of mental life.* New York: Harper & Row.

Richards, J. C. (1985). *The context of language teaching.* Cambridge: Cambridge University Press.

Rutherford, W. E. (1987). *Second language grammar: Learning and teaching.* New York: Longman.

Rutherford, W. E., & Sharwood Smith, M. (Eds.). (1988). *Grammar and second language teaching.* New York: Newbury House.

Selinker, L. (1972). Interlanguage. *IRAL 10*(3), 209-231.

Stern, S. L. (1991). An integrated approach to literature in ESL/EFL. In M. Celce-Murcia (Ed.), *Teaching English as a second or foreign language* (2nd ed., pp. 328-346). New York: Newbury House.

Tomasello, M., & Herron, C. (1988). Down the garden path: Inducing and correcting overgeneralization errors in the foreign language classroom. *Applied Psycholinguistics, 9*(3), 237-246.

Tomiyama, M. (1980). Grammatical errors and communication breakdown. *TESOL Quarterly, 14*(2), 71-79.

van Ek, J. A. (1976). *The threshold level for modern language learning in schools.* London: Longman.

Wechsler, R. (1987). *An inquiry into interview analysis as a fine tuning technique.* Unpublished master's thesis, University of California, Los Angeles.

Widdowson, H. G. (1978). *Teaching language as communication.* Oxford: Oxford University Press.

Wilkins, D. A. (1976). *Notional syllabuses.* Oxford: Oxford University Press.

Winitz, H. (Ed.). (1981). *The comprehension approach to foreign language instruction.* New York: Newbury House.

Winitz, H. (no date). *The learnables.* (Picture-books and cassettes for learning English, French, Spanish, German, Hebrew; available from the International Linguistics Corporation, Kansas City, MO)

Witbeck, M. (1976). Peer correction procedures for intermediate and advanced ESL composition lessons. *TESOL Quarterly, 10*(3), 321-326.

The Pronunciation Component in Teaching English to Speakers of Other Languages

JOAN MORLEY
The University of Michigan

This paper reviews the nature of changing patterns in pronunciation teaching over the last 25 years.[1] It then describes in detail six instructional features of a multidimensional teaching process: a dual-focus communicative program philosophy, learner goals, instructional objectives, the role of the learner, the role of the teacher, and a framework of three instructional practice modes.

Recent discussions of "pronunciation"[2] teaching principles have examined a number of important rationale issues including: questions of whether pronunciation should (or can) be taught and, if so, what should be taught and how; expressions of the need for more controlled studies of changes in learner pronunciation patterns as the result of specific instructional procedures; views on whether and how research in second language phonology can inform classroom practices. These and many other pertinent concerns have been ably discussed in thorough and insightful state-of-the-art papers by Leather (1983) and Pennington and Richards (1986). When it comes to classroom practice, however, as Yule (1990) has observed, it may have appeared to novice teachers that the only classroom choice available is one between teaching pronunciation as articulatory phonetics or not teaching pronunciation at all. But could this limited choice of options be more apparent than real? Clearly, on the positive side of the picture, some creative and principled contributions to alternatives have come on the scene in recent years, with a small but steady movement toward some "new looks" in pronunciation teaching. This does not mean that there are not many remaining questions about a number of issues, and more

---

[1] The focus of this discussion is pronunciation teaching and is not intended to include a review of research in areas of second language phonology.

[2] The term *pronunciation* means different things to different people. In this paper, I refer to a range of pronunciation teaching practices.

than a few leaps of faith in mounting classroom practices without a clear theory of pronunciation teaching. Nonetheless, it does seem that there is reason for optimism.

It is the intent of this paper to approach the topic of pronunciation teaching with this spirit of optimism, devoting one section to a search for signs of changing patterns and agents of change over time, and a second section to summary descriptions of some of the major instructional strands found in many innovative programs, with a multidimensional look at the pronunciation teaching process. A final section considers some continuing needs. Specifically, Part 1 presents a short background introduction focused on the broad sweep of growth and development in TESOL, the profession. This is followed by a review of changing patterns of emphasis in the teaching of the pronunciation component in ESL/EFL[3], concluding with a look at two important catalysts of change: the urgent needs of adult (and near-adult) learners and the emergence of a number of shifts in instructional focus, ones that are formulated here as programming principles. Part 2 describes six important instructional features in detail. Part 3 considers some present/future needs.

PART 1: CHANGING PATTERNS

TESOL AT TWENTY-FIVE: EXTENSIVE GROWTH AND DEVELOPMENT

The first observation that must be made in any reflection on the ESL profession today is one that recognizes at the outset its extensive growth and development—in size, in diversity, in complexity of learner clientele and of professional substance.

In the last quarter century we have witnessed an enormous "population explosion" in student numbers the world over, and especially in adult and near-adult learner groups. Strevens (1988) reported that estimates of the number of people in the world who use English for some purpose range between 750 million and a billion and a half. But, and of special interest to us, only approximately 300 million of them are native speakers (NSs), leaving a staggering number of nonnative speakers (NNSs). With this turn of events has come new instructional demands in new situations and we have needed to turn our attention more and more to carefully focused assessments of specific student needs and subsequent design of effective instructional programs. This has

---

[3] The designation "English as a second language" (ESL) is used throughout and is taken to include both "second" and "foreign" settings.

proved a special challenge for the planning of effective pronunciation programs.

As for professional substance, a second explosion, a veritable knowledge explosion in both our own field and in resource disciplines, presents changing perspectives on the nature of language, language learning, and language teaching and provides a multiplicity of options for setting our pedagogical, assessment, and research agenda. This last quarter century also has produced an instructional technology revolution, one that has been especially advantageous to pronunciation work, with a variety of audio, video, and computer capabilities applicable to classroom and learning center laboratories.

CHANGING PERSPECTIVES ON LANGUAGE AND LANGUAGE LEARNING

As perspectives on language learning and language teaching have changed, there has been a gradual shift from an emphasis on teaching and a teaching-centered classroom to an emphasis on learning and a learning-centered classroom, with special attention to the individual learner as well as the group of learners. At the same time, there has been a shift from a narrow focus on linguistic competencies to a broader focus on communicative competencies, within which linguistic competencies (i.e., grammar, pronunciation, etc.) remain an essential component albeit only one of several critical competencies (Canale & Swain, 1980).

The following significant changes in theoretical paradigms—in learning models, in linguistic models, in instructional models—inform much of the state-of-the-art work in the field today (including current directions in the principles and practices of pronunciation work).

1. From a language learning perspective of outside-in, to one of inside-out; that is, a changed concept of language acquisition that views the learner as the active prime mover in the learning process (Corder, 1967), and an emerging paradigm shift in which learners are seen as active creators, not as passive recipients, in a process which is cognitively driven.

2. Following from this altered conceptualization of the learning process, a movement from a focus on the group, to an increasing focus on individual learner differences and individual learning styles and strategies (Naiman, Fröhlich, Stern, Todesco, 1978; O'Malley & Chamot, 1989; Oxford, 1990; Rubin, 1975; Stern, 1975; Wenden & Rubin, 1987).

3. From a focus on language as simply a formal system, to a focus on language as both a formal system and a functional system, one that exists to satisfy the communicative needs of its users (Halliday, 1970, 1973, 1978).

4. From linguistic preoccupation with sentence-level grammar to widening interest in semantics, pragmatics, discourse, and speech act theory (Austin, 1962; Searle, 1970).

5. From an instructional focus on linguistic form and correct usage to one on function and communicatively appropriate use (Widdowson, 1978, 1983).

6. From an orientation of linguistic competence to one of communicative competence (Hymes, 1972).

7. From a global competence concept to detailed competency specifications and the introduction of an especially useful model that brings together a number of viewpoints in one linguistically oriented and pedagogically useful framework: grammatical competence, sociolinguistic competence, discourse competence, and strategic competence (Canale & Swain, 1980).

These developments and others have led to a wide variety of changes in virtually all aspects of ESL including the area of pronunciation teaching.

PRONUNCIATION TEACHING PAST AND PRESENT

The 1940s, 1950s, and into the 1960s

Not much question about it: In the 1940s, 1950s, and into the 1960s pronunciation was viewed as an important component of English language teaching curricula in both the audiolingual methodology developed in the U.S. and the British system of situational language teaching. In fact, along with correct grammar, accuracy of pronunciation was a high-priority goal in both systems.

Although these two schools of language teaching developed from different traditions, as Richards and Rodgers (1986) point out, they reflected quite similar views on the nature of both language and language learning. In general, language was viewed as consisting of hierarchies of structurally related items for encoding meaning. Language learning was viewed as mastering these forms, the building blocks of the language, along with the combining rules for phonemes, morphemes, words, phrases, sentences. The pronunciation class in this view was one that gave primary attention to phonemes and their meaningful contrasts, environmental allophonic variations, and combinatory phonotactic rules, along with structurally based attention to stress, rhythm, and intonation. Instruction featured articulatory explanations, imitation, and memorization of patterns through drills and dialogues, with extensive attention to correction. One text that was very widely used and served as a source of much imitation in the preparation of pronunciation teaching materials was an oral approach volume produced under the supervision of Robinett (Lado, Fries, & Robinett, 1954).

Actually, the use of the past tense here is misleading since both audiolingual and situational language teaching continue to flourish in programs throughout the world, and many make use of the traditional approach described above. The major change that has occurred today in many innovative programs is one that abandons the notion of an articulatory phonetics approach as the conceptual basis for teaching pronunciation, but integrates attention to the sound system into an expanded and more comprehensive framework, one that focuses on communicative interactions and functional language use.

The 1960s, 1970s, and into the 1980s

Beginning in the late 1960s and continuing through the 1970s and into the 1980s, and in quite sharp contrast to the previous period, a lot of questions were raised about pronunciation in the ESL curriculum. There were questions about the importance of pronunciation as an instructional focus, questions about whether or not it could be taught directly at all, questions about the assumption it could be learned at all under direct instruction. The effect was that more and more programs gave less and less time and explicit attention to pronunciation; many programs dropped it entirely. While the number of textbook and teacher reference publications in other segments of the ESL curriculum increased dramatically, very little new material on pronunciation appeared.

The elimination or reduction of the pronunciation component developed amid growing dissatisfaction with many of the principles and practices of the traditional approach to pronunciation. Factors involved included changing models of second language learning, changing foci in second language teaching, and changing models of linguistic description. The familiar ways and means of teaching pronunciation no longer seemed appropriate as new pedagogical sights were set on language functions, communicative competencies, task-based methodologies, and realism and authenticity in learning activities and materials. Moreover, both the process and the product were seen as flawed. The process, viewed as meaning-less noncommunicative drill-and-exercise gambits, lost its appeal; likewise, the product, that is the success ratio for the time and energy expended, was found wanting.

Through the decade of the 1970s, however, there were some indications of change. The agents of change were a number of ESL professionals who began to raise issues and suggest expansions and changes of emphasis in classroom practices. In retrospect, many of these perspectives foreshadowed things to come: Prator (1971) examined issues relating to phonetics versus phonemics in pronunciation teaching; Allen (1971) wrote on intonation, providing practice suggestions that continue to be cited today; Bowen (1972) focused on contextualizing practice in the classroom, with a classic format that is still recommended, for example, by Celce-Murcia and Goodwin (1991) who refer to it as "Bowen's Technique"; Kriedler (1972), W. Dickerson (1975), and Dickerson and Finney (1978) stressed the importance of the spelling/pronunciation link for learners; Morley (1975) emphasized the need for learner-involvement and speech self-monitoring; Robinett (1975) suggested ways to present information in a manner that appeals to students' cognitive involvement; Stevick (1975) turned attention to a view of the learner's feelings and the importance of the affective dimension in learning; L. Dickerson (1975) and W. Dickerson (1976) looked at aspects of variability in L2 pronunciation performance; Cathcart and Olsen (1976) reported on teachers' and students' preferences for correction; Parrish (1977) and Stevick (1978) presented viewpoints on a practical philosophy of pronunciation with attention to issues involving linguistic, affective, social, and methodological con-siderations; G. Brown (1977, 1978) underscored the importance of focusing listening attention on prosodic patterning; Beebe (1978) provided some sociolinguistic perspectives on "teaching pronuncia-tion, why we should be"; Smith and Rafiqzad (1979) investigated mutual intelligibility among speakers from different cultures.

These articles all addressed topics that were to be issues of continuing concern into the 1980s: (a) basic philosophical consider-ations for teaching pronunciation; (b) the importance of meaning and contextualized practice; (c) learner involvement, self-monitoring, and learners' feelings; (d) learner cognitive involve-ment; (e) intelligibility issues; (f) variability issues; (g) correction issues; (h) increasing attention to stress, rhythm, intonation, reductions, assimilations, etc.; (i) expanded perspectives on listening/pronunciation focus; (j) attention to the sound-spelling link.

Through the 1980s and into the 1990s

Beginning in the mid-1980s and continuing into the 1990s there has been a growing interest in revisiting the pronunciation component of the ESL curriculum for adults and young adults. An important part of this movement has been pronunciation developments in several ESP areas: that is, programming for specific-purpose attention to pronunciation (i.e., academic, occupational, etc.).

The modest number of pronunciation-focused papers of the 1970s was followed in the 1980s by a significant increase in both journal articles and teacher resource books, clearly a reflection of renewed interest in pronunciation teaching principles and practices. First of all, a number of insightful review articles were published in the eighties, including: Leather in *Language Teaching* (1983), with a thorough state-of-the-art article on second language pronunciation learning and teaching, one that raised pertinent issues that a rationale for L2 pronunciation teaching ought to address, then reviewed the status of each; Pennington and Richards (1986), in the *TESOL Quarterly,* with a careful reexamination of the status of pronunciation in language teaching and a call for a broader focus on pronunciation within the context of discourse in both second language acquisition (SLA) research and ESL teaching; von Schon (1987) in the 25th-anniversary edition of the *English Teaching Forum,* with a close look at pronunciation in the international context of English as a foreign language (EFL), and an examination of the roles of English and the issue of what models should be taught; Grant (1988) in *TESOL in Action,* a Georgia TESOL publication, with a discussion of the problems and the possibilities for innovative pronunciation planning for the adult learner; Anderson-Hsieh (1989) in *Cross Currents,* with a succinct history of approaches toward teaching pronunciation with special reference to Japan, but with useful applicability to other EFL contexts; Yule (1989) and Riggenbach (1990) in *Annual Review of Applied Linguistics (ARAL)* with reviews of a number of aspects of teaching the spoken language, including pronunciation.

A number of teacher resource books on teaching pronunciation and/or speaking skills appeared during the 1980s as well: Brown and Yule (1983), a broad "armoury of strategies and tools" (p. ix), with a concentration on the communicative use of language by speakers; Bygate (1987), a useful source of ideas on teaching speaking, with both practical and theoretical perspectives; Morley (1987) a variety of "current perspectives on pronunciation teaching: practices anchored in theory"; Kenworthy (1987), solid information on pronunciation teaching, including a section reviewing the main problems experienced by speakers of nine selected languages; Avery and Ehrlich (1987) (a TESL Canada *Talk* volume), papers on classroom methodology and a section on problems of eight language groups; Wong (1987b), focus on English rhythm and intonation in pronunciation teaching; Swan and Smith (1987), 24 contributors provide a comprehensive teachers' guide to "learner English" in terms of typical interlanguages of speakers of several dozen different languages: A. Brown (1991), a collection of 29 papers published between 1956 and 1986; Celce-Murcia, Brinton, and Goodwin (in press), a reference book on English pronunciation for ESL/EFL teachers; Comrie (1987), linguists provide descriptions of "the world's major languages," including sections on phonology.

In addition, a number of excellent English language reference books were published during the 1980s: Wells (1982), three volumes that contain detailed descriptions of a wide variety of the English dialects found around the world; Ladefoged (1982), a course in phonetics with substantial information on English sounds, patterns, and suprasegmentals; Bauer, Dienhart, Hartvigson, and Jakobsen (1980), a careful description of "American English," with very useful comparative notes on "British English" as well; Brazil, Coulthard, and Johns (1980), a British discourse intonation and language teaching text which stresses the "learnability" (p. 118) of four intonational categories and their associated meaning; Brown, Currie, and Kenworthy (1980), a challenge to previous assumptions and models of sentence-level intonation, using data from interactive discourse; Wolfram and Johnson (1982), a volume on phonological analysis, with a "focus on American English"; Kriedler (1989), a phonology course with comprehensive presentation of the pronunciation of English.

Taken together, the reviews and the teacher references reveal a number of important developments and many continuing questions. An especially significant trend is an increasing number of programs engaged in developing new looks in pronunciation teaching, ones that are concerned with an expanded pronunciation/speech/oral communication component of the ESL curriculum.

Overall, with today's renewed professional commitment to empowering students to become effective, fully participating members of the English-speaking community in which they communicate, it is clear that there is a persistent, if small, groundswell of movement to write pronunciation back into the instructional equation but with a new look and a basic premise: *Intelligible pronunciation is an essential component of communicative competence.*

As Beebe (1978) observed, in this era of emphasis on meaningful communication, it is important for ESL professionals to take note of the fact that "pronunciation—like grammar, syntax, and discourse organization—*communicates* [italics added] . . . . the very act of pronouncing, not just the words we transmit, are an essential part of what we communicate about ourselves as people" (p. 121). She reported that NSs often label NNS pronunciation errors derisively, as sounding comical, cute, incompetent, not serious, childish, etc.

In this review, it becomes clear that the decades of the seventies and eighties were important periods of development. A number of changing views on pronunciation learning and teaching emerged. Coincidentally, some of the need to rethink both principles and practices came about as the result of the pressing urgency of student needs. In the following section, student needs and principles guiding changes in pronunciation learning/teaching practices will be discussed.

MAJOR INFLUENCES ON CHANGING PATTERNS OF PRONUNCIATION TEACHING

As noted earlier, changes in perspectives on second language learning and teaching over the past two and a half decades have impacted every facet of second language study. In the case of pronunciation, an early and rather wholesale movement in TESL toward eliminating or reducing attention to pronunciation instruction presently seems to be undergoing something of a trend reversal. Part of the reason for this may lie in the fact that it has become increasingly clear in recent years that ignoring students' pronunciation needs is an abrogation of professional responsibility. In programs for adult (and near-adult) ESL learners in particular, it is imperative that students' educational, occupational, and personal/social language needs, *including reasonably intelligible pronunciation*, be served with instruction that will give them communicative empowerment—effective language use that will help them not just to survive, but to succeed. Moreover, with an increasing focus on communication, has come a growing premium on oral comprehensibility, making it of critical importance to provide instruction that enables students to become, not "perfect pronouncers" of English (which, as we shall see later is neither reasonable or necessary), but intelligible, communicative, confident users of spoken English for whatever purposes they need.

Two developments have been catalysts in bringing about changes in pronunciation teaching in recent years. One is the increasing pressure of the urgent needs of special groups of ESL learners.

Second, there are a number of emerging principles that seem to reflect an underlying belief system shared by many new pronunciation programs.

Groups of Learners in Special Need of Attention to Pronunciation

Wong (1986), Morley (1987, 1988), Anderson-Hsieh (1989), Celce-Murcia (1991), and others have expressed concerns about particular groups whose pronunciation difficulties may place them at a professional or social disadvantage. In response to this need, a number of accent reduction programs have appeared, especially in the United States; some are run by solidly trained language professionals, some by less well-informed instructors. For all groups of learners profiled below, a broadly-constructed communicative approach to teaching pronunciation/speech is likely to be much more effective than a narrowly constructed articulatory phonetics approach.

In ESL Settings

1. Adult and teenage refugees in vocational and language training programs. For this clientele of ESL learners, not only the initial stage of developing survival language skills (including reasonably intelligible speech), but continuing oral communicative development is crucial for education and employment, for conducting personal business, and for personal/social interactions.

2. Immigrant residents who have been in an English-speaking country for 5 to 15 years. This refers to those residents who have passed through the educational system and graduated into the workplace, only to find that their spoken language, and particularly their intelligibility, prohibits them from taking advantage of employment opportunities or from advancing educationally. Helping these ESL learners work to modify their pronunciation/speech patterns toward increased intelligibility is especially challenging—for both student and teacher—for the patterns are likely to be well entrenched and resistant to change. As Wong (1986) observed "the long-term effects of neglecting pronunciation are most dramatically exemplified by the accountants, programmers, police officers, telephone operators, and engineers enrolled in accent improvement and effective communication courses" (pp. 232-233). She goes on to note that

these long-term residents who demonstrate so well that pronunciation is not simply picked up through interaction with English speakers have to pay a high price to untangle the linguistic morass that is strangling their ability to communicate at the level demanded by their jobs.

3. A growing population of nonnative speakers of English in technology, business, industry, and the professions in English-speaking countries. Each year increasing numbers of NNSs are employed by both large corporations and small companies in English-speaking settings. Indeed, the United States Congress in 1991 passed legislation that raised the immigration quota for skilled foreign professionals from 55,000 to 140,000 a year. And more and more, employers and employees in business and industry are finding that job-related oral use of English is a must, with a premium on intelligible speech and good communication skills.

4. College and university faculty members and research scholars in virtually every field of higher education. Along with skilled professionals in business and industry, there are growing numbers of NNSs among the ranks of college and university faculty members and research associates, not only in science and engineering fields but in the social sciences and humanities as well. Significant oral language demands (including requirements of reasonably intelligible pronunciation) are placed on NNS faculty members including possessing not only the requisite language skills for lectures, seminars, and interactions with students and colleagues, but also the speaking skills needed in public presentation contexts on campus and at national and international conferences.

5. Graduate and undergraduate students in higher education in English-speaking countries. These include international teaching assistants and NNSs who are pursuing a master's degree in teaching English as a second language (MATESL). Achieving the proficiency score required for admission to an institution of higher education gains NNS students admission and may reflect sufficient command of English to enable them to survive, but growing college and university demands on both oral and written English skills may make it more and more difficult for many to really succeed without special English for academic purposes (EAP) attention to language skills. In addition, some of the NNS graduate students who become teaching assistants (TAs) may have difficulties due to significant language

deficiencies, including pronunciation intelligibility problems, that need special instructional attention. NNSs in MATESL programs are a special group of learners who need attention to speech intelligibility.

In EFL Settings

1. International business personnel, scientists, technologists, and other professionals whose careers demand the use of both effective written and spoken English as a lingua franca. More and more today, in countries throughout the world, careers in commerce and trade, banking, science and technology, health care, transportation, industry, manufacturing, and many other fields place high English language demands on employees, both in their home country and in assignments around the world. In fact, these professionals may find that their families need to become English students as well, in the case of long-term overseas assignments. Many international companies have found it necessary to mount English language programs in both the home country and in the English-speaking country.

2. College and university professors and academic research scholars in many disciplines in higher education. The increasing role of English as the world's international language of scholarship and research is well documented (Swales, 1991). In fact, English is today the dominant language of international conferences and of scholarly and research publications in a significant number of the major professional journals that circulate worldwide.

3. Students who ultimately wish to enter English-speaking colleges and universities to pursue undergraduate and/or graduate degrees. The better prepared NNS students are with effective written and oral skills (including reasonably intelligible speech) before they enter English-speaking colleges and universities, the better their chances not just for survival but for success. In particular NNSs whose career goals include teaching English as a second/foreign language need special attention paid to communicative skills in general and to pronunciation intelligibility in particular.

Programming Principles

A survey of the pronunciation literature of the past several years—teacher reference books, articles in journals and collections, conference papers, student texts—reveals a number of shifts in instructional focus. Taken together, the themes found in new programs seem to reflect a shared underlying belief system. Some of the principles guiding current directions in pedagogy are the following. (See Morley, 1987, preface.)

1. A focus that views the proper place of pronunciation in the second language curriculum as an integral part of communication, not as an isolated drills-and-exercises component set aside from the mainstream; in short, a growing trend toward communicative approaches to teaching pronunciation.

2. A redirection of priorities within the sound system to a focus on the critical importance of suprasegmentals (i.e., stress, rhythm, intonation, etc.) and how they are used to communicate meaning in the context of discourse, as well as the importance of vowel and consonant sounds (segmentals) and their combinations. (Yule, 1989, has observed that perhaps this direction is best described as the prosodic (or suprasegmental) approach, and that it has its intellectual roots in the intonation work of Bolinger, 1964, and the extensive treatment of paralinguistic features by G. Brown, 1977.)

3. A focus on an expanded concept of what constitutes the domain of pronunciation, one that incorporates not only attention to (a) segmentals and (b) suprasegmentals, but also (c) voice quality features such as the phenomena referred to as *voice-setting features* by Pennington and Richards (1986); as *voice quality settings* by Laver (1980), Esling and Wong (1983) and Esling (1986); as *paralinguistic features* by G. Brown (1977) (as a rubric for certain vocal features); and as *articulatory settings* by Honikman (1964), and (d) elements of body language used in oral communication (e.g., facial expressions and gestures; eye contact; head, arm, and hand gestures; body stance, posturing, and use of space; and upper body movements, which Acton, 1984, discusses in detail in connection with teaching rhythm).

4. A focus on some revised expectations in both learner involvement and teacher involvement. Current perspectives on learner involvement in the pronunciation learning/teaching process include an emphasis on speech awareness and self-monitoring, while a revised characterization of teacher involvement is drawn along the lines of facilitator-coach and organizer of instructional activities.

    Learner involvement through overtly labeled self-monitoring is not a new focus in pronunciation (Acton, 1984; Morley, 1975,

1979). Acton stresses giving constant attention to the individual's own resources and puts the responsibility for success in the course on the student. Wong (1986) notes that by giving students specific means to develop independently, the responsibility falls on those who have the actual power to make the necessary changes. Firth (1987) presents a variety of techniques for developing self-correcting and self-monitoring strategies as a way of dealing with the serious problem of "carry-over" (p. 48). Crawford (1987) examines a number of pronunciation learning/ teaching issues including perspectives on monitoring. Kenworthy (1987) emphasizes sensitizing learners to their own potential as active participants in the process and describes the teacher's role as primarily supportive of the learner's own efforts. Yule, Hoffman, and Damico (1987) point out the need for patience and support of learners who, as they are engaged in developing their L2 pronunciation skills, may go through a period of deteriorating performance as they give up old ways and have not yet become fluent with new ways. W. Dickerson (1989) makes the case for a natural ability for self-monitoring of language and the importance of activating it systematically in pronunciation teaching. Riggenbach (1990), in a section on self-monitoring of speaking activities, reviews a number of techniques for self- and peer analysis.

5. A focus on meaningful practice and especially speech-activity experiences suited to the communication styles and needs of the learners' real-life situations. Suggestions for contextualized work with segmentals and suprasegmentals are found in Bowen (1972, 1975), Celce-Murcia (1983, 1987), English (1988), Celce-Murcia and Goodwin (1991), and Morley (1991a). Meaningful practice activities, of course, go hand in hand with the focus on commu- nicative approaches to teaching pronunciation. Suggested speaking activities that can be adapted for special pronunciation focus as well are found in Ur (1980), Rooks (1987), Brown and Yule (1983), Porter, Grant, and Draper (1985), Bygate (1987), Riggenbach and Lazaraton (1991).

6. A focus on the link between listening and pronouncing/speaking and a need to expand the nature and the range of pronunciation- oriented listening activities. Attention to pronunciation-oriented listening instruction was an important component of traditional pronunciation teaching with a primary focus on sound discrimi- nation and identification exercises. Many of today's texts and teaching references continue to include this focus among a wider range of listening/teaching foci. Gilbert (1984), who stresses a

dual focus on pronunciation and listening comprehension apprises students that, "How you *hear* English is closely connected with how you *speak* English" (p. 3). Wong (1987a) focuses on ways to make a language-rich pronunciation classroom in which students hear a variety of speakers engaged in diverse real-world communicative events in order to develop active listening skills and a comfortable level of fluency. Mendelson-Burns (1987) advocates teaching pronunciation through listening and suggests a variety of activities.

7. A focus on a range of important sound/spelling relationships. Substantial attention to the utilization of spelling information in adult ESL pronunciation teaching was slow to appear in course books until relatively recently, although Kriedler (1972) and W. Dickerson (1975) had emphasized its importance, and some attention to spelling was included in student texts by Bowen (1975), Morley (1979), and Prator and Robinett (1985). More recently W. Dickerson (1989) presents an extensive treatment of English orthography as a key tool in teaching pronunciation, especially in stress and rhythm instruction, and a number of new texts have included a spelling section in lessons on segmentals. Recent teacher reference materials on spelling include papers by Temperley (1983, 1987) and a chapter in Kenworthy (1987) on spelling, including how the morphological regularity of English spelling can be exploited for pronunciation purposes.

8. A focus on the uniqueness of each ESL learner. Each has created his or her own personal pattern of spoken English, which is unlike that of anyone else and the product of influences from both the L1 and the L2, the student's personal learning and communicability strategies, as well as the impact of input and instruction. And Eckman (1991) has provided convincing evidence over the years to show that L2 pronunciation is going to be subject to universal forces quite distinct from rules of the L1 or the L2. This unique pattern now needs to be modified in some way(s) in order to reach goals of intelligibility, communicability, and self-confidence.

Flege (1980) noted that L2 learners produce sounds that are not typically found in either their native or the second language. Beebe (1984), reporting on a study of variability, noted that her results suggested that there is a high level of inherent variation in interlanguages, just as there is in native languages, as indeed was revealed in earlier variability work done by L. Dickerson (1975) and W. Dickerson (1976). And Prator (1971) suggested that the safest solution for teachers is to regard *un*intelligibility not as a result of *phonemic* substitution but as the cumulative effect of many little departures from the *phonetic* norms of the language.

PART 2: PUTTING IT ALL TOGETHER: SOME INSTRUCTIONAL FEATURES OF A MULTIDIMENSIONAL PRONUNCIATION TEACHING PROCESS

This section will look at some of the intersecting strands of a process—the teaching of pronunciation—which often is rather narrowly regarded as one dimensional. As discussed in Part 1, current developments demonstrate the contrary, that in fact the pronunciation teaching process is a multifaceted domain. With urgent needs of learners and the principles summarized in Part 1 as key considerations, six features will be discussed. Information has been drawn from published accounts and from personal communications about current practices in a variety of developing programs.[4]

A FOCUS ON PROGRAM PHILOSOPHY

The basis for planning in many new programs has been to take the pronunciation class out of isolation, conceptually speaking as well as practically speaking, where it often has been set aside out of the mainstream, and to reconstitute it in both learning/teaching form and function as an *integral part of oral communication*. A variety of communicative pronunciation teaching practices of a general nature are included in Celce-Murcia (1983, 1987), Pica (1984), Kenworthy (1987), Naiman (1987), English (1988), Celce-Murcia and Goodwin (1991), and Celce-Murcia, Brinton, and Goodwin (in press). In addition, publications available with an English for specific purposes (ESP) focus include international teaching assistant (ITA) and English for science and technology (EST) work. Byrd, Constantinides, and Pennington (1989) present five specialized chapters of ITA pronunciation teaching materials, and Schwabe (1988), Wennerstrom (1991, in press), Stevens (1989), and Anderson-Hsieh (1990) report on specialized pronunciation-focused ITA activities and methods. Huckin and Olsen (1983) include a special section on pronunciation in their EST handbook for nonnative speakers; Browne and Huckin (1987), and Browne (in press) discuss corporate-level communicative ESP pronunciation training for NNS scientists and engineers; Imber and Parker (1991) present a program framework and communicative teaching ideas for "milieu-specific" pronunciation teaching which can be applied to a wide variety of ESP situations.

[4] Portions of this section have appeared in Morley (1988).

Outlining a Dual-Focus Program:
Speech Production and Speech Performance

From a philosophy of pronunciation teaching as an integral part of communication it is possible to construct a dual-focus framework as shown in Figure 1. The dual framework combines a *microlevel* focus on *speech production* (i.e., a focus on discrete elements of pronunciation in a bottom-up sense) and a *macrolevel* focus on *speech performance* (i.e., a focus on general elements of communicability in a top-down sense). Either the microlevel or the macrolevel can be given priority attention at a given time, or they can share the classroom focus.

At the microlevel (or discrete level) the focus is on contextualized modification of vowel and consonant sounds (and their reductions,

FIGURE 1

Dual Focus: Speech Production and Speech Performance

From *Rapid Review of English Vowels and Selected Prosodic Features* by Joan Morley, in press, Ann Arbor: The University of Michigan Press. Copyright by The University of Michigan Press. Adapted by permission.

SPOKEN ENGLISH

SPEECH PRODUCTION	SPEECH PERFORMANCE
[A focus on specific elements of pronunciation[a]]	[A focus on general elements of oral communicability[b]]
Pronunciation: *Microfocus*	*Oral Communication:* *Macrofocus*
• Clarity and precision in articulation of consonant and vowel sounds	• Overall clarity of speech, both segmentals and suprasegmentals
• Consonant combinations both within and across word boundaries, elisions, assimilations, etc.	• Voice quality effectiveness for discourse-level communication
• Neutral vowel use, reductions, contractions, etc.	• Overall fluency and ongoing planning and structuring of speech, as it proceeds
• Syllable structure and linking words across word boundaries, phrase groups, and pause points	• Speech intelligibility level
• Features of stress, rhythm, and intonation	• General communicative command of grammar
• Features of rate, volume, and vocal qualities	• General communicative command of vocabulary words/phrases
	• Overall use of appropriate and expressive nonverbal behaviors

[a] A focus on *discrete features* of voice and articulation.

[b] A focus on *global patterns* of spoken English.

combinations, elisions and assimilations, etc.); on the specific features subsumed under the rubric of stress, rhythm, and intonation; and on features of rate, volume, and vocal qualities. Within communicative activities, specific attention is given to stabilizing a student's emerging abilities to adjust vowel and consonant pronunciation and to manipulate prosodic and vocal features *at will* with ease and accuracy, to express intended meaning, and to increase intelligibility.

At the macrolevel (or global level) the focus is on the synthesis of many components of communicative oral discourse. This encompasses a variety of elements including appropriate and expressive nonverbal behaviors, increasingly facile communicative command of grammar and appropriate vocabulary, enhanced ability to sustain speech (i.e., for fluent ongoing structuring and planning of speech as it proceeds), as well as developing aspects of overall intelligibility, discourse-level vocal effectiveness, and overall clarity of speech.

A FOCUS ON LEARNER GOALS, STANDARDS, AND OUTCOMES

Traditional pronunciation goals, by and large, exhort ESL students to strive for "perfect pronunciation," and/or near-native pronunciation, and/or mastery of pronunciation. While these aspirations sound attractive to many students (and their teachers), the path to these high levels of performance is a tortuous one, on both sides. The truth is that they are virtually unattainable for the vast majority of ESL learners. In fact, there is a widely held consensus that few persons, especially those who learn to speak a second language after the age of puberty, can ever achieve native-like pronunciation in that second language; Scovel (1969) and others believe *never*. The factors involved in answering the question of why this is so are many and varied—neurological, psychomotor, cognitive, affective—but clearly, the current consensus is that this is the case for most learners. (But see Hill, 1970, and Neufeld, 1978).

At best, perfectionistic performance goals turn out to be unrealistic; at worst, they can be devastating: They can defeat students who feel that they cannot measure up, and they can frustrate teachers who feel they have failed in their job. How fortunate it is that perfect or native-like pronunciation is *not* a necessary condition for comprehensible communicative output. In fact, it may not always even be desirable. As Leather (1983) observed, in some situations learners who do well in acquiring a very good L2 accent may get mixed responses from NSs. He reports Christophersen's (1973) description of one possible NS reaction to too-perfect pronunciation in an L2 speaker may be that of "a host who sees an uninvited guest making free with his possessions" (p. 199). In another dimension, perfect L2 pronunciation is not desired by some learners who wish—consciously or unconsciously—to retain accent features to mark their L1 identity and to insure that they are not perceived as betraying their loyalty to their L1 community.

Pushing perfection issues a bit further, in addition to the fact that it is not a realistic expectation, nor a necessary condition for effective NNS communication with NSs or other NNSs, nor necessarily a desirable goal for everyone, there is a further concern here. Notions of perfection and native-like pronunciation may be imposing and perpetuating false standards, standards difficult to define, let alone uphold, because these are slippery concepts with basic questions of, What is perfect? and Which native speaker are we talking about? since everyone speaks their language with an accent. This is particularly significant today with many serviceable and respected Englishes existing throughout the world. In fact, in a cross-cultural communication intelligibility study involving 1,383 people from 11 countries, Smith and Rafiqzad (1979) report that a most important result is that "the native speaker was always found to be among the least intelligible speakers" (p. 375). Nakayama (1982) reports that in the business sector in Japan, some language training programs actively seek and employ NNSs as well as NSs as instructors in order to help the students become accustomed to English dialects other than British and U.S.

What, then, are reasonable and desirable goals? In view of the preceding considerations, four learner goals have been formulated (see Figure 2).

Perhaps a few further notes on intelligibility are in order, as it is a key ingredient in goal setting in new programs and a bit of a shift from traditional views. Like perfection and native-like pronunciation, the notion of intelligibility is a slippery concept. Judgments about intelligibility are strongly influenced by the listener's preconceived ideas about NNSs in general (including their accent) and the personality and accent of any individual NNS in particular. Moreover, it is undoubtedly the case that an individual listener's norms for what makes attractive L1 speech also have a core involvement here. Indeed, intelligibility may be as much in the mind of the listener as in the mouth of the speaker.

Chastain (1980), in looking at the general concept of comprehension judgments of NNSs by NSs, made some interesting discoveries.

FIGURE 2
Learner Goals

Goal 1: Functional intelligibility

The intent is to help learners develop spoken English that is (at least) reasonably easy to understand and not distracting to listeners. (See Figure 3, Speech Intelligibility Index.)

Goal 2: Functional communicability

The intent here is to help the learner develop spoken English that serves his or her individual communicative needs effectively for a feeling of communicative competence.

Goal 3: Increased self-confidence

The intent here is to help learners become more comfortable and confident in using spoken English, and to help them develop a positive self-image as a competent nonnative speaker of English and a growing feeling of empowerment in oral communication.

Goal 4: Speech monitoring abilities and speech modification strategies for use beyond the classroom

The intent here is to help learners develop speech awareness, personal speech monitoring skills, and speech adjustment strategies that will enable them to continue to develop intelligibility, communicability, and confidence outside class as well as inside.

He found that depending upon NS factors such as the NS's linguistic tolerance, insight, interest, and patience, student language errors will be viewed as (a) comprehensible and acceptable, (b) comprehensible but not acceptable, or (c) incomprehensible (in the case of failure to comprehend). Chastain noted that while these reactions will vary from person to person and situation to situation, this does not diminish the importance of the contribution made by the listener in the communicative process.

An example of this is found in elements of the so-called ITA problem, that is, teaching difficulties experienced by some international teaching assistants in colleges and universities. The reported "foreign accent" or "unintelligible speech" of the ITAs is often the first complaint of their students, but pronunciation per se may be a problem that is more apparent than real: Consider Chastain's observations about the role of the listener as well as the subtle (and sometimes not so subtle) elements of prejudice and xenophobia (Hofer, 1990) known to impinge on the judgments of some of the NS undergraduate population. (Recall the derisive speech labels reported by Beebe, 1978.)

Looking carefully at assessments of the "ITA problem," Hinofotis and Bailey (1980) reported that out of 12 subcategories of problems, pronunciation was ranked first by undergraduate student raters as well as by TESL and TA-training raters. The two latter groups also pointed out that there seemed to be a threshold of intelligibility in the subjects' pronunciation. That is, beyond a certain point, as yet undetermined, pronunciation ceases to be a factor, but up to a given speaking proficiency level, the faulty pronunciation of the NNS can severely impair the communication process. This work points directly to the need for serious study of the intelligibility factor. The Speech Intelligibility Index in Figure 3 is part of a project exploring ways to identify both discrete and global features that impinge positively/negatively on an individual learner's communicability, with an additional focus on the role of compensatory communication strategies that may raise the perceived intelligibility level.

A FOCUS ON LEARNING DIMENSIONS AND INSTRUCTIONAL OBJECTIVES

Within communicative approaches to pronunciation teaching it is important to focus on critical dimensions of learning and to formulate instructional objectives that include whole-person learner involvement. Three important dimensions of learning are an intellectual involvement, an affective involvement, and a physical or performative involvement.

Information Objectives: Serving the Intellectual Component of Learning

These objectives relate to an intellectual or cognitive component of learning. Adult and near-adult learners seem to be helped enormously by attention to intellectual frameworks. Information objectives are intended to contribute to the development of *speech-awareness* and *study-awareness* in order to engage the intellectual involvement of learners in their learning process.

Language Information

Short, carefully selected pronunciation/speech descriptions and explanations help learners develop speech awareness and focus on modifications of specific features of (a) pronunciation/speech production, (b) pronunciation/speech performance, (c) intelligibility, and (d) communicability. Pronunciation/spelling information and analysis tasks help learners unlock some of the mysteries of sound/spelling interpretations and help them reduce inaccurate spelling-pronunciation infelicities.

FIGURE 3
Speech Intelligibility Index: Evaluation of Student Communicability
From *Rapid Review of English Vowels and Selected Prosodic Features* by Joan Morley, in press, Ann Arbor: The University of Michigan Press. Copyright by The University of Michigan Press. Adapted by permission.

Level	Description	Impact on Communication
1	Speech is basically unintelligible; only an occasional word/phrase can be recognized.	Accent preludes functional oral communication.
2	Speech is largely unintelligible; great listener effort is required; constant repetitions and verifications are required.	Accent causes severe interference with oral communication.

Communicative Threshold A

3	Speech is reasonably intelligible, but significant listener effort is required due to speaker's pronunciation/grammatical errors which impede communication and cause listener distraction; ongoing need for repetitions and verifications.	Accent causes frequent interference with communication through the combined effect of the individual features of mispronunciation and the global impact of the variant speech pattern.
4	Speech is largely intelligible; while sound and prosodic variances from NS norm are obvious, listeners can understand if they concentrate on the message.	Accent causes interference primarily at the distraction level; listener's attention is often diverted away from the content to focus instead on the novelty of the speech pattern.

Communicative Threshold B

5	Speech is fully intelligible; occasional sound and prosodic variances from NS norm are present but not seriously distracting to listener.	Accent causes little interference; speech is fully functional for effective communication.
6	Speech is "near-native"; only minimal features of divergence from NS can be detected; near-native sound and prosodic patterning.	Accent is virtually nonexistent.

Notes on speech evaluation:

1. Elicit a speech sample of several minutes. The sample should be sustained impromptu speech, not just answers to simple questions or rehearsed biographical comments. The sample should be spontaneous speech, perhaps on a topic such as: (a) What are your career plans in the next 5 years? (b) What makes your life interesting? (c) What makes a happy family?

2. Try to listen to the speech sample as if you were an untrained language listener. Err on the conservative side, with consideration of the "lay" listeners whom the student will meet.

3. In a few descriptor phrases summarize the student's strengths and weaknesses in three areas: (a) use of vowel and consonant sound segments, their combinations, and reductions, contractions, elisions, assimilations, etc.; (b) use of features of stress, rhythm, and intonation, and vocal quality features, rate, volume, etc.; (c) features of general "communicability." (Use Figure 1 as a reference.) Comment on how each of these factors impacts communicative intelligibility, and assign a Speech Intelligibility Level (SIL), using [+] and [−] notations as necessary. Monitor student progress through periodic SIL reevaluation.

Procedural Information

Explicit directions and goal-related participatory guidelines help students develop study awareness; they help students understand what they will do, how, and why.

Students can develop a useful degree of speech awareness and study awareness in a surprisingly short time. Even very young students profit from a little information which can be presented in brief descriptions and simple charts and diagrams. *Simplicity, selectivity,* and *moderation* are the keys to effective use of both language information and procedural information.

Affective Objectives: Serving the Psychological Component of Learning

These objectives relate to the powerful affective or psychological component of learning.

Learner Self-Involvement

Pronunciation/speech study is most profitable (and most pleasant) when students are actively involved in their own learning, not passively detached repeaters of drills. Research has shown that self-involvement is a primary characteristic of good language learners. However, learner self-involvement cannot be left to chance; it must be actively shaped, early and continually, throughout ESL course work. Teachers and materials can help students become involved in the following four areas.

1. Recognition of self-responsibility. Learners can be guided toward taking responsibility for their own work not just by exhorting them, but by providing ways and means: (a) clear directions and explicit participatory guidelines so that students know the what, the how, and the why of their work; (b) carefully defined tasks, outcomes, and responsibilities for class and small-group activities; (c) substantive and sharply focused cues for self-monitoring and pronunciation/speech modification.

2. Development of self-monitoring skills. Self-monitoring can begin as gentle consciousness-raising with the goal of helping students develop speech awareness, self-observation skills, and a positive attitude toward them: (a) by giving concrete suggestions for monitoring (i.e., observing) their own speech on one or two production or performance points at a time; (b) by helping them

develop a simple self-rehearsal technique—talking to yourself and listening to yourself—as the way to self-monitor; (c) by helping them shift gradually from the dependent mode of teacher-monitoring (in imitative practice and guided self-practice) to the independent mode of self-monitoring (in independent rehearsed practice and extemporaneous speaking practice).

3. Development of speech modification skills. Negative feelings about correction as a bad thing, a punishment, *need to be eliminated*. (Actually, I like to substitute the word *modification* for *correction*). And, of course, it is the learner, not the teacher, who modifies (i.e., corrects) pronunciation. It is important to help learners develop a positive understanding of roles: the student role is to modify (i.e., adjust, alter, correct) a microlevel or macrolevel feature of speech/pronunciation; the teacher role is to give cues to help the student identify what, where, and how to modify and to give support, encouragement, and constructive feedback. From the first, it is useful for teachers to shift from repeated modeling to cueing for student modification.

4. Recognition of self-accomplishment. Improvement is a gradual process with much variability, neither an overnight phenomenon, nor an overall development, and it may be difficult for learners to perceive changes in speech patterns. It is important for learners to become aware of small successes in modifying features of pronunciation/speech in a given task. Many teachers use audio and/or video recording and guide students in recognizing speech changes in themselves and in their classmates. Assessment of achievements should be based on degrees of change, not absolutes. The emphasis should be on self-comparisons over time, not on student-to-student comparisons.

A Comfortable, Supportive Classroom Atmosphere

In pronunciation/speech work, perhaps more than any other part of language study, a comfortable classroom atmosphere is essential for maximum achievement. Classroom interactions need to be enjoyable and supportive with a focus on strengths as well as weaknesses. The learning climate needs to be one where even the most retiring (and the most unintelligible) students can lose their self-consciousness and embarrassment about "sounding funny" as they work to modify pronunciation/speech features of their oral communication skill.

1. Supportive teacher/student interactions. (See the section below on teacher involvement.)

2. Supportive student/student interactions. The Speech Intelligibility Index can be very useful in helping students assess their own strengths and weaknesses and those of others. Pair and small-group work with audio- or videotape analysis of *specified* speech production and/or speech performance features can be very effective, but it is essential that critiquing be constructive, not destructive, with an emphasis on positive features as well as features that need modification.

Practice Objectives: Serving the Physical or Performative Component of Learning

These objectives relate to the *physical* or performative component of speech/pronunciation study.

Pronunciation/Speech Practice

For maximum effect, pronunciation/speech instruction must go far beyond imitation; it calls for a mix of practice activities. Three kinds of speech practice can be included from the very beginning: imitative practice, as needed (dependent practice); rehearsed practice (guided self-practice and independent self-practice); extemporaneous speaking practice (guided and independent self-practice). (See also the section below on instructional planning.)

Pronunciation-Oriented Listening Practice

Specialized speech-oriented listening tasks can help learners develop their auditory perception, their discriminative listening skills for dimensions of pronunciation/speech communicability, and their overall aural comprehension of English. Attention needs to be given to prosodic features and vocal features including the fast speech phenomena found in authentic speech patterns as well as vowel and consonant sounds and their combinations.

Spelling-Oriented Pronunciation Practice

It is essential that ESL students learn to relate spoken English and written English quickly and accurately if they are to become truly literate in English. A variety of kinds of sound/spelling work can prepare them to do this. Learner awareness of spelling patterns as cues to stress/rhythm patterning can be tremendously useful. (See W. Dickerson, 1989 and elsewhere, for extensive work in this area.)

A FOCUS ON THE LEARNER AND LEARNING INVOLVEMENT

Research on learner strategies, that is those measures (either tutored or untutored) which a learner undertakes to facilitate his or her own language learning, has been reported by Stern (1975), Rubin (1975), Naiman et al. (1978), Wenden and Rubin (1987), O'Malley and Chamot (1989), and Oxford (1990). Among the strategies found to be most successful for learners is self-involvement in the learning process. How can a goal of learner self-involvement be reached in the pronunciation teaching process?

Learner Awarenesses and Attitudes

Adult learners seem to benefit most when they are involved, consciously, in the speech modification process as they work to become intelligible, communicative, confident speakers of English. Teachers can assist learners in developing useful awarenesses and attitudes, including those listed in Figure 4.

FIGURE 4

Learner Awarenesses and Attitudes

1. Speech awareness
2. Self-awareness of features of speech production and speech performance
3. Self-observation skills and a positive attitude toward self-monitoring processes
4. Speech-modification skills (i.e., self-"correction") and the elimination of negative feelings that correction is a punitive thing
5. Awareness of the learner role as one of a "speech performer" modifying, adjusting, or altering a feature of speech/pronunciation, and the teacher role as one of assisting students as a "speech coach" who gives suggestions and cues for speech modification, support, encouragement, and constructive feedback
6. A sense of personal responsibility for one's own learning, not only for immediate educational and occupational needs, but for future career, social, and personal goals
7. A feeling of pride in one's own accomplishments
8. Building a personal repertoire of speech monitoring and modification skills in order to continue to improve speaking effectiveness in English when the formal instructional program is finished

A FOCUS ON THE TEACHER AND TEACHER INVOLVEMENT

Programs that are committed to helping learners modify pronunciation/speech patterns and develop effective communicable speech skill often reflect a philosophy of learner/teacher partnership. In pronunciation work, perhaps more than in any other facet of second language instruction, clearly the teacher doesn't "teach," but facilitates learning in a very special learner-centered way.

The Teacher as Pronunciation/Speech "Coach"

In programs with the partnership philosophy, the role of the teacher is viewed as one of assisting learners something like a coach, a speech coach, a pronunciation coach. The work of a pronunciation/speech coach can be viewed as similar to that done by a debate coach, a drama coach, a voice coach, a music coach, or even a sports coach. A coach characteristically supplies information, gives models from time to time, offers cues, suggestions and constructive feedback about performance, sets high standards, provides a wide variety of practice opportunities, and overall supports and encourages the learner.

The pronunciation/speech coach has the critical role of monitoring and guiding modifications of spoken English at two levels, as noted earlier: (a) speech production (i.e., the microlevel) and (b) speech performance (i.e., the macrolevel). Note again that articulatory phonetics is not abandoned, but takes a place as one part in the larger communicative picture of getting the message across.

The teacher-as-coach has a challenging task made up of diverse responsibilities, including those listed in Figure 5.

A FOCUS ON THE INSTRUCTIONAL PLANNING

This final portion will look at instructional planning for a pronunciation/speech curriculum that encompasses (a) a cognitive dimension, with attention to selected information about both language and study procedures, as appropriate; (b) an affective dimension, with encouragement of learner self-involvement and self-monitoring, and a classroom atmosphere which is positive and supportive; and (c) a practice dimension with speaking tasks and activities through which learners can work toward modifying pronunciation/speech patterns in spoken English. The discussion will focus on specifics of the practice objective.

FIGURE 5

Teacher-as-Coach Responsibilities

1. Conducting pronunciation/speech diagnostic analyses, and choosing and prioritizing those features that will make the most noticeable impact on modifying the speech of each learner toward increased intelligibility

2. Helping students set both long-range and short-term goals

3. Designing program scope and sequence for an entire group of learners; designing personalized programming for each individual learner in the group

4. Developing a variety of instructional formats, modes, and modules (e.g., whole-class instruction, small-group work, individual one-on-one tutorial sessions; prerecorded audio and/or video self-study materials; both in-class and out-of-class self-study rehearsal recordings in audio and/or video formats; work with new computer program speech analysis systems, and more). Overall, providing genuine speech task activities for practice situated in real contexts and carefully chosen simulated contexts

5. Planning out-of-class field-trip assignments in pairs or small groups for real-world extemporaneous speaking practice, with panel discussions as follow-up

6. Structuring in-class speaking (and listening) activities with invited NS and NNS guests participating

7. Providing models, cues, and suggestions for modifications of elements in the speech patterning for each student

8. Monitoring learners' speech production and speech performance at all times, and assessing pattern changes, as an ongoing part of the program

9. Encouraging student speech awareness and realistic self-monitoring

10. *Always* supporting each learner in his or her efforts, be they wildly successful or not so successful

The Challenge of Fulfilling the Practice/Performance Objective

Some Questions About Practice

The big challenge pronunciation/speech teachers face lies in fulfilling the practice objective by providing meaningful and productive speaking experiences within which learners can monitor and modify their speech patterns without disrupting communication. Questions of what to practice, how to practice, and how much to practice must be faced. Moreover, the question of why learners should practice needs to be examined through two related questions, Does practice work? and if so, How can we evaluate the impact of practice on changes or improvement?

A Carry-Over Consideration

How can we determine how much practice will bring about modifications that will carry over into the learner's speaking experiences in myriad domains outside the classroom? How does practice relate to students' needs, especially those students who clearly *must* have effective instructional assistance in order to alter speech patterns which are virtually unintelligible to speech patterns which are functionally intelligible? As a working guideline for the present, three modes of practice are presented here.

Three Modes of Practice

A pronunciation/speech syllabus can be planned to provide a variety of speaking and listening tasks and activities using an integration of three practice modes. The three modes can be characterized as follows.

Imitative Speaking Practice

This kind of practice should be used only as necessary and, in fact, may be introduced as a short-term component within a rehearsed or extemporaneous practice context, especially with advanced or intermediate students. The purpose of the practice is to focus on controlled production of selected pronunciation/speech features. It includes contextualized practice (see Bowen, 1972, 1975; Celce-Murcia, 1983, 1987; Celce-Murcia & Goodwin, 1991; English, 1988; Gilbert, 1984; and Morley, 1991a). It can include self-access audio- and/or videotaped materials for individual use or for assigned pair and small-group study sessions outside of class as well as computer program speech-analysis systems that transform speech input into a visual display on the computer screen (see Browne, 1991, and Molholt, 1988); should *not* be used beyond the point where the learner can produce the given feature(s) easily at will, at which time the practice activity should shift immediately to rehearsed and extemporaneous speech practice modes.

Rehearsed Speaking Practice

This kind of practice can be used in a variety of ways as a practice mode in its own right as well as an interim step between imitative and extemporaneous practice. The purpose of the practice is to work toward stabilization of modified pronunciation/speech patterns (i.e., discrete-point features, global features, etc.) so that the learner can manipulate them easily at will. Practice can include oral reading scripts of a wide variety, either teacher-selected or self-selected or composed by teachers and/or students (e.g., simulated radio or TV broadcast scripts of all kinds; excerpts from famous speeches, plays, narrative poems, novels, role-play skits and playlets, etc.; preplanned (relatively short) oral presentations of a wide variety, with topics self-selected); in-class dress rehearsal and final performance with audio- and/or videotaping (and feedback critique sessions either immediately or later); out-of-class self-study rehearsals or paired/small-group rehearsal study sessions with audio- and/or videotaping; one-on-one individual speech work-out study sessions with the speaking teacher (i.e., speech coach). Practice can move into the next mode (extemporaneous speech practice) by adding audience-participation in the form of question-and-answer and discussion interactions. (In addition, see the following for materials which can be adapted for both imitative and rehearsed pronunciation focus: Archibald, 1987; Maley & Duff, 1978; Stevens, 1989; and Via, 1980, 1987), for drama techniques; Graham, 1978, for rhythmic chants; Maley, 1987, for poetry and song; Gilbert, 1984, and Morley, 1991a, 1991b, for oral reading materials.)

Extemporaneous Speech Practice

This kind of practice can be used with a wide variety of speaking tasks and activities, and is for the purpose of working toward integration of modified speech patterns into naturally occurring creative speech in both partially planned and unplanned talks (monologues). It can include small-group panel discussion presentations, both formal and informal (preplanned outside of class or planned relatively spontaneously during class time in small-group work sessions and presented immediately); audience-interaction follow-up dialogue sessions in a question-and-answer format; in-class presentations with audio- and/or videotaping; out-of-class self-study rehearsals individually, in pairs, or in small-group preparation sessions; one-on-one individual work-out speech sessions with the teacher with audio- and/or videotaping and feedback sessions. (Many speech activity texts cited earlier can be adapted for use with this pronunciation/speech practice mode including Brown & Yule, 1983; Bygate, 1987; Morley, 1991b; Porter, Grant, & Draper, 1985; Rooks, 1987; Ur, 1980.)

These practice modes move from dependent practice (with a model given) to guided practice (with self-initiated, rehearsed speech) to independent practice (with both partially planned and extemporaneous speech practice) with the content self-generated and developed by the learners to meet their personal educational or occupational needs.

PART 3: LOOKING AHEAD

It was the intent of Part 1 of this presentation to look at pronunciation teaching over the past quarter century, to review some of the patterns of change, and to identify some of the agents of change—that is, a relatively small but committed cohort of pronunciation specialists who are dedicated to the development of new instructional alternatives that can be programmed into effective course work. Part 2 directed attention to multiple dimensions of the pronunciation teaching process with a discussion of six major instructional features. This final portion focuses on continuing needs.

THE FUTURE OF PRONUNCIATION TEACHING: THE 1990S AND INTO THE TWENTY-FIRST CENTURY

Optimism and positive developments in teaching pronunciation were featured in the two preceding sections. In this final segment optimism prevails, but attention must be turned to perplexing issues and research and development needs. As observed by many colleagues in references already cited, the needs for future explorations are many. A few are listed here.

1. A need to equip ESL teachers (in both initial and in-service training) with a very specific kind of background in applied English phonetics and phonology, one that gives detailed attention to suprasegmentals and voice-quality features and their forms and their functions in interactive discourse (in addition to segmentals information) and one that stresses application in communicative approaches to pronunciation teaching. (As urged by Gilbert, 1984, Wong, 1986, and others, this is an area where communication between language teachers and linguists is critical.)

2. A continuing need for development of pronunciation/speech activities, tasks, materials, methodologies and techniques across the spectrum of imitative, rehearsed, and extemporaneous speaking practice experiences—that is, more of the kinds of things now available in some of the references cited above. (One tool now becoming an economic and practical possibility is self-study computer programming both for student practice and for assessment through the use of visual displays of speech parameters. As laboratory speech analysis and synthesis capabilities have become more accessible for instructional uses, Leather (1983) notes the potential for creative uses—while

guarding against misuses—is great. (See Browne, 1991; de Bot, 1980; de Bot & Mailfert, 1982; Gilbert, 1980; Molholt, 1988.)

3. Together with the need for continuing development of creative and effective practice experiences is the need for more definitive evaluative measures and methods to quantify changes and improvements in the learner's intelligibility and communicability. (Celce-Murcia & Goodwin, 1991, stress student assessment as both formative, or ongoing, and summative, or final; Morley, 1991a, suggests the development of a Speech Intelligibility Index that makes use of behavioral descriptors correlated with impact on communication.)

4. A need for controlled studies of changes in learner pronunciation patterns as the result of specific instructional procedures. (This is a particularly difficult area for research because, as Pennington & Richards, 1986, have pointed out, there is not likely to be a one-to-one relationship between teaching and learning, since learning "is a gradual process involving successive approximations to the target language system over time in a progression from controlled to automatic processing" [pp. 218-219].)

5. Finally, a continuing need for research (as noted in the reviews by Leather, 1983, and Pennington & Richards, 1986) into aspects of second language phonology and the nature and course of development of an L2 phonological system. A review of these areas of research has not been the focus of this discussion. Information on a range of interlanguage phonology topics, and phonological theory and L2 phonological issues is available in the papers in Ioup and Weinberger (1987) and James and Leather (1986) and in articles in *Language Learning, Studies in Second Language Acquisition, Applied Linguistics*, and other periodicals.

CONCLUSION

Beginning slowly in the early 1980s and gathering momentum into the 1990s, there has been a growing movement of renewed concern for and excitement about the learning and teaching of pronunciation in the field of TESL. A major concern has been the urgent needs of several special groups of adult and near-adult learners who are seriously disadvantaged without effective second language oral skills, including intelligible communicative speech patterns. The excitement has been in the challenging work of expanding the horizons of pronunciation learning and teaching, redefining basic concepts (philosophy, learner goals, instructional objectives, roles of learner and teacher), and constructing communicative approaches featuring creative classroom and self-study instructional activities and procedures.

An increasing number of ESL professionals are engaged in studying issues and developing programs grounded in new perspectives. Much has been accomplished but much more development is needed. It is clear that pronunciation can no longer be ignored; today intelligible pronunciation is seen as an essential component of communicative competence. The challenge to teachers and researchers is to develop an informed expertise directed toward facilitating learners' development of functional communicative speech/pronunciation patterns.

■

ACKNOWLEDGMENTS

I am grateful to D. E. Morley, Maria Parker, Betty Wallace Robinett, John Swales, and George Yule for their comments on an earlier version of this article. Special thanks to Sandra Silberstein for her thorough and insightful editing.

THE AUTHOR

Joan Morley is Associate Professor of Linguistics at The University of Michigan. She is Past President of TESOL and served on its Executive Board for 10 years. Her interests are applied linguistics, ESL instructional research, and the development of ESL materials and methodologies. She has written a number of articles and books in the areas of pronunciation, aural comprehension, and speaking activities. Her books in press are *Rapid Review of English Vowels and Selected Prosodic Features, Intensive Consonant Pronunciation Practice*, and *Extempore Speaking Practice* (all from The University of Michigan Press).

REFERENCES

Acton, W. (1984). Changing fossilized pronunciation. *TESOL Quarterly, 18*(1), 71-85.

Allen, V. (1971). Teaching intonation, from theory to practice. *TESOL Quarterly, 5*(1), 73-81.

Anderson-Hsieh, J. (1989). Approaches toward teaching pronunciation: A brief history. *Cross-Currents, 16*, 73-78.

Anderson-Hsieh, J. (1990). Teaching suprasegmentals to international teaching assistants using field-specific materials. *English for Specific Purposes, 9*, 195-214.

Archibald, J. (1987). Developing natural and confident speech: Drama techniques in the pronunciation class. In P. Avery & S. Ehrlich (Eds.), The teaching of pronunciation: An introduction for teachers of English as a second language [Special issue]. *TESL Talk, 17*, 153-159.

Austin, J. L. (1962). *How to do things with words*. Cambridge, MA: Harvard University Press.

Avery, P., & Ehrlich, S. (Eds.). (1987). The teaching of pronunciation: An introduction for teachers of English as a second language [Special issue]. *TESL Talk, 17*.

Bauer, L., Dienhart, J. M., Hartvigson, H., & Jakobsen, L. K. (1980). *American pronunciation*, New York: Gyldendal Boghandel.

Beebe, L. (1978). Teaching pronunciation (why we should be). *IDIOM, 9*, 2-3.

Beebe, L. (1984). Myths about interlanguage phonology. In S. Eliasson (Ed.), *Theoretical issues in contrastive phonology* (Studies in Descriptive Linguistics No. 13, pp. 51-61). Heidelberg: Julius Groos Verlag.

Bolinger, D. (1964). Around the edge of language: Intonation. *Harvard Educational Review, 34*, 282-293.

Bowen, D. (1972). Contextualizing pronunciation practice in the ESOL classroom. *TESOL Quarterly, 6*(1), 83-94.

Bowen, D. (1975). *Patterns of English pronunciation*. Rowley, MA: Newbury House.

Brazil, D., Coulthard, M., & Johns, C. (1980). *Discourse intonation and language teaching*. London: Longman.

Brown, A. (1991). *Teaching pronunciation: A book of readings*. London and New York: Routledge.

Brown, G. (1977). *Listening to spoken English*. London: Longman.

Brown, G. (1978). Understanding spoken English. *TESOL Quarterly, 12*(3), 271-283.

Brown, G., & Yule, G. (1983). *Teaching the spoken language*. New York: Cambridge University Press.

Brown, G., Currie, K., & Kenworthy, J. (1980). *Questions of intonation*. London: Croom Helm.

Browne, S. (in press). A pedagogy of corporate-level ESP training for international scientists and engineers. In J. Alatis (Ed.), *Georgetown University Round Table on Languages and Linguistics 1991*. Washington, DC: Georgetown University Press.

Browne, S., & Huckin, T. (1987). Pronunciation tutorials for nonnative technical professionals: A program description. In J. Morley (Ed.), *Current perspectives on pronunciation: Practices anchored in theory* (pp. 41-57). Washington, DC: TESOL.

Bygate, M. (1987). *Speaking*. Oxford: Oxford University Press.

Byrd, P., Constantinides, J., & Pennington, M. (1989). *The foreign teaching assistant's manual*. New York: Macmillan.

Canale, M., & Swain, M. (1980). Theoretical bases of communicative approaches to second language teaching and testing. *Applied Linguistics, 1*, 1-47.

Cathcart, R., & Olsen, J. (1976). Teachers' and students' preferences for correction of classroom conversation errors. In J. Fanselow & R. Crymes (Eds.), *On TESOL '76*. Washington, DC: TESOL.

Celce-Murcia, M. (1983, May). Activities for teaching pronunciation communicatively. *CATESOL News*, pp. 10-11.

Celce-Murcia, M. (1987). Teaching pronunciation as communication. In J. Morley (Ed.), *Current perspectives on pronunciation* (pp. 1-12). Washington, DC: TESOL.

Celce-Murcia, M., & Goodwin, J. (1991). Teaching pronunciation. In M. Celce-Murcia (Ed.), *Teaching English as a second or foreign language* (2nd ed., pp. 136-153). New York, NY: Newbury House.

Celce-Murcia, M., Brinton, D., & Goodwin, J. (in press). *English pronunciation: A reference for ESL/EFL teachers.* Cambridge: Cambridge University Press.

Chastain, K. (1980). Native speaker reaction to instructor-identified student second-language errors. *The Modern Language Journal, 34,* 210-215.

Christophersen, P. (1973). *Second language learning: Myth and reality.* Harmondsworth, U.K.: Penguin.

Comrie, B. (1987). (Ed.). *The world's major languages.* New York: Oxford University Press.

Corder, S. P. (1967). The significance of learners' errors. *International Review of Applied Linguistics, 5,* 161-170.

Crawford, W. (1987). The pronunciation monitor: L2 acquisition considerations and pedagogical priorities. In J. Morley (Ed.), *Current perspectives on pronunciation: Practices anchored in theory.* Washington, DC: TESOL.

de Bot, K. (1980). The role of feedback and feedforward in the teaching of pronunciation. *System, 8,* 35-47.

de Bot, K., & Mailfert, K. (1982). The teaching of intonation: Fundamental research and classroom applications. *TESOL Quarterly, 16*(1), 71-77.

Dickerson, L. (1975). The learner's interlanguage as a set of variable rules. *TESOL Quarterly, 9*(4), 401-408.

Dickerson, W. (1975). The WH question of pronunciation: An answer from spelling and generative phonology. *TESOL Quarterly, 9*(3), 299-309.

Dickerson, W. (1976). Phonological variability in pronunciation instruction: A principled approach. *TESOL Quarterly, 10*(2), 177-191.

Dickerson, W. (1989). *Stress in the speech stream: The rhythm of spoken English.* Urbana and Chicago, IL: University of Illinois Press.

Dickerson, W., & Finney, R. (1978). Spelling in TESL: Stress cues to vowel quality. *TESOL Quarterly, 17*(1), 89-95.

Eckman, F. (1991). The structural conformity hypothesis and the acquisition of consonant clusters in the interlanguage of ESL learners. *Studies in Second Language Acquisition, 13,* 23-41.

English, S. (1988). *Say it clearly.* New York: Collier Macmillan.

Esling, J. (1986, March). Techniques for presenting voice quality settings. Paper presented at the 20th Annual TESOL Convention, Anaheim, CA.

Esling, J., & Wong, R. (1983). Voice quality settings and the teaching of pronunciation. *TESOL Quarterly, 17*(1), 89-95.

Firth, S. Developing self-correcting and self-monitoring strategies. In P. Avery & S. Ehrlich (Eds.), The teaching of pronunciation: An introduction for teachers of English as a second language [Special issue]. *TESL Talk, 17*, 148-152.

Flege, J. (1980). Phonetic approximation in second language acquisition. *Language Learning, 30*, 116-134.

Gilbert, J. (1980). Prosodic development: Some pilot studies. In R. Scarcella & S. Krashen (Eds.), *Research in second language acquisition* (110-117). Rowley, MA: Newbury House.

Gilbert, J. (1984). *Clear speech.* New York: Cambridge University Press.

Graham, C. (1978). *Jazz chants.* New York: Oxford University Press.

Grant, L. (1988). Enhancing pronunciation skills in the adult learner. *TESOL in Action, 3*(3), 1-10. Atlanta, GA: Georgia TESOL.

Halliday, M. A. K. (1970). Language structure and language function. In Lyons (Ed.), *New horizons in linguistics* (pp. 140-165). Harmondsworth, U.K.: Penguin.

Halliday, M. A. K. (1973). *Explorations in the functions of language.* London: Edward Arnold.

Halliday, M. A. K. (1978). *Language as social semiotic.* London: Edward Arnold.

Hill, J. (1970). Foreign accents, language acquistion and cerebral dominance revisited. *Language Learning, 20*, 237-248.

Hinofotis, F., & Bailey, K. (1980). American undergraduate reactions to the communication skills for foreign teaching assistants. In J. Fisher, M. Clarke, & J. Schacter (Eds.), *On TESOL '80: Building bridges* (pp. 120-133). Washington, DC: TESOL.

Hofer, B. (1990, November 8). TAs try to break language barrier. *The Michigan Daily.*

Honikman, B. (1964). Articulatory settings. In D. Abercrombie, D. B. Fry, P. A. D. MacCarthy, N. C. Scott, & J. L. M. Trim (Eds.), *In honour of Daniel Jones* (pp. 73-84). London: Longman.

Huckin, T., & Olsen, L. (1983). *English for science and technology: A handbook for nonnative speakers.* New York: McGraw-Hill.

Hymes, D. (1972). On communicative competence. In J. Pride & A. Holmes (Eds.), *Sociolinguistics* (pp. 269-293). Harmondsworth, U.K.: Penguin.

Imber, B., & Parker, M. (1991, March). Milieu-specific pronunciation. Paper presented at the 26th Annual TESOL Convention, New York.

Ioup, G., & Weinberger, S. (Eds.). (1987). *Interlanguage phonology: The acquisition of a second language sound system.* Cambridge, MA: Newbury House.

James, A., & Leather, J. (Eds.). (1986). *Sound patterns in second language acquisition.* Dordrecht, Netherlands: Foris.

Kenworthy, J. (1987). *Teaching English pronunciation.* Harlow, U.K.: Longman.

Kreidler, C. (1989). *The pronunciation of English.* Oxford: Basil Blackwell.

Kreidler, C. (1972). Teaching English spelling and pronunciation. *TESOL Quarterly, 5*(1), 3-12.

Ladefoged, P. (1982). *A course in phonetics* (2nd ed.). New York: Harcourt Brace Jovanovich.

Lado, R., Fries, C. C., & Robinett, B. W. (1954). *English pronunciation.* Ann Arbor, MI: The University of Michigan Press.

Laver, J. (1980). *The phonetic description of voice quality.* Cambridge: Cambridge University Press.

Leather, J. (1983). State of the art: Second-language pronunciation learning and teaching. *Language Teaching, 16,* 198-219.

Maley, A. (1987). Poetry and song as effective language-learning activities. In W. Rivers (Ed.), *Interactive language teaching* (pp. 93-109). Cambridge: Cambridge University Press.

Maley, A., & Duff, A. (1978). *Drama techniques in language learning.* Cambridge: Cambridge University Press.

Mendelson-Burns, I. (1987). Teaching pronunciation through listening. In P. Avery & S. Erlich (Eds.), The teaching of pronunciation: An introduction for teachers of English as a second language [Special issue]. *TESL Talk, 17,* 125-131.

Molholt, G. (1988). Computer-assisted instruction in pronunciation for Chinese speakers of American English. *TESOL Quarterly, 22*(1), 91-112.

Morley, J. (1975). Round robin on the teaching of pronunciation. *TESOL Quarterly, 9*(1), 81-88.

Morley, J. (1979). *Improving spoken English.* Ann Arbor, MI: The University of Michigan Press.

Morley, J. (Ed.). (1987). *Current perspectives on pronunciation: Practices anchored in theory.* Washington, DC: TESOL.

Morley, J. (1988). How many languages do you speak? Perspectives on pronunciation-speech-communication in EFL/ESL. *Nagoya Gakuin University Roundtable on Linguistics and Literature Journal, 19,* 1-35. Nagoya, Japan: Nagoya Gakuin University Press.

Morley, J. (1991a). *Intensive consonant pronunciation practice.* Ann Arbor, MI: The University of Michigan Press.

Morley, J. (1991b). *Extempore speaking practice.* Ann Arbor, MI: The University of Michigan Press.

Naiman, N. (1987). Teaching pronunciation communicatively. In P. Avery & S. Ehrlich (Eds.), The teaching of pronunciation: An introduction for teachers of English as a second language [Special issue]. *TESL Talk, 17,* 141-147.

Naiman, N., Frohlich, M., Stern, H. H., & Todesco, A. (1978). *The good language learner* (Research in Education Series No. 7). Toronto: Ontario Institute for Studies in Education.

Nakayama, Y. (1982). International English for Japanese people: Suggesting "multinationalization." *TESL Reporter, 15,* 63-72.

Neufeld, G. (1978). On the acquisition of prosodic and articulatory features in adult language learning. *The Canadian Modern Language Review, 34,* 163-174.

O'Malley, J. J., & Chamot, A. (1989). *Learning strategies in second language acquisition.* New York: Cambridge University Press.

Oxford, R. (1990). *Language learning strategies.* New York: Newbury House.

Parish, C. (1977). A practical philosophy of pronunciation. *TESOL Quarterly, 11*(3), 311-317.

Pennington, M., & Richards, J. (1986). Pronunciation revisited. *TESOL Quarterly, 20*(2), 207-226.

Pica, T. (1984). Pronunciation activities with an accent on communication. *English Teaching Forum, 22*(3), 2-6.

Porter, P., Grant, M., & Draper, M. (1985). *Communicating effectively in English: Oral communication for non-native speakers.* Belmont, CA: Wadsworth.

Prator, C. (1971). Phonetics vs. Phonemics in the ESL classroom: When is allophonic accuracy important? *TESOL Quarterly, 5*(1), 61-72.

Prator, C., & Robinett, B. W. (1985). *Manual of American English pronunciation* (4th ed.). New York: Holt, Rinehart & Winston.

Richards, J., & Rodgers, T. (1986). *Approaches and methods in language teaching.* Cambridge: Cambridge University Press.

Riggenbach, H. (1990). Discourse analysis and spoken language instruction. *Annual Review of Applied Linguistics, 11,* 152-163.

Riggenbach, H., & Lazaraton, A. (1991). Promoting oral skills. In M. Celce-Murcia (Ed.), *Teaching English as a second or foreign language* (2nd ed., pp. 125-136). New York: Newbury House.

Robinett, B. W. (1975). Round robin on the teaching of pronunciation. *TESOL Quarterly, 9*(1), 81-88.

Rooks, G. (1987). *The non-stop discussion workbook* (2nd ed.). Rowley, MA: Newbury House.

Rubin, J. (1975). What the "good language learner" can teach us. *TESOL Quarterly, 9*(1), 45-51.

Schwabe, G. (1988, March). A pronunciation course for foreign student teaching assistants. Paper presented at the 22nd Annual TESOL Convention, Chicago, IL.

Scovel, T. (1969). Foreign accents, language acquisition and cerebral dominance. *Language Learning, 19,* 245-254.

Searle, J. (1970). *Speech acts.* Cambridge, MA: Cambridge University Press.

Smith, L., & Rafiqzad, K. (1979). English for cross-cultural communication: The question of intelligibility. *TESOL Quarterly, 13*(3), 371-380.

Stern, H. H. (1975). What can we learn from the good language learner? *Canadian Modern Language Journal, 1,* 304-318.

Stevens, S. (1989). A "dramatic" approach to improving the intelligibility of ITA's. *English for Specific Purposes, 8,* 181-194.

Stevick, E. (1975). Round robin on the teaching of pronunciation. *TESOL Quarterly 9*(1), 81-88.

Stevick, E. (1978). Toward a practical philosophy of pronunciation: Another view. *TESOL Quarterly, 12*(2), 145-150.

Strevens, P. (1988). ESP after twenty years: A re-appraisal. In M. L. Tickoo (Ed.), *ESP: State of the art* (pp. 1-13). Singapore: SEAMEO Regional Language Centre.

Swales, J. (1991). International graduate students in anglophone research worlds. *Rackham Reports*, 72-88.

Swan, M., & Smith, B. (Eds.). (1987). *Learner English: A teacher's guide to interference and other problems*. Cambridge: Cambridge University Press.

Temperley, M. (1983). The articulatory target for final -*s* clusters. *TESOL Quarterly, 17*(3), 421-436.

Temperley, M. (1987). Linking and deletion in final consonant clusters. In J. Morley (Ed.), *Current perspectives on pronunciation: Practices anchored in theory* (pp. 59-82). Washington, DC: TESOL.

Ur, P. (1982). *Discussions that work: Task-based fluency practice*. Cambridge: Cambridge University Press.

Via, R. (1976). *English in three acts*. Honolulu: The University of Hawaii Press.

Via, R. (1987). "The magic if" of theater: enhancing language learning through drama. In W. Rivers (Ed.), *Interactive Language Teaching* (pp. 110-123). Cambridge: Cambridge University Press.

von Schon, C. (1987). The question of pronunciation. *English Teaching Forum, 25*(4), 22-27.

Wells, J. C. (1982). *Accents of English* (Vols. 1, 2, & 3). Cambridge: Cambridge University Press.

Wenden, A., & Rubin, J. (1987). *Learner strategies in language learning*. Englewood Cliffs, NJ: Prentice Hall Regents.

Wennerstrom, A. (1991). *Techniques for teachers: A guide for nonnative speakers of English*. Ann Arbor, MI: The University of Michigan Press.

Wennerstrom, A. (in press). Content-based pronunciation. *TESOL Journal*.

Widdowson, H. (1978). *Teaching language as communication*. Oxford: Oxford University Press.

Widdowson, H. (1983). *Language purpose and language use*. Oxford: Oxford University Press.

Wolfram, W., & Johnson, R. (1982). *Phonological analysis: Focus on American English*. Washington, DC: Center for Applied Linguistics.

Wong, R. (1986). Does pronunciation teaching have a place in the communicative classroom? In D. Tannen & J. Alatis (Eds.), *Georgetown University Round Table on Languages and Linguistics 1986* (pp. 226-236). Washington, DC: Georgetown University Press.

Wong, R. (1987a). Learner variables and prepronunciation considerations in teaching pronunciation. In J. Morley (Ed.), *Current perspectives on pronunciation: Practices anchored in theory* (pp. 13-28). Washington, DC: TESOL.

Wong, R. (1987b). *Teaching pronunciation: Focus on English rhythm and intonation*. Englewood Cliffs, NJ: Prentice Hall Regents.

Yule, G. (1989). The spoken language. In R. Kaplan (Ed.), *Annual Review of Applied Linguistics, 10*, 163-173.

Yule, G. (1990). [Review of *Teaching English pronunciation; Current perspectives on pronunciation: Practices anchored in theory;* and *Teaching pronunciation: English rhythm and stress*]. *System, 18,* 107-111.

Yule, G., Hoffman, P., & Damico, J. (1987). Paying attention to pronunciation: The role of self-monitoring in perception. *TESOL Quarterly, 21*(4), 765-768.

Twenty-Five Years of Contrastive Rhetoric: Text Analysis and Writing Pedagogies

ILONA LEKI
University of Tennessee

In the years since Robert Kaplan's ground-breaking work on contrastive rhetoric in the 1960s, the study of how different cultures put together texts has undergone considerable refinement. Despite the difficulty of finding comparable writing contexts across cultures, contrastive rhetoric studies have focused on such features of text as the logic of textual organization, the relative responsibility of writer and reader in written communication, the function of writing in a culture, cultural preferences for literary or poetic language, and standards of proof for assertions. This article reviews recent work in contrastive rhetoric, in particular, advances in methodologies for contrastive rhetoric research and discusses the role of contrastive rhetoric findings in teaching second language writing.

Contrastive rhetoric studies with implications for the ESL writing classroom began with Robert Kaplan's 1966 study of some 600 L2 student essays. This work was exploratory and, to a degree, more intuitive than scientific, but valuable in establishing contrastive rhetoric as a new field of inquiry.

It has also created controversy. Kaplan's diagrams of rhetorical patterns have been widely reprinted, appearing even in ESL composition textbooks. Indeed, it is in L2 writing classes that contrastive rhetoric work has the greatest potential practical application. The diagrams, with their implications in regard to patterns of written discourse, readily place contrastive rhetoric into the current traditional approach to teaching ESL writing (Silva, 1990), but contrastive rhetoric has not found much favor with those who adopt a process orientation to teaching writing.

Proponents of process approaches maintain that contrastive rhetoric research examines the product only, detaching it from and ignoring both the contrastive rhetorical context from which the L2 writers emerge and the processes these writers may have gone through to produce a text. Furthermore, as a result of this research orientation toward the product, when the findings of contrastive rhetoric have been applied to L2 writing, they have, almost by definition, been prescriptive: In English we write like this; those who would write well in English must look at this pattern and imitate it.

Modern contrastive rhetoric researchers, hoping to reconcile contrastive rhetoric to teaching composition, insist, perhaps somewhat defensively, that text-oriented research does not equal product-oriented writing instruction (Grabe & Kaplan, 1989). While that may be the case, in practice the diagrams have, in fact, been used to justify prescriptive approaches to teaching writing. Even more unfortunately, perhaps because of the simplicity of the diagrams, the findings of early contrastive rhetoric studies were whole-heartedly embraced in many ESL writing classes, which actually taught that English speakers think in a straight line while Asians think in circles and others think in zigzags.

On the other hand, by turning their backs on contrastive rhetoric, process-oriented researchers and writing teachers are logically compelled to argue that L2 writing problems are, in fact, those of any developing writer, a position that Mohan and Lo (1985) take when they suggest that problems of Chinese students writing in English do not result from the influence of Chinese rhetorical patterns but are the usual difficulties of inexperienced writers.

Several objections to that position might reasonably be raised. Those who ignore the insights of contrastive rhetoric imply that students come to L2 writing without any previously learned discourse schemata. Yet writing conventions are taught in schools. While many children already can read when they start school and many read outside school for entertainment, few can write when they enter school and, except for letters and lists, few write outside school. In other words, writing, for most school children, is nearly always school sponsored and inevitably, therefore, reflects the culture of the school system and reproduces culturally preferred discourse styles. Furthermore, if we consider the age and level of education of the many ESL graduate students studying in English-speaking countries, it is difficult to take the position that these L2 writers are inexperienced in writing in L1.

Another difficulty with the anticontrastive rhetoric position is its implication that L1 writing strategies are not transferred to L2 writing situations. While sufficient research does not exist to establish firmly to what degree L1 writing strategies transfer to L2, Jones and Tetroe (1987) conclude from a study of Spanish-speaking writers writing in English and Spanish that transfer of higher level planning skills in writing does occur, particularly with writers beyond a certain threshold of proficiency in L2. Hall (1990) also concludes that some revising strategies appear to function across languages. The Carson, Carrell, Silberstein, Kroll, and Kuehn (1990) study of both Chinese and Japanese students revealed a complex pattern of interactions between L1 and L2 reading and writing skills. If writing strategies do transfer across languages, presumably ESL students might then employ strategies learned for specific L1 writing contexts to their L2 writing. The L1 strategies might differ from those appropriate in, for example, English-medium universities, proving, therefore, to be ineffective in the new context.

It seems reasonable to assume that different cultures would orient their discourse in different ways. Even different discourse communities within a single language, such as those constituted by different academic disciplines, have different writing conventions: preferred length of sentences, choice of vocabulary, acceptability of using first person, extent of using passive voice, degree to which writers are permitted to interpret, amount of metaphorical language accepted. If different discourse communities employ differing rhetorics, and if there is transfer of skills and strategies from L1 to L2, then contrastive rhetoric studies might reveal the shape of those rhetorical skills and strategies in writers from different cultures.

Contrastive rhetoric studies have become considerably more complex over the last 25 years and have explored a number of different directions related to written discourse across cultures. This article (a) provides an overview of these changes and research problems associated with them, (b) reanalyzes the concerns of process-oriented teachers and researchers in light of these changes, and (c) examines the extent to which the findings of modern contrastive rhetoric can play a more legitimate, less prescriptive role in L2 writing classrooms.

DEVELOPMENT OF CONTRASTIVE RHETORIC STUDIES

For years after the introduction of the idea of contrastive rhetoric little progress was made in this type of text analysis. During the 1970s the development of text linguistics or discourse analysis might have given contrastive rhetoric a more scientific, less intuitive base, but it did not in fact have much effect. Discourse analysis of the 1970s focused either on spoken discourse, rather than written, or analyzed such features of written text as anaphora or cohesive links between propositions. This focus yielded atomized, disparate bits of information that seemed either to be incapable of explaining differences in larger segments of discourse or almost to trivialize the differences. Patterns of usage emerging from text linguistics studies did not seem generalizable or broad enough to have much pedagogic function. The failure to contribute much to pedagogy may have come from what Carrell (1984b) describes as text linguists' attempt to extend linguistic methodology to full texts and to create "a kind of 'grammar' for texts, with texts viewed simply as units larger than sentences, or as a sequence of sentences" instead of examining "the linguistic properties of texts (e.g., cohesion), but also the social-psychological, interactive properties of texts" (p. 111).

The 1980s, however, thanks to developments like the work of de Beaugrande (1980) in discourse analysis and text linguistics, sparked renewed interest in contrastive rhetoric and in the exploration of more than the strictly surface features of discourse although, like anaphora or nominalization, these less immediately obvious features may still be quantifiable. John Hinds published extensively on Japanese rhetoric (1976, 1980, 1984, 1987); Alan Purves and colleagues with the International Association for Evaluation of Educational Achievement (IEA) Study of Written Composition began in 1980 to collect and analyze the high school exit essays of 20,000 12-, 14-, and 18-year-old students in 14 countries (Purves & Takala, 1982). In 1984 the *Annual Review of Applied Linguistics* devoted an entire issue to contrastive rhetoric (Kaplan, 1984). The middle to late 1980s saw the publication of Ulla Connor and Robert Kaplan's *Writing Across Languages* (1987) and Purves' *Writing Across Language and Cultures* (1988). Several unpublished manuscripts, theses, and dissertations on contrastive rhetoric also attest to a renewed interest in contrastive rhetoric.

Most of these studies have continued to explore Japanese, Chinese, Arabic, and Spanish, thus reflecting our student populations, but work has also appeared on Korean, Thai, and Hindi; there have been surprisingly few studies of European languages other than Spanish, however.

MODERN CONTRASTIVE RHETORIC STUDIES: WRITING IN L1

The recent research approaches taken to contrastive rhetoric have been varied, making comparison of the findings across the analyses difficult. Some researchers continue to focus on L2 student writing, but the two main approaches to contrastive rhetoric now seem either (a) to examine L1 texts from different cultures, often professional, published work, written for native speakers, and the rhetorical contexts in which these tests are inscribed; or (b) to establish textual criteria and search for those qualities in samples of success-ful and unsuccessful texts by students writing in their L1.

Some researchers (Ostler, 1988; Santana-Seda, 1975) have con-tinued Kaplan's approach, examining the English writing of non-native-English-speaking students to detect systematic textual dif-ferences in their written English style and that of native speakers. Taking the position that L1 writing skills are transferable and are transferred to L2 writing tasks, studies of this kind face the burden of addressing Mohan and Lo's argument (1985) that what is being identified as non-English is, in fact, merely nonskilled, develop-mental writing.

Another more dubious intuitive research approach has been to describe the "temperament" of a culture and attempt to deduce how writers from that culture will write or, alternatively, to use the writing of a culture to draw conclusions about the temperament of the culture. Hamady (1960) and Shouby (1951), for example, wrote about the influence of Arabic on the so-called Arab personality, and although this work is quite old, references to these two articles have continued to appear in the contrastive rhetoric literature.

From essays by Thai and U.S. high school students on the generation gap, Bickner and Peyasantiwong (1988) draw conclu-sions about differences in world views of U.S. and Thai young people; young people from the U.S. are said to see themselves as the center of the universe, whereas Thai teens supposedly see the teen years as transitions to real life, adult life, where they are patiently waiting to take their rightful places. In another study of Thai and U.S. high school students' writing (Indrasutra, 1988), the two groups of students were asked to write on the topics "I Made a Hard Decision" and "I Succeeded at Last." The researcher explains the Thai students' greater focus on internal struggle as stemming from Buddhist training, which emphasizes human inability to affect external events and which, as a result, causes Thais to focus inwardly. Edamatsu (1978) uses examples of Japanese writing to make the case that the Japanese have difficulty thinking "democrat-ically" (p. 18). A problem with this type of approach to contrastive rhetoric is obviously the serious danger of stereotyping and over-generalizing.

The dominant line of inquiry in contrastive rhetoric studies has been to look at discourse in L1 and compare it with English, or more exactly, with what English is said to look like. Rather than looking at actual English writing for his description of English, Kaplan (1967), for example, relied on style manuals from the 1960s instructing students how to write proper paragraphs. In fact, one criticism of contrastive rhetoric's descriptions of English is directed at this reliance on style manuals or textbook writers to describe English writing. Researchers since Kaplan's time (Braddock, 1974) have made it clear that professional native-speaker English writers do not, in fact, necessarily write in a straight line beginning with a topic sentence and moving directly to support, and so on. There are numerous variations apparent in a normal English text.

Nevertheless, many who describe English writing still refer to the straight line pattern as though it fully accounted for English practices, comparing texts from another L1 to this pattern. Pandharapande (1984) explains Marathi texts with a diagram of small spirals within a circle. Basing the discussion on a traditional view of the English paragraph, this author notes that Marathi does not follow the English pattern of paragraphs but rather probably uses the *tarka*, a traditional Sanskrit unit of organization which consists of "a logical hypothesis which is examined by providing evidence to support or reject the hypothesis" (p. 130), thus permitting opposing points of view in the same paragraph or unit of discourse. The author regards this type of approach as uncharacteristic of English, which the author views as developing only one self-consistent idea per paragraph.

Like Pandharapande's research, recent studies of L1 writing have focused primarily on textual analysis of L1 writing published by professionals for consumption by native-speaker readers (Clyne, 1984, for German; Dantas-Whitney & Grabe, 1989, for Brazilian Portuguese; Eggington, 1987, for Korean; Hinds, 1980 & 1987, for Japanese; Kachru, 1988, for Hindi; Pandharapande, 1984, for Marathi; Tsao, 1984, for Mandarin; Zellermayer, 1988, for Hebrew). In this kind of analysis, obviously the researcher must know the L1 very well, but it is also important to select the text carefully. Grabe (1987) warns that researchers examining or comparing expository texts, for example, must be sure that they are comparing the same type of text across cultures. In his examination of texts in English, Grabe found that the single category of expository writing covered several subgenres he was able to identify as text types within the category of expository writing: humanities, general information, and two different types of natural science texts.

Another problem arising from the comparison of texts across cultures is related to the frequency of a particular text type in a particular culture. Hortatory (exhortational) texts are common in Iran, for example, but uncommon in the U.S. (Houghton & Hoey, 1984). A comparison of that text type in these two cultures then would yield skewed or invalid results since that type of text appears with very different frequencies in the two cultures.

Eggington's work (1987) with academic Korean writing further illustrates the difficulty in selecting appropriate texts across cultures for comparison. He finds that Korean academic texts may be written either in a style similar to that of academic English or in a more Korean style, depending on whether or not the Korean author of the text has been trained in an English-speaking country, as apparently many have. Both text types commonly appear in journals written for other Korean academics. Clearly, depending on whether the contrastive rhetoric researcher fell upon one or the other of these two common text types, the research conclusions would be quite different. In examining Hindi writing, Kachru (1984) also finds both Hindi style and English style texts, a situation stemming from India's colonial history. Similarly, Clyne (1984) makes the point that German writing on math and engineering resembles English style but that writing on chemistry looks more German, characterized by a greater freedom to bring in broader issues not directly related to the discussion at hand.

On the other hand, Tsao (1984) explains the text characteristics specific to Chinese writing and then cites Mo (1982), who finds those same patterns in English paragraphs! Thus, when examining professional writing across cultures, it is clearly important to move beyond the texts themselves to an examination of the rhetorical context in which they are embedded.

CONTRASTS IN THE TEACHING OF WRITING AND RHETORICAL TRADITION

Part of the rhetorical context is educational and rhetorical tradition. Thus, rather than looking directly at L1 texts, other researchers have investigated writing prescriptions in different cultures by looking at current rhetorics or style manuals. However, while English fairly bulges with style manuals and rhetorics, there appear to be few style manuals or composition texts for school use in other cultures, and most of those address specific formal text features of specific text types, like business letters, or contain grammatical prescriptions (Kachru, 1988). This approach is, of course, open to the same criticism directed against dependence on English style manuals to characterize English prose style.

Other difficulties arise with this approach as well; it is not always clear how to interpret the manuals' prescriptions. Attempting to establish that writing in the People's Republic of China (PRC) is not characterized by indirectness, Mohan and Lo (1985) cite a Chinese style manual's exhortations to seek directness and clarity and to avoid repetition. However, since no examples are given of texts fulfilling these injunctions, it is difficult to know if these manuals mean the same thing that English manuals mean by directness and clarity. Matalene's descriptions (1985) of her PRC students' essays characterized them as full of concrete detail; it is not unreasonable to speculate that such concrete detail might well be what is referred to by the writers of the Chinese style manual as direct and clear. The manual's injunction to avoid repetition might be displayed in a text which draws no conclusion at the end if the conclusion is taken to be obvious from the exposition. Yet the possible repetition implied by an explicit conclusion is expected in English.

Similarly, Eggington (1987) points out that a Korean expository pattern looks like the typical English introduction-body-conclusion pattern but that the content and function of those three sections are different in Korean rhetoric.

In addition to examining writing manuals to learn how writing is taught, other investigators have attempted to look directly at school writing instruction, but the results are inconclusive. Although schools are clearly the dominant influence on student writing, according to some investigators, few young people in other cultures are explicitly taught how to write in school. Kachru (1984), Eggington (1987) and Hinds (1987) note that in India, Korea, and Japan, respectively, there is little or no direct instruction in writing in the L1. Hinds (1987) reports that Japanese children study writing only to the sixth grade.

On the other hand, Liebman-Kleine (1986) surveyed 77 international students on their experiences learning to write in their own languages. Most of these students report having studied writing in school and, interestingly, report having been instructed to write in patterns similar to what they were later told was the appropriate pattern to use in English. While it is possible that these students were projecting backward their experiences in writing classes in English, they reported that their school teachers had told them good writing had an introduction, development with support, and a conclusion. French school children are also specifically taught how to write (Bassetti, 1990), but the textual style they learn is not similar to English patterns; French children learn to write literary textual studies called *explications de textes* and to rely in other school sponsored writing on a rigid tripartite text structure of thesis-antithesis-synthesis.

However young people are initiated into their cultures, the careful investigation by Carson (in press) of literacy instruction in Japan and the PRC makes clear that reading and writing are complexly and variously inscribed in cultures, and simple descriptions of reading and writing instruction in schools are probably inadequate and perhaps misleading.

In an effort to see how school writing instruction is realized in actual texts, student writers from different cultural backgrounds have been assigned the same writing task, and the texts examined for differences. Indrasutra (1988), and Bickner and Peyasantiwong (1988) looked at the writing of Thai and U.S. students writing on the same subjects. Connor and Lauer (1988) examined groups of native-speaker students writing in English from the U.S., Britain, and New Zealand and noted systematic differences even among these speakers of English.

Beyond the examination of manuals and direct instruction in writing, another approach to contrastive rhetoric studies has been to look more broadly at education in different cultures. Purves' IEA project, covering 14 countries, investigates types of writing assignments in high schools (Purves & Takala, 1982). Regretta-bly, only about one quarter to one third of the school systems cooperating in the project are Asian, African, or Middle Eastern, the rest being Western (including locations such as New Zealand).[1]

Some researchers have examined student discourse in L1 and correlated text characteristics with high and low ratings within the L1 educational system. Jie and Lederman (1988) discuss entrance exams for Chinese universities. Despite claims that China's rhetori-cal preferences are shifting (Hinds, 1987), these authors note that essays with more traditional features like elaborate metaphors and literary references are still the ones rated highly in these exams.

Further broadening the examination of the context in which L1 writing takes place, some researchers have looked at a country's economic, social, and political history in an attempt to explain text development. Kachru (1984, 1988), writing about Hindi, points out that while oral exposition was common in Sanskrit and has influ-enced Hindi, Hindi expository writing did not really exist before British colonization and therefore can be expected to show the influ-ences both of oral Sanskrit exposition and written British exposition.

Matalene (1985) cites Oliver's discussion (1971) of the historical political function of rhetoric in ancient China, one quite different

---

[1] Another, ultimately unsuccessful, direction taken by researchers in this project asked students to indicate preferences for bipolar sets of adjectives describing a text and to attempt to predict their teachers' preferences for the same group of texts and descriptors. Degenhart and Takala (1988) hoped with this research to be able to develop a simple system that would tabulate cultural preferences for some 24 textual characteristics of a good essay as perceived by high school students in several different countries. The descriptors included such terms as ("a good essay should be") narrowed to one point, exhaustive of the subject, humorous, formal, precise, abstract, etc. Unfortunately, the research was unsuccessful because the students were inconsistent in their preferences over time—about five weeks—and this line of research was dropped.

from the rhetorical tradition in the West. Oliver points out that rhetoric in the Western tradition had as its goal to convince political equals in a public forum of some political position and, as a result, placed a great deal of emphasis on the individual speaker's ability to reason and to marshal evidence. The Asian tradition Oliver cites grows out of political relationships entirely different from those influenced by ancient Greek civilization and therefore imposed a different duty on the rhetor, who was called upon less to convince than to announce truth and to arrange the propositions of the announcement such that it might be easily and harmoniously agreed upon by referring to communal, traditional wisdom. This type of research, then, looks at the effect of rhetorical traditions on modern texts.

IDENTIFYING TEXT FEATURES

All these studies constitute one line of inquiry in contrastive rhetoric, which has been to analyze the form the texts from various cultures take. The other major strand in contrastive rhetoric studies is more data-driven and seems to come more directly from linguistics. In this approach, researchers target certain features of discourse and then analyze L1 texts written in a variety of cultures to see how those languages compare on those features. This is the basis of Purves' (1986) analysis of writing samples from the IEA study, for example. Purves has been able to classify the writing style of 14 different participating countries using categories like personal versus impersonal, ornamented versus plain, abstract versus concrete, single versus multiple focus, and propositional coherence strategies (if this, then this, for example) versus appositional coherence strategies (chronological patterns). Thus, Australian writing style is characterized as highly personal, figurative, single focus, and propositional; while Finnish is impersonal, plain, multiple focus, and appositional.

Dantas-Whitney and Grabe (1989) analyzed editorials in Brazilian Portuguese in the *Jornal do Brazil* and in English in the *Christian Science Monitor* using three criteria: the presence or absence of narratives, the orientation (that is, the relationship between the writer and reader), and the formality of the presentation of the information. They found that the Portuguese and English texts were similar on the first and third characteristics but differed on the orientation they exhibited. The English tendency was information-oriented with a responsibility on the part of the writer to accommodate the reader, whereas the Portuguese orientation was interactional, interpersonal, using more concrete and colloquial language.

Hinds' (1987) focus is also on reader versus writer responsibility for successful communication. He hopes to categorize the rhetorics of various cultures according to the degree to which the reader is required to make inferential bridges between propositions and to deduce meaning from a text, as opposed to the degree of the writer's duty to explicitly provide explanations of propositions. Thus, he analyzes Japanese as using a *reader-responsible* rhetoric, English as using a *writer-responsible* rhetoric, and Chinese as being in transition from a *reader-* to a *writer-responsible* rhetoric. Similarly, from an examination of translations of Hebrew to English and English to Hebrew, Zellermayer (1988) concludes that by evoking shared context between reader and writer, Hebrew writing requires more reader involvement than does English.

Along similar lines, but in far greater detail, Biber's (1988) analyses of different text types and genres in English suggest a potential direction for contrastive rhetoric studies for both diachronic and synchronic examinations of text. Biber investigated the degree to which various English text types might be characterized with reference to the presence or absence of categories of linguistic features. Heavy use of deictics, for example, indicates a context-dependent type of writing which implies considerable interactive reader involvement. This detailed examination of the linguistic features of a text in order to distinguish text types informs Grabe's (1987) study of English subgenres of expository prose. Although cross-linguistic comparisons of this type are as yet extremely limited (Biber cites a single example of such a study), if clear and objectively defined linguistic features of texts can distinguish among text types in English, presumably these same features might be defined for other languages, contributing to the descriptive characterization of text types across languages. These researchers have thus elaborated a potentially rich methodology for data-based contrastive rhetoric studies.

Connor's approach (1987) is somewhat different. Connor establishes a series of three sets of criteria for argumentative texts: the text structure (problem-solution), the text's successive speech acts (asserting a claim, justifying the claim, and inducing the original claim from observations), and evidence of awareness of audience. Essays written in L1 from Finland, Germany, the U.S., and Britain were then rated holistically. An examination of the highest and lowest rated essays from each language group reveals that the best rated essays fulfilled cross-cultural expectations implied by Connor's original criteria. In other words, she notes a correlation between the presence or absence of the features she identifies and a high or low independent rating, thus implying the existence of a universal argumentation style which transcends cultural boundaries. As we see with all these approaches, contrastive rhetoric textual studies expanded a great deal in the 1980s. While they continue to examine contrasts in the smallest features of texts, they now also include investigations of the broad political and historical contexts for writing and recognize that not simply rhetorical style but also purpose, task, topic, and audience are culturally informed. Furthermore, textual studies regard as their domain both diachronic and synchronic study; Hinds (1987) suggests, for example, that Chinese is becoming a writer-responsible language having been reader-responsible. Such analyses are provocative in their implications for claims about oral and literate cultures by writers such as Ong (1982) and Olson (1977); the latter argues that the ideal Western text, unlike texts from oral cultures, is the least context-dependent, that is, as writer-responsible as possible. Contrastive rhetoric studies can, thus, add to our understanding of the structure of texts and perhaps eventually to a deeper understanding of cultures. The question remains how these understandings translate into classroom practice.

PEDAGOGICAL CONCERNS OF TEXTUAL AND PROCESS ORIENTATIONS

The findings of modern contrastive rhetorical studies are much less immediately importable into the ESL writing classroom than they once seemed. In a sense, this change is positive since rhetorical patterns of any culture are surely more complex than they were once thought to be, more dynamic and protean, responding to the interaction between discourse communities and individual writers over time and in varied contexts. When this characterization of written texts from any culture, or any discourse community, is acknowledged, it becomes much less likely that contrastive rhetoric can be put to use prescriptively in the classroom. It appears to be this prescriptive and simplistic application of contrastive rhetoric insights to which process-oriented teachers and researchers most object. Thus, as contrastive rhetoric studies become more sophisticated, an important objection to their pedagogical implications is addressed.

A second doubt about the applicability of contrastive rhetoric studies to writing classrooms, indeed, an objection to the validity of the entire enterprise raised by process-oriented teachers and researchers concerns the rhetorical contexts from which the texts studied are drawn. As shown in the warnings and analyses by Grabe, Eggington, and Clyne, contrastive rhetoric researchers have become aware of this problem and are attempting to designate with greater exactness the complex network of textual types, purposes, readers, places of publication, and other specifics of context from which their texts are drawn. Clearly, some of the designations will make the findings of contrastive rhetoric studies inapplicable to ESL writing classrooms; there is little pedagogical purpose in discovering the prevalence of a particular style of writing in, for example, Japanese magazine articles if Japanese students are not writing magazine articles.

In suggesting different slants on the development of schemata or on other goals of writing classrooms, I do not wish to imply that a textual orientation is the polar opposite of a process orientation or that these orientations are mutually exclusive. They certainly do not have to be, and most teachers probably focus on different aspects of text study and text creation at different times and to different degrees depending on the particular class. Nonetheless, it is worthwhile to note that these approaches imply different pedagogical foci.

A writing pedagogy that embraces the textual orientation of contrastive rhetoric would work to actively foster the construction in students of rhetorical schemata which hopefully correspond to those of English-speaking readers. A difference, then, between such a pedagogy and one less likely to be interested in contrastive rhetoric findings, a process orientation, for example, would center on the approach taken for the development of schemata. A textual orientation suggests that schemata can be directly taught while a process orientation would hope to induce the construction of schemata indirectly, perhaps through student contact with target language (or, more precisely, target discourse community) readings. A process pedagogy appears to assume that schemata are or can be absorbed unconsciously, perhaps in somewhat the same way as comprehensible input is thought to promote acquisition of grammatical forms (Krashen, 1981). In a process-oriented classroom, if L2 readings are used, they do not typically serve as examples of successful target language communication but rather as sources for ideas or touchstones for personal interactions and reactions. Their content is to be evaluated against personal experience. The questions asked of a text are likely to be: What does the author mean? Does it make sense to you? Do you agree? Have you had similar experiences? A writing class with a greater textual orientation, an English for Academic/Specific Purposes class, for example, is more likely to ask: What are the main sections of the piece? What is in each section? What textual devices are used to advance the argument? What is the tone? These questions echo those of contrastive rhetoric research.

This is not to say that a process pedagogy ignores structure, but that the focus of such a writing course would privilege the structure of the student's evolving text rather than the structure of an outside text. By the same token, a textual orientation does not require students to ignore content but rather might attempt to discover how structures promote meaning in texts—by comparing them, analyzing them, looking for ways in which they duplicate each other, trying to uncover patterns and variations on patterns, patterns which advance meaning.

Although a textual orientation appears at first glance to concern itself primarily with form, the true or ultimate focus of a textual orientation, and of contrastive rhetoric studies, and an appropriate pedagogical agenda of a textual orientation in a writing class, is a focus not on form but on audience. At their most pedagogically useful, contrastive rhetoric studies concern themselves with the social construction of knowledge within discourse communities. In other words, an appropriate textual pedagogy does not construe audience simplistically as merely a reader or readers with particular preferences or opinions which must be accommodated by the writer, but rather implies an attempt "to tap into the consensual construction" (Rubin, 1988, p. 28) of such matters as how, when, and where a point is established and supported in a text within the target discourse community. Similarly, contrastive rhetoric attempts to articulate the parameters of that consensual construction.

This is the core of the problem ESL students face. How can they tap into the dynamic *consensual* construction of knowledge-through-discourse when they are precisely *not* participants in that consent. Donald Bartholomae (1985) makes the point that native-English-speaking writing students are initiates into the discourse community of the university.[2] When they write for that community, of which they are not yet full-fledged members, they are required to *imagine* themselves as members, to take on the role of members of the community, and, as Bartholomae says, to "invent the university," that is, to attempt to represent that community to themselves, and to hold that representation in mind as they write. ESL students are also inventing the university, in Bartholomae's sense, but in most cases are likely to have already in place at least the beginnings (and

---

[2] For the sake of simplicity, I refer to a university "discourse community" as though there were a single community. Clearly, this is not the case even within a single university in a single English-speaking country, not to mention across the many countries and academic settings in which advanced writing in English is taught.

for graduate students perhaps quite an elaborate version) of another competing representation of the university and of the discourse expectations of that community. At their most pedagogically useful, contrastive rhetoric studies simplify the students' task by offering glimpses into the differences between those two representations. These glimpses are intended to help students present themselves (i.e., their texts) as *already* part of the discourse community they are addressing.

It should be clear that the distinction between a process orientation and a textual orientation in a writing pedagogy is not the simple distinction between form and content. Both attempt to create appropriate text schemata in writing students, both work to initiate students into the target discourse community, and both focus on the discovery of meaning—but in different ways. One is not innately more prescriptive than the other, but each draws its ability to lighten the student writer's load from a different source: one from idea exploration and the exploitation of students' own cognitive resources, the other from an exploration of how other writers have solved meaning problems and from a recognition that different cultures have evolved different ways of solving those problems. It should also be clear that a primary focus on one of these approaches to teaching writing in no way, in and of itself, must entail the exclusion of the other.

PEDAGOGICAL IMPLICATIONS OF CONTRASTIVE RHETORIC

Contrastive rhetoric and contrastive rhetoric methodology are still in their "formative stages" (Purves, 1988, p. 15). In theory, contrastive rhetoric studies potentially have a great deal to offer classroom teachers. In the case of EFL writing teachers dealing with groups of EFL students from a single native language and educational background, the benefits of contrastive rhetorical analyses are perhaps more obvious, particularly if the students have consciously learned contrasting text forms in their native languages, as might be the case, for example, with the French students mentioned earlier.

At this point, however, the immediate practical uses of the findings of contrastive rhetoric for ESL writing teachers are not altogether clear. But these immediate, practical pedagogical implications are an issue worth raising. What are ESL writing teachers to do with the information that cultures approach writing differently? Obviously, whether their pedagogy is process oriented or textually oriented, teachers will most likely not be trained in the specific rhetorics of various cultures and will probably simply more or less impose typical English forms on all nonnative speakers, regardless of their L1, in much the same way English grammar is "imposed," in most cases, without regard to a contrastive analysis of the L1 and L2.

If this is the case, does contrastive rhetoric have anything to contribute now, during its formative stages, to classroom teaching? Ideally, contrastive rhetoric studies will help avoid stereotypes based on failing to recognize that preferences in writing styles are culturally informed. More practically, however, perhaps teachers will, in fact, retain and use information on a variety of L1s: that Spanish rhetoric requires longer introductions than English does; that Japanese employs a reader-responsible rhetoric while English favors a writer-responsible one; that certain ways of structuring arguments appear to be admired in a variety of cultures. This information is not trivial and can potentially lead teachers to a deeper understanding of text structure, which will help both teachers and students analyze qualities of texts that are admired and considered to represent successful communication. Furthermore, as many teachers will attest, when conveyed to L2 student writers, the findings of contrastive rhetoric often produce instant enlightenment about their writing in English, as students suddenly become conscious of the implicit assumptions behind the way they construct written ideas and behind the way English does.

Unfortunately, this sudden enlightenment does not, however, mean sudden improvement, as Schlumberger and Mangelsdorf (1989) show in their research. They directly lectured on some of the findings of contrastive rhetoric studies to one group of students, but this attention focused on contrastive rhetoric seemed to have no effect on the students' subsequent writing compared with that of a control group. This finding is consistent with the results of research with native speakers which shows that clear, even profound cognitive awareness of rhetorical strategies does not necessarily translate into the ability to use that knowledge in actual writing situations (Quick, 1983). As language and writing teachers well know, the ability to understand may far exceed the skill to use that understanding.

Nevertheless, contrastive rhetoric can bring a different kind of benefit. Students who are having trouble writing in English and who are made aware of cultural differences in rhetoric suddenly view themselves, not as suffering from individual inadequacies, but as coming from a particular rhetorical tradition, which they must retain of course, but which cannot be applied wholesale to English writing. To help her students make their own rhetorical traditions visible to themselves, Liebman (1988) has had writing classes do ethnographic research, looking for the supposedly preferred writing style of their own cultures by analyzing published texts or letters in their L1. The metacognitive awareness students can develop in this way is one more step along the road to the realization that writing consists of making choices, an important insight for young writers to develop.

As for changing students' native writing style preferences, it seems clear that ESL teachers have a responsibility to teach the expectations of the English audience to L2 writers. Research in reading shows that readers understand better what they are familiar with and that applies both to content and to form, that is, to rhetorical patterns of development (Carrell, 1984a). Recall studies (Carrell, 1984a; Connor, 1984) show that readers recall texts better if the information is presented in a form they expect or are familiar with. This means that our students' texts will be easier for their professors to read if the writers show the kind of audience awareness that comes from knowing what the rhetorical expectations of the reader are and whether these student writers provide for them. While it is always difficult, even for a native-speaker writer, to anticipate reader needs, for nonnative speakers this problem is exacerbated, and yet misjudging the amount of explicit bridging the reader needs may result in textual incoherence. Directly confronting the issue of the varieties of rhetorics and resulting expectations of native-speaker readers may help ESL students become more aware of themselves as members of a variety of discourse communities.

The exploration of rhetorical contrasts across cultures may also help us to avoid uncritically adopting techniques from native-speaker composition classrooms into TESL contexts. In a touching personal account of the confrontation between differing rhetorical expectations, Fan Shen (1989), a Chinese graduate student in the U.S., describes her reaction to being told, in her literature class, to write naturally, to be herself, to find her own voice. She quickly realized that she could not possibly "be herself," her Chinese self, and write a text that would be acceptable, or even comprehensible, to an English-speaking audience. Instead, she found herself forced to develop an English "self," one that would correspond to the expectations of "self" in the U.S. academic discourse community.

Contrastive rhetoric studies help us to remember that the idea of "being yourself," or writing elegantly, or communicating clearly and convincingly has no reality outside a particular cultural and rhetorical context and that our discourse community is only one of many.

■

ACKNOWLEDGMENTS

I would like to thank Tony Silva and two anonymous *TESOL Quarterly* reviewers for their careful readings and insightful comments.

THE AUTHOR

Ilona Leki is Associate Professor of English at the University of Tennessee. Her publications include *Academic Writing: Techniques and Tasks* (St. Martin's Press, 1989); *Reading in the Composition Classroom: Second Language Perspectives* (Ed., with Joan Carson, Newbury House, 1993); and *Understanding ESL Writers: A Guide for Teachers* (Boynton-Cook, 1992). She is coeditor (with Tony Silva) of the *Journal of Second Language Writing*.

REFERENCES

Bartholomae, D. (1985). Inventing the university. In M. Rose (Ed.), *When a writer can't write* (pp. 134-165). New York: Guilford Press.

Biber, D. (1988). *Variation across speech and writing.* New York: Cambridge University Press.

Bassetti, C. (1990). *How do students coming from a French schooling system adapt themselves to the American composition style?* Unpublished manuscript, University of Tennessee, Knoxville.

Bickner, R., & Peyasantiwong, P. (1988). Cultural variation in reflective writing. In A. Purves (Ed.), *Writing across languages and cultures* (pp. 160-174). Newbury Park, CA: Sage.

Braddock, R. (1974). The frequency and placement of topic sentences in expository prose. *Research in the Teaching of English, 8,* 287-302.

Carrell, P. (1984a). The effects of rhetorical organization on ESL readers. *TESOL Quarterly, 18*(2), 441-469.

Carrell, P. (1984b). [Review of *Introduction to text linguistics*]. *Language Learning, 34,* 111-117.

Carson, J. E. (in press). Becoming biliterate: L1 influences. *Journal of Second Language writing.*

Carson, J. E., Carrell, P. L., Silberstein, S., Kroll, B., & Kuehn, P. (1990). Reading-writing relationship in first and second language. *TESOL Quarterly, 24*(2), 245-266.

Clyne, M. G. (1984). English and German. In R. Kaplan (Ed.), *Annual Review of Applied Linguistics, 3,* 38-49.

Connor, U. (1984). Recall of text: Differences between first and second language readers. *TESOL Quarterly, 18,* 239-256.

Connor, U. (1987). Argumentative patterns in student essays: Cross-cultural differences. In U. Connor & R. Kaplan (Eds.), *Writing across languages* (pp. 57-72). Reading, MA: Addison-Wesley.

Connor, U., & Kaplan, R. (Eds.). (1987). *Writing across languages: Analysis of L2 text.* Reading, MA: Addison-Wesley.

Connor, U., & Lauer, J. (1988). Cross-cultural variation in persuasive student writing. In A. Purves (Ed.), *Writing across languages and cultures* (pp. 138-159). Newbury Park, CA: Sage.

Dantas-Whitney, M., & Grabe, W. (1989). *A comparison of Portuguese and English newspaper editorials.* Paper presented at the 23rd Annual TESOL Convention, San Antonio, TX.

De Beaugrande, R. (1980). *Text, discourse, and process: Toward a multidisciplinary science of texts.* Norwood, NJ: Ablex.

Degenhart, R. E., & Takala, S. (1988). Developing a rating method for stylistic preference: A cross-cultural pilot study. In A. Purves (Ed.), *Writing across languages and cultures* (pp. 79-106). Newbury Park, CA: Sage.

Edamatsu, F. (1978). The Japanese psycho-social barrier in learning English. *TESL Reporter, 12,* 4-6, 17-19.

Eggington, W. G. (1987). Written academic discourse in Korean: Implications for effective communication. In U. Connor & R. Kaplan (Eds.), *Writing across languages* (pp. 153-168). Reading, MA: Addison-Wesley.

Grabe, W. (1987). Contrastive rhetoric and text-type research. In U. Connor & R. Kaplan (Eds.), *Writing across languages* (pp. 115-137). Reading, MA: Addison-Wesley.

Grabe, W., & Kaplan, R. (1989). Writing in a second language: Contrastive rhetoric. In D. Johnson & D. Roen (Eds.), *Richness in writing* (pp. 263-283). New York: Longman.

Hall, C. (1990). Managing the complexity of revising across languages. *TESOL Quarterly, 24(1),* 43-60.

Hamady, S. (1960). *Temperament and character of the Arabs.* New York: Twayne.

Hinds, J. (1976). A taxonomy of Japanese discourse types. *Linguistics, 184,* 45-54.

Hinds, J. (1980). Japanese expository prose. *Papers in Linguistics, 13,* 117-158.

Hinds, J. (1984). Retention of information using a Japanese style of organization. *Studies in Language, 8,* 45-69.

Hinds, J. (1987). Reader vs. writer responsibility: A new typology. In U. Connor & R. Kaplan (Eds.), *Writing across languages* (pp. 141-152). Reading, MA: Addison-Wesley.

Houghton, D., & Hoey, M. (1984). Linguistics and written discourse: Contrastive rhetorics. In R. Kaplan (Ed.), *Annual Review of Applied Linguistics, 3,* 2-22.

Indrasutra, C. (1988). Narrative styles in the writing of Thai and American students. In A. Purves (Ed.), *Writing across languages and cultures* (pp. 206-226). Newbury Park, CA: Sage.

Jie, G., & Lederman, M. J. (1988). Instruction and assessment of writing in China: The National Unified Entrance Examination for Institutions of Higher Education. *Journal of Basic Writing, 7,* 47-60.

Jones, S., & Tetroe, J. (1987). Composing in a second language. In A. Matsuhashi (Ed.), *Writing in real time* (pp. 34-57). New York: Longman.

Kachru, Y. (1984). English and Hindi. In R. Kaplan (Ed.), *Annual Review of Applied Linguistics, 3*, 50-77.

Kachru, Y. (1988). Writers in Hindi and English. In A. Purves (Ed.), *Writing across languages and cultures* (pp. 109-137). Newbury Park, CA: Sage.

Kaplan, R. (1966). Cultural thought patterns in intercultural education. *Language Learning, 16*, 1-20.

Kaplan, R. (1967). Contrastive rhetoric and the teaching of composition. *TESOL Quarterly, 2*(1), 10-16.

Kaplan, R. (Ed.). (1984). *Annual Review of Applied Linguistics, 3*.

Krashen, S. (1981). *Second language acquisition and learning*. Oxford: Pergamon Press.

Liebman, J. (1988). Contrastive rhetoric: Students as ethnographers. *Journal of Basic Writing, 7*, 6-27.

Liebman-Kleine, J. (1986). *Towards a contrastive new rhetoric: A rhetoric of process*. (ERIC Document Reproduction Service No. ED 271 963)

Matalene, C. (1985). Contrastive rhetoric: An American writing teacher in China. *College English, 47*, 789-808.

Mo, J. C. (1982). A study of English reading comprehension from the point of view of discourse function. *English Teaching and Learning, 6*, 39-48. (In Chinese)

Mohan, B. A., & Lo, W. A-Y. (1985). Academic writing and Chinese students' transfer and developmental factors. *TESOL Quarterly, 19*(3), 515-534.

Oliver, R. (1971). *Communication and culture in ancient India and China*. Syracuse, NY: Syracuse University Press.

Olson, D. R. (1977). From utterance to text. *Harvard Educational Review, 47*, 257-281.

Ong, W. (1982). *Orality and literacy*. London: Methuen.

Ostler, S. (1988). A study of the contrastive rhetoric of Arabic, English, Japanese, and Spanish. *Dissertation Abstracts International, 49*(2), 245A-246A.

Pandharapande, R. (1984). English and Marathi. In R. Kaplan (Ed.), *Annual Review of Applied Linguistics, 3*, 118-136.

Purves, A. (1986). Rhetorical communities, the international student, and basic writing. *Journal of Basic Writing, 5*, 38-51.

Purves, A. (Ed.). (1988). *Writing across languages and cultures*. Newbury Park, CA: Sage.

Purves, A., & Takala, S. (Eds.). (1982). *An international perspective on the evaluation of written composition*. Oxford: Pergamon Press.

Quick, D. M. (1983). *Audience awareness and adaptation skills of writers at four different grade levels*. Unpublished dissertation, State University of New York at Albany. *Dissertation Abstracts International, 44*, 2133-A. (University Microfilms No. DA 8325612)

Rubin, D. L. (1988). Introduction: Four dimensions of social construction in written communication. In B. A. Rafoth & D. L. Rubin (Eds.), *The social construction of written communication* (pp. 1-33). Norwood, NJ: Ablex.

Santana-Seda, O., Sr. (1975). A contrastive study in rhetoric: An analysis of the organization of English and Spanish paragraphs written by native speakers of each language. *Dissertation Abstracts International, 35,* 3862A.

Shen, F. (1989). The classroom and the wider culture: Identity as a key to learning English composition. *College Composition and Communication, 40,* 459-466.

Schlumberger, A., & Mangelsdorf, K. (1989). *Reading the context.* Paper presented at the 23rd Annual TESOL Convention, San Antonio, TX.

Shouby, E. (1951). The influence of the Arabic language on the psychology of the Arabs. *Middle East Journal, 5,* 284-302.

Silva, T. (1990). ESL composition instruction: Developments, issues and directions. In B. Kroll (Ed.), *Second language writing: Research insights for the classroom.* NY: Cambridge University Press.

Tsao, F-F. (1984). English and Mandarin. In R. Kaplan (Ed.), *Annual Review of Applied Linguistics, 3,* 99-117.

Zellermayer, M. (1988). An analysis of oral and literate texts: Two types of reader-writer relationships in Hebrew and English. In B. A. Rafoth & D. L. Rubin (Eds.), *The social construction of written communication* (pp. 287-303). Norwood, NJ: Ablex.

ORGANIZATIONAL PERSPECTIVES

TESOL and Applied Linguistics in North America *

ROBERT B. KAPLAN
University of Southern California

The TESOL organization has played a central role in the development of applied linguistics in North America. The development of applied linguistics results both from the evolution of paradigmatic differences between applied and general linguistics and from the influence of TESOL. The role of the paradigmatic differences and of our organization need to be made explicit, and the 25th anniversary of TESOL seems an appropriate time to do so.

At the end of TESOL's 25th year, it seems appropriate for me, as retiring President, to bracket the year by looking at the relationship between TESOL and the field of applied linguistics in North America and the important role TESOL has played as a supporting mechanism for the development of applied linguistics.

It is difficult to isolate applied linguistics exclusively to North America; the discipline arose almost simultaneously in the U.S. and in the U.K., though in more recent years, there has been some divergence across the Atlantic. As Strevens (1992) has pointed out:

> Considering that applied linguistics as a unified field of study came into being only in the late 1950s, it has blossomed and diversified in a remarkably rapid way. . . . The term *applied linguistics* . . . has been used at least since the founding of the University of Edinburgh School of Applied Linguistics in 1956, and of the Center for Applied Linguistics in Washington, D.C., in 195[9]. (p. 13)

The invention of the term is sometimes attributed to an unknown group of language teachers in the U.S. during the 1940s; they wanted to be identified as scientists rather than as humanists, to separate themselves from literature teachers, and to ally themselves with scientific linguists (Palmer, 1980; see also Mackey, 1966). But the term did not acquire substance until the late 1950s and the early 1960s. A chronology of key events may be useful at this point:

---

* This is a revised version of a featured address presented at the 26th Annual TESOL Convention in Vancouver, Canada.

1956   Inauguration of the School of Applied Linguistics, University of Edinburgh (Ian Catford, Director)

1959   Opening of the Center for Applied Linguistics, Washington, D.C. (Charles Ferguson, Director)

1964   Formation of the International Association of Applied Linguistics (AILA); Peter Strevens appointed first Professor of Applied Linguistics in the U.K., at the University of Essex

1966   TESOL organized

1967   International Association of Teachers of English as a Foreign Language (IATEFL) organized; British Association for Applied Linguistics (BAAL) organized

1973   S. Pit Corder's *Introducing Applied Linguistics* published by Penguin; J. P. B. Allen and S. Pit Corder's *Readings for Applied Linguistics* (The Edinburgh Course in Applied Linguistics, Vol. 1) published by Oxford University Press; Robert B. Kaplan appointed first Professor of Applied Linguistics in the U.S., at the University of Southern California

1975   Allen and Corder's *Papers in Applied Linguistics* (The Edinburgh Course in Applied Linguistics, Vol. 2) published by Oxford University Press

1977   American Association for Applied Linguistics (AAAL) organized

1980   *Applied Linguistics* begins publication from Oxford University Press; *Annual Review of Applied Linguistics* begins publication from Newbury House, subsequently published by Cambridge University Press; Kaplan's *On the Scope of Applied Linguistics* published by Newbury House

This is not intended to suggest that nothing else of significance occurred between 1956 and 1980 or that nothing of significance has occurred since 1980; on the contrary, acknowledging a number of key events in the last decade, this chronology is only intended to suggest a few of the occurrences that shaped the field in its first quarter century.

Although applied linguistics was initially nearly inextricably tied to language teaching, it has gradually diversified to subsume a number of areas. In a paper delivered before the AAAL, Angelis (1987) reported on a number of empirical indices of the contemporary scope of applied linguistics. He examined the titles of articles published in the journal *Applied Linguistics* over the first 8 years of its existence, the titles of articles in the *TESOL Quarterly* over the first 10 years of its existence, as well as the descriptors employed in the ERIC system under the broad category applied linguistics. Grabe and Kaplan (1992) augmented that exploration by looking at the titles included in the *Annual Review of Applied Linguistics* between 1980 and 1990, at the applied linguistics categories included in the *Oxford International Encyclopedia of Linguistics*, edited by Bright (1992), and at the titles of the scientific commissions of AILA. Something on the order of half of the items in these several indices are in some way related to language teaching and learning, including second language acquisition (SLA, which has in the recent past spun off as an area in its own right) and educational language testing (which has also spun off into independent status). Thus, language pedagogy has remained a significant focus of applied linguistics. In addition, about 5% of the titles implicate discussions of the field itself—items like this paper or Angelis' paper cited above. The remaining 45% of the material seems to fall into five broad categories—in no particular order: language and language-in-education policy and planning; the uses of languages in various professions and occupations (as distinct from the teaching of language for special purposes, counted under language teaching); language assessment and aberrant language behavior; discourse analysis (broadly defined to include both oral and written language); and the complex of areas subsumed under bilingualism, multilingualism, multiculturalism, and literacy. But even this empirically supported breadth probably does not do justice to the field.

In North America, at least, there have, historically, been two quite different ways of looking at the nature of language, and these divergent views have supported the independent development of applied linguistics. On the one hand, in what has been called general linguistics (or sometimes formal, autonomous, or even theoretical linguistics, though the latter is a misnomer because a variety of alternative views are also concerned with theory), the object of inquiry has traditionally been seen as an independent language system composed of unique and invariant structural and semantic rules. In contemporary thinking, this system has been seen as innate to human beings—a species-specific phenomenon encoded into the human genetic structure. Given this biological explanation of its ontogeny, it has been perfectly reasonable, in this paradigm, to investigate language as a separate entity because it has an independent existence unrelated to human production or use. The relationship in that system between the investigator and language is quite straightforward and unproblematic—subject → object. The objective of formal inquiry is systematic description in "neutral" scientific language quite isolated from the value-laden characteristics of everyday language. Such neutral description is seen to give rise to rational predictions about the internal operations of the system and about the directions of its future development. This perspective derives from the traditions of logical positivism and scientific realism and is thought to provide parsimonious and invariant description.

Although there is no question that this approach to the study of language has produced useful information and has given rise to certain cognitive-linguistic structures that appear invariant, there are also problems. As Sridhar (1990, p. 171) points out:

Formal linguistics . . . identifies language with grammar and linguistic theory with grammatical theory, leading to an exclusive preoccupation with form and disregard of, or skepticism toward, language use and function. If linguistics is defined as the scientific study of language, why should it be limited to the study of . . . syntax, semantics, morphology, and phonology? . . . . Chomsky has [for example] steadfastly asserted the autonomy of grammar and its independence from considerations of language use and function. He has even stated that "language is not a task-oriented device" (Chomsky, 1980, p. 53) . . . .

There is no intent in this description to disparage that view, only to differentiate it from an alternative view. Nevertheless, as Sridhar (1990) says, "the claim that grammar is independent of context is disingenuous" (p. 172), and further,

while the successes of formal linguistics in discovering structural regularities are impressive, they have come at a price: It is arguable that linguistic theory may have become a science at the expense of its subject matter, namely language as an instrument of communication in real-life situations. (p. 172)

There is an alternative, more applied view, but it should not be conceived as a single powerful theoretical thrust, though various segments do hold in common certain basic assumptions. From this perspective, language is seen not as an independent system, but rather as a human product and a social tool. The ontogenesis of this syndrome of views is influenced by hermeneutic philosophy—a position essentially antagonistic to scientific realism and logical positivism. The perception is that, whereas the physical sciences deal with inanimate objects outside the human sphere, language is the product of the human mind and is therefore inseparable from it and the attendant subjectivity, value-orientation, and emotion. In scientific realism, the object of empirical research is to capture an invariant objective reality through repeated testing of hypothetical correspondences that occur between models and observed phenomena; that is, empirical research is a tool through which to test, repeatedly, the consistency of any observed correspondences and thus to verify their validity. In the alternative view, deriving at least in part from the ideas of Husserl, that sort of empiricism was conceived as an error traceable to Gallilean systematization, because the notion hypothesis → test → verification is based on an assumption of the constancy of any given phenomenon. Such an assumption ignores even the practical problems inherent in setting up a consistent measurement system with respect to language. In the alternative view, the investigator is simultaneously both the subject and the object of inquiry; the study of language is the study of human beings, and the relationship between the researcher and the object of study, therefore, must be defined as subject → subject. Such a perception challenges, on logical grounds, the notion of the independent existence and objectification of language as well as the possibility of devising an invariant abstract model. Given the complexity of language, given the fact that language changes over time, and given the fact that language exists within various cultural systems, it would be impossible to discover invariant laws as in the physical sciences. Thus, the study of language, at certain levels at least, must be descriptive rather than predictive and explanatory. In addition, it would be impossible, from this perspective, to describe language in a context-free, neutral scientific sense because there is constant movement between the parts and the whole and because there are no clearly identifiable beginning and ending points. Language, furthermore, cannot be perceived as ahistorical. As long as language is perceived as invariant and independent of human activity, it cannot be examined in historical perspective; as long as language is perceived as genetically conditioned and independent of human agency, history is irrelevant. But as soon as language is perceived as a product of the human mind and as a tool, its continuing existence over time constitutes a theoretical problem.

Applied linguistics, then, has, at least in North America, refused to limit itself to the analysis of syntax, semantics, morphology, and phonology, but rather has concerned itself with the solution of human problems based in language. This rather different orientation has led to internecine warfare between the two divisions of the field. Departments of linguistics in North America are constantly reconfiguring themselves, and the dominant group has been inclined to push the minority out of the nest. As a result, some few departments of applied linguistics have come into independent existence, but the realities of academic financing in general have mitigated against the emergence of independent departments of applied linguistics and have tended to exacerbate the internecine warfare.

The concern of the field of applied linguistics with human problems has led it to become more clearly political in its activities.

It has, for much of its existence, concerned itself with the issue of language rights, for example. In the past decade, this broad concern with language rights has aligned segments of the North American applied linguistic community in opposition to the "English only" movement in the United States and with the francophone movement in Canada. Furthermore, the specificity of the political issues has caused a divergence between the development of applied linguistics in North America and the development of the field in the U.K. and in Europe.

Much of the intellectual and political discussion summarized in these comments has gone on within TESOL. At the TESOL Conference in San Juan, Puerto Rico, in 1973, a small group of people came together to discuss the desirability of forming an association of applied linguists in the United States. It seemed clear to that nucleus of people that an organization was necessary. For example, it was a bit awkward that the U.S. had no affiliate of AILA, TESOL by definition not being in a position to serve that purpose. In the latter months of 1973, an effort to form such an association was mounted. Some 100 applied linguists throughout the U.S. were polled, and the poll showed a clear sentiment in favor of developing such an association. On the basis of the results of that poll, a more general open meeting was convened in conjunction with the Summer Institute of the Linguistic Society of America (LSA) in Ann Arbor, Michigan, in August 1973.

The reaction in that open meeting was somewhat less enthusiastic, and the following day, at the LSA business meeting, a resolution was passed requesting that the LSA Executive Committee study the possibility of convening a subsection within the LSA concerned with applied linguistics. At the annual conference of the LSA in San Diego just after Christmas 1973, the matter was raised again, and the LSA Executive Committee suggested that applied linguists would be welcome at LSA conferences so long as they adhered to the quality standards of the LSA. It was agreed that there would be no special subsection of the LSA and that for at least a couple of years no further action would be taken in the context of forming a separate association. During that probationary period, the receptivity of the LSA would be evaluated on the basis of experience.

In the interim, the constitution of TESOL was amended to permit the existence of special interest groups. One of the special interest groups (SIGs) created early on was the Applied Linguistics SIG. Its first appointed chair was Bernard Spolsky, and its subsequent elected chairs over the next several years included Robert B. Kaplan, David Eskey, Thomas Buckingham, Joe Darwin Palmer, and Eugene J. Briere. For a time, it was hoped that the existence of this new special interest group within TESOL would obviate the need for a separate association. At the same time, the LSA did include in its annual meeting in San Francisco in 1975 a section on language acquisition intended to serve the interests of applied linguists. The Applied Linguistics SIG of TESOL also mounted a program segment at the TESOL conventions in New York (1976), Miami (1977), and Mexico City (1978). The first two of these were predominantly concerned with English for special purposes and were organized with the close cooperation and assistance of the British Council.

It gradually became clear that these various efforts could not serve the broader needs of applied linguists and that a new independent organization was desirable. At the TESOL convention in Miami in 1977, a panel discussion on the scope of applied linguistics was organized under the auspices of the Applied Linguistics SIG. The participants on that panel were H. Douglas Brown, S. Pit Corder, Paul D. Holtzman, Robert B. Kaplan, Tony Robson, Bernard Spolsky, Peter Strevens, and G. Richard Tucker. In addition, David Eskey and Thomas Buckingham, acting as the officers of the TESOL Applied Linguistics SIG, collected a set of statements from 10 well-known individuals in the field, some of whom also participated in the panel, thereby adding the views, in absentia, of Edward Anthony, Thomas Buckingham, Russell Campbell, Francisco Gomes de Matos, Stephen Krashen, and John Oller to those expressed at the panel discussion. (It is an interesting sidelight on the history of applied linguistics in North America that, if memory serves me, of the 14 individuals involved in this activity, 5 have been presidents of TESOL and an additional 4 have held other offices within TESOL. In addition, 3 have held office in AAAL.) At the end of the panel discussion, the question of forming an association was broached again, and a mandate emerged from the participants and the audience to move forward toward the formation of an independent body. During the summer of 1977, several interim committees were organized. A formal constitutional meeting was held in conjunction with the American Council on the Teaching of Foreign Languages (ACTFL) meeting in San Francisco in November of 1977, and the American Association for Applied Linguistics came into being, with Eugene J. Briere as its first president. The papers from the panel discussion appeared as *On the Scope of Applied Linguistics* from Newbury House (Kaplan, 1980).

In 1977, BAAL and IATEFL celebrated their respective 10th anniversaries, and planning was well along towards the fifth world congress of AILA scheduled to be held in Montreal (its first venture into North America) in 1978. AAAL sought and gained affiliation with AILA soon thereafter, and its officers have played important leadership roles in AILA over the intervening years. AAAL met for a number of years in conjunction with LSA, but for the last few years it has returned to TESOL.

During these important years in the political life of applied linguistics, the discussions that resulted in the eventual publication both of the journal *Applied Linguistics* and of the *Annual Review of Applied Linguistics* took place within the framework of TESOL. The idea of the journal *Applied Linguistics* took initial shape at the same 1973 TESOL meeting in San Juan where the notion of an applied linguistics association was born, and the developmental steps in the evolution of that journal took place almost entirely within TESOL. The first discussions leading to the birth of the *Annual Review* also took place within TESOL, beginning in 1978, and to this day the editorial board of the *Annual Review* meets regularly at the annual TESOL Conference.

It is clear that were there no TESOL, there would be no AAAL. TESOL has been the womb within which applied linguistics in North America was nurtured. Not only has TESOL given birth to the organization and publications of applied linguists but it has also been the spawning ground for other subconfigurations of applied linguistics interest—in language assessment and in SLA research. It is important, at this moment in TESOL's history, to recognize the enormously important role that this association has played not only in the development and promotion of language teaching but in the conceptualization of the closely allied field of applied linguistics.
■

THE AUTHOR

Robert B. Kaplan is Professor of Applied Linguistics and Past Director of the American Language Institute at the University of Southern California. He is also Past President of TESOL and President of the American Association of Applied Linguistics. He is author or editor of 25 books, has authored more than 100 articles, and has lectured at universities in some 25 countries around the world.

REFERENCES

Allen, J. P. B., & Corder, S. P. (Eds.). (1973). *The Edinburgh course in applied linguistics: Vol. 1. Readings for applied linguistics*. London: Oxford University Press.

Allen, J. P. B., & Corder, S. P. (Eds.). (1975). *The Edinburgh course in applied linguistics: Vol. 2. Papers in applied linguistics*. London: Oxford University Press.

Angelis, P. (1987, December). *Applied linguistics: Realities and projections*. Paper presented at the 1987 Annual Conference of the American Association for Applied Linguistics, San Francisco.

Bright, W. (Ed.). (1992). *International encyclopedia of linguistics*. New York: Oxford University Press.

Corder, S. P. (1973). *Introducing applied linguistics*. Hammondsworth, England: Penguin.

Grabe, W., & Kaplan, R. B. (Eds.). (1992). *Introduction to applied linguistics*. Reading, MA: Addison-Wesley.

Kaplan, R. B. (Ed.). (1980). *On the scope of applied linguistics*. Rowley, MA: Newbury House.

Mackey, W. F. (1966). Applied linguistics: Its meaning and use. *English Language Teaching, 20*(3), 197-206.

Palmer, J. D. (1980). Linguistics *in medias res*. In R. B. Kaplan (Ed.), *On the scope of applied linguistics* (pp. 21-27). Rowley, MA: Newbury House.

Sridhar, S. N. (1990). What are applied linguistics? *Studies in the Linguistic Sciences, 20*(2), 165-176.

Strevens, P. (1992). Applied linguistics: An overview. In W. Grabe & R. B. Kaplan (Eds.), *Introduction to applied linguistics* (pp. 13-31). Reading, MA: Addison-Wesley.

Building an Association: TESOL's First Quarter Century

JAMES E. ALATIS with CAROL LeCLAIR
Georgetown University

TESOL has been a dynamic organization, responding to the changing needs of an expanded constituency and the developing role of English worldwide. This paper outlines the history of our professional organization from its beginnings in the mid-1960s to the multifaceted organization we find today. TESOL has grown from a small learned society to an effective professional organization.

BACKGROUND

It was only early in the 20th century that classes and methods for teaching English to nonnative speakers began to demand the systematic attention of U.S. educators and only in the second quarter of the 20th century that this matter became a concern of the U.S. government. In 1933, President Franklin D. Roosevelt set forth principles of cooperation, known as the Good Neighbor Policy, at the Pan-American Conference. As partial implementation of this policy, by the end of the 1930s, the U.S. Department of State evinced a strong interest in teaching English in Latin American countries. The State Department followed through on its interest with support for the English Language Institute (ELI), which was opened at the University of Michigan in June 1941. The Rockefeller Foundation also assisted with a grant. The first 10 years of its existence saw the training of U.S. teachers to go abroad, the establishment of an English Language Institute in Mexico City under the direction of Albert H. Marckwardt, and the teaching of 2,100 international students in intensive courses at the ELI itself. This first decade was also marked by important research and by publication of key works in the field: a classroom textbook series under the direction of Charles C. Fries (Fries, 1952–1957); a work on intonation by Kenneth L. Pike (1945); a volume on testing by Robert Lado (1961); as well as the first and for many years the only U.S. journal in the field of TESOL, *Language Learning: A Journal of Applied Linguistics*.

In the 1950s and 1960s, ELI expanded its work. Under contracts and grants from government agencies and private institutions such as the Ford Foundation, it undertook projects for teacher education in Indonesia; the improvement of English instruction in Laos, Thailand, and Vietnam; and teacher training in Japanese universities. Annually it trained Peace Corps volunteers assigned to English teaching. It was from experience gained in the institute that Robert Lado (1957) wrote *Linguistics Across Cultures*, which led to wide recognition that learning cultural behavior is a necessary accompaniment to the learning of another language.

By 1969, the Institute for International Education (IIE) reported 23 institutions offering graduate work and certificate programs in TESOL and about 40 other institutions offering at least methods courses in TESOL. Many of these institutions in turn undertook projects for English language teaching in various parts of the world, usually with support from a foundation or government agency. Involved in these programs were persons with backgrounds in foreign language teaching and others lacking that experience but convinced of the great value of linguistic theory in teaching English to nonnative speakers. To bring about mutual understanding between these two types of educators, the Ford Foundation supported a conference on linguistics and TESOL at the University of Michigan in 1957. Out of this conference came the clearinghouse in Washington, D.C. known as the Center for Applied Linguistics (CAL), established in 1958 by a Ford Foundation grant to the Modern Language Association (MLA). CAL has continued to operate independently of the MLA and with expanded linguistic interests but with its central concern remaining TESOL. Among many other projects, the center served as secretariat for the National Advisory Council on the Teaching of English as a Foreign Language (NACTEFL), a nine-member group set up in 1961 to advise federal agencies that undertake the teaching of English.

The efforts described thus far were concerned mainly with the teaching of English outside the U.S. In the late 1940s, following World War II, there was a great increase in the numbers of international students matriculating in U.S. universities. Gradually, authorities became aware that special English classes were needed for these students. In some places, instructors were drawn from English departments, in other places from the modern languages departments. In 1953, about 150 institutions had English programs for international students.

As more persons received specialized instruction in teaching ESOL, a sense of belonging to a special discipline began to take hold. In 1948, a committee of such instructors was formed within the new National Association of Foreign Student Advisers (NAFSA). In 1952, this committee, chaired by Robert Lado, held a meeting of ESOL instructors at the NAFSA convention, and in 1956, NAFSA formally organized its English Language Section, with David P. Harris as first chair. That section, which is now known as the Association of Teachers of English as a Second Language (ATESL), holds regular meetings at NAFSA conventions and publishes professional papers. This growing concern with teaching English outside the U.S. and to international students in the U.S. gradually led to a realization that a need for this special discipline existed in U.S. elementary and secondary schools, where pupils whose native tongue was not English, including Native Americans, were grouped in the same classes with native English speakers. A survey sponsored by the U.S. Office of Education and the National Council of Teachers of English (NCTE), showed that there was little awareness in the school systems "that teaching English to children with other first languages is a discipline calling for professional competence and specialized textbooks and other educational materials" (H. Allen, 1970, p. 310).

The federal government began providing support for teacher training in TESOL under Title VI of the 1963 National Defense Education Act and continued it under the 1967 Education Professions Development Act. This teacher training was supplemented by the preparation of specialized textbooks and other educational materials for use in the ESOL programs in the school systems. Special attention was given to the programs for learning English in the schools under the aegis of the Bureau of Indian Affairs (BIA).

With specialized training, materials, classes and programs, as well as support from foundations and the federal government, the sense of a professional discipline emerged and the need was recognized by members of this discipline for cohesion, a publication, and a professional home of their own. Although sections of NAFSA and NCTE devoted themselves to the concerns of the teachers of English to international students and to international cooperation, neither had shown concern with the problems of teaching English to non-English speakers in the U.S.

Upon Harold Allen's initiative as a member of NCTE's executive committee and with Robert Allen's cooperation, NCTE and NAFSA agreed to sponsor a joint spring conference for the discussion of ESOL problems and, specifically, the possibility of creating a new ESOL journal. (At the same time—September 1963—NACTEFL affirmed a decision supporting the establishment of a quarterly journal for teachers of ESOL.) In order to make the conference truly interorganizational, CAL acted as a neutral organizing agent. In September 1963, a Washington, DC, meeting called by CAL agreed to plan a series of annual conferences. The first national conference in the U.S. devoted solely to the teaching of English to speakers of other languages was held in Tucson, Arizona, May 8-9, 1964. It was jointly sponsored by NCTE, NAFSA, MLA, CAL, and SAA (Speech Association of America). Its expressed purpose was

> to establish lines of communication between the various interested groups who are at present represented in a number of organizations; to bring to bear the body of interdisciplinary knowledge which is relevant to the teaching of English to speakers of specific languages; and to give consideration to a professional status for those who teach English as a second language. (Center for Applied Linguistics, 1963)

Although a good attendance from a variety of disciplines had been expected, the organizers were amazed at the large numbers who came representing many groups and institutions, showing clearly the opportunities such conferences could provide for contacts and the exchange of professional information. Official registrants numbered 680, but the total in attendance was estimated at 800. Participants came from 31 states, the District of Columbia, and Puerto Rico as well as Canada, Mexico, the Philippines, the Netherlands, and Japan. There were professors of linguistics, anthropology, sociology and sociolinguistics, English, education, psychology, and psycholinguistics as well as teachers of ESL/EFL and teacher trainers. There were directors of TESOL programs in government agencies, official personnel from federal and state education departments, school principals, coordinators of adult education, supervisors, and consultants. "One of the interesting features of the conference was an informal get-together with representatives of eighteen associations and agencies . . . who were available to answer questions and give general information on the work of their organizations (V. Allen, 1965). This "organizational get-together" was to become a distinguishing feature of TESOL conventions.

The enthusiasm of the participants was evident, and on the second day of the Tucson conference, representatives of the five sponsoring organizations met to plan the next step. They readily agreed to hold a similar conference the following year in another location where the problem of non-English-speaking students in the school system existed. It was generally believed, however, that it would be premature to move toward the formation of an independent professional organization.

Shortly after the Tucson Conference, Mamie Sizemore, a classroom specialist in the Arizona Department of Public Instruction wrote:

> It is the most marvelous thing that has ever happened for education of our Mexican-American and Indian students in the Southwest. Administrators as well as teachers were inspired to go back to their own schools and attack the very important problem "of teaching English to speakers of other languages" with renewed vigor and new ideas. (personal correspondence to C. A. Ferguson, 1964)

In August 1964, the Steering Committee met, and the following month the planning group met to work on the next annual conference, to take place in San Diego, California. (The Steering Committee consisted of one permanent staff member of each organization plus one extra member, possibly rotating, and its function—carefully distinguished from the Program Committee's work—was to guide the overall affairs of the conferences, e.g., publication, site selection, and finances.)

In October 1964, NACTEFL met. On the second day of the meeting, the council affirmed four decisions, the second of which was destined to influence the planning of the TESOL conferences and precipitate the forming of a new association. The council recognized the need for a register of teachers of English to speakers of other languages and believed that it should be established and maintained within the framework of an independent professional association. The council therefore recommended "that immediate steps be taken by appropriate individuals within the profession toward the formation of an independent national association of teachers of English to speakers of other languages" (NACTEFL, 1964). The council felt that the immediate need for a register made it desirable to proceed without further delay and therefore recommended "that a concrete proposal for the organization of such an association be prepared and presented to participants at the Second Annual Conference on the Teaching of English to Speakers of Other Languages, to be held in San Diego, California, March . . . 1965."

A NEW ORGANIZATION

As a result of the NACTEFL decisions, therefore, Allen, Lado, and Sirarpi Ohannessian, acting as individuals connected with NACTEFL rather than as representatives of organizations, called a meeting in Chicago for January 30, 1965, to which they invited all members of the Steering Committee plus others in the field. The 18 persons attending the meeting decided that (a) a need existed for a separate organization, and steps should be taken to form one; (b) a report of the meeting should be given to registrants at the coming San Diego conference; and (c) a questionnaire should be prepared for participants in that conference, the results of which would provide information for drafting a constitution which could be presented at the following conference, to be held in New York in 1966.

The first meeting of the planning committee for the proposed new association was held in July 1965, following the San Diego conference. In attendance were Allen, Ferguson (Chair), Robert F. Hogan, Mary McDonald, Ohannessian, Clifford Prator, and Sizemore. This committee suggested a name, discussed the register, the annual meetings, the journal with its editor and advisory board, constitution, officers, executive board, location of secretariat, and amount of dues. The constitution prepared by Hogan was revised by the group and further revised at a joint meeting with the TESOL conference steering committee in January 1966. It was presented to the business meeting at the Third TESOL Conference, March 18, 1966 in New York City. Two changes were made, and the constitution was then unanimously adopted. Thus the organization called Teachers of English to Speakers of Other Languages: A Professional Organization for Those Concerned with the Teaching of English as a Second or Foreign Languages (TESOL) was born. The meeting then proceeded to elect officers for the new organization. Its first convention was held in Miami Beach, Florida, in 1967.

TESOL Announced

In June 1966, the *TESOL Newsletter* (*TN*) was dispatched from the University of Minnesota's Department of English by Allen. In it he announced the birth of the association and the appointment of an executive secretary, James E. Alatis, incoming associate dean of the Institute of Languages and Linguistics (ILL) at Georgetown University. Allen, through the good offices of Lado, who was both first vice president of TESOL and the dean of the ILL at Georgetown, arranged with the university administration to house the TESOL office at the university and to reimburse the university for one third of Alatis's salary as associate dean in exchange for his being released to devote one third of his time to TESOL.

A Newsletter

A good deal of the history of the TESOL organization in its first 21 years can be gleaned from the pages of the *TN*. Edited on a volunteer basis by TESOL professionals whose rewards were a token honorarium and the personal satisfaction coming from such service, the *TN* was a cohesive force in the profession.

As a matter of course, the *TN* kept members informed about their organization's conventions, both by previews and postconvention reports; about meetings and conferences in related fields; about programs for teacher training in ESOL and bilingual education, scholarships, publications and job opportunities. It also kept members abreast of developments in the TESOL organization itself, for example, establishment and growth of affiliates, the activities of groups within the organization focusing on particular professional interests, proposed and actual revisions in the constitution and bylaws, and candidates for election to TESOL's governing board. In addition to this kind of factual information, the *TN* was also a source of short articles on teaching techniques and methodology, book reviews, bibliographies, and articles about various aspects of the profession.

For a number of years the *TN* varied in terms of size and frequency. It was in 1979, under the editorship of John Haskell, that a bimonthly frequency was standardized. Although the *TN* was superceded in February 1991 by the tabloid newspaper *TESOL Matters* (TM), the newer publication has continued the mission of its predecessor, keeping TESOL members apprised of the association's activities and abreast of news related to the profession.

A Journal

Already announced in the first issue of the *TN* was the appointment of Betty Wallace Robinett (then of Ball State University in Muncie, Indiana) as first editor of the forthcoming TESOL journal, *TESOL Quarterly*. It would continue for 6 years under the editorship of Robinett, who set the high professional quality for which it would be known.

The *Quarterly*, unlike the *TN*, has always been published four times yearly, beginning in March 1967. It has undergone significant evolution in the size of the issues and the addition of various departments such as The Forum and Research and Teaching Issues. As in the case of the *TN*, the *Quarterly* has been edited by professionals on a volunteer basis.

A Second Journal

TESOL Journal (TJ), a magazine offering articles on teaching and classroom research, began publication in Autumn 1991, under the editorship of Elliot Judd, of the University of Illinois at Chicago. The *TJ* has offered members short articles on teaching techniques and methodology, book reviews, and opinion pieces about various aspects of the profession.

A Convention

A third organ that TESOL established from the beginning was a large annual convention, which in turn would be known as a mini-university, so intent were the participants on learning. In fact, it was said that at no other convention save TESOL's would one likely find the meeting rooms packed session after session in Miami Beach, San Juan, or Honolulu, with the ocean only yards away. From the beginning, the conventions featured three or four prominent leaders in the field as invited speakers, who could energize and inspire their listeners. In addition, the hours of each day and every available meeting room were tightly scheduled with presentations where veterans and newcomers alike learned methods and techniques from their colleagues. One of the significant benefits of a TESOL convention was the informal mixing with colleagues from all over the world, which encouraged the fruitful exchange of ideas.

Early in TESOL's history it was decided that the annual convention would be held in a large metropolitan area which had a great demand for teaching English to nonnative speakers and that it should move around to locations throughout North America. Over the period of 25 years, participants in the annual conventions increased from about 800 to nearly 5,000. Special landmarks in convention locales were offshore sites—Puerto Rico in 1973 and Hawaii in 1982—and countries other than the U.S.—Mexico in 1978 and Canada in 1992. Many participants felt that attending conventions where English was not the first language, for example, San Juan and Mexico City, was especially beneficial. TESOL veterans have attended conventions year after year, many taking pride in not missing a year. At the same time, every convention has had great numbers of eager newcomers as participants. Every site has had its particular group(s) of nonnative English speakers and something unique in the way of training programs. Thus an offering at each convention has been school visits, the opportunity to observe local programs, whether at public or private schools, colleges, universities, or proprietary establishments. Another feature of TESOL conventions has been publishers' exhibits—an unparalleled opportunity for teachers to view the latest material in the field and annually examine textbooks before purchasing.

By the time of the first annual convention of the organization in Miami Beach, April 1967, scarcely more than a year after its founding, TESOL could boast a constitution, duly elected officers and executive committee, a one-third time executive secretary, headquarters at a university in the U.S. capital, a scholarly journal and informative newsletter with their respective editors, and a membership approaching 1,000 (up from the initial 357 who had joined in New York). At that time the annual dues for membership in TESOL were set at US$6.

STRUCTURE

Affiliated Groups

In addition to the yearly TESOL conventions, teachers wanted to band together on a local level where they could learn from each other and give mutual support. During an informal meeting of the Executive Committee (EC) of the new organization held at a NAFSA convention only 2 months after the founding of TESOL and before the executive secretary was engaged, the six members present "agreed that a committee on regional affiliates should be formed immediately, in order to build up membership among school people who cannot travel to the national conferences" (Allen, 1966).

A revision of constitution and bylaws providing for affiliates with geographical boundaries was adopted at the Chicago convention in 1969. In the revised bylaws, the first vice president would be given responsibility for promoting relationships with the affiliates. At that same convention, First Vice President Harris (1969) recommended to the EC that

> TESOL devote all possible energies to the development of regional affiliates. . . . An organization with as diverse a membership as ours has much to benefit from a strong regional setup, whereby special local interests may be served and "local talent" identified and fed into the national association.

One year later at the 1970 San Francisco convention, the president and the executive secretary reported that five affiliates had joined TESOL in this first year following the constitutional revision: New Mexico, California, New Jersey, Texas, and Puerto Rico. The February 1971 *TN* listed five additional affiliates: Arizona; Florida; Illinois; Washington, DC; and New York.

In May 1970, the idea of affiliates from outside North America (specifically from South America) was introduced to the EC, but it was agreed that this matter needed further study. Bernard Spolsky, president of the New Mexico Association for TESOL and Bilingual Education, wrote a justification for the formation of local affiliates in the September/December 1970 *TN*. He wrote that the need for local affiliates stemmed from the importance of the area concerned, namely, the intersection of language and education. The New Mexico Association facilitates understanding at the grass roots, he said, between teachers and parents and between school and community. At the 6th Annual TESOL Convention in Washington, DC, in 1971, representatives of the affiliates met as a group, including the first affiliate from outside the U.S., Venezuela. A column called Affiliate Notes in the November 1971 *TN* listed activities of various affiliates and included notice of the affiliation of another group from outside the U.S., from Ireland. From that time, news from affiliates became a regular department in the newsletter. More or less steadily, new affiliates were added to the roster, until in 1992, the number stood at 78, among them 35 from outside the United States. Whereas the usual pattern was for a U.S. affiliate to have its boundaries coterminous with those of a state, there were several exceptions to the pattern. For example, the state of Texas provided five autonomous geographical affiliates, while only one affiliate encompassed the states of Utah, Idaho, Wyoming, and Montana. Groups that affiliated from outside the U.S. usually represented an entire country, such as Japan or Mexico. In the case of Canada, however, affiliates represented individual provinces.

The relationship of affiliates to TESOL was a two-way street. Advice and assistance in organizing, along with the existing pattern and structure, came to the petitioning affiliate from TESOL. The new group would receive a boost at one of its very early meetings with the presence of and an address by the president, first vice president, or executive secretary. In the early years of a small struggling affiliate, the central organization would often send a recognized expert in the field (usually a member of the board) to speak to annual meetings, thus providing stimulation and attracting new members. It would assume part or all of the related expenses until the affiliate was financially able to support these costs. The central organization stood ready, on an ad hoc basis to assist the affiliate in particular problems, such as establishing a newsletter, providing a noninterest loan for an unforeseen need or even providing assistance in a lawsuit. In turn, affiliates provided geographical diversity and interests, new members to the central organization especially classroom teachers and, not least, a proving ground for future leaders of TESOL.

After the affiliates had grown strong, numerous, and experienced, a movement began among them which was approved and encouraged by the parent organization: to group together in an area to hold a regional conference. While not nearly as large as the international TESOL conventions, such regional conferences could provide much more extensive opportunities for participation and learning than did a one-affiliate meeting. The first such event was the first Midwest Regional Conference held in Champaign-Urbana, Illinois, in April 1981, with 11 midwestern organizations participating. The Midwest Regional Conference became an annual event. The pattern was adapted for use in other areas in the following years: the Rocky Mountains, Pacific Northwest, Southeastern U.S., and the Caribbean. TESOL offered to help groups organize such regional conferences by granting interest-free loans.

Professional Interests

As affiliates began to participate in the affairs of the central organization, it became obvious that another way of grouping members was needed, namely, by teaching level or professional interest. The organization was not only spread out geographically but served members with many divergent interests, all under the banner of TESOL. Members taught students on every level from kindergarten to adult. They taught English for survival, for travel, for academic or technical/scientific use. Some were primarily researchers; some taught in bilingual education programs; some were testing experts. These various professional interests of members, of course, were being addressed in convention presentations as well as in the *Quarterly* and the *TN*.

As early as 1968, however, the EC, meeting in San Antonio, recognized that as TESOL grew it might well "be desirable to have sections representing educational levels" (TESOL Executive Committee, 1968, p. 14). The time had come to provide an organizational framework for members according to professional interests, to enable them to meet together, address their concerns, and act together in the governance of TESOL. Thus another revision of the constitution and bylaws was brought before the Legislative Assembly (LA) of TESOL in San Juan, Puerto Rico, in May 1973. A related bylaws revision was presented to the LA in Denver in 1975. It was adopted and immediately put into action with the appointment of the first officers of the seven special interest groups (SIGs): EFL in Foreign Countries, EFL for Foreign Students in the U.S., ESL for U.S. Residents in General, ESL in Bilingual Education, ESL in Adult Education, Standard English as a Second Dialect, and Applied Linguistics. Each group was to have a business meeting at the convention, elect its own officers, and prepare a 2-hour academic session for the convention.

At the Honolulu convention in 1982, a major restructuring of the organization was effected by constitutional and bylaws revision. A great part of this affected the SIGs. They were renamed interest sections—although the acronym *SIG* remained—because it was felt that both terms, *special* and *group*, were "inappropriate descriptors of what are professional concerns of formally established bodies in the organization" (TESOL Executive Committee, 1981). There had been a moratorium on the formation of additional SIGs for 5 years. The bylaws adopted in Honolulu provided for the formation of new interest sections, with explicit procedures for initiating and maintaining them.

Membership Representation

Also according to the revised bylaws of 1982, the Advisory Council, composed of representatives of both affiliates and SIGs, was replaced by separate bodies, an Affiliate Council and a Section Council. The Interest Sections were allotted proportional representation, between one and three members, on the Section Council. Each council prepared half of the slate from which the Legislative Assembly elected the members of the Nominating Committee. Each council prepared a slate of three candidates to be placed on the mail ballot sent to all members, one of the three to be elected to serve a 3-year term on the Executive Board (or EB, formerly known as EC; terminology changed in the 1982 constitutional revision). The Nominating Committee's responsibility was to provide the slate from which TESOL members would choose the first vice president (who succeeded to the presidency) and second vice president (who organized the annual convention).

Thus did the membership of the organization have its voice in policy making through direct vote on policy at the LA, through direct election of the officers, board members, and nominating committee members. In turn, delegates from the membership, representing geographical and professional interests, prepared the slates from which members were entitled to make their choices.

Committees

Another way in which TESOL functioned and served its members was through committees. The original constitution mentioned only two committees: executive and nominating. But only 2 months after the founding of TESOL members of its EC discussed the formation of standing committees, one on regional affiliates and another on professional standards. Revisions of the constitution and bylaws the following year allowed establishment of committees by the EC, with appointment of members by the president. As the need was reconciled, standing committees were established to deal with membership, publications, resolutions, coordination of schools and universities, research, sociopolitical concerns, and awards. In addition, as temporary needs arose, ad hoc committees were set up, among them editorial search committees, constitutional revision committees, a committee on the international concerns of TESOL, a committee on ESL in bilingual education, and others. The organization was exceedingly flexible, and even the standing committees evolved as times changed.

In 1985, the EB decided to put into effect a new committee structure for TESOL, and proposed a bylaws revision which was adopted by the LA in 1986. The names of standing committees became a part of the bylaws, and a Long Range Planning and Policy Committee as well as a Finance Committee (subcommittee of the EB) were established.

SERVICES

Publications

TESOL began to serve the profession through publications very early in its history. The first *TN* included a four-page bibliography compiled by the editor. In the second *TN*, there was a four-page supplement to this bibliography as well as a list of 20 publications, with prices ranging from US$0.10 to $3, which could be purchased from TESOL's Central Office (CO). Through the years, TESOL would continue to provide this service: buying quantities of materials from other publishers at a discount and making them available for purchase. One example of this was *Adapting and Writing Language Lessons* by Earl Stevick (1971). Published by the Foreign Service Institute of the U.S. Department of State, it could be a lengthy and inconvenient process for individuals to purchase this volume from the Government Printing Office. But TESOL could purchase 100 copies at a time at the quantity discount.

The fledgling organization was eager to begin its own publishing, and in March 1970, at the San Francisco convention, its first title was displayed, *TESOL, 1967-68: A Survey*, prepared by Kenneth Croft, chair of the Bibliography Committee. The following year, a bibliography of ERIC reports and abstracts, compiled by Anna Maria Malkoc, and a revised edition of *A Handbook of Bilingual Education* by Muriel Saville and Rudolph Troike were published. Both stemmed from work by CAL. Relatively early in TESOL's history, an attempt was made to create a series of works on techniques for teachers. Unfortunately, only two volumes appeared: *Classroom Practices in ESL* (Muriel Saville-Troike [Ed.], 1973) and *Bilingual Education and Classroom Practices in ESL and Adult Education* (Donna Ilyin & Thomas Tragardh [Eds.], 1978).

The first *Membership Directory of TESOL* appeared in 1973. It continued to appear annually until 1981, when the EB directed that it should appear biennially, as a matter of economy. In the 1970s, it had been sent without charge to all members; since the 1980s, it has been available for a fee to those who order it. In the Spring of 1972, *TESOL Training Program Directory, 1971-72* appeared, compiled and edited by Charles H. Blatchford, then of the University of Hawaii. This directory listed programs in the U.S. and Canada for training teachers of ESL/EFL and included requirements, tuition, faculty, courses, and descriptions. Blatchford continued to compile updated and expanded issues of the directory every 2 years until 1985-1986, when the work was subsumed by the director of publications at CO.

Today, TESOL publishes a diverse collection of teacher resource books, boasting more than 20 titles in print. The TESOL Publications Committee works closely with CO to develop an ongoing publications program with titles of interest to members of TESOL and sister organizations.

Placement Information Services

Another service TESOL has provided, both to its members as job seekers and to the profession as prospective employers, was a placement information service. A list of positions available in the field was mailed at regular intervals to those who wished to receive it, for a modest fee. Job seekers in turn submitted biodata to CO. Although the staff did not attempt to match positions with candidates, it did allow employers access to candidates' files. It was only in 1977 that TESOL began to provide space at conventions where employers could interview job seekers, on the model of the MLA's placement service. It began very modestly in Miami Beach with the provision of two booths in the exhibit area, which were obviously not sufficient. Two years later, the job interview headquarters in suites at the Sheraton-Boston was overrun with the influx of EFL teachers returning from revolutionary Iran and in need of new positions. The following year (1980), in San Francisco, the placement service hosted for the first time delegates from the Foreign Experts' Bureau in Beijing, who were seeking to recruit

English teachers for China. This service of making job interviews possible has been much in demand at TESOL conventions; it became an annual challenge to find ever larger space, more volunteers, and improved procedures. At the same time, the year-round service was continued and expanded: Bimonthly job opportunities were mailed to those who subscribed, and abbreviated job announcements were carried in the *TN*, with fees charged to non-TESOL members. In 1991, the bimonthly *Placement Bulletin* (PB) replaced previous job announcements. The *PB* is currently available for a fee to TESOL members.

Summer Institutes

When the EC met at the Denver convention in 1974, it appointed an ad hoc committee to look into the possibility of a TESOL Summer Institute (TSI) in 1975. The idea remained in the investigative stage for 2 years. At the New York convention in 1976, the EC authorized Alatis to carry on negotiations "with proper consultation with the Executive Committee," aiming at the goal of organizing a TSI for 1977.

Two years later, J. Donald Bowen offered on behalf of the University of California, Los Angeles (UCLA) to prepare plans for an institute in the summer of 1979 if TESOL would provide $10,000 for the salary of one professor and some scholarships. After committee approval, plans accelerated. In September, the EC formally approved sponsorhip of three TSIs—at UCLA in 1979, at the University of New Mexico in 1980, and at Georgetown University in 1981, with TESOL contributing $10,000 to each. It was decided that a summer meeting sponsored by TESOL would be held in conjunction with each institute. William R. Slager, evaluator of the 1979 TSI at UCLA, wrote: "The first annual TSI held at UCLA was a milestone in the history of [the] profession" (TESOL Executive Committee, 1979). There were more than 200 participants, including practicing teachers from around the world.

The following summer, the TSI was held at the University of New Mexico, jointly with the Summer Institute of the LSA. In the meantime, John Fanselow, at Teachers College, Columbia University, came forward with a proposal for the summer of 1981. This was the first TSI to which TESOL was able to award fellowships; thereafter, such awards were offered annually.

The TSI held at Teachers College was quite successful financially, and Teachers College actually returned to TESOL the $10,000 grant. The consortium of universities in Chicago which mounted the 1982 TSI requested an advance of $15,000, and from that time

TESOL provided $15,000 to the host university with the stipulation that the amount or any part of it be returned if the institution came out financially ahead when the accounts were closed.

Over the years of the TSIs, the expectations of TESOL's EC/EB have changed. At the beginning, the sum of $10,000 was seen as an outright contribution to assist the host institution in mounting the TSI. Then the EB began to hope, to expect, and eventually to require that the advance be returned to TESOL. Today (1993), TESOL offers loans of up to $15,000 at 3% interest to planners of TSIs. This work of cosponsoring summer institutes was seen by early leaders of the organization as one of the most important functions it could undertake to serve the profession.

Professional Standards

Standards for teachers. At San Francisco, in March 1970, the EC learned that CONPASS (Consortium of Professional Associations for the Study of Special Teacher Improvement Programs) had awarded TESOL a grant of $4,000 to hold a Conference on Guidelines for Teacher Preparation in English as a Second Language. Invited to the conference were members of TESOL's EC and many others with expertise in the field. Thirty persons representing public schools, universities, government, and private agencies from all over the country met together for 2 days and agreed to eight broad guidelines which stated the personal qualities, proficiency, understanding, experience, and knowledge which the teacher of English to speakers of other languages should possess. These guidelines were published in the September/December 1970 *TN.* Following this first and most important step accomplished by the conference, President Mary Finocchiaro, a conference participant, undertook to more fully develop the eight broad guidelines. This was a lengthy process allowing for considerable input and revision. Later Alatis, and still later William Norris (also a conference participant) continued, and at the 1972 Washington TESOL convention, a revised version was distributed. Further input was invited in the following edition of the *TN.* These guidelines were published by TESOL in booklet format and widely distributed.

Employment Issues

Because of the serious professional and economic issues in the field, in 1980, at the LA in San Francisco, the Washington, DC–area affiliate and the ESL in Higher Education SIG cosponsored a resolution which was passed by the membership. It was resolved that in-depth studies be undertaken of the following areas: (a) benefits, contracts, and salaries; (b) job security; (c) grievance procedures; (d) bargaining organizations; (e) program approval; (f) management training for administrators; (g) job market survey; and (h) lobbying. Reports and possible solutions to problems were to be presented in writing to the TESOL president at or before the beginning of the 1981 convention. The committee, composed of several subcommittees under the general leadership of Carol Kreidler, requested wider distribution of the report and action—some immediate, some long-term—on their resolutions. The EC agreed to continue the Ad Hoc Committee on Employment Concerns, together with a mandate and financial support, for another year.

A column called "The Standard Bearer" appeared for the first time in the August 1981 issue of the *TN*. It had been prepared by the Ad Hoc Committee on Employment Issues and would become a regular feature in the newsletter. It functioned not merely as a column, but also as a forum for members.

The committee undertook a broad survey of employment conditions in the field, work which was financially supported jointly by TESOL and Georgetown University. A four-page "ESL Employment Survey Form" was inserted in the December 1981 *TN* in order to reach all TESOL members.

As a part of the general reorganization process approved in Honolulu in 1982, the Schools and Universities Coordinating Committee and the Ad Hoc Committee on Employment Concerns were subsumed into one, called the Committee on Professional Standards (CPS). Kreidler served as the first chair. TESOL published and distributed the results of the employment survey in a booklet with a preliminary statement from the EB. In addition to this booklet, the committee also prepared, and TESOL published, two booklets reporting on employment conditions in specific types of programs: ESL in higher education, and English in non-English-speaking countries. These booklets have been superceded by up-to-date manuals revised annually by the field services department at CO.

Accreditation. Immediately upon becoming the CPS, the group began its study on the topic of accreditation. It reported two possible procedures: (a) establish an accrediting body, or (b) develop evaluation guidelines. The first would be costly, complicated, and unpopular. The latter, implying self-study, would be more popular and less costly. In either case, guidelines for professional standards would need to be developed. For this purpose, several meetings of committee members and EB representatives were held in 1982-1983. Open hearings were held at the 1983 convention in Toronto to obtain member input. The committee recommended the method of program self-evaluation and drafted a set of core standards sufficiently general to be used in any level of program. By October of 1984, 68 programs around the world had endorsed the core standards, and a year later, 175 program endorsements had been received. In the summer of 1986, CO received the first report on a self-study initiated by Teachers College, Columbia University. Since then, nine programs have received certificates of completion.

Certification. After TESOL had adopted and promoted its "Guidelines for Teacher Preparation and Certification," it began actively to promote the notion that all state departments of education should adopt certification both for English as a second language and for bilingual education at all levels of education. Public-advocacy activities with state governments were carried on by local affiliate representatives, with materials, support, and encouragement supplied by the association. In the December 1975 *TN*, an article announced that the state of New Jersey had approved certification in both ESL and bilingual education as a result of a statewide subcommittee's year-long planning and deliberation. In New York, in 1976, the LA passed a resolution that called on the TESOL organization to "take an energetic lead in the area of teacher certification." This was to be accomplished chiefly through the first vice president, the affiliates, and a special task force of the Schools and Universities Coordinating Committee. A report in the December 1976 *TN* revealed that very few states (5) had certification in ESL; slightly more (11) had certification in bilingual education. It was to be a slow process. Two and one-half years later, a report showed 11 states plus the District of Columbia and Puerto Rico with ESL certification, and 17 states plus the District of Columbia with bilingual certification.

A guide was prepared by Gina Cantoni-Harvey, chair of the Schools and Universities Coordinating Committee, for affiliates to use in advocating ESL certification in their states. The guide listed nine discrete steps, from forming a committee to preparing a written proposal and contacting legislators and other key people. This was published in a separate brochure and was printed in the August 1980 *TN*. In a comprehensive article in the April 1981 *TN*, Cantoni-Harvey reported that the figures then stood at 19 states with ESL certification and 22 with bilingual certification (Frank-McNeil, 1986). The committee under Cantoni-Harvey's leadership was active in promoting the adoption of certification, and the biennial issue of the *Training Program Directory* listed those states that had certification and provided pertinent information. This promotion of certification was looked upon as an ongoing project in which the central organization would assist and support the affiliates until such time as certification would be adopted in all states. Certification remains an ongoing issue.

Liaison with Other Organizations

Article II of TESOL's constitution states that one of the organization's purposes is "to cooperate in appropriate ways with other groups having similar concerns." At the second meeting of the EC—in Miami in 1967—the committee approved a resolution "that TESOL actively offer its assistance to all organizations attempting to deal with the problem of TESOL and that this be an active policy." It soon established a committee to develop liaisons with other organizations. At times in the early history of TESOL, specific members were appointed to this committee; at other times, it was accepted practice that officers and other EC members who were active in related professional organizations would assume liaison responsibility in the course of their activities. Cooperation was carried on principally with the five founding organizations: NCTE, MLA, SCA, CAL, and NAFSA. The American Council on the Teaching of Foreign Languages (ACTFL) spun off from MLA soon after TESOL's founding, and TESOL began to work closely with ACTFL as it later did with the National Association for Bilingual Education (NABE), when it was established.

Collaboration took on different forms with different organizations and included delegates to assemblies, exhibits at conventions, program segments sponsored at conventions, invited speakers, organizational and logistical advice, joint publishing, joint advocacy efforts, joint sponsorship of meetings or institutes. Other associations with which TESOL particularly collaborated were the International Reading Association (IRA), Linguistic Society of America (LSA), the International Association of Teachers of English as a Foreign Language (IATEFL; headquartered in the U.K.), and the International Federation of Modern Language Professors (FIPLV).

Such cooperation arguably reached a high point when TESOL became one of the organizations in the Joint National Committee on Languages (JNCL). JNCL was an umbrella of professional language organizations formed to attempt to influence the U.S. government to establish a national language policy. It created a spinoff, the Council on Languages and Other International Studies (CLOIS; later renamed the Council on Languages and International

400

Studies, or CLIS), to serve as a legally registered advocacy arm with the congress and executive agencies of the government. Not having individual memberships, JNCL was dependent upon assessed fees from its member organizations. Active collaboration with sister organizations continues today.

Political Activities

Bilingual education. TESOL strove to promote a very positive view of bilingual education: It favored bilingual education not only for the speakers of other languages so that they could learn the English of their adopted country while maintaining and enriching their native languages but also for English-dominant children so that they too could have the enriching experience of learning another language and becoming familiar with another culture. TESOL held that learning other languages and cultures would promote understanding and peace among the peoples of the world and advocated a policy of bilingual enrichment.

At the 5th Annual TESOL Convention in New Orleans in 1971, the membership passed the following resolution:

> Whereas we recognize that any human being's language constitutes his link with the real world, and
>
> Whereas we are collectively engaged in teaching another language to human beings who already possess a fully articulated and developed linguistic system,
>
> Therefore, be it resolved that TESOL affirms
>
> 1. That bilingual education must be assumed to mean education in two languages;
> 2. That this in turn presupposes full recognition by every available means of the validity of the first language;
> 3. That such recognition includes positive attitudes of all teachers and administrators toward the student's language;
> 4. That the validity of that language not only as a communication system but as a viable vehicle for the transfer and reenforcement of any subject content in the classroom must be central in curricular policy, and
> 5. That, where numbers of individuals justify such concern, the student's own language must specifically constitute a segment of the curriculum.

The January/March 1974 *TN* reported the U.S. Supreme Court decision *Lau v. Nichols,* which was to become known in ESL and bilingual circles as the *Lau* decision. The Court ruled unanimously that school systems which do not provide meaningful education for non-English-speaking pupils are in violation of the 1964 Civil Rights Act. The decision, based on a case involving 1,800 Chinese children in the San Francisco schools, declared that the same education for all children does not satisfy the law when some pupils are effectively foreclosed from any meaningful education because of a language barrier. It was left to the executive branch of government to determine what precise form(s) meaningful education should take in such cases.

In December 1975, the *TN* excerpted from an article appearing in the October issue of the *Linguistic Reporter*, announcing that the Office of Civil Rights (OCR; part of the U.S. Department of Health, Education, and Welfare [HEW]) had issued a set of guidelines for schools to comply with the *Lau* decision. These guidelines required a bilingual education program at the elementary and intermediate levels wherever a school district had 20 or more pupils of a single language group and declared that ESL was not appropriate. In a footnote, however, the guidelines stated that ESL was a necessary component of all the "aforementioned programs." With these guidelines and a new group of activities promoting bilingual education, there began to emerge among language professionals rumors of incompatibility or confrontation, a notion of ESL versus bilingual education. TESOL strove to lay such rumors to rest.

In the June 1976 *TN*, the lead article, "Is ESL Appropriate?" Buckingham and Haskell sought to clear up the confusion that persisted in regard to implementing the *Lau* decision. The "confusion, anger, frustration and continued disappointment" referred to in the article could be traced to the government's requirement of stating that ESL was not appropriate, yet stating that ESL was a component of any such program. It only seemed to add to the confusion when a subsequent memo from HEW to regional directors pointed out that bilingual education programs had not been mandated. The *TN* article attempted to inject some clarity into the situation by (a) emphasizing that ESL does positively promote the affective and cognitive development of elementary school pupils, contrary to what was asserted in the OCR guidelines, and (b) pointing out that ESL is a course with a content, like French or mathematics, whereas bilingual education is not a course with a content, but an approach to education, or a way to organize a total curriculum. Thus, ESL and bilingual education are not alternatives and hence are not in competition.

In March 1976, meeting in New York City, the TESOL EC approved and adopted the "Position Paper on the Role of English as a

Second Language in Bilingual Education," which had been prepared by an ad hoc committee under Carmen Perez. The paper stated unequivocally that the international organization "endorses and supports the bilingual approach to education, recognizing that it provides students of limited English proficiency with equal educational opportunities." It also stated that "bilingual teachers and teachers of ESL must accept a partnership relationship in bilingual education." It outlined nine specific steps the organization was prepared to take in order to promote and achieve understanding and cooperation among educators in both fields. This position paper was published by TESOL as a companion brochure to the guidelines on teacher preparation and certification, distributed widely, and reprinted several times.

In September 1977, the *TN* printed a group of editorials and letters to the editor from the *New York Times* and from affiliate newsletters under the heading "Bilingual Education (The Continuing Problem of Communication)," providing members with an opportunity to continue the discussion. In April 1978, a front-page article in the *TN* gave an historical overview of bilingual education in the U.S.

Then in August 1980, U.S. Secretary of Education Shirley M. Hufstedler released for public comment a revised set of regulations describing the responsibilities of the public schools to serve students whose primary language was not English. These were proposed to replace the "*Lau* remedies" (OCR guidelines) which had been promulgated in 1975 with much resulting confusion. Public hearings on the proposed regulations were held in September in New York, Chicago, Denver, New Orleans, San Antonio, and San Francisco. At the New York hearing, oral statements were made by TESOL's executive secretary, the president of the New York State affiliate, and the chair of TESOL's Sociopolitical Concerns Committee. The president of the Illinois affiliate made an oral statement at the Chicago hearings. The CO communicated with the officers of all U.S. affiliates, sent materials, and urged that they give testimony at hearings in their areas if possible, or at least submit their written reactions to the head of the Office of Civil Rights. TESOL also prepared an official statement in response to the proposed regulation. This statement supported the goals of the regulations, while pointing out certain inadequacies in them and recommending the use of qualified teachers, provision for the continuous development of English language skills, and the maintenance of skills in the students' first languages.

In December 1984, JNCL/CLOIS was able to report that the Bilingual Education Reauthorization Act had become law, reauthorizing funding for bilingual education for the next 4 years, with an increased funding level, and that the law included a section which addressed learning a second language as a primary educational goal. The law also authorized grants for adult English literacy programs. The 1988 reauthorization act remains in effect through fiscal year 1994. The next reauthorization debates are expected to take place during the 103rd session of the U.S. Congress. There will undoubtedly be debate about the role of English language instruction.

Learning other languages. Toward the end of 1982, TESOL endorsed the Sanibel Statement of Principles for a National Multiple Language Policy. This statement had been originally drafted by a group of language-related organizations in Florida and revised with the assistance of representatives of leading national organizations. It promoted the principle that in the U.S., there should be maximum opportunity provided for all to learn to function in both English and other languages.

President's commission. Another thread of political activity in which TESOL became involved was the commission established by President Jimmy Carter on April 21, 1978, known as the President's Commission on Foreign Languages and International Studies (PCFLIS). The commission was established to (a) recommend means for directing public attention to the importance of foreign languages and international studies for understanding among nations, (b) assess U.S. need and market for foreign language and area specialists, (c) recommend appropriate programs and support at all academic levels, and (d) recommend effective legislative changes. The commission also held regional meetings which affiliate members were encouraged to attend; affiliate representatives did attend in San Francisco, Houston, Raleigh, and Boston. It was reported that the commission was uncertain if ESL should be included in their mandate. In November 1979, the commission made its report to the president, proposing that the federal government encourage foreign language study with new incentive grants and promote knowledge of other countries through a variety of programs that would provide opportunities to work and study abroad. The persistent input of TESOL was at least partially responsible for the inclusion of ESL/EFL in the final draft of the commission's report. This type of activism continues today.

Resolutions. Another avenue by which TESOL members sought to influence public policy was the adoption of resolutions at the annual LA. As early as 1971 in New Orleans, the TESOL membership adopted a resolution supporting bilingual education and promoting recognition of the student's first language. In 1976 in New York, a resolution was adopted expressing the concern that the Financial Assistance to Elementary and Secondary Education Act then before the Congress, which called for a block grant approach, might give short shrift to the adult, migrant, bilingual, and Native American education populations which needed ESL components.

In 1979 in Boston, the members passed a resolution reaffirming the need for qualified teachers of ESL and condemning their replacement by unqualified personnel. Another resolution was passed supportive of the aim of Native American education, promoting greater participation and encouraging maintenance of native languages.

In Detroit in 1981, a resolution was passed directing the president and executive secretary to establish a relationship with the secretary of education and other government officials whereby TESOL could have input into educational matters which affect limited-English-proficient and nonstandard-English-speaking students. Another resolution directed TESOL to create a special task force to deal with refugee concerns; a third, that TESOL would show support for the teaching of standard English to speakers of nonstandard dialects; and a fourth resolution supported the proposition that a significant majority of a program's faculty be full-time qualified professionals.

In Honolulu in 1982, a resolution was passed opposing two Senate bills which would "violate the intent of Congress in creating the Bilingual Education Act" and "seriously hinder the future implementation of educational programs that have proved successful" (TESOL, 1982). At each subsequent convention, TESOL members have passed resolutions on timely issues related to the profession and mission of TESOL.

Political movements. The "English Only" movement began with the proposal of Senator Hayakawa to declare English the official language of the U.S. TESOL saw this movement as mistaken patriotism and as potentially detrimental to the multilingual, multicultural policy it favored and to the bilingual education programs it supported. It expressed its opposition through input to JNCL and through advice to its affiliates.

Awards

In 1972, the Asia Foundation made a grant of $1,000 to TESOL to supply memberships to teachers and students from Asia. In 1973, it doubled the grant so that TESOL could award some financial support to Asians studying English in the U.S. to attend the TESOL convention. In 1974, TESOL received the first grant of funds from the U.S. Department of State, through IIE, to make awards to international students (not from Asia) studying in the U.S. to attend the convention; it was able to make 10 awards through this grant and eight through the Asia Foundation's grant. The seventh grant from the Asia Foundation was received in November 1977, and this proved to be the final one. From that time on, awards were made to Asian students as well as to other students and professionals from the annual IIE grants.

The November/December 1976 *TN* carried the announcement that TESOL had established a Memorial Fund in honor of Albert H. Marckwardt, who had died the previous year. TESOL made the initial contribution of $1,000. The announcement stated:

> The intent is to use monies from this fund to assist graduate students in TESOL/TEFL/TESL to attend the annual convention. Such awards already exist for graduate students from foreign lands, through the Asia Foundation and the Institute for International Education. We would now like to make similar help available to graduate students who are U.S. citizens. (TESOL, 1976, p. 17)

The first group of 11 award recipients under the Marckwardt Memorial Fund were given assistance to attend the 1978 convention in Mexico City (appropriately, because Marckwardt had established the first English Language Institute in Mexico City). Contributions to this fund were solicited regularly from the TESOL membership.

Although the Asia Foundation and IIE grants ceased, students continue to receive financial assistance to attend TESOL conventions through USIA grants and the Marckwardt Fund. In addition to these grants, TESOL offers the TESOL/Longman/Robert Maple Memorial Travel Grant, an award established in memory of Robert Maple, a materials writer for Longman, who died in 1988. This latter award supports an EFL professional who wishes to attend a TESOL convention.

On October 31, 1979, TESOL's President, Ruth Crymes, was aboard the Western Airlines flight which crashed in Mexico City. She had been on her way to address the MEXTESOL annual convention in Oaxaca, her year as president only half completed. The EB established a trust fund in her memory to provide scholarship money for one or two fellows to the TESOL Summer Institutes. This was felt to be a fitting way to remember Ruth Crymes, who had been especially devoted to helping classroom teachers. Contributions to the Ruth Crymes Memorial Trust Fund were sought from publishers and affiliates as well as individual

TESOL members. In the summer of 1981 the first two fellowships were awarded under this fund, to attend the TSI at Teachers College, Columbia University (again appropriately, because Teachers College was Ruth Crymes' alma mater). Each year after 1981, either one or two persons received fellowships from this fund to attend the TSI, and the scholars receiving awards represented several countries.

Until this time the various awards had been administered by CO staff. In 1983, the EB began to consider naming a special group to oversee and coordinate these various awards, and an ad hoc group was established under Darlene Larson's leadership. In September 1984, this group became the Awards Committee, a standing committee of TESOL with the charge to oversee, coordinate, develop, and promote awards. At this time also, two new awards were announced, each with funds contributed by publishers and using publishers' names. The first was the $1,000 TESOL Research Interest Section/Newbury House Distinguished Research Award. The second was to be a fellowship whereby Regents Publishing Company would annually contribute an award of $5,000 to assist a qualified candidate in the pursuit of his or her academic career. This came to be known as the TESOL/Prentice Hall Regents Publishing Company Fellowship for Graduate Study. By 1986, Newbury House Publishers had contributed another annual award: $1,000 to honor individuals considered by their colleagues to be excellent teachers. Also in 1986, the EB approved a new award to honor Mary Finocchiaro, with specifics to be determined later, and directed that a fund be established for the award. In 1987, to honor James E. Alatis for his 21 years of service as TESOL's first executive director, the James E. Alatis Award for Service to TESOL was established.

In addition to these specific awards, TESOL set up a general awards fund, for which it solicited contributions from its members. CO funds specific awards from this general fund based on need.

GROWTH
Grants and Contracts

There are two objectives of a professional association in obtaining a contract or grant: one professional, the other financial. The BIA made a grant to TESOL in its early years for the purpose of evaluating ESL teaching on the Navajo Reservation in Arizona and New Mexico. Site visits were made by two teams, each visiting five schools at various levels. The teams also met with policy-making committees of the Navajo Area Office, hoping through that meeting to initiate improvements in teaching ESL to the children. The teams' final report to the BIA was published.

In September 1983, Lois Roth of the Educational/Cultural Division of the United States Information Agency (USIA) approached TESOL in regard to a new English Language Teaching by Broadcast series. A series which the agency had produced long before was now outdated. The agency had finally earmarked funds to get the project started. Roth proposed that the funds be granted to TESOL for the research, planning, development, and early production phases of a new series on English Teaching by Broadcast. Under this grant, the agency continued to do the planning, organizing, and decision making, while TESOL served as the banking agent or administrator of funds, also providing professional consultants and logistical/clerical services.

In the research stage, a team of TESOL/broadcast/USIA experts visited 10 countries to acquire background information regarding needs, market, and regulations, among other factors. After their return, a conference was held with participants from the U.S. and around the world to advise on a form for the series. Sample segments were commissioned, produced, and reviewed. Publishers and producers were invited to a meeting at USIA headquarters in Washington, DC, for a conference after the proposed series was opened for bid. In December 1985, USIA awarded the contract for production of the broadcast series to Macmillan Publishing Company.

The significance of the above-described grant from USIA lay largely in the fact of the agency's official recognition of TESOL as the responsible professional association in the field. There had already been a great deal of informal cooperation between USIA and TESOL on various levels. Many personnel in the English teaching branch of USIA were TESOL members, some having served on TESOL's EC/EB or as officers of special interest groups. There had been cooperation in regard to employment opportunities as well. But this was the first evidence of official recognition by the agency.

Long-Range Planning and Policy

In the first decade of TESOL's existence, the EC met only once a year, at the annual convention, with two exceptions. By 1977, the volume of business demanded more meeting time. Beginning in 1978, therefore, a midyear meeting was scheduled in addition to the one held at the convention.

At this first regularly scheduled midyear meeting, the EC authorized the president to establish a six-member committee for a period of 2 years with a possible 1-year extension, to do long-term planning for TESOL. TESOL continues its long-range planning, continuously monitoring these and other issues facing a dynamic organization.

Internationalism

TESOL was founded in the U.S., by language professionals who were U.S. citizens, from five existing U.S. organizations. Although at that time, it was almost totally concerned with matters relating to teaching English to non-English speakers in the U.S. or elsewhere by U.S. expatriates, its founders intentionally omitted "American" or "national" from the title of the organization in order "that the door be left open for memberships from abroad, and in order to retain the organization's international character" (TESOL Executive committee, 1971).

In 1970, an EC member brought up the matter of possible affiliates from South America. The EC responded by requesting the first vice president to investigate the implications. In 1971, the matter of affiliates from outside the U.S. was broached again, and the EC determined that the organization should not actively seek to attract affiliates from abroad. The EC was clearly aware of the problems in teaching English overseas that called for professional solutions and intended the organization to maintain its international character, but at that point in TESOL's development, the EC did not feel TESOL had the resources to serve international affiliates adequately.

In the early years of the *TN*, international news was limited to such items as employment opportunities in Australia, Peace Corps volunteers needed in Malaysia and the Congo, or USIA positions in Latin America.

By the summer of 1972, TESOL had accepted two overseas affiliates: the first one from Venezuela, the second from Ireland. At least three times (1977, 1983, and 1985), a motion was introduced to the EC/EB that the word *international* be added to TESOL's official name, and the motion always failed. However, the term was officially added to the subtitle.

In the October 1982 *TN*, a letter from Liz Hamp-Lyons of Edinburgh, Scotland, suggested an international exchange to share information through the *TN*. As a result, the International Exchange column was inaugurated in the February 1983 issue. In addition, a "rap session" specifically for international affiliates was held at the

1983 convention in Toronto. Out of this grew a study group formed to explore the needs and interests of affiliates and individual members outside the U.S. Their concerns included more representation on the EB, the difficulty of paying fees in U.S. dollars, regional conferences, making the annual conventions more relevant to international participants, the high costs of attending conventions in the U.S., and sharing information in both directions. Also at the Toronto convention, the affiliate from Quebec issued a statement asking (perhaps rhetorically) what specific, concrete advantages an international affiliate of TESOL has that an individual member does not have. This statement was printed in the June 1983 *TN*.

The following October, the EB, meeting in Fredericksburg, Virginia, changed the study group formed in Toronto into the Ad Hoc Committee on International Roles and Concerns of TESOL, provided for a larger committee membership, allowed an expense budget, and gave it a charge with a schedule of expected reports. In addition to establishing the ad hoc committee, the EB took other actions at its October 1983 meeting which were in direct response to some of these international concerns: It approved seed money up to $3,000 (contingent upon specific requirements) to groups wishing to hold regional conferences; it provided for a leadership workshop at the convention for affiliate leaders, with partial financial support; and it encouraged the nomination of non-U.S. members for positions on the EB.

In the International Exchange column in the *TN* for October 1983, an article by Thomas Robb and Kenji Kitao of the Japan affiliate, Japanese Association of Language Teachers (JALT), listed five major aspects of perceived inequities in service between U.S. and international members. Robb and Kitao paid tribute to what TESOL had accomplished on the international scale and admitted the formidable obstacles to making all benefits equal. They suggested that "it may be time for TESOL to perform parthenogenesis upon itself; to divorce the domestic issues from the international by setting up two distinct entities, a U.S. TESOL . . . and a truly *International TESOL*" (p. 26).

The ad hoc committee submitted a report at each EB meeting. It prepared a questionnaire on international issues which it circulated at the New York convention in 1985. It prepared an international speakers' list. It asked for input on various committees of TESOL and requested specific financial information. When financial information was compiled showing how much money had been spent by TESOL to subsidize speakers to U.S. affiliates as compared to the amount spent to subsidize speakers to non-U.S.

affiliates, it was found that significantly more was spent on the latter, both in actual dollars and when considered in proportion to the numbers of each. (At that time, there were 44 affiliates in the U.S. and 17 outside.)

At the Anaheim convention in 1986, the ad hoc committee, having functioned for 2 years, reported to the EB that they perceived that change had occurred mainly in the raising of consciousness but also reported concrete advances including the following:

1. More international candidates for the Executive Board
2. More international awareness in the statements of Executive Board candidates
3. More frequent requests for international input from TESOL committees and interest sections
4. More addressing of international issues within the convention (as exemplified by the 1986 plenary topics)
5. A more international orientation to *TESOL Newsletter* (TESOL Executive Committee, 1986)

The committee listed potential objectives yet to be met, under the headings of professional standards, professional resources, professional development, and teaching/learning contexts, and parallel with each objective, the mechanism to be employed in obtaining the objective. The Ad Hoc Committee on International Concerns continued for the coming year on a reduced level as a monitoring body, and, with favorable progress, was dissolved at the end of that time. The committee observed that it was then looking at international concerns from a different perspective than heretofore, namely from a professional rather than an organizational point of view. And it saw no "evidence that TESOL's international goals cannot be achieved within existing structures" (TESOL, 1986).

The history and accomplishments of the Ad Hoc Committee on International Concerns were summarized in "A Brief Report from the Executive Board." In it, Past President Jean Handscombe thanked the committee and reported that President Morley had established a subcommittee of the EB to complete the following tasks by March 1988:

1. To study TESOL policy decisions and actions taken during the past several years on items that involve aspects of international concerns
2. To study the recent work of the various components of TESOL vis-à-vis items of international concerns
3. To review the final report of the Ad Hoc Committee on International Concerns (1984-1986), as amended by the Executive Board . . ., to

recommend appropriate actions for specific components of TESOL, and to summarize the report for publication in the *TESOL Newsletter*

4. To prepare a guideline document (i.e., a stylesheet) on terminology to be used in all official TESOL documents and reports vis-à-vis international concerns (Handscombe, 1986, p. 21)

Tangible changes were evident in the number of countries represented in candidates for election, members of committees, authors of articles in TESOL publications, presenters at conventions, and holders of office. Two presidents and several board members have had citizenship outside the U.S.

Transition Process

In 1983, the EB held its midyear meeting in Fredericksburg, Virginia. At the spring meeting which had preceded it in Toronto, President Larson requested that Alatis and his staff prepare an analysis and recommendations concerning the organization's needs, especially in the matters of staff and office space, suggesting that he select EB members to assist him. This was done, and the task force so formed presented its one-page report to the EB at the Fredericksburg meeting. The most important recommendation was that additional staff be hired for the CO, the first priority being a convention coordinator, then a field services coordinator, and eventually a publications manager. Secondly, additional staff would require additional office space.

By July 1, 1987, TESOL entered into a new era with its first full-time executive director and fully independent, no longer under the wing of a university.

CONCLUSION

Leonard D. Goodstein (1988), CEO of the American Psychological Association, has theorized that all discipline-based membership organizations begin as learned societies and tend to move toward becoming professional organizations. They start out with a small membership, modest dues, a periodical or two, an annual meeting, and are usually run out of a university office or a spare bedroom. Then, more or less slowly, because of growth in membership and the services demanded by the members, they evolve toward large professional organizations. The latter, in addition to the services rendered by learned societies, strive to enhance and protect the discipline by such means as establishing criteria of competence, setting up mechanisms to implement standards, engaging in advocacy on behalf of their members on both local and national levels of government, actively marketing the discipline, and offering a range of auxiliary services to members.

It is clear from the preceding that TESOL has followed such a model throughout its development. Growth in membership and budget followed a more or less steady increase. In other areas, growth could be marked in gradual steps, such as the development of professional standards, the establishment of TSIs, public advocacy, provision for member insurance, reorganization of governance, and expansion of headquarters and staff.

Finally—that is, for this first segment of TESOL's history—in 1983, the governing board decided that 21 years of growth did indeed mark a "coming of age" for TESOL and that it was time to take another important step, from a volunteer ED who had guided the organization through its beginnings and growth, to a full-time, paid ED. It would be impossible to mark the precise time when an evolving organization passes the threshold from learned society to professional association, but certainly TESOL already has most of the characteristics which Goodstein ascribes to the latter. Its growth has been rapid because of the nature of the discipline affected by world events and the spread of English and because of the dynamism of TESOL members. That growth, however, has not been so rapid as to put balance, integrity, dignity, and quality at risk.

■

THE AUTHORS

James E. Alatis, Dean of the School of Languages and Linguistics and Professor of Linguistics and Modern Greek at Georgetown University, served as Executive Director of TESOL from its founding until 1987, and as President of the Joint National Committee for Languages (JNCL), 1980-1988. Previously, Alatis held positions at the U.S. Office of Education and the Department of State.

Carol LeClair worked with James E. Alatis in the formation of TESOL headquarters at Georgetown University during the years of its growth, 1973-1987. She now serves on the administrative staff of the Georgetown University main campus library.

REFERENCES

Allen, H. B. (1966, May). *Written account of informal meeting of the TESOL Executive Committee*, Chicago, IL.

Allen, H. B. (1970). English as a second language. In T. A. Sebeok (Ed.), *Current trends in linguistics 10: Linguistics in North America* (p. 310). The Hague: Mouton.

Allen, V. F. (Ed.). (1965). Introduction. *On teaching English to speakers of other languages*. Unpublished draft.

Center for Applied Linguistics. (1963, September). [Unpublished report of pilot conference]. Washington, DC: Author.

Fries American English series. (1952–1957). Boston, MA: D.C. Heath.

Frank-McNeil, J. (1986). *Directory of professional preparation programs in TESOL in the U.S. 1986-1988*. Washington, DC: TESOL.

Goodstein, L. D. (1988, Autumn). From learned society to professional association. *ACLS Newsletter*, pp. 5-6.

Handscombe, J. (1986, October). The international concerns of TESOL: A brief report from the Executive Board. *TESOL Newsletter*, p. 21.

Harris, D. P. (1969). Report of the First Vice President. In *Proceedings of the 4th Meeting of the Executive Committee*. The 3rd Annual TESOL Convention, Chicago, IL.

Lado, R. (1961). *Language testing*. London: Longman.

Lado, R. (1957). *Linguistics across cultures: Applied linguistics for language teachers*. Ann Arbor: University of Michigan Press.

National Advisory Council on the Teaching of English as a Foreign Language (NACTEFL). (1964, October). *Decisions of Meeting 5*, Warrenton, VA.

Pike, K.L. (1945). *The intonation of American English*. Ann Arbor, MI: University of Michigan Press.

Robb, T., & Kitao, K. (1983, October). How international is TESOL? A view from Japan. *TESOL Newsletter*, pp. 25-26.

TESOL. (1976, November/December). TESOL establishes memorial fund. *TESOL Newsletter*, p. 17.

TESOL. (1982, May). *Proceedings of the legislative assembly*, 15th Annual TESOL Convention, Honolulu, HI.

TESOL Executive Board. (1986). *Proceedings of the 32nd Meeting of the TESOL Executive Board*, 20th Annual TESOL Convention, Anaheim, CA.

TESOL Executive Committee. (1968, March). *Proceedings of the 3rd Meeting of the TESOL Executive Committee*, 2nd Annual TESOL Convention, San Antonio, TX.

TESOL Executive Committee. (1971, October). *Proceedings of the 8th Meeting of the TESOL Executive Committee*, Washington, DC.

TESOL Executive Committee. (1979, September). *Proceedings of the 18th Meeting of the TESOL Executive Committee*, Chicago, IL.

TESOL Executive Committee. (1981, September). *Proceedings of the 23rd Meeting of the TESOL Executive Committee*, Washington, DC.

Also available from TESOL

All Things to All People
Donald N. Flemming, Lucie C. Germer, and Christiane Kelley

A New Decade of Language Testing Research:
Selected Papers from the 1990 Language Testing Research Colloquium
Dan Douglas and Carol Chappelle, Editors

A World of Books:
An Annotated Reading List for ESL/EFL Students
Dorothy S. Brown

Common Threads of Practice:
Teaching English to Children Around the World
Katharine Davies Samway and Denise McKeon, Editors

Coherence in Writing:
Research and Pedagogical Perspectives
Ulla Connor and Ann M. Johns, Editors

Current Perspectives on Pronunciation:
Practices Anchored in Theory
Joan Morley, Editor

Dialogue Journal Writing with Nonnative English Speakers:
A Handbook for Teachers
Joy Kreeft Peyton and Leslee Reed

Dialogue Journal Writing with Nonnative English Speakers:
An Instructional Packet for Teachers and Workshop Leaders
Joy Kreeft Peyton and Jana Staton

Directory of Professional Preparation Programs
in TESOL in the United States, 1992-1994
Helen Kornblum, with Ellen Garshick, Editors

Diversity as Resource:
Redefining Cultural Literacy
Denise E. Murray, Editor

Ending Remediation: Linking ESL and Content in Higher Education
Sarah Benesch, Editor

New Ways in Teacher Education
Donald Freeman, with
Steve Cornwell, Editors

New Ways in Teaching Reading
Richard R. Day, Editor

*Students and Teachers Writing Together:
Perspectives on Journal Writing*
Joy Kreeft Peyton, Editor

*Video in Second Language Teaching:
Using, Selecting, and Producing Video for the Classroom*
Susan Stempleski and Paul Arcario, Editors

For more information, contact

Teachers of English to Speakers of Other Languages, Inc.
1600 Cameron Street, Suite 300
Alexandria, Virginia 22314 USA
Tel 703-836-0774 • Fax 703-836-7864

3851